ANATOMY
of
SOUTH AFRICA

———◦———

WHO HOLDS THE POWER?

Richard Calland

ZEBRA

Published by Zebra Press
an imprint of Struik Publishers
(a division of New Holland Publishing (South Africa) (Pty) Ltd)
PO Box 1144, Cape Town, 8000
New Holland Publishing is a member of Johnnic Communications Ltd

www.zebrapress.co.za

First published 2006

1 3 5 7 9 10 8 6 4 2

Publication © Zebra Press 2006
Text © Richard Calland 2006

PUBLISHING MANAGER: Marlene Fryer
MANAGING EDITOR: Robert Plummer
EDITOR: Ronel Richter-Herbert
PROOFREADER: David Merrington
TEXT DESIGNER: Natascha Adendorff-Olivier
TYPESETTER: Monique van den Berg
INDEXER: Robert Plummer
PRODUCTION MANAGER: Valerie Kömmer

Set in 10 pt on 14.2 pt Legacy Serif ITC

Reproduction by Hirt & Carter (Cape) (Pty) Ltd
Printed and bound by Paarl Print, Oosterland Street, Paarl, South Africa

ISBN 13: 9 781868 729036

ISBN 10: 1 86872 903 6

To Gaye, Jack and India Jane

Contents

Preface

The title of this book is either stolen or borrowed, depending on your viewpoint, from Anthony Sampson's seminal book on who ran Britain, *Anatomy of Britain*. First published in the early 1960s, it was revitalized in May 2004 as *Who Runs this Place? The Anatomy of Britain in the 21st Century*. Given that Sampson was Nelson Mandela's biographer and had deep links with this country, perhaps he would not have minded. Sadly, Sampson died in December 2004. In *Anatomy of South Africa*, I try to present a vivid, up-to-date picture of who runs South Africa in the second decade of democracy – much like Sampson did with Britain.

With the first twelve years of democracy safely under its belt, it is a good moment to reflect on how democracy has changed the face of power and power relations. Or has it? One of the core themes of the book is to examine whether democracy has, in fact, made such a profound difference. In each chapter I try to trace not only the changing power, but also the changing people. People make politics; institutions are made by the people who inhabit them, something we are all prone to forget. So, this is a book about people, and I have not hesitated to depict individuals as I see them, set against the organizations they work within, and with all the wonderful contradictions that human nature conjures up.

This is an extraordinary country that has beguiled and bewitched me since I first set foot in it. The colours of the Rainbow Nation remain vivid and the stories are many. Despite the media's failure to capture the vibrant essence and energy of politics in South Africa, it is alive, and luminously so. My main aim with this book, therefore, is to bring that political world to life through a set of mini-narratives. I make no apology for my fly-on-the-wall approach. Like Sampson before me, 'I offer myself as an informal guide to a living museum, describing the rooms and the exhibits as I found them, giving basic hard facts and frequent quotations from others, but not hesitating to add my own comments.'

In this, I do want to make one thing very clear: while there are short-comings to the book, which I willingly concede below, it should not be judged as a history book. Its point is not to provide an academically accurate account of what happened; it does not seek to provide a comprehensive analysis of any one or other important event or set of events. Rather, it dips in and out of the trail of events that together comprise the political story of a society in order to serve the primary purpose – namely, to elucidate the way in which power operates in the new South Africa. Moreover, because it seeks to provide a contemporaneous 'X-ray' of power relations at the point at which I signed off on the edited manuscript (July 2006), it is also a hostage to fortune: new events may intercede and change things, perhaps dramatically – not least in relation to Jacob Zuma – and/or people may leave their jobs and move on to new ones. Even the biggest events, however, are unlikely to seriously undermine the rationale of the book – more than anything, if it is successful, it will be because it provides readers with the tools to assess the nature of political power in South Africa for themselves in the future. In this sense, it is less of a map and more of a compass.

Like Sampson, I too have concentrated on the basic anatomy of power: the brain, the bones and the bloodstream. There are, therefore, omissions. Others can correct them; I would welcome that. This is just one X-ray. Different equipment focused from different angles may provide a different physiology. In particular, I have not tried to capture every part of the politi-cal system. While I focus on the national executive, there is little discussion of the other two spheres of government – provincial and local – except in passing. A future volume would need to remedy this by covering both properly.

Further, the so-called quangos – the quasi-autonomous non-governmental organs of state, such as the Human Rights Commission or the Financial and Fiscal Commission – deserve a full chapter, but are allotted none. Instead, the Introduction provides an overview of the governance system and the main institutions that it comprises. It sketches rather than analyses a range of institutions whose influence – except perhaps in the case of the National Economic Development and Labour Council (NEDLAC) – does not quite match their constitutional importance. In a future volume or edition, the armed services, the parastatals and the Reserve Bank would all merit proper attention, as would the National Intelligence Agency – and I regret not including a chapter on the NIA, because the spooks continue to interfere with the 'normal' operation of power in South Africa, exerting significant influence.

Nor does this book attempt to go much beyond public power, unlike Sampson's works. Although my Conclusion focuses on the compelling and, as I term it, congealing embrace between public and private power, time constraints have prevented me from giving the corporate world the separate chapter it requires. Other segments of society that are both interesting and important are omitted in this volume: the Churches (except for a brief reference in the chapter on civil society), culture and sport, which plays such a prominent part in South Africa's psyche, the professions and the universities. Like the quangos, they must wait until next time.

Last in this litany of concessions, I must note that there are constraints that arise from my own background and class. For example, I speak only one language: English. So, in Chapter 8, when I discuss the most influential radio interviewers, I am speaking mainly of my own experiences and making my own assessment. Because I don't speak isiZulu or isiXhosa, for example, I have not been able to assess interviewers on radio stations that specialize in those languages. That is one of the problems of such a socially diverse nation, a challenge that Sampson was largely spared with his subject, Britain. I also wanted to make this book a distinctly personal account. Because I have been working in and around politics in South Africa for over ten years, I felt justified in bringing my own experiences and opinions to bear. I hope this approach also helps to personalize and humanize the narrative. At times there is an element of autobiography. I suppose there were certain experiences I wanted to get off my chest; I hope this is neither too self-indulgent nor too intrusive to the reader.

In my determination to bring South African politics vividly to life, I have sought to emphasize its personal, human side, probably at the expense of hard, dry, empirical analysis. Hence, I have limited citations and academic references to a bare minimum so as not to clutter the narrative; in a couple of places I have drawn from my own columns in the *Mail & Guardian*. A future edition, should there be one, will need to redress this imbalance. I hope critics will take account of my central purpose when they assess the book's merit: to provide an accessible keyhole into the working life of politics and the politicians – in the broad meaning of the term – who operate the wheels of power. Personalizing politics is a fairly precarious exercise, and so there are certain risks involved in my approach, especially those places where I have taken a little dramatic licence – again, the purpose is to bring things to life and not to paint an inaccurate picture of some-one or something. In any case, a mark of a strong democracy is its capacity to accept parody and to construct satire. South Africa does tend to take itself a little too seriously – especially those with power and in power. Hence, if there is more than a touch of irreverence in my observations, I make no apology, but nor do I mean to offend. The 'fantasy left cabinet', presented at the end of Chapter 6, is offered in this, more playful, spirit. I greatly respect this country of which I am now a citizen, as well as its people, including – and often especially – those working in the public domain.

One of the more obvious conclusions that I reach is that the African National Congress (ANC) is *the* key political entity in the country. I was a member of the ANC for a while and worked for the party's campaign in the Western Cape when I first came to South Africa in early 1994. But I resigned when I joined the Institute for Democracy in South Africa (Idasa) in March 1995, as my role there was to build a specialist parliamentary monitoring capability, and it was therefore essential that I be seen to be impartial, which I have earnestly sought to be. Therefore, when it comes to the ANC, while I have many good friends in the organization, I am essentially an outsider looking in, with all the attendant advantages and disadvantages of such independence. Those who are 'on the inside' will obviously have a much clearer view of how the organization works, but if further light is shed upon this critical organization in response to my account, then so much the better. I realize that, inevitably, some mistakes will be made, and I will be grateful for any corrections from readers that can be incorporated into a later edition.

It is notable that not a single 'insider' account of democratic government has emerged since 1994. Unlike Britain, say, where former cabinet ministers and advisors rush to publish as soon as they leave Westminster or Whitehall, there has been no such clamour for self-publicity here. That may be a mark of the greater dignity of politics in South Africa; regrettably, British politics is so media-driven that the urge to expose tends to eclipse the no less important need to respect the confidentiality of government. I say this not in defence of illegitimate secrecy – on the contrary, I am a strong advocate for government transparency – but because the consequences of such published 'revelations' tend to reduce trust within government and, at times, to drive it 'underground' for fear that open communication within government will be revealed to the public.

What I am looking for in South Africa is the publication of a sort of grand historical work, such as the British Labour politician Dick Crossman's famous diaries, or Tony Benn's three-volume autobiographical studies of life in politics and government in the 1970s and 1980s. I would have hoped and expected a Pallo Jordan or Kader Asmal to have contemplated and delivered such a work by now (perhaps they soon will). The consequence is that very little is really known about how politics, and government in particular, works in practice. Without such accounts, it is hard for ordinary citizens to understand what is going on. The absence of knowledge in the end represents a shortcoming in the democracy as a whole; in darkness, rumours prosper, and sinister and often unflattering accounts of power predominate. This book is an attempt to shed some light and to help allay such perceptions.

Like Sampson's last version of *Anatomy* (his 2004 volume), this book is written 'with urgency'. I share the angst of British human rights lawyer Helena Kennedy when she writes in the Preface to her book, *Just Law*: 'Whenever I was studying for exams I used to find myself saying, "Dammit, if only I had more time." I feel that about this book.'

My book is about people with power at a time when power is definitely changing hands as a part of South Africa's ongoing transformation as a society. It does not deal with people who do not have formal political power – the so-called 'ordinary people'. Indeed, the principal question for us all is this: Having won the vote in 1994, do the people have power and do they govern? Regrettably, despite the dramatic change of 1994, the great majority of South Africans remain marginalized from real power and excluded from full participation in society due to chronic unemployment and poverty. Thus, I say, all the more reason to understand better who does control the power that washes over and around them.

I want to thank and acknowledge a number of people: first of all, my brilliant wife Gaye Davis, and my two charming, witty children, Jack and India Jane, whose company I enjoy as much as I love them. I wrote the first draft of this book in 2004 while continuing to honour all my other work commitments; I was only able to summon the necessary time and focus to complete the final draft by taking a sabbatical in Cambridge in late 2005 and early 2006 (accordingly, I would also like to thank Jean September of the British Council: Southern Africa for helping to make the sabbatical possible, as well as the Lauterpacht Research Centre for International Law and Robinson College, Cambridge University, and John and Saskia Barker of each Cambridge institution, respectively). Even though it thus meant sacrificing precious time with my family, they were understanding and very supportive. When I first met her, Gaye was a leading political journalist, and one of the best; despite her sojourn into 'talk radio', there is still no one I know with a better instinctive feel for politics in this country. She provided the initial guidance through the minefield of South African politics, and I would not have made it through without her.

Second, I wish to acknowledge all the people who lent me their valuable time so that I could pick their brains about the issues I cover in the book. All of them are busy and important people, including several past and present members of the cabinet. Almost all spoke to me on a background basis for ease of discussion, applying 'Chatham House' rules, which meant that I had to go back to them to secure their agreement to use the quotes that I attribute to individuals. Except where I have provided a specific reference, the source of the comments attributed to any individual is my interview with them.

Towards the end of the book I express my optimistic assessment that those in power are becoming more open in their attitudes and more comfortable with their power, as greater security in tenure is found. That is a very good development, if it is true (although it was an outlook that was being shaken by the waves of division and paranoia that washed around the succession battle as this book went to print). People in politics tend to be very cautious and somewhat nervous about what they say publicly. Though it is easy for me to say, I think perhaps they are *too* cautious and fearful. Skins are thicker than they may think; the debate can afford to be more robust. I hope I am right about this, and that no one suffers any sort of reprisal as a result of this book. If there were real justification for fearfulness, then that would be a very bad sign indeed.

Third, I must thank Zebra Press for wanting to publish a book about politics, and specifically Steve Connolly, Marlene Fryer, Robert Plummer and the book's excellent editor, Ronel Richter-Herbert (and, in passing, thanks too to my old mate Dan Ford, now founder of the Two Dogs publishing label for facilitating at Steve's behest my first meeting with him in my favourite local, the Fireman's Arms, in January 2003). Showing considerable vision, they have seen that there is a market for accessible books about public life. The fact that so few people buy books in this country is an outrage. For me, it is not the illiteracy statistics that are so alarming – horrifyingly high though they are – it is the *literacy* figures: if 4 000 represents a 'good' sales figure for a book, then there is something seriously wrong. The 'affluent masses' – a wonderful phrase I heard on the radio recently – don't buy books. They don't read! I suspect that this poverty of the mind is as much a danger to democracy in South Africa as the abject material deprivation that afflicts around a third of the population.

Fourth, certain friends and colleagues deserve specific mention. Researcher Jonathan Faull and his manager at Idasa's Political Information and Monitoring Service (PIMS), Judith February, kindly agreed to tailor certain research conducted by Jonathan on parliament, and the cabinet in particular, in such a way that it was directly useful for this book. Jonathan, one of the country's most astute young analysts, provided valuable, incisive commentary on the first draft. My dear colleague Judith was also very helpful in reviewing the chapter on the judges. Also, another excellent PIMS researcher, Ralph Mathekga, enthusiastically and skilfully filled the gaps that needed filling as the final deadlines loomed. My researcher, Catherine Musuva, also helped with final research queries, along with Andrew Schalkwyk, as did Bianca Valentine, Joe Fine and Helen Watkinson with much earlier ones. My thanks also to Professor Harry Boyte and my British friends, Dr Fernanda Pirie of Oxford University, and Jonathan Oates.

My superb personal assistant, Ilse Toerien, carefully stored chapter drafts in her sub-file marked 'Richard the Author', organised appointments and the checking of quotes by interviewees – and persuasively reassured them that their refinements would be heeded – and generally held the world at bay. I would not cope without her.

My sincere thanks and acknowledgements therefore go to my principal employers, Idasa, and my current boss, our executive director Paul Graham, whose wisdom and skill as a leader are evidenced at least partly by giving me a sufficiently long leash to enable me to pursue projects such as this one! His and Idasa's trust in me is something I am profoundly grateful for. Coming to work for Idasa in 1995 changed my life completely and has provided me with the greatest opportunity that anyone could wish for. For all that its detractors may have to say, Idasa is an extraordinary organization doing extraordinarily varied work across the continent of Africa, with many extraordinary staff members – it is a privilege to work with them.

I would also like to thank my great friends Lawson Naidoo, Sahra Ryklief and Ebrahim Fakir, as well as Sean Jacobs, not just for reading and commenting on either the whole draft manuscript or certain chapters, but for the significant guidance they have provided in relation to the pitfalls of South African politics over the years. And thank you to Ronald Segal for his words of wisdom and encouragement over the years, especially when I first decided to come to South Africa.

Six of my most significant interviewees also kindly gave me even more of their valuable time and read and commented on certain chapters. They know who they are, but it is probably best that they remain nameless lest they are unfairly associated with the shortcomings of the book, which are entirely my own responsibility.

Finally, while I remain an outsider here, I have very rarely been made to feel like one. People are incredibly warm and generally very kind. In fact, I feel far more at home here than in Britain; in an uncomplicated way, I feel far freer. Before I came to South Africa in early 1994, I was a barrister in London, with a growing yet strangely unsatisfying practice in human rights law, and an even more frustrating experience as an active member of the Labour Party. The intellectual corruption of the British legal system, a microcosm of the suffocating constraints of the deep-rooted class ruts of wider society, was beginning to suck me in. The shades of grey were oppressive. Though it is painful to miss my parents and oldest friends, I have never once regretted moving to South Africa. I have learnt so much, and my life is far richer.

Hence, this book is dedicated simply, and with humility, to the people of South Africa. I can never repay my debt to them and to this country, but if this book makes even the slightest contribution to a collective understanding of democratic politics and to enhancing people's participation in public life as active citizens, then I would be very glad indeed.

RICHARD CALLAND
Cape Town
August 2006

Abbreviations

ACDP: African Christian Democratic Party

AFT: Advocates for Transformation

ANC: African National Congress

APF: Anti-Privatization Forum

ASGISA: Accelerated and Shared Growth Initiative of South Africa

AZAPO: Azanian People's Organization

BEE: black economic empowerment

BIG: basic income grant

CCS: Centre for Civil Society

CEC: central executive committee

CEPPWAWU: Chemical, Energy, Paper, Printing, Wood and Allied Workers Union

CIA: Central Intelligence Agency

CIU: Coordination and Implementation Unit

CODESA: Convention for a Democratic South Africa

COSATU: Congress of South African Trade Unions

CWU: Communication Workers Union

DA: Democratic Alliance

DDG: deputy director-general

DENOSA: Democratic Nursing Organization of South Africa

DG: director-general

DP: Democratic Party

DPP: Directorate of Public Prosecutions

DPSA: department of public service and administration

FA: Federal Alliance

FAWU: Food and Allied Workers Union

FFC: Financial and Fiscal Commission

FOSAD: Forum of South African DGs

FRELIMO: Frente de Libertação de Moçambique (Liberation Front for Mozambique)

GCIS: Government Communication and Information Service

GEAR: Growth, Employment and Redistribution

HSRC: Human Sciences Research Council

ICFTU: International Confederation of Free Trade Unions

ID: Independent Democrats

Idasa: Institute for Democracy in South Africa

IEC: Independent Electoral Commission

IFP: Inkatha Freedom Party

ILO: International Labour Organization

JSC: Judicial Services Commission

LPM: Landless People's Movement

MDM: Mass Democratic Movement

MEC: member of the executive council

MINMEC: meeting of MECs and DGs

MK: Umkhonto we Sizwe

MP: member of parliament

MUSA: Musicians Union of South Africa

NACTU: National Council of Trade Unions

NADECO: National Democratic Convention

NAIL: New Africa Investments Limited

NALEDI: National Labour and Economic Development Institute

NCOP: National Council of Provinces

NEC: national executive committee

NEDLAC: National Economic Development and Labour Council

NEHAWU: National Education Health and Allied Workers Union

NEPAD: New Partnership for African Development

NGC: National General Council

NIA: National Intelligence Agency

NICOC: National Intelligence Coordinating Committee

NICRO: National Institute of Crime Prevention and Reintegration of Offenders

NNP: New National Party

NP: National Party

NUM: National Union of Mineworkers

NUMSA: National Union of Metalworkers of South Africa

NWC: National Working Committee

OKM: Operation Khanyisa Movement

PAC: Pan Africanist Congress

PAGAD: People Against Gangsterism and Drugs

PAWE: Performing Arts Workers' Equity

PCAS: Policy Coordination and Advisory Service

PFMA: Public Finance Management Act

PFP: Progressive Federal Party

PIMS: Parliamentary Information and Monitoring Service

PLAAS: Programme for Land and Agrarian Studies

POPCRU: Police and Prisons Civil Rights Union

PSC: Public Service Commission

PSU: Presidential Support Unit

RDP: Reconstruction and Development Programme

SAAPAWE: South African Agricultural Plantation and Allied Workers Union

SABC: South African Broadcasting Corporation

SACCAWU: South African Commercial, Catering and Allied Workers Union

SACP: South African Communist Party

SACTWU: South African Clothing and Textile Workers Union

SADC: Southern African Development Community

SADF: South African Defence Force

SADNU: South African Democratic Nurses' Union

SADTU: South African Democratic Teachers Union

SAFPU: South African Football Players Union

SAMA: South African Medical Association

SAMWU: South African Municipal Workers Union

SARFU: South African Rugby Football Union

SARS: South African Revenue Service

SASAWU: South African State and Allied Workers Union

SASBO: The Finance Union

SASS: South African Secret Service

SATAWU: South African Transport and Allied Workers Union

SCOPA: standing committee on public accounts

SECC: Soweto Electricity Crisis Committee

TAC: Treatment Action Campaign

TRC: Truth and Reconciliation Commission

UCDP: United Christian Democratic Party

UCT: University of Cape Town

UDF: United Democratic Front

UDM: United Democratic Movement

UNDP: United Nations' Development Programme

UNISA: University of South Africa

WECAEC: Western Cape Anti-Eviction Campaign

Wits: University of the Witwatersrand

WTO: World Trade Organization

Introduction

Cracking the Mbeki Code

Trevor Manuel, South Africa's minister of finance, woke, rubbed his eyes and contemplated his day. It did not inspire him. Thirty-six hours had passed since his Budget Speech to parliament on Wednesday 18 February 2004, and he was now suffering his usual sense of anti-climax. Weeks of detailed planning and adrenalin-infused late nights of preparation were over for another year. Would there be another one? He had been in the job for ten years – South Africa's first black finance minister. Rumours were circulating that the Boss had decided it was time for Manuel to move on, and that the time had come for a 'real black man' in the job.

To Manuel's fury, a couple of weeks before his Budget Speech, a national newspaper had reported that President Thabo Mbeki was going to move Jabu Moleketi, Gauteng province's highly regarded finance minister, into the job, and made the mistake of writing that such a person would be 'South Africa's first black finance minister'. Manuel, who under apartheid's appalling brand of racial categorization had been classified as 'coloured' (i.e. mixed race), was justifiably incensed. '*I* am South Africa's first fucking black finance minister,' he bawled down the phone to a friend, and later to the editor of the errant newspaper.

Isobel Frye, a young woman in her early thirties, was awoken by the sound of her alarm clock, 1400 kilometres away. Frye is not at her best first thing in the morning. Catching the 6 a.m. red-eye flight to Johannesburg provides a stern test of resolve and dedication, not to mention cosmetic dexterity. But on this Friday in late February 2004, she knew she had to get her act together and make the flight. As she fired up her carefully crumpled VW Beetle and pointed its multicoloured nose towards Cape Town airport, something inside her – perhaps a sixth sense – told her it was going to be an important day.

Back in Johannesburg, Manuel thought that perhaps he had overreacted to the article. Times were a-changin', he could sense that; perhaps he was just feeling unsettled. President Mbeki's first term was almost up. Throughout Mbeki's tenure, Manuel had enjoyed an almost first-among-equals status in the cabinet; his ministry, by the same token, a sort of government within a government (see Chapter 2). In politics, this sort of primacy can never last forever – the pendulum of luck and personal favour will usually swing the other way eventually. His personal circumstances had also changed. In the distance, Manuel could hear his partner, Maria Ramos, bustling about, already prepared for the day. She had been beside him professionally for a number of years as his director-general in the department of finance. They had formed a rare bond – and not just because of their love affair – which had provided cohesion and an immensely powerful foundation stone at the very heart of Mbeki's most powerful ministry. Now, Ramos had moved on, professionally, to be the new head of Transnet, the state-owned transport parastatal.

Whatever the reasons – the upcoming elections and the possibility of a subsequent cabinet reshuffle, Maria's career move or just the post–Budget Speech blues – Manuel felt lethargic. His troublesome shoulder injury was precluding his usual exercise routine, including his beloved golf. He certainly badly needed his first cup of coffee, black with just a splash of milk; he, too, was not at his best in the early morning. Surely his mood could not be caused by a sense of unease about his morning's appointment at the National Economic Development and Labour Council (NEDLAC), where, in a closed session, he would have to explain and defend his Budget. Manuel remained unconvinced by NEDLAC's role and power. Yet it was an important body, and potentially influential as well. It provided direct communication channels with all three main sectors: business, labour and civil society.

The meat and drink of NEDLAC is its use of process as an instrument of power. Although the pressures of high executive office have made him less patient when in its close proximity, Manuel, from his days at CODESA,[1] still respected the value of good process – a quintessential and highly distinctive characteristic of post-1990 South African politics. And so, despite his torpor, he knew that he should put on a good, convincing show for the worthy denizens of this New South African political institution. As so often in the past eight years, Manuel would be speaking with forked tongue. Multi-forked, in fact. NEDLAC comprises four 'chambers': business, labour, government and the development community. To the business sector, he must continue to sound prudent, effective and in control, and, above all, 'pro-enterprise'. To the unions, he must demonstrate that he has not lost sight of their core concerns, around growth, jobs and proper protection in the labour market. And to the civil society chamber, the sector that at times has caused Manuel the most frustration, he must sound as if he was at least prepared to listen.

Manuel had done it all before; in fact, he was a master at it. With great technicians such as Ramos by his side, and with his charm, gift of the gab and innate grasp of political reality, he was now regularly described in the media as South Africa's 'finest-ever minister of finance'.

Oh, it will be fine, Manuel reassured himself. He had held them all at bay until now. After all, had he not been elected at number one in the ANC elections for its national executive committee (NEC) at its national conference in Stellenbosch just over a year before, in December 2002? Why, yes, he certainly had. When the announcement was made, friends and colleagues from the Western Cape delegation to the conference had mobbed Manuel. For a minute or two he was submerged, but not before I had seen his look of pure joy; it had given him more pleasure than just about anything. Tears were unashamedly running down his cheeks as he jogged to the podium to take the first seat in the 2002–07 NEC of the ANC – the party's most important and influential structure.

Golf is a relatively new passion for Trevor Manuel. Soon after his NEC victory, he bagged a hole-in-one at the 13th hole at Rondebosch Golf Club in Cape Town, where he is a member. It was quite a remarkable feat, given his still somewhat uneven golf swing. I bumped into Manuel at a private conference on the Middle East soon after and cheekily asked him: 'Which gave you more pleasure, the hole-in-one or being voted number one in the NEC ballot?' His eye-twinkling laugh told me that it was a close thing. Such is the power of golf.

When Manuel got up to speak in the NEDLAC conference room in Johannesburg, Frye had only just picked up her rental car. By the time she arrived, Manuel had commenced his thirty-minute presentation. No sooner had she settled in than it was over, and one of the members of the council was calling on Frye to respond on behalf of the Development Chamber. Although she had been nominated to represent the Chamber at this special meeting, no one had told her that this, in effect, meant that she would have to address the minister of finance. Only two years ago, Isobel Frye had been a corporate lawyer – and a very bored one. Not any more. Immersed in politics, the geography of her life was transformed. Her friends included South African Communist Party (SACP) treasurer Phillip Dexter, the former chief executive of NEDLAC, and Neil Coleman, head of the Congress of South African Trade Unions' (COSATU) parliamentary office, a veteran labour lobbyist and now a persistently influential voice in parliamentary debates.

She was then head of advocacy for the Black Sash Trust, a well-respected welfare rights pressure group, and was the chair of the board of a new non-governmental organization (NGO), the Open Democracy Advice Centre. In two years she had learnt a lot, including the ability to wing it, and had gained the confidence to trust her instincts. Frye stood up and asked Manuel if he was prepared to consider a basic income grant (BIG), the across-the-board welfare payment that the BIG Coalition had lobbied for unsuccessfully for three years.

Though you would be unable to detect it, Manuel groaned inwardly. If he had to listen to yet another whinge about BIG, he would throw up. Because of the HIV/AIDS debate, he had avoided a major political showdown with the BIG Coalition. And the Democratic Alliance (DA) had also made it part of their policy platform, thus harming the prospects of the idea being well received at the ANC's December 2002 national conference. At that conference, as well as at the preceding 'policy conference' in October 2002, the ANC had voted against adopting BIG per se, opting instead for a more ambivalent set of resolutions, calling on government to 'continue with plans towards a comprehensive social security system ... [including] expanding existing pro-grammes such as the child support grant'.[2] For the umpteenth time, Manuel spelt out government's policy on welfare and, thereby, its opposition to BIG.

After taking a few more questions, he handed over to his cabinet colleague, the then minister of trade and industry, Alec Erwin. Apart from President Mbeki and Manuel himself, no other member of the cabinet has exerted more influence over the government's crucial macroeconomic policy decisions than Erwin. Whether it was the notorious arms deal, the controversial and fundamental switch to the Growth, Employment and Redistribution (GEAR) policy from the previously pivotal Reconstruction and Development Programme (RDP) in the dark of night in the middle of 1996, Erwin's imprimatur can always be found. Erwin is politically courageous, with a rhinoceros-like skin. Hence Frye was, as always, interested to hear him speak.

But when Manuel left the stage and walked out of the room, Frye followed her instinct and went after him, hoping that he was not heading for the bathroom. He wasn't. They made tea together and then, undisturbed, conversed for twenty minutes. For Frye, it was a heaven-sent opportunity to speak directly to power. For Manuel, it was probably a bit of a nuisance. Although he rarely feels intellectually intimidated these days, so lauded has his tenure in the Treasury been, he was immediately put on the defensive. No, he told Frye, he would not entertain any further dialogue with the BIG Coalition. Not until they had something *new* to say, he qualified.

This was the chink, the gap, and Frye took it. 'I think we do,' she said, as she quickly related the most recent research findings. In a situation such as this, she knew the 'meeting' could end as suddenly as it had begun. Okay, Manuel said, if you can put the new issues together, then I will consider meeting you.

When I lobbied in parliament, I often did not even try to make an appointment to see a minister or an MP. Instead, I would simply work out when they would next be in parliament, and where. Then I would ambush them. Trying not to cause undue anxiety to their bodyguards if they were cabinet ministers, I would approach them with caution and politely raise the relevant issue. If you are good at your job, you can make your point in less than two minutes. At the very least, I would hope to extract a promise to take up dialogue.

'Okay, okay,' a minister once said to me when I trapped him in the lobby of the National Assembly. 'Speak to my secretary and come and see me later in the week to discuss the issue properly.' And he was true to his word.

This is what Frye achieved in her twenty minutes with Manuel. Their talk may not in itself have changed policy, or changed anything at all, but it created the *possibility* of change – a change of mind or a change in attitude that may tip a delicately balanced issue in a different direction. This is what *influence* amounts to. As the *Oxford English Dictionary* explains, it is the act of exerting influence on something or someone that contains within it the promise or possibility of effecting or impacting.

This is the crux of what this book is about: influence. Who and what exert influence on political power in South Africa? Understanding power is a complex undertaking. There are individual and institutional dimensions. Power operates in different ways – economic, political, social and cultural – as the academic literature on the subject shows. One approach focuses on individual behaviour.[3] As one theorist writes, 'One can conceive of power – influence and control are serviceable synonyms – as the capacity of one actor to do something affecting another actor, which changes the probable pattern of specified future events. This can be envisaged most easily in a decision-making situation.'[4] This represents a 'positive' expression of power; where an individual or a group *prevents* the resolution of issues, there is a negative expression of power.[5] Power can also be seen as that which shapes the discursive field by the advancing or silencing of certain issues.[6]

These approaches have been subject to several critiques. First, a post-structuralist critique that posits that power is encoded – hidden, so to speak – within the micro-culture of, for example, the professions through their formal rules and informal lores and identities. The second, an insight especially developed in community and union organizations, represents a challenge to the idea of power as something that simply happens *to* people. Instead, citizens and communities, even if they feel powerless, have some 'relational power' – power that increases as citizen agency deepens.[7] A third critique supports this approach by emphasizing the generative, productive power of people – suggested by the phrase *we are the ones that we have been waiting for* (from an American civil rights song by Dorothy Cotton).[8] This has special resonance in South Africa, with its rich tradition of active citizenship and social mobilization.

My own approach is to distinguish between two dimensions of power. The one is *importance*, the other *influence*. Institutions and individuals derive their importance from their cultural authority – broadly defined to include constitutional and legal authority and the authority of a particular office. Influence, in contrast, has no such roots. It represents the operation of raw power, cutting across the bows of those that are important. So, while there is a greater legitimacy embedded in something or someone that is important, someone or something with influence can trump it.

So, the chapters that follow outline the institutional geography of the political landscape, but they do so against a two-dimensional matrix, with *importance* and *influence* at each axis. This is my own, two-dimensional view of power. Understanding the distinction and having the capacity to differentiate the one from the other is axiomatic to understanding political power everywhere; being able to delineate the two commodities is pivotal to good lobbying.

At the back of this book, the reader will find my 'Power Matrix', a simple two-by-two matrix, with importance as one axis and influence as the other. The main institutions and players are located in one quadrant or other. Something or someone may be important but not influential, or vice versa, or important and influential – i.e. the big top-right quadrant, where our attention should be riveted.

Metaphors are a writer's device, a tool for illustration and clarification. The anecdote about Manuel and Frye acts as such a metaphorical device. One such metaphor could not capture the many strands that comprise political power in South Africa, but it does touch upon a significant number. The paradox of accessibility on the one hand – a product of a still fluid, transitional, political environment – and of process orientation on the other – of institutions designed, like NEDLAC, to ensure that the heat of deeply opposed interest groups can be extracted and turned towards a common purpose. The relationship between individuals and institutions. The contest between ideology and ideas; technocracy and mechanics; idealism and realism; caution and ambition. The overlap between money and politics, capital and government. The personal element too: of history and happenstance, and of opportunism or courage; sometimes, of love and sex. The ever-present shadow of the ANC and its own central pivot: the divide between the exiles and 'inciles' (someone who was in the struggle against apartheid but not in exile from South Africa, e.g. the UDF). All of these are themes of great importance in understanding political power in the South Africa of the 2000s; all of them are touched on, to a greater or lesser extent, in the chapters that follow.

In governance terms, South Africa is unrecognizable from ten years ago. As noted in Chapter 4, 1994–96 was a 'golden age' for parliament, primarily because it was the period in which it wrote one of the finest modern constitutions, which is internationally admired. It is ornately crafted, with carefully weighted counterbalances to power. It creates a network of new institutions, all of which are now up and running. Although the transformation of the public service is not yet all one would want it to be, the institutional geometry is spectacular. From an academic perspective, it is wonderful. But does it work in practice? Does it release democratic power to serve the people, or merely tie it up in a procedural and institutional labyrinth?

The centrepiece of the constitutional jigsaw is the Constitutional Court itself. In a constitutional democracy, the Constitutional Court is the Supreme Court, and the ultimate repository of both legal and political power. As Chapter 9 explains, although its direct political influence is non-existent, its indirect, latent power is derived from its authority, from the intellectual integrity of its membership and the credibility of its judgments, some of which represent robust offensives against executive unconstitutionality.

In keeping with the overall aim of this book, the purpose at that point is not to outline the whole judicial picture. Instead, it focuses on the Constitutional Court's relationship with political power, examining its structure and membership in the context of its judgments thus far, against the backdrop of a massive public furore about the independence of the judiciary and perceived threats to it caused by draft government legislation intended to inject greater administrative accountability into the judicial arm of government.

A core theme of the book is that importance may not translate into influence. So, while its supremacy in terms of importance is constitutionally established, the political influence of the Constitutional Court is circumscribed. Executive power has no such inhibitions; indeed, the main part of the book examines the extent to which executive power, in the presidency and in the cabinet, is circumscribed, if at all.

Therefore, the first stop is the presidency. In the South African system, which is something of a hybrid, the president is both head of state and head of the executive – both president and prime minister (although not, curiously, a member of parliament). Accordingly, Thabo Mbeki has built up his office and advisory staff, but arguably it is still not strong enough. He likes systems and bureaucracy, and there is now plenty of that in the presidency. Debates rage in the media about the quality of the advice he receives from his immediate team, but they are a little-known entity. So, the most influential people around the president are identified in Chapter 1, and two key figures are discussed: Mojanku Gumbi, the president's legal advisor, who is rarely far from Mbeki's side; and Joel Netshitenzhe, head of the president's policy unit, a remarkable intellect who has had fingers in several giant political pies. His role and influence are elaborated on in Chapter 2, which describes how the cabinet operates.

Thus, the interplay between powerful individuals and powerful institutions is illuminated. Netshitenzhe is identified as the most influential individual aside from President Mbeki, partly because of who he is and partly because of the remarkable range of authority and responsibility he enjoys, but, institutionally, there is a 'government within the government' – the National Treasury. The Treasury derives its exceptional power from the inherent pre-eminence of its role and responsibilities, and, secondly, from the built-in technical and procedural advantages it enjoys, which pivot around the Budget process. While both of these characteristics are typical of finance ministries throughout the world, especially in the modern era, a third decisive component is less common: the character of the minister and the level of support he receives from the president.

One of the greatest challenges that has faced the ANC government since 1994, along with the transformation and growth of the economy and national reconciliation, has been transformation within the public service. I do not dig too deeply into this complex and fairly technical subject; rather, Chapter 3 explains the role of the special advisors and the directors-general, the key figures in each ministry and department. A fascinating, though opaque, process is unfolding in relation to the directors-general. On the one hand, rightly, it has been seen as an absolutely strategic priority to attract the best people as directors-general. Yet, equally, there is a concern that, in doing so, a Frankenstein's monster is being created – an elite group of individuals with too much power. In theory, the ministers make the political judgments, and the directors-general implement them through their departments. But it is not so clear-cut. In essence, the chapter asks, and explores, the question: Is there a new 'Mandarin' class? (Mandarins were high public officials in imperial China, and the term is now used in many countries to denote the most powerful government bureaucrats.)

Politicians are human beings. Some are lazy, but many of them work hard; some of them work too hard. Chapter 4 begins with the moment that now–deputy justice minister, Johnny de Lange, realized he was having a stroke. As chair of the parliamentary justice committee, De Lange was a leading light, along with dedicated parliamentarians such as Pravin Gordhan, Blade

Nzimande, Gill Marcus, Barbara Hogan and Yunus Carrim, in turning the National Assembly from a part-time rubber stamp of the old apartheid regime into a full-time, professional place of work.

Parliament has been a roller-coaster ride since 1994, however. There are structural flaws, mainly flowing from the Westminster system, whereby the parliament overlaps with the executive. As the ANC has got bigger and bigger, and as the 'brain drain' from its parliamentary caucus has intensified, so parliament's ability to exert influence and power has become more precarious. The pivot is the ANC, which enjoys a vast and convincing majority. It is a large party in every sense of the word, and its tentacles now spread far and wide. It attracts all manner of people seeking fame, fortune and safety beneath its generously proportioned wings. And it has a long and proud tradition, with all the cultural idiosyncrasies that accompany such a history. It now dominates the centre ground of South African politics, a moderate party in close touch with middle South Africa, and, once again, following the success of its grassroots election campaign in early 2004, the social and economically excluded majority: 'We are a movement of the poor,' Mbeki proclaimed in his election victory speech.

Understanding the ANC is a task of Sisyphus. Just as you reach the top of the hill and think you are getting close to grasping what makes it tick, some-thing inexplicable happens that pushes you back down. For many people, the ANC is an entirely obscure and impenetrable organization. Chapter 5 tries to shed some light; it identifies some of the key traditions and organizational design features that help explain how the ANC operates, reaches the decisions it does and uses its power. Most importantly, it also draws a distinction between the ANC as an organization and the ANC in government.

As I completed the first draft of this book, the post-2004 election honey-moon period was not yet over, so the love-in that election campaigns encourage was still casting its seductive spell over the tripartite alliance partners (the ANC, SACP and COSATU). As I completed my revisions and the final draft, two years later, the local government elections of 1 March 2006 were on the immediate horizon. The ANC needed – and realized it needed – the alliance partners, especially COSATU, for their dedication, manpower and organizational capacity, not to mention credibility in local working-class communities. After the 2004 elections, senior figures on both sides were claiming a qualitative shift, and pointing to government and

ANC comments about the end of the privatization programme and a more interventionist government approach to public works, public services and job creation. By the time I came to proofread the manuscript, in July 2006, the ANC alliance was at war – ostensibly over Jacob Zuma and the succession battle, but with deep-rooted causes beneath the surface.

It is not this book's job to make any policy assessments or predictions. What is important is whether the power of the left, as represented by COSATU and the SACP, which appeared to be in terminal decline, ravaged by the offensives of Thabo Mbeki in 2002, has been restored to better health. Chapter 6 considers the influence and power of the two alliance partners – COSATU and the SACP. Clearly, both have a certain degree of importance and influence, but the question is, how much? Do they represent a counter-vailing force, and, if so, are they the predominant countervailing force? Though it may not be the most apt of analogies, given their ideological discomfort with capitalism's premier institutions, there is a sort of stock exchange in operation. Some months, the stock of the alliance partners is up; other times, it drops. As a general rule, their value diminishes when the ANC is feeling strong and confident. When it is feeling weaker and more vulnerable, such as in the run-up to an election, the ANC's stock falls and that of its alliance partners increases.

Pivotal though alliance politics are to South Africa's anatomy of political power, COSATU and the SACP are not the only other 'centres of power', as veteran Stellenbosch academic Professor Sampie Terreblanche refers to them, that compete with the ANC and the executive arm of government for primacy. There are others that time precluded me from covering, but the book does consider the other principal political actors: in Chapter 7, the opposition; in Chapter 8, the media; in Chapter 9, the judges; and, in Chapter 10, civil society. And last but by no means least, in the Conclusion, business – the 'captains of industry', old and new. There I synthesize my exploration of political power in relation to 'The New Establishment' – the overlapping of business with politics, what I call the congealing embrace.

As mentioned in the Preface, a deeper analysis of the power of capital is necessary if a full assessment of the 'balance of forces', as Marxists call it, can be made. Nonetheless, the book reaches an interim conclusion. The Constitution created a multitude of new institutions that now populate the governance firmament, which are not covered by this book. Many of them – such as the Public Protector, the Gender Commission, the Human Rights Commission – are important, but not yet terribly influential. None of them has been especially convincing in establishing a public sense of its core role and purpose. Rather like the courts, their influence, such as it is, appears to be rooted in the negative rather than the positive – reacting, through their constitutional mandates, to particular political events. Indeed, they are having to live their formative years in relation to the ANC's primary instinct, which I've heard described as a 'Malthusian version of hegemony'; it likes to control everything. Those ANC leaders who take a 'live-and-let-live' approach are probably in the minority.

For example, although the Public Service Commission (PSC) is a constitutional body, it is, in reality, an extension of the department of public service and administration (DPSA). Although the relationship is a 'messy one that needs to be cleaned up', according to a source close to the minister, Geraldine Fraser-Moleketi, she treats the two as a 'part of the same team'. In turn, the PSC has failed to clearly delineate its own role, though it tends to emphasize matters of compliance rather than those of organizational values.

A far more serious failure to respect constitutionally assigned roles appears to have occurred at the Public Protector's office. The first Public Protector, Selby Baqwa, was a canny operator. Painfully aware of the need to move cautiously and not upset too many political apple carts too early in the life of a new institution, prudence was the watchword of his investigations. But while he could on occasion be accused of fudging, he did not evade the issues, as his successor, Lawrence Mushwana, chose to do in 2005 with his pathetic 'investigation' into the so-called 'Oilgate' scandal – where the *Mail & Guardian* exposed evidence of a collusion between the ANC and the parastatal PetroSA, whereby R11 million was paid through a compliant middle company, Imvume.

Mushwana, the current Public Protector, is a former ANC member of the National Council of Provinces (NCOP). As I know from direct experience – I accompanied him on a study visit to the UK in 1997 – he is both genial and decent. But he lacks backbone and intellectual rigour, and self-evidently is prone to bend too easily to political pressure. Whereas Baqwa – such as in the case of his investigations into Penuell Maduna and, later, the arms deal – was able to send important signals about conduct for the future, Mushwana's

Oilgate report is quite simply a whitewash. As I wrote in a column at the time, 'a dismal, depressing, disingenuous display of intellectual dishonesty'. Meanwhile, the Human Rights Commission has been hampered by internal ructions and a failure to convince parliament that it needs more resources to perform the broad mandate that it has been assigned.

These sorts of weaknesses in terms of strategy, resources and smart leadership limit power and influence. So much in politics depends on the individual and not the institution. Much as modern management and bureaucratic theory would like us to believe that we can 'institutionalize' things, and much as the philosopher Max Weber's great theory of bureaucratic 'character' is compelling, in the end the personality and integrity of leadership make an enormous difference. One institution that resists such vulnerability is NEDLAC, which brings together labour, government, business and the development sector.

As the opening anecdote in this chapter illustrates, it creates a forum for the exchange of views and the mediation of interests, all within a carefully prescribed statutory setting. According to NEDLAC's former executive director, Phillip Dexter, 'not only does this create a culture of dialogue, but in turn the culture of dialogue creates a shift in power'. Whether on privatization, HIV/AIDS, or growth and development strategy, NEDLAC provides a forum for negotiation and debate. It both diffuses power and creates an opportunity for its realignment. Command of process is one of the ways of securing political influence.

As the new constitutional order has settled down over the past ten years, it is those who have adapted best to this new culture of dialogue and process that have sustained or acquired political power. As Dexter points out, NEDLAC derives its approach from the culture of dialogue that was established during the negotiations leading up to the first democratic elections in 1994. Individuals matter hugely; but so, here, does *process*. It is *The South African Way*.

I

The Presidency

Inside South Africa's West Wing

It was trademark Thabo. At a typical policy-making meeting. In the cabinet room at the Union Buildings, sunlight streaming in, around ten people were gathered. An informal subcommittee, hastily pulled together the previous evening by Frank Chikane, director-general in the presidency, to discuss the worsening crisis in the Middle East in 2003.

'So,' began Mbeki. 'What position do we take on this?'

There was silence from the collection of ministers and advisors. Then one of the advisors raised his hand and began to speak.

'Mr President, I think ...'

'No,' interrupted Mbeki, 'you speak last.'

On this issue, Mbeki knew the advisor's position already. Moreover, he knew that the two of them shared the same view, and he wanted to avoid a phenomenon known as 'groupthink' – a psychological concept adapted by an American political scientist in the 1960s to explain the failure of President John F Kennedy's Cuban policy at the time of the Bay of Pigs. This phenomenon occurs when a small group of like-minded people meet to make a key decision and, instead of testing hypotheses or fundamental assumptions and analyses, end up simply affirming each other's preconceived views, thus promoting a poor decision-making process.

Ronnie Kasrils, minister of water affairs and forestry, but a man with strong views on the Middle East, spoke instead. Kasrils has been a courageous defender of the human rights of Palestinians, regularly attacking the self-defeating oppressive policies of the Israeli government.

As a Jew, he has been viciously attacked by Zionist Jews in South Africa, who accuse him of being anti-Israel and anti-Jew. This is nonsense. Kasrils, in line with South African government policy, is pro-Palestinian, but certainly does not buy into the destruction of Israel. Perhaps he is too close to the subject, for although Kasrils addressed the heart of the issue on the table – South Africa's relationship with Israel – his meandering assessment of what to do next soon elicited Mbeki's irritation.

'Minister' – in formal meetings of government, Mbeki is never anything other than formal; he would never address Kasrils as 'Ronnie' – 'come on, take a position!'

Mbeki is very hands-on, very 'engaged'. Some would say too much so. By definition, heads of government are powerful, usually pivotal and sometimes all-consuming. Mbeki is all three. By 'all-consuming', I mean that Mbeki rarely if ever permits alternative centres of power to grow and flourish within his own constellation.

Trevor Manuel is a partial exception because, as minister of finance, he is largely left to get on with the job. As the next chapter suggests, Manuel himself roots his mandate and authority entirely in the president – on a personal, political, ideological and policy basis.

In Mbeki's determination to modernize both government and the ANC, he knows that alternative foci of power – a minister, institution or faction with excessive power, such as the left, the ANC or the 'Zuma camp' – will only serve to distract him and his government from the task at hand. Intellectually, he is very engaged. Everyone I spoke to agrees that Mbeki is a voracious reader. He consumes everything, develops a better understanding of the subjects – often better than even the minister whose responsibility it is – and so is several steps ahead of everyone else around him.

Thus, to understand political power in South Africa, you have to understand Mbeki, and the way he thinks and wields political power. This is no easy undertaking. He is a complex individual, and his style of leadership rarely conforms to the norms of modern politics. However, this book is not about Thabo Mbeki, although any attempt to 'anatomize' the South African body politic cannot get very far without a necessary digression: to try to explain how the politics and ideology of the South African president[1] inform his decision-making, and thereby his use of political power.

First and foremost, Mbeki is a pragmatist. His ideological ambiguity infuriates his detractors from both the left and right, but especially the left, some of whom interpret his pragmatism as conservative ideology masked as something less dangerous; what leftist academics such as Patrick Bond would call his tendency to 'talk left and walk right'.[2]

There is also a 'Socratic' inquisitiveness to which Mbeki is predisposed and which underpins his leadership style and management practice. In this regard, his thinking finds expression in *questions*. He holds no concept or view sacred and aims at it a quiver of questions, all of which have to be answered before he is content to move on. He generally leads debates with a lot of questions, and his speeches are often littered with them – especially when dealing with discontent. This is a powerful intellectual asset for any president, but can also be dangerous, as we have seen in his overt curiosity in unorthodox approaches to understanding the causes of the HIV/AIDS pandemic.

This is Mbeki the Thinker and Mbeki the Strategic Manager. There is also Mbeki the Political Operator. The latter can be even more uncompromising than the former. I do not propose to dwell on the subject, but it is worth recalling the way in which Mbeki has dealt with potential challenges to his leadership within the ANC.

In autumn 2001, with the December national conference of the ANC less than eighteen months away, the minister of safety and security, Steve Tshwete, a Mbeki loyalist, went on national television and casually mentioned that his police force was investigating rumours of a plot against the president by three major ANC figures, Cyril Ramaphosa, Mathews Phosa and Tokyo Sexwale. Speaking in Zulu on SABC 2, Tshwete actually used the word 'assassinate'.

It is hard to imagine a more ruthless and cynical use of state authority for the execution of an intra-party political purpose. But it was effective. All three were, at least temporarily, disabled. The allegations were withdrawn once the 'investigation' was complete. Though Ramaphosa and Phosa were re-elected to the NEC at the Stellenbosch national conference in December 2002, their wings had been clipped – not in any manifest way, but in the knowledge that the plot ploy showed how far Mbeki would be prepared to go to keep them firmly in their place.

As wealthy men, with wide crosscutting networks and power bases within the movement, all three were potentially serious rivals to Mbeki. Shots were fired across their bows. All three took to port. The fourth, Jacob Zuma, was in a different category, and was dealt with later. Mbeki certainly knows how to consolidate his power.

The political *handlanger*

All political leaders have a *handlanger* (sidekick). As always, the Afrikaans word captures the essence more through its natural sound and onomatopoeia than by the literal meaning. Essop Pahad is no 'bag carrier', but he is a *handlanger*. He has been by Mbeki's side for as long as anyone can remember. Plenty has already been written about their close historic relationship – he was best man at Mbeki's wedding, and they studied together at Brighton. But to hear some people speak of him, you would think he was Count Dracula. He is almost more maligned than Mbeki.

For the left especially, Pahad is a hypocrite with devious intent, although I remember the long interview I had with him in around 1998, during which he kept insisting that he was and always would be a socialist. If he is, the left certainly does not recognize the 'socialism' in the policy and politics of the ANC government of today. As William Gumede's book asserts, the ANC has been taken over by fervent capitalists, perhaps selling its soul in the process.[3]

Like Mbeki, Pahad is the ultimate realist, an ultra-realist, so to speak, deeply schooled in the doctrine of politics that, to coin the famous phrase, asserts that politics is best defined as 'the art of the possible'. Pahad is important because he is in the cabinet, as minister in the presidency, and because part of his function is to handle a basket of policy issues that have important and potentially influential implications – women, the disabled and government communication. He is also charged with the administration of the National Youth Commission Act. He meets with the executive of the commission on a two-monthly basis. His duties are well captured in one of his Budget vote speeches, on 15 April 2005, in which he talked about a South Africa where 'various social forces work together towards shared development goals'. His job description is general and broad, anchoring all forces of the society towards one goal.

Though he can be as charming in private as he is sometimes boorish in public, as swift to pull out his mischievous wide smile as he is a bottle of malt whisky, Pahad is not universally popular within the ANC, though no one will voice complaints publicly. In the National Assembly I have regularly seen him destroy members of the opposition with brutally worded interventions; clearly, Pahad had learnt from the least attractive debating traditions in Westminster while he was in exile in the UK.

There is no doubt that his long-term loyalty means he is deeply trusted by Mbeki, who knows that Pahad has no external political strength and is therefore no threat – an axiomatic characteristic of the true political *handlanger* (something that, because of her PAC past, also characterizes presidential legal advisor Mojanku Gumbi – but more on her later).

But it is hard to know what precise influence Pahad has over Mbeki today. As other people establish themselves around Mbeki and he looks for new ideas, there is a definite sense that Pahad's influence is waning. Other advisors and cabinet ministers with whom I spoke are somewhat vague. Some brief – that is to say, they comment off the record – heavily against him, partly because it is clear that they resent his style and historical proximity to Mbeki; some regard him as a prime minister, a first among equals.

If so, they are wrong. If there is a first among equals, it is finance minister Trevor Manuel; and, if there is a new *handlanger* on the block, it is Mojanku Gumbi.

So, whereas Pahad was once indisputably in the top five – even three – most influential and, therefore, powerful people in South Africa, he has since slid lower down the league table.

One insider compares Pahad to Harry Hopkins, the 'political fixer' of US president Franklin Delano Roosevelt. Tony Blair had Alastair Campbell, although, according to another presidential advisor, Pahad is 'in fact more of a Peter Mandelson', thus implying that Pahad operates at a more deeply political and strategic level. Giving a highly personal view, former *Cape Times* editor Tony Heard, currently a special advisor in the presidency, offers the following assessment of Pahad:

> Dr Pahad eats, sleeps and drinks politics. The energy he devotes to the job is phenomenal. A senior member of the Communist Party for years, he is an ANC loyalist to the core. But despite an ideologically committed and robust, even blunt, nature, he is capable of flashes of laconic humour and deep personal concern (for example in cases of death or illness); and there is a certain pragmatism in his make-up. He is obviously totally trusted in the councils of power, and with good reason. Generally, I have found, in an advisory capacity in government for a number of years, that, more often than not, the Communist Party members tend to work hardest, have the deepest sense of social responsibility and commitment, and are more meticulous about matters of personal ethics and morality.

No less pertinently, he adds a rhetorical question with which it is hard to disagree if one is realistic: 'How can you run a country like South Africa, with its history of neglect, racial compartmentalism and centrifugal forces, without a firm hand at the centre, but, of course, with respect for due process and freedom?' Amen to that, whether Dr Pahad is your cup of tea or not.

Letter from the President

Like Pahad, Mbeki's closest advisors are very loyal to him. Most see Mbeki as not only an intellectual giant and a great strategist, but also as a man with a deeply ideological component. Most often they cite his leadership on the 'African Renaissance', as it is popularly called. So, let us use that project – for project it is – to describe Mbeki's approach to power.

Mbeki is seeking a historical role for himself; he sees his part in history as shifting attitudes towards Africa and recasting the continent in the global political firmament. He wants to 'restore Africa as one of the major civilizations'; he wants to challenge the structural inequality – what he has often described as 'global apartheid' (talking left, again). To achieve this requires a long-term strategy and, because he is so well versed in the realpolitik of the northern capitals (London, Washington, DC, and Berlin), a careful, step-by-step pragmatism.

For those wanting a clearer insight into the workings of Thabo Mbeki's mind, unencumbered by the clutter of intermediary analysis, there is a simple and accessible solution: the weekly 'Letter from the President', which appears on the ANC's website, www.anc.org.za. It is important to precede this observation with the qualification that the letter is in essence an elite exercise – to read it you need not only be literate and proficient in English, but have access to the Internet, and in this sense the letter does little to quell the accusation that he is a 'distant philosopher king'. It nonetheless represents a decisive riposte to those of his detractors who tend to criticize him for being vague and obscure in communicating policy. Which other heads of government around the world pen such a topical and candid expression of their views? None that I know of.

In December 2003, at the conclusion of the Commonwealth Heads of Government meeting in Nigeria, Mbeki was infuriated. Africa was split on Mugabe, and Mbeki's view, which was that Zimbabwe should be restored to membership of the Commonwealth, did not prevail. Mbeki was livid. Most political leaders teach themselves to count to ten in order to avoid blurting out an indelicacy in public, and Mbeki made no comment to the media. Later in the week, he let the Southern African Development Community (SADC) statement do the formal talking for the South African government. *His* outlet was his weekly letter, which, technically, he writes as president of the ANC and not the country.

Still furious on the aeroplane back from Abuja, he vented his feelings on his laptop. It was the longest, most vehement, passionate and, therefore, insightful of Mbeki's 'Letter from the President' missives.

The title of the letter is uncompromising and says it all: 'We will resist the upside-downing of Africa.' He lashes out at the Commonwealth heads of government, the West and the media for their 'disinformation' and 'spin' on the Zimbabwean dialogue. He expresses discontent that the dialogue has been taken away from Africans themselves as it became a political tool used by the West to attain a 'regime change' in Zimbabwe.

Known for his punchy quotes, Mbeki pulls out Ngugi wa Thiong'o, a revered Kenyan writer, carefully showing how some African intellectuals have played a part in perpetuating the view that Africa is incapable of solving its own problems. Taking on the media and the intellectuals, Mbeki writes: 'There are some among us, those that have the possibility to occupy the media spaces, who claim that they are Africans, among them intellectuals, who now rationalize this upside-down way of looking at Africa …'

Generally, he writes the entire letter himself. It is obvious when he doesn't, as the writing style departs from that which is so distinctly Mbeki's – an intoxicating mixture of elegance, clarity of expression and ideological obfuscation.

Similarly with his speeches. Unlike most leaders around the world, Mbeki not only amends, but will also draft large parts of his speeches. This is partly because he does not trust others to get it right, and partly because he is a workaholic who loves to write. As his former spokesman, Bheki Khumalo, confirms: 'He is a prodigious writer. Most nights when he is not travelling, and even sometimes when he is, he will work in the early hours.'

He writes often for his ministers too – an equally unusual occurrence. His style and turn of phrase, not to mention his frequent use of literary allusions, give the game away. Aziz Pahad's attack on Professor Sampie Terreblanche's book *A History of Inequality in South Africa*, on 13 December 2002, was one such obvious example. The ANC's submissions to the Human Rights Commission's hearings into racism in the media, on 5 April 2000, were presented by Jeff Radebe, a speaker not well known for quoting Shakespeare and JM Coetzee.

The shift from the Mandela presidency

The contrast between the Mandela presidency and the Mbeki presidency is both interesting and striking, but, more importantly, it is now useful in helping to understand the evolution of Mbeki's presidency and the way it wields its power. During his five-year term, from 1994 to 1999, Nelson Mandela probably had the smallest office of any president in the world. Essentially, he had a staff of four: Jakes Gerwel, the chief of staff and director-general; Fink Haysom, the presidential legal advisor; Parks Mankahlana, the presidential spokesperson (or senior spin doctor); and, lastly, long-time confidant and fellow Robben Islander Ahmed Kathrada, the parliamentary counsellor. Together these men comprised the 'big four' – truly 'all the president's men'.

In addition to the obvious administrative, protocol and security officials, there was also a small public relations unit, comprising Joel Netshitenzhe and Tony Trew ('a propagandist stroke speech writer', according to one of the big four). Netshitenzhe occupied a unique space, which he still does in 2006. He is close to the president and attached to the president's office, yet also somehow distinctively independent. He is probably the only individual in South Africa to have such a high level of influence as well as such a relatively high level of independence (a point on which I elaborate in the next chapter).

Relations between Mandela's office and Mbeki's, as the executive deputy president, were uncomfortable from the outset. The two offices had to share Tuynhuis in Cape Town and, as in any organization, the matter of space can be very controversial. There were early disputes about office allocation, which intensified as Mbeki's office rapidly expanded. Mandela did not try to compete.

His chief of staff, Jakes Gerwel, took the view that 'small is manageable; less is more'. Mbeki, perhaps with an eye on the day that he would succeed Mandela as president, decided to build up a 'presidency-in-waiting'. Lest he be accused of gratuitous empire building, the astute Mbeki realized that it would be necessary to muster independent support for the expansion. He appointed a commission, headed by the respected academic Vincent Maphai, to investigate the options for reform, including expansion.

The Maphai Commission's report, one of the most important in the institutional history of the South African government, reached the inevitable conclusion that the presidency needed much greater capacity.

Giving evidence to the Maphai Commission, Zola Skweyiya, then minister for public service and administration (DPSA), made the following incisive observation:

> There is a problem in so far as the coordination of the policy. We inherited a Cabinet Secretary from the old Apartheid Regime. Literally Comrade Mandela just went into the same office that Mr de Klerk, Mr Botha and their predecessors had previously occupied. There were no changes whatsoever – completely none. The only thing that really happened there is that the office was divided into three – one for Mandela, the other for De Klerk and the third for Mbeki ... De Klerk's office was better resourced than the others in so far as personnel and everything was concerned. The office of Mandela is the smallest office of a President I've ever seen in my life. That of Mbeki was about the same, with the most senior public servant there being a Chief Director. There was nobody really politically responsible for running the administration of the Presidency, due specifically to the nature in general of the Government of National Unity. There was also nobody senior enough to take decisions there on the questions of administration in general.[4]

The Maphai Commission was quickly convinced that the task of modern government required capacity at the very top, and it accordingly recommended the following:[5]

Strengthening direction and coordination at the centre of government
- In the view of the Commission the principal objectives of reform are (i) to formulate policies which meet the needs of the people, and which are well-founded on relevant data, coherent and well coordinated, fully and prudently costed to ensure value for money, and prioritized within available resources; and (ii) to facilitate the efficient and effective implementation of such policies, and to ensure that they are regularly monitored and reviewed.

- The Commission is firmly of the opinion that these objectives **cannot be fully realised without significant change at the apex and core of government**. National departments and provincial administrations will not be able to achieve these objectives if they continue to function as at present. By themselves they do not have the capability or authority to remedy the way government works.
- The Commission believes, therefore, that the transformation and development of the governance of South Africa requires a radical reappraisal of the functions, structures, personnel and management of the **Office of President**, taken together with the Office of the Deputy President, to ensure greater direction and coordination in government policy at all levels.
- In addition to the private office and a number of existing units, the Commission recommends that the Office of the President should be restructured to include:
  - An **Office of the Cabinet Secretariat (OCS)**, to coordinate Cabinet policy.
  - An **Office of Public Management (OPM)**, under the oversight of a minister, which would take on the functions of the DPSA and incorporate the existing offices on the Status of Women and Persons with Disabilities.
  - An **Organisational Review Agency (ORA)**, which would be located within the Office of Public Management and would carry out the ongoing process of evaluating and reconfiguring the structural organs of government.
  - An **Office of the Public Service Commission (OPSC)**, which would replace the current PSC, whilst retaining its independence and continuing to carry out the functions laid down by the Constitution.
  - The **Coordination and Implementation Unit (CIU)**, which would be transferred from the Office of the Deputy President and which might eventually be incorporated into the Cabinet Secretariat.
  - A **Coordinating Agency for Inter-Governmental Relations**, which would deal with inter-sectoral and inter-governmental relations but not local government. This body would take over the coordinating functions currently carried out by the Department for Constitutional Development.
  - An **Information Management and Systems Agency**, to coordinate all public service IMST [information management, systems and technology] initiatives.

- In the view of the Commission, the idea needs to be reinforced that the public service is essentially a unitary entity, operating at both national and provincial levels. Accordingly, the Office of the President should be restructured to avoid overlap and potential conflict. **In our view, there should be one DG for the offices of the President and Deputy President combined**, and a smaller office for the Deputy President. We recommend in particular that machinery is put into motion to assess whether or not senior personnel in the Presidency have been appropriately deployed and that, where necessary, appropriate corrective measures for the deployment and redeployment of staff be adopted as a matter of urgency.

> - The thrust of all the PRC's task team reports is that there is likely to be increasing delegation from the DPSA to the departments and provinces. Once the major elements of transformation have been broadly achieved, therefore, and the public service is more 'stabilised' at national and provincial levels, the Commission believes that there will no longer be a continuing need for a large department of public service and administration. We therefore recommend that a leaner Office of Public Management (OPM), strategically located in the Office of the Presidency, and under the oversight of a minister, would be more appropriate and would provide the Office with the necessary authority to engage more effectively with other departments and with the provinces.

- As indicated above, the Commission recommends that a more appropriate location for the offices on the Status of Women and Disabled Persons would be within the proposed Office of Public Management, where their contributions to policy could be more effectively integrated into the overall strategic planning processes.
- Our recommendation for the restructuring of the Public Service Commission is on the grounds of efficiency and effectiveness. In the view of the Commission, a less elaborate and more professionally managed body, led by no more than three Commissioners (rather than the fourteen laid down in the Constitution), would be more suitable for carrying out most of the monitoring and standards preserving functions outlined in the Constitution. Such a body would have a

limited staff, supplemented according to need, and would report the findings to the President, as well as to parliament (particularly through the relevant parliamentary portfolio committees).

- We recommend the creation of a stronger portfolio for the Secretary to the Cabinet as **Head of the Public Service**. An important role for this person would be to coordinate Cabinet inputs, follow up decisions taken, and ensure that policy is being implemented and communicated effectively.

Not all of these recommendations were implemented, but the main ones were. At the time, the outcome of the report provoked a largely cynical reaction from the press and other political commentators. An extraordinary process of Mbeki demonization started, much of which was unfair and lacking in contextual analysis. In my opinion, Mbeki was experiencing the 'Mandela-the-saint' factor: commentators were reluctant to disturb the halo-embossed narrative of Mandela and the feel-good factor that accompanied his accession to the presidency.

In truth, Mbeki is often his own worst enemy. He eschews the trappings of modern politics and cares little for presentation and 'spin'. At times, his stubbornness suggests that he actually takes pleasure in the bad press he invariably attracts. The growth of his staff provided perfect proof to the cynics that he was the ultimate centralist, a man determined to control everything from the top.

The irony of much of the commentary was lost on both the commentators and the public at large. Most of those who complained about Mbeki's 'empire building' also complained about the lack of coordination and good management in government. This was precisely Mbeki's – and Maphai's – argument: that, in order to manage properly and to enhance government's ability to deliver efficiently on its electoral mandate, it needed sufficient capacity to do so at the very top.

In any case, the comparison with Mandela's office was like comparing apples with oranges. It is not so much that Mandela and his team were amateurish – although this was how one of Mbeki's most loyal lieutenants disapprovingly described it to me at the time – but that they were 'Corinthian' – meaning old-style: not because they weren't professional, but because they were performing a labour of love. Much like Gerwel himself, they were an unpretentious lot, with no precious delusions of grandeur, no great plans for the future, merely a simple determination to deliver a reliable and uncomplicated service to the man they all treasured: Madiba.

In this straightforward objective, they succeeded. Mbeki increasingly filled the role of 'prime minister' or 'CEO' to Mandela's state president or chairman of the company, while Mandela was content to lead by example and delegate, focusing on the Big Issue, which was, at least during the first three years, national reconciliation and race relations.

Gerwel's opposite number in the deputy presidency was the Reverend Frank Chikane, a senior leader from the United Democratic Front (UDF), an appointment that contradicts the theory that Mbeki is only surrounded by former exiles; indeed, Murphy Morobe, another very prominent 'incile', is now Mbeki's director of communications in the presidency. Mbeki wanted a black African to head his office in the long term, someone with a reach into the Black Consciousness movement. It is far from clear whether Chikane has delivered; on that front, Mojanku Gumbi has been a much more potent link.

Like Gerwel, Chikane neither seeks nor gets the limelight. Though he attends cabinet meetings, as cabinet secretary – as had Gerwel before him – he prefers to be a 'backroom boy', also just like Gerwel. In managerial terms, those who have worked with him describe Chikane as collegial and congenial, but often slow in reaching a decision, and sometimes weak when faced with a tough one.

For example, they point to his failure to make two pivotal senior appointments in the presidency. The position of deputy head of the policy unit was vacant for several months in 2003 before Chikane finally made an internal appointment, promoting Goolam Aboobaker. And the position of director of communications remained vacant after the death of Parks Mankahlana in 2000 until May 2004, when the highly regarded Morobe, previously head of the important Financial and Fiscal Commission from 1994 to 2004, was appointed.

The answer to the question of who is more powerful, the cabinet ministers or the president's advisors, depends on whom you ask. One advisor tells me that the line managers – the cabinet ministers – are the president's main advisors. This may be true in policy terms, but in political terms certain key advisors wield immense power.

Fink Haysom, Mandela's legal advisor, recalls that, as the secretary of cabinet and head of the presidency, Jakes Gerwel was 'as powerful as any minister'. He recalls how the ministers quaked when Gerwel, on Mandela's authority, sent out questionnaires to each minister halfway through his term of office demanding to know what progress had been made in relation to policy implementation. Mbekite critics of the Mandela presidency cite this incident as a typical example of a lack of austere professionalism. The missive caused consternation because it was so unexpected. Until that point, ministers had largely been able to drift along, without clear targets or timelines.

Things are very different now, even though Frank Chikane is less assertive than Gerwel and less likely to send out such a questionnaire. Now there is a carefully crafted system, which is mainly overseen by the policy unit.

Mojanku Gumbi, however, has on occasion summoned cabinet ministers to meetings, which, according to a presidential source, 'they hate, but have to [attend]'. Public enterprises minister Alec Erwin begs to differ.

'If,' he says, 'I can't speak to the president, I am very happy to talk to one of his close advisors, either Mojanku Gumbi or Alan Hirsch.'

Much more than a legal advisor

Gumbi is a fascinating member of the inner circle. Every single person I have spoken to about Mbeki's core of advisors cites her as the top advisor and most powerful of them all. Without noise or fanfare she has glided into position as the president's right-hand woman. Asked about this, Joel Netshitenzhe, head of the presidential policy unit, says her constant interaction with the president is partly because 'the legal area has a tendency of impacting on everything'. Also because she is a 'very good lawyer and a bloody good negotiator', according to Alec Erwin.

Gumbi now stands head and shoulders above all the other advisors. Seldom does Mbeki meet anyone, or go anywhere, without her by his side. When the president-elect of Bolivia, Evo Morales, made an impromptu visit to South Africa in early January 2006, Mbeki agreed not only to meet with him, even though it was not a formal state visit – Morales had not yet been inaugurated – but greeted him at the bottom of the red-carpeted stairs of the west wing of the Union Buildings as if it were, in fact, a formal state visit.

By Mbeki's side was Gumbi – tall, slim, elegant, sharp-suited and sharp-eyed, but with a broad, warm smile. The protocol for the meeting had been agreed, as usual, in advance. One plus two on the South African side; one plus one on Bolivia's. Morales brought his economics advisor, Carlos Villegas; Mbeki, Gumbi and deputy minister for foreign affairs, Sue van der Merwe.

What happened next is instructive. Idasa was hosting Morales's visit and I was accompanying this remarkable, historic figure – the first indigenous president of Bolivia – on three days of meetings. Mbeki offered warm congratulations to Morales and, more importantly, concrete offers of help. Set for half an hour, the two men talked a full hour on global politics, and in particular US reaction to Morales's victory.

In the run-up to the previous Bolivian election in 2002, the United States had described Morales as a 'narco-terrorist' in the light of his history as leader of the Cocalero – the coca leaf farmers of his native region of Cochabamba in central Bolivia. Morales was moved by the strength of Mbeki's words of support, and touched by his concern and commitment to do all he can to ensure that Morales will get a fair hearing in the international arena. At one point Mbeki leant forward and asked Morales: 'What is this American obsession with Chàvez?' (He was referring to the controversial president of Venezuela, who persistently challenges US influence in the Andes.)

Mbeki then moved fast. He proposed a bilateral agreement between South Africa and Bolivia. Such agreements have become a central instrument of South African foreign policy – there are now more than twenty such agreements with nations as diverse as the United States and Germany on the one hand, and Mozambique and the Democratic Republic of Congo on the other. Van der Merwe was instructed to get the Mozambique document, 'Tippex' out all the details specific to that country and present it to Morales before he left South Africa a day later.

As we drove in convoy towards Johannesburg after the meeting had finished, the message arrived that Van der Merwe would join the meeting with Essop Pahad later that afternoon at his Houghton house in order to present the draft. Pahad took up from where Mbeki had left off. Van der Merwe had phoned him and they had discussed a further idea – assisting Morales to strengthen his presidency. On this, Pretoria now believes it speaks with authority, having experimented in a concerted fashion for eleven years and having learnt the hard lesson that, to guide a modern, democratic government effectively, you need strong capacity at the very top.

In the event, bad traffic prevented Van der Merwe from joining the meeting, so instead she met with Morales the next day in Cape Town, where she efficiently ran through the structure of the document in twenty minutes. Morales and his Bolivian colleagues were suitably impressed; they were dealing with a government that not only talked, but also acted. He was not yet president, but had already forged a new, potentially strategically valuable relationship for his impoverished country.

But back to the President's Men and Women. It is clear that, in terms of influence, Gumbi's role now extends far beyond that of legal advisor. As a lawyer, she received bad early press, due to her rather clumsy presentation of a report that inquired into Allan Boesak's culpability in financial mal-administration and fraudulent accounting at the Foundation for Peace and Justice. Boesak, a Cape Town–based cleric and one of the main leaders of the UDF during the days of the struggle, was also the ANC's candidate for premier during its ill-conceived Western Cape election campaign in 1994.

Feebly drafted and argued – later described by the *Sunday Times*'s Hogarth column as 'ill-considered and written with unseemly haste'[6]– the conclusions of the Gumbi report prematurely suggested that there was no prima facie evidence against Boesak and that he should be permitted to continue in public life by taking up the position of ambassador to the UN in Geneva. Following a criminal trial, in May 2000, Boesak was convicted and sentenced to prison.

The report did not do justice to Gumbi's raw intelligence, which I encountered when she headed the Open Democracy Task Force, established by Mbeki in 1995.[7] In any case, when it comes to presidential legal opinion forming, the politics often eclipses the law, as Haysom would himself readily accept. Haysom cites the example of the infamous South African Rugby Football Union (SARFU) case, in which Louis Luyt sued Nelson Mandela for 'failing to apply his mind' when he established the commission of inquiry into South African rugby in 1998. Ironically, although Mandela prevailed on the main issue, law triumphed over politics, in the dry and levelling form of a lengthy but incisive judgment on the nature and extent of presidential powers.

The Open Democracy Task Force provides a rather intriguing case study. Mbeki is often cited as being both innately secretive and inclined towards centralism. Yet it was he, as deputy president, who appointed a high-level committee headed by Gumbi, which included academics such as Professors Etienne Mureinik and Mandla Mchunu, later the CEO of the Independent Electoral Commission (IEC) and now director-general in the premier's office in KwaZulu-Natal, to do founding work on transparency policy.[8] It produced a progressive, in places even radical, draft law – the Open Democracy Bill. Moreover, Mbeki instructed Gumbi to put together an expansive civil society sounding board.

At a first meeting in July 1995, the so-called Open Democracy Advisory Forum was convened. It was too big and its membership too distracted by its 'daily agenda' to play the sort of role that was intended. It was subsequently eclipsed by a smaller but more effective group of ten organizations, which self-styled itself as the Open Democracy Campaign Group.[9]

Perhaps Mbeki knew that the larger forum would not work; perhaps, as one of the participants suggested at the first meeting, it was an attempt to co-opt civil society. But, given that the law had been so strongly drafted and was later diluted after a three-year round of consultations within the executive, with cabinet ministers such as Kader Asmal chipping away at its more sweeping provisions, I am not inclined towards this cynical interpretation.

The fact is that the committee produced a very strong, far-reaching draft law under Gumbi's leadership. During this period, the task force declined in strength after Mureinik's premature and tragic death, and Mchunu's appointment to the IEC. Gumbi became increasingly frustrated, and then uninterested. Perhaps her boss had lost interest as well. Or perhaps he had been ground down by the drip-drip of his colleagues' attempts to dilute the draft law; perhaps he was not really too keen on it anyway. In any case, at some point between 1996 and 1999, Mbeki washed his hands of the law, and it became a line-function responsibility of the minister of justice (at that time, Dullah Omar).

By way of a postscript, the law – renamed the Promotion of Access to Information Act, 2000 – did finally wend its weary way to the statute book, thanks to a Constitution-imposed deadline of February 2000, the hard work of Johnny de Lange and his justice committee in parliament, and Advocate Empie van Schoor, the remaining active and attentive member of the task force. Using the Act, Idasa launched legal proceedings in late 2003 against the ANC and the then three other largest political parties (the DA, the NNP and the IFP), asserting the public's right to know who secretly bankrolls their activities.

And, despite a certain amount of predictable bureaucratic inertia, the law continues to be useful to organizations and citizens who wish to extract accountability from those in power. Indeed, the law is widely admired internationally for its far-reaching and unique coverage of the private sector: information held by a private body, including a company or an individual, must be disclosed where access is 'necessary to protect or exercise another right'.

During the Open Democracy Bill process, I found Gumbi to be both reasonably accessible and candid. She would rile against the judiciary's opposition to her idea of a specialist Information Court, and express her dismay at the slow pace of the law's progress through the cabinet consultation process. She profoundly dislikes Cape Town. I will never forget the sight of her, coat collar turned up against the August rain and wind, making her way across the few yards separating the ministerial block at 120 Plein Street from the National Assembly building, screaming, 'I hate this place!'

Gumbi was in Cape Town because Mbeki had temporarily deployed her to work with the doomed 2004 Cape Town Olympic bid. It is clear that Gumbi is less lawyer and more political fixer. She is, as another advisor in the wider presidency put it, 'an all-rounder now. She is quite competent, and clearly the president has a lot of confidence in her. She has tremendous access and is close to him. She travels everywhere with him all the time.'

The same source confirms that Gumbi is 'still AZAPO', and that there is a meeting of minds between the president and her on issues that are generally termed 'African nationalism'.

Partly because of this meeting of minds, she is very loyal to Mbeki, but I suspect that some of her strength and appeal to the president is that she is no 'yes-man'. She has the power to walk away, which enhances her ability to wield influence by looking him in the eye while talking to him frankly on a range of issues. Given her access, the value that Mbeki attaches to her views, and the natural advantages that lawyers have in both the domestic and international policy arena, Gumbi is now the president's most influential advisor, which makes her one of the top five most powerful people in the country.

Other members of the inner circle

Apart from Gumbi, the other special advisors in the presidency are Titus Mafolo (political), Cunningham Ngcukana (NEPAD – the New Partnership for African Development), appointed in May 2004, and Wiseman Nkuhlu, although he has been on almost permanent secondment to the NEPAD secretariat since 2002. The appointment of Ngcukana, the charismatic former head of the National Council of Trade Unions (NACTU), with a specific NEPAD brief, indicates that Nkuhlu will not be returning to his old position. Nkuhlu will continue to enjoy very good access to the president's ear. Given the importance of NEPAD in Mbeki's African Renaissance agenda, his influence remains substantial.

Ngcukana offers competition and probably a very different approach from Nkuhlu's. It is safe to say that Ngcukana will push for a far stronger pan-Africanist line with the president. NACTU was a non-COSATU federation, with a more regional bent. A trade unionist who knows all the union leaders well describes Ngcukana as 'a very good diplomat, very bright, but lunatic, who professes to be a socialist, with an ego equal to Peter Marais''.

Nkuhlu, on the other hand, is an economist's economist, and was central to the vision of NEPAD as an instrument of economic, rather than political, change. But this is not the place to canvass or resolve these sharply different perspectives on NEPAD.

No one seems entirely clear what exactly Titus Mafolo does; he is very low-profile. Speechwriting is part of his responsibilities, but, like Bill Clinton, Mbeki takes a very firm hand on the tiller of his speeches. According to one former member of Mbeki's immediate team: 'I was never really sure where Mafolo was or what he did, and I'm not really sure what value he adds.'

In 2006, Mafolo was attributed as the driving force behind the creation of the 'Native Club' – a private group of black intellectuals loyal to the president – which attracted snide ridicule from a wider group of public intellectuals and other commentators.

Even after two years, it is too early to say how distinctive a contribution is being made by the director of communications, Murphy Morobe. On his appointment in 2004, the idea was for him to play a greater role in trying to develop an approach to communications that matches the strategic emphasis of Mbeki's approach to governance. In other words, that there would be a bigger plan for communicating the presidential message, as opposed to fire fighting. I explore the role of 'spin doctors' more closely in Chapter 8, given the very important role they play in modern politics.

Before Morobe was appointed, his position lay vacant for a long period of over two years. This was curious, to say the least, and explains the many difficulties in communication the presidency faced after Mbeki took office in 1999. During the hiatus, the role was partly filled by the presidential spokesman, Bheki Khumalo. Khumalo is an immensely talented man, with an approachable and instantly likeable manner, who won and held the respect of the great majority of the media, a topic I return to in the chapter on spin doctors and the media. Due to an unresolved dispute about allowances, Khumalo moved on to a very senior position at Siemens in mid-2005.

The final advisor in the presidency is John Jeffrey – or 'JJ', as he is more commonly and colloquially known – who holds the position of parliamentary counsellor. Armed with a mischievous sense of humour and a rhinoceros-like skin, Jeffrey's appointment is intriguing. Previously, he held the same position in the deputy presidency – serving, loyally, as he had for many years, Jacob Zuma. Yet despite this, he survived the culling of Zuma from the deputy presidency and the ensuing power struggle within the ANC, and in effect swapped camps. As a long-time MP in the KwaZulu-Natal provincial legislature and then the National Assembly, he is well placed to ensure that there is proper coordination and communication between parliament and the presidency, as well as acting as Mbeki's eyes and ears in the ANC parliamentary caucus.

The previous office holder was Manne Dipico. After eight years as premier of the Northern Cape and having headed the ANC's election campaign in 2004 – to great acclaim, given the outcome – it was widely assumed that Dipico would get a cabinet post. Commentators were confused by his appointment to parliamentary counsellor. But they underestimated both the position and the power of being part of Mbeki's immediate team. One only has to look at Dipico's predecessors to understand that his star is in the ascendant: Essop Pahad, Willie Hofmeyr (now head of the Special Investigating Unit of the DPP) and Charles Nqakula (minister of safety and security).

Dipico moved into the private sector, and is now the deputy chairperson of De Beers, following a black economic empowerment (BEE) deal involving top government brass and the mining giant. The deal has a staggering price tag of R3.8 billion, one of the biggest – if not *the* biggest – to involve a senior ANC politician.

When Sue van der Merwe was appointed to parliamentary counsellor in 1999, a joke did the rounds that Mbeki had wanted to add to the number of Afrikaners in government. On seeing her name, he assumed that she fitted the bill, when, in fact, she is as English-speaking as they come. She is now deputy minister of foreign affairs, with the important brief of ensuring that there is proper internal capacity to enable the department to fulfil all the many international obligations that Pretoria has accrued since 1994. This liberates the minister, Nkosazana Dlamini-Zuma, and the long-standing other deputy, Aziz Pahad, to focus on diplomacy and longer-term strategic issues.

According to one former member of Mbeki's advisory team, Aziz Pahad is, in fact, the more influential of the two brothers, contrary to received wisdom. Aziz Pahad and Mbeki speak often about foreign policy issues, and they go back a long way. Indeed, according to someone who knew them at the time, Aziz Pahad actually did carry Mbeki's bag to lectures on occasion when they studied together at the University of Sussex in the UK in the 1960s. A former Mbeki staffer puts it simply: 'Aziz is President Mbeki's best personal friend.'

Presidential units, councils and spies

One of the Maphai Commission's very specific recommendations (set out on pages 23 to 26) was that the policy advice and oversight function within the presidency should be enhanced. The idea of a Coordination and Implementation Unit (CIU) was raised and then implemented, with Dr Punday Pillay as its first head.

On one level, it has not worked out. Pillay left in 2000, apparently frustrated at the unit's lack of influence and its inability to forge an oversight role for itself. Pillay's idea was that it would, in effect, be looking over the shoulder of cabinet ministers, checking that what they were doing was what the president wanted them to do.

If so, this was an entirely unrealistic and politically naive notion. Mbeki, if he originally shared Pillay's vision, clearly retreated from it. After Pillay left, the position remained, as mentioned, unfilled for a long period; while Netshitenzhe is the de jure head, the de facto head is now Goolam Aboobaker as deputy director-general.

Aboobaker's journey to such a potentially important role is unusual. A former UDF activist and a physicist at the University of the Western

Cape, he was brought into the presidency by his old mentor Jakes Gerwel during the early years of the Mandela administration. Aboobaker soon read the tealeaves and engineered a transfer into the deputy presidency, having spotted its growth trajectory. A former colleague says that this was 'the act of an opportunist, which is what he is; he is not vituperative enough to be a viper', which sounds like a backhanded compliment if ever I heard one.

Everyone who knows Aboobaker from the old days says that intelligence, eccentricity and paranoia jostle for predominance; more laid-back now, yet still somewhat furtive and restless, as if he still expects to turn around and find a knife in his back, Aboobaker may not be the likeliest manager of such a unit. From another viewpoint, he may be ideally suited to the Byzantine intricacies of institutional politics at the highest level.

Unlike Pillay, Aboobaker sees the role of the policy unit as a 'modest one – we don't have any pretensions about a highfalutin role'. The policy unit deals, he says, with very specific tasks, such as the preparation of answers to parliamentary questions, cabinet memoranda, which they scrutinize ahead of cabinet, specialist reports, such as the poverty and inequality report, or the coordination of a special study on spatial development and investment, which Aboobaker cites as one of their most significant pieces of work to date.

Preparing a critique of a cabinet memorandum, whether Aboobaker chooses to portray it as a 'modest' task or not, is manifestly influential. Cabinet ministers tend to know very little about the detail of the subject matter they are being asked to make decisions on, other than their own policy areas. In most cases, they will only get to read the cabinet memorandum and any critique of it. There is no time to undertake a detailed examination of the issues. Hence, the 'critiquing' process is not so much a major technical exercise but rather 'to prepare brief analytical notes that attempt to get at the heart of the matter', according to Aboobaker. The purpose is to allow the cabinet to see the political wood from the trees, and, having got to the *political* heart of the matter, reach a political decision.

Much of the rest of the work of the Policy Coordination and Advisory Service (PCAS) is considered at director-general (DG) level, when the ministries get together in the clusters that shadow the full cabinet (see Chapter 2). For big pieces of work, such as the spatial development report, the policy unit will hire specialist consultants. (Interestingly, this report has not yet been published, even though it deals with the politics of the issue, on the basis that it might be 'misunderstood' – this according to a presidential source.)

So, for the influential 'Ten-Year Review', which played a major role in setting the ruling party's agenda and campaign line going into the 2004 general elections, a consultant named Andrew Merrifield was contracted to oversee the preparation of the report. The report represents a comprehensive and laudably self-reflective appraisal of the first ten years of democratic government.[10]

The political influence of the report in terms of settling some key policy issues, or raising new ones, such as the greater emphasis on industrial policy that the second Mbeki administration is aiming for, should not be underestimated. And nor, by the same token, should the power and influence of Joel Netshitenzhe. If any one piece of work underlines his influence, it is that the 'Ten-Year Review' was, in effect, a joint piece of work by the policy unit and the Government Communication and Information Service (GCIS), with Netshitenzhe's deputy at GCIS, Tony Trew, also playing a significant role.

Trew had been a member of Mandela's advisory team, and he and Aboobaker worked well together there; as in any organization, personal relationships matter greatly in government. Aboobaker says they were 'nervous ahead of the finalization of the report'. Although they briefed the national directors-general, as usual, they wanted to elicit a response from the cabinet ministers, because of the anticipated high-profile nature of the document. It certainly caught the eye of the more perspicacious ministers, who recognized an opportunity to blow their own (ministries') trumpet. Interestingly, the report was not presented as the government line – although that is what it became in the end because of the excellence of the work and its general acceptance by the cabinet. Such an approach would not have been possible without the political weight of Netshitenzhe behind it.

Despite the trajectory of growth created by the Maphai report and Pillay's grand vision, the policy unit has remained small in size. Under Aboobaker there are five deputy directors-general, again matching the cluster configuration: Dr Percy Mosieleng (international relations), Kefiloe Masiteng (governance and administration), Dr Yasmin Dada (social affairs), Alan Hirsch (economics) and Loyiso Jafta (justice, peace and crime prevention).

The policy unit may be small in size, but it is high-powered intellectually.

Aboobaker is smart and prudent enough to believe that it is through the credibility of the unit's work, and the members' ability to marshal the arguments, especially with their bureaucratic counterparts at the head of the national departments, that the policy unit will exercise the greatest influence.

In a sense, given the false start of the Pillay period and the relatively recent appointment of Aboobaker, it is still too soon to say how great an influence the unit will have in the future. Given the technocratic and unassuming outlook of Aboobaker, it is likely to be influential at certain moments in relation to certain policy decisions, rather than a persistent sphere of power at the heart of government. In a sense, the more structured vision presented by the Maphai report has been replaced by a more organic diffusion of influence, as Mbeki has increased his own direct team of advisors.

The Maphai vision was of the policy unit comprising the whole of the presidential advisory capability. Now, rather, there are two parts to it – the more technical, more structured PCAS unit, and Mbeki's direct, core group of advisors.

There is another unit within the presidency, aside from the policy unit and the private and cabinet offices, and that is the Presidential Support Unit (PSU). It is a wonderfully understated nomenclature. It suggests logistics – travel arrangements and paper clips – but nothing could be further from the truth. In so far as it is about travel, it represents an advance party gathering intelligence for Mbeki's international wanderings and interventions.

As noted, Mbeki is preoccupied by international affairs. Indeed, he would have made a very fine foreign minister had Mandela not wanted to anoint his successor so clearly when appointing him deputy president in 1994. However, Essop Pahad's spin doctor, Tony Heard, went out of his way to point out to me that the perception that Mbeki travels incessantly is not matched by the facts. According to Heard, Mbeki spent an average of 15 per cent of the time outside the country's borders in 2003 – the height of the media clamour on the issue. But another advisor accepts that 'with his concern for international affairs, we are neglecting our world here in South Africa – or at least that is the perception we have created'.

The PSU is a free-limbed, nimble creature of modern politics. First headed by Welile Nhlapo, a former intelligence operative, most of the other members have intelligence backgrounds. However, they no longer do any spying. Spies collect information; they do not sort it. The PSU do a certain amount of collecting, but their real role is in the sorting – the analyses that will help Mbeki make a decision about a course of action.

Due to turf wars arising from the fact that its work cut across several departments – most obviously intelligence and foreign affairs – the five members of the PSU have recently been redeployed: two have become ambassadors, and Nhlapo is now at the United Nations. So, at least for the time being, the PSU as an entity within the presidency exists only on paper, though its function lives on, but now under a different institutional heading – the National Security Council (NSC). The NSC is headed by Barry Gilder, the former director-general of home affairs, and is part of the National Intelligence Agency.

For example, Dr Andre Zaaiman, a former intelligence operative in the liberation movement and a key policy thinker on the Middle East, is working on the same issues as before from within the NSC along with the others, often reporting directly to the president.

Typically, Zaaiman and his colleagues will fly to wherever in the world there is an issue – the Middle East, Sri Lanka, the Great Lakes, western Sahara – and talk to the key players. Then they will do some thinking and analysis before reporting back to the president.

The creation of the PSU was by no means a secret, but it was hardly well advertised either. Look on the government website and it does not appear in the organograms or descriptions of the presidency. Google it, and the first mention is on a website called somalilandnet.com – reporting a fact-finding mission by Nhlapo. The second mention is on a Sri Lankan site named tamilnet.com, which reports on a visit to South Africa in April 2005 by LTTE (Tamil Tiger) leaders.

'We are troubleshooters and code-breakers,' a PSU member told me in its third year of operation.

It's nice work if you can get it; certainly the one job in government I am more than willing to admit I would love to have. Set up in 2001 to provide Mbeki with direct information and advice free from the bureaucratic impediments of foreign affairs and the intelligence services, the PSU is supposed to operate in a free but somewhat controversial space between the presidency and these two line-function departments. The structural issues are clearly obstacles to its longer-term future, but the need will always be there for high-level, skilled people who can 'move fast and think politically in ways that traditional advisors and bureaucrats can't', according to a former PSU member.

Finally, there are the presidential councils, which have spawned rapidly over the past five or so years since 2000. The councils are self-selecting; that is to say, there are no set lists. But there are regular and very influential attendees, for example Zwelinzima Vavi and Ebrahim Patel from labour, and Michael Spicer and/or Tony Trahar from Anglo American, on the business council. Mbeki does not always attend, though he tries to. The agendas are equally vague; they represent freewheeling, off-the-record opportunities to exchange ideas and debate points of view.

The SACP regards the presidential councils as significant, remarking on them in its epic May 2006 discussion paper: 'Established capital, for instance, by and large boycotts parliament, preferring to deal directly with a series of presidential councils (the business council, the investment council, etc.).'[11]

The big pivot

Naturally, the president is the most powerful man in the country. That may not be as obvious as it seems. There are plenty of what are fashionably known as 'failed states' around, especially in Africa, where the head of government is a proxy or puppet for another, invariably external corporate, but sometimes military, interest. As the Conclusion suggests, Mbeki is contesting political ground with some serious political and commercial interests, most notably domestic and transnational capital. His hold on political power is complete in the sense that he has painstakingly sidelined all serious internal opposition within the ANC, whether individual or collective – though Jacob Zuma has shaken his sense of security and control.

Although the alliance partners – COSATU, in particular – cannot by any means be totally discounted (see Chapter 6), Mbeki has defeated the left and, having taken control of the centre ground of South African politics, is busy imposing his own version of modern social democracy on government. Armed with an increasingly competent advisory team and the cabinet of men and women that he wants, he is the dominant pivot in government. The question of whether his dogged dedication to remain fully abreast of all of his cabinet's agenda and the progress of his line managers – the cabinet ministers – is a help or hindrance to effective government is impossible to say at this point.

Whatever his faults, Mbeki is a man with a devotion to long-term strategy and an egocentric view of his own epic place in history; he knows his own mind, stubbornly so at times (as on HIV/AIDS). His advisors and his government have to live with that. As with any dominant boss, the manager must be managed. History has still to define the impact that Mbeki will make on South Africa and beyond. But it is already clear that his influence is substantial; even his greatest detractors know that he is a serious force to be reckoned with.

Access to Mbeki from outside the immediate circle is not easy, so access through the advisors is crucial if the president's course is to be influenced in any way. Advisors draw their strength from their principal. Thus, Mbeki's power increases their potential influence. Though they are all essentially chips off the same block as the president, to whom they are so loyal, a number of them exert special influence.

Certain individuals, such as Mojanku Gumbi, and certain sub-institutions, such as the policy unit, stand out. The presidency – as opposed to the president, who is pre-eminent – is a centrifugal centre of influence in the new anatomy of the new South Africa, sucking power from the surrounding atmosphere with its ornate array of presidential councils.

2

The Cabinet

All the President's Men ... and Women

Part of Mbeki's 'Socratic' predisposition is not to talk much when chairing cabinet. He prefers to sit back and listen, unleashing the occasional arrow-like question that invariably goes to the heart of the matter, sometimes bringing the minister who holds the floor to an abrupt halt. When public servants make presentations to cabinet, as they quite often do, Mbeki will be even quieter, inviting the relevant minister to lead the discussion, and sometimes actually handing the chairing of the meeting to another minister.

For the public servant concerned, this can be a deeply off-putting experience. As one told me: 'The president was like a ticking bomb in the corner. Completely silent, but somehow I could sense his brain turning over and I just wanted him to say something, anything! But you can hardly scream at your president, "For God's sake, say something!"'

Despite his impatience with waffle, Mbeki prefers to let a discussion take its full course. Whereas Tony Blair's cabinet meetings typically last less than an hour, Mbeki's will start at 8.30 a.m. on alternate Wednesday mornings and nearly always last until lunchtime, sometimes into the afternoon. As a chair, he has the ability to give the dialogue space, but also to remain firmly in control. It is quite an art, at which Mbeki is very adept, and now also very experienced.

He chaired the majority of the Mandela government's cabinet meetings between 1994 and 1999, even though Mandela hated that Mbeki was considered the 'prime minister', as in reality he was. Mbeki is also fully on top of the issues, despite the fact that the briefing papers from his staff are rarely up to scratch. According to one of his former cabinet colleagues, Kader Asmal, he has 'the knack of asking all the tough questions'. To Asmal, Mbeki's style meant that the experience of being in cabinet was at times like being in an 'Oxbridge seminar'.

Ministers present their draft laws and policies. The debates are serious. In one of the early cabinet meetings in the Mbeki presidency, during a fairly intense discussion, Mangosuthu Buthelezi said, 'Once our leader has spoken, we defer.' Winning the instant respect of her ANC colleagues, Nkosazana Dlamini-Zuma, the minister of foreign affairs, spoke up and said, 'In our party we do things differently; we may challenge our leader.'

For Marthinus van Schalkwyk, the former New National Party leader who dissolved the NNP and joined the ANC and was rewarded with a cabinet appointment as minister for environmental affairs and tourism in April 2004, this is also unfamiliar ground: 'Although the president is very strong intellectually, he is not afraid to put something on the table and say "Now criticize this idea." That is not what I am used to. In the National Party we were used to deferring to our leader. Mbeki challenges us to challenge him.'

In a parliamentary system, cabinet is an important institution. The way that President Mbeki runs it, it is also very influential. In terms of the actual meetings, there are two tiers of influence. One group of ministers will confine their contributions to those subjects that have some bearing on their own line function. Then there are those who will speak on a range of subjects: Trevor Manuel will intervene in almost every subject, as there is a budgetary implication to almost every issue (just as he sits on each and every one of the cabinet cluster committees for the same reason).

Alec Erwin, too, often intervenes. Like Kader Asmal, minister of education from 1999 to 2004, who was left out of the second Mbeki cabinet, Erwin is a former academic, familiar with a broad range of subjects. So, too, is the formidably talented Thoko Didiza of the younger brigade, who may one day become South Africa's first woman president. According to their peers, it could be either Didiza or Deputy President Phumzile Mlambo-Ngcuka.

Mbeki's commitment to women is noteworthy and admirable. The 2003 United Nations' Development Programme (UNDP) report on South Africa not only criticized the government's macroeconomic approach, but also observed that South African men are the laziest in the world. South African women work 22 per cent harder than the men, almost the highest differential globally.

Perhaps Mbeki did not need the UNDP to point this out to him. He pays more than lip service and rhetorical justice to women: he actually appoints them to positions of power. His current cabinet contains twelve women (out of thirty cabinet ministers, including Mbeki and his deputy president); and of the twenty-one deputy ministers, nine are female. Moreover, while Tony Blair increased the number of women in cabinet when he came to power in 1997, they occupied relatively minor positions. Not so with Mbeki: women are at foreign affairs, home affairs, justice, health, housing, public service and administration, and mineral and energy affairs – all key, senior posts – as well as Phumzile Mlambo-Ngcuka as deputy president. Pen portraits of all the current cabinet members (as at June 2006, following Mbeki's reshuffle of his cabinet after the death of Stella Sigcau) can be found in Appendix A.

Gender accounting: Cabinet and deputy ministers (excluding president and deputy president)[1]

	1994	1996	1999	2003	2004	2005
Male	35	28	23	26	28	28
Female	5	12	16	17	21	22
Total	40	40	39	43	49	50

Choosing the cabinet is a complex process for the president. In addition to merit – ability and performance – Mbeki has to take into account other considerations, such as provincial bias, racial and ethnic mix, and language. The ANC hates to talk about it, but the evidence indicates that the Nguni language group is very prominent (see table below). The first caller into SAfm's midday show after the announcement of the cabinet on 28 April 2004 bemoaned the influence of the 'Xhosa Nostra', as he put it, and the lack of Tswana-speaking ministers (Joe Modise having been the only one since 1994).

Ethnic accounting: Cabinet and deputy ministers (excluding president and deputy president)

	1994	1996	1999	2003	2004
Coloured	2	2	2	3	3
Indian*	6	7	5	5	4
Pedi	0	1	0	1	2
Sotho	0	0	2	2	2
Swazi	1	1	1	1	1
Tsonga	1	2	1	1	1
Tswana	1	1	0	0	0
Venda	1	1	2	2	2
White**	12	4	4	5	8
Xhosa	8	11	12	14	18
Zulu	8	10	10	9	7
Total	40	40	39	43	49

*   In 1994: 2 x Hindu, 4 x Muslim; 1996: 2 x Hindu, 5 x Muslim; 1999: 5 x Muslim; 2003: 5 x Muslim; 2004: 1 x Hindu, 3 x Muslim

** In 1994: 8 x Afrikaner, 4 x English (2 x Jewish); 1996: 1 x Afrikaner, 3 x English (2 x Jewish); 1999: 1 x Afrikaner, 3 x English (1 x Jewish); 2003: 2 x Afrikaner, 3 x English (1 x Jewish); 2004: 5 x Afrikaner, 3 x English (2 x Jewish)

	1994	1996	1999	2003	2004	2005
Nguni	17	22	23	24	26	25
Other African	3	5	5	6	7	7
Minorities	20	13	11	13	16	18

Nguni: Zulu, Xhosa, Swazi, Ndebele
Other African: Pedi, Sotho, Tsonga (Shangaan), Tswana, Venda
Minorities: White, Indian, Coloured

Note: The number of Afrikaners represented in cabinet has increased dramatically this term.

The constitutional authority and role of cabinet

The Constitution describes who is in the cabinet, how they are appointed and whom they are accountable to. That is the easy bit: the cabinet consists of the president, as head of the cabinet, a deputy president and ministers;[2] they are appointed by the president, who 'assigns their powers and functions'[3] – and 'may dismiss them'; and the members of the cabinet are 'accountable collectively and individually to parliament for the exercise of their powers'.[4]

It is a classic statement of a liberal democratic parliamentary democracy. The 'president' is really a 'prime minister', as 'head of the cabinet', and the ministers are (in the great majority) drawn from parliament, to which it is accountable. Such a system is to be contrasted with a 'presidential' system, where the legislature (parliament) and the executive (departments and presidency) are elected separately, and, although the latter can be called to account by the former, there is no overlap in functions, power or personnel.

This is especially important for understanding the power relations between the legislature and the executive: in parliamentary systems, the executive is always far more powerful than the legislature, and there is a mountain of academic literature to back up this assertion. In both, the president or prime minister is very powerful – in the presidential system he or she draws particular succour from the fact that he or she has been directly elected; in a parliamentary system the power of the prime minister is entrenched by the built-in power he or she can exercise over the legislature through his or her control of the majority party. These are crucial themes that I will return to in the coming chapters on parliament and the ANC itself.

But what exactly does the cabinet do and how does it operate? Its narrow role is as a political decision-maker. At its fortnightly Wednesday morning meeting in the Union Buildings (sometimes, if parliament is in session, it will meet in Tuynhuis in Cape Town, the presidential building next to the National Assembly), it must make and review policy, forming *political* judgments on the issues that emerge, which it does with the help of cabinet memoranda. As I mentioned in Chapter I, these are prepared by the cabinet secretariat in close consultation with the responsible line-function department and are supposed to be circulated the Friday before the cabinet meeting. In most cases, however, the cabinet secretariat operates far more as an administrative function, with memoranda drafted by the minister and his or her staff.

At that point, numerous drafts will have been subjected to technical revisions, as well as the budgetary and implementation considerations that arise. This occurs through an intricate process of inter- and intra-departmental committees, culminating in a review by the appropriate cabinet cluster committee (considered in a little more detail below), although some policy proposals, such as the mining charter legislation, come direct to cabinet. Where there is a labour consideration, the proposal will have to go through NEDLAC. Lastly, the Policy Coordination and Advisory Service of the presidency will have critiqued the policy and its memorandum.

Thus, by the time the policy idea reaches the cabinet table, it should be in a finely tuned condition. And yet there may still be tough political decisions to make. The political judgment is the culmination of a non-technical process that usually runs parallel to the technical side of the policy-making. This is more organic and less structured, and will include engagement with a wider group of sometimes non-governmental stakeholders, including the ANC's allies COSATU and the South African Communist Party (SACP). A parliamentary study group – the ANC membership of a parliamentary committee – may intervene if and when it has taken the opportunity to appraise itself of the policy development.

Sometimes a more elaborate policy-making process must unfold. Kader Asmal recalls how in the case of his Higher Education Bill it was necessary to consult every institution: 'I sent people around and then met with the vice-chancellors.' A Green Paper setting out the parameters of the idea followed, then a cabinet submission prepared by the department; there were discussions with COSATU because of the employment issues; it also therefore went to NEDLAC. There was controversy, so the president suggested a further month of consultation and debate. Thus, each policy process may involve slight variations according to its particular political needs.

In recent years, Mbeki has added an additional policy-making and implementation round to the overall process: the January and July *lekgotlas*. According to one former cabinet minister, 'they are absolutely dreaded'. It is a meeting of the cabinet, but with all directors-general and most special advisors present. It is, in essence, a grand governmental think tank. For the non-cabinet ministers, especially the DGs, it is a chance to shine; personal agendas are ruthlessly pursued, but the overall value is accepted – it helps government work more effectively across departments.

The golden rule for any lobbyist is: Get in early! Changing a government's mind is far harder than influencing the original decision. So, making a mark during the 'thinking' period is key, especially before the government goes public and announces its policy choice. It is one of the less attractive outcomes of competitive democratic systems that changing one's mind is generally regarded as a sign of weakness.

Hence, once a decision or a policy view is published, it is hard to get a substantial reversal. One of the main complaints of the ANC alliance partners, not to mention those of us who work in policy think tanks in civil society, is that the government tends to operate at times with insufficient consultation during the policy-making process. Ideas are kept inside the executive, perhaps as a result of the complex governmental decision-making apparatus that has now been assembled.

Notwithstanding this, the political decision will be informed to some degree or other by wider ideological and strategic considerations. How do they get funnelled into the cabinet process? Through three main channels: first, the presidency, which has its own policy-making capacity, as described in the previous chapter; second, the department of finance – a 'government within a government', as described later on; and, lastly, through the ANC.

Mbeki is obviously the key player and representative of the presidency's position in cabinet, though, as noted, his key advisors are extremely influential in this regard. Trevor Manuel, as minister of finance, is the key player from the government-within-a-government's perspective, again for obvious reasons. As to the ANC, it is more complex, but the key person and the lynchpin for all of this is Joel Netshitenzhe.

Jewel in the crown

Netshitenzhe is *the* most extraordinary person. It is not unusual for professionals in contemporary South Africa to hold down more than one
job, but not to hold down two *huge* jobs. Netshitenzhe is head of the PCAS
– the president's own policy unit, with both access and, therefore, direct
influence at the very apex of government.

Until June 2006, Netshitenzhe was for several years the CEO of the
government's communication arm, GCIS. (Former ANC MP and businessman, Themba Maseko, is the new CEO of GCIS.) Put these two positions
together and this is what they add up to: Netshitenzhe is the most senior
policy advisor and coordinator in the country, and was for a long time
responsible for the packaging and marketing of the government's collective
message. It is hard to imagine a more powerful combination of roles – one
that has created a reservoir of political capital and influence from which
he will be able to draw for a long time to come. Netshitenzhe attends all
cabinet meetings and, as secretary to the cabinet, takes overall responsibility
for recording decisions and compiling the cabinet minutes, sometimes
taking the chair or leading discussions. He is also a member of the ANC's
NEC and, far from being the technocratic manager that his two positions
suggest, he is also one of the ANC's leading thinkers and intellectuals,
drafting many of the most influential internal discussion papers of the past
fifteen years. Indeed, Netshitenzhe laments the decline of intellectualism
in the broader movement and the emphasis on technocracy.

'There should be a battle of ideas,' he says, 'but too many of our intellectuals are doing practical jobs, not "thinking". Why was it so difficult to
persuade Pallo Jordan to apply for a vice-rectorship at a university? What is
Penuell Maduna [former minister of justice, 1999–2004] doing in private legal
practice and not teaching law? Why has Rams Ramashia left government
[he was director-general at the department of labour] and gone to the private
sector [BP] and not to a university?'

Netshitenzhe partly answers his own question, noting the paradox: the
government needs good people so as to give leadership to society and must
compete in the market; but people get used to a new lifestyle and 'you cannot
deploy a talented DG as a town clerk somewhere, even if you need to, because
the lifestyle that a DG's package provides cannot be sustained in other areas,
seemingly of a lower status but in fact quite strategic in the order of things'.

Besides, Netshitenzhe adds, the ANC has not mastered the challenge of deployment to give leadership in the various 'loci of power in a polity'. Nelson Mandela decried this in his opening speech to the 1994 national conference of the ANC: 'Seldom before have we experienced such dislocation as in the few months after the elections … Ours was not a planned entry into government. Except for the higher echelons, we did not have a plan for the deployment of cadres. We were disorganized, and behaved in a manner that could have endangered the revolution.' But, according to Netshitenzhe, the problem persists.

Despite this awesome array of responsibilities and the power that accompanies it, Netshitenzhe is a remarkably nice person. Once one has got through the innate reserve and shyness, there is warmth and humanity, and a willing smile. It is all but impossible to find someone with a bad word to say about him; incredibly, he commands the respect of a huge range of people across the whole of the ANC-alliance spectrum. Almost everyone will, without prompting, mention his influence and intellectual integrity. To one former cabinet minister, Netshitenzhe is 'elliptical, but independent – definitely not a lackey, though GCIS is absolute crap', while to a current cabinet minister he is 'a recessive character, very professional, very loyal, who does not often invoke his status. Because he does not throw his weight about, though he could, he keeps friends and rarely makes serious enemies.'

Netshitenzhe's main office in downtown Pretoria is high above the hustle and bustle of street level and has a quiet serenity, encouraged by a view towards a nearby park and the simple but elegant African furniture. On the wall hangs a certificate of appreciation from a company called Inroads, whose sales line is 'developing brands'. This is apt: in a sense, Netshitenzhe has spent the past eleven years developing one brand: Mbekite government.

'Joel would die for the president,' says Bheki Khumalo, Mbeki's spokesman from 1999 to 2005.

It may be unfair to attach him so closely to Mbeki, but one cannot help but feel that they are brothers in all but name. They share a disinclination for the limelight, yet they do not shun responsibility and take on huge amounts of work; they write prodigiously; they philosophize as much as they strategize; both men turn to Marxist theory to help explain political economy, yet they are both conspicuously determined to ensure that capital remains 'onside'.

It is in these terms that he responds to my first question: Is the government in office but not in power?

'Any state has limitations, especially in the realm of economic policy,' he says. 'Capital lies in private hands and so, in some areas of social activity, we have also to depend on the cooperation and even the leadership of others.'

Citing job creation as the prime example, Netshitenzhe argues that much therefore depends on whether the private sector 'plays ball' – a phrase he mentions often. It is, he concedes, an open, unresolved question, critical to the future prosperity of South Africa. Netshitenzhe refers to a recent invitation to address the board of Anglo American. Netshitenzhe made the presentation – not Mbeki or Manuel – and sought to persuade Anglo that there is a joint action with government in the realm of job creation. Again: developing – and selling – the brand. A brand based on the South African Way – talking and consulting and negotiating, although Netshitenzhe admitted to me that he is concerned about overdoing the consultation for fear that it will encourage the status quo ahead of change, and states that Mbeki's second term is more assertive than his first, with less emphasis on consultation and more on taking action.

Continuity and change

This adjustment in the overall strategy and approach of government since 2004 is subtle, yet decisive. We will come to recognize 2004 as the end of the beginning (but hopefully not the beginning of the end). The 1994–99 and 1999–2004 administrations were in many ways an extension of what preceded the ANC's coming to power in 1994 – reflected in both policy and personnel.

If there is one figure that embodies this, it is Alec Erwin. When I interviewed Erwin for this book, it was notable how he grounded his points in the period leading up to 1994.

'The key to our success,' says Erwin, 'was the work done before 1994, the preparatory work, especially in the economic arena.'

He lists the men who built policy during that period, along with himself: Trevor Manuel, Tito Mboweni (now Reserve Bank governor), Jay Naidoo, Moss Ngoasheng and Derek Hanekom. Others, such as Blade Nzimande, worked on education policy, contained in a famous 'yellow book'. Hence, argues Erwin, the first cabinet of 1994 came in 'knowing roughly what we wanted to do' – though as a former cabinet minister points out, 'While some of us were "fish to water", and we swam, others nearly sank – they were terribly dependent on Mbeki; if there was a problem, it was always "go and see Thabo". People like Stella Sigcau and Ivy Matsepe-Casaburri would virtually camp outside his office.'

The point of this brief excursion into history is merely to illustrate that there was a core group of people who had worked together for a long period of time, preparing for government, with strong contacts internationally. 'A fairly cocky bunch,' says Erwin. 'We didn't feel intimidated.' This produced a cohesive cabinet in the early years after 1994, with few major debates, willing to dip into what Erwin calls the ANC's 'long tradition of pragmatism' and able to make incisive decisions, such as the adjustment in macroeconomic policy in 1996 (as discussed further on).

Alec Erwin was one of the central figures during this period, but he concedes that it is much less about big policy-making now and far more about the 'nitty-gritty' of government. People have moved on. There is a different group of ANC leaders coming through whose experiences are less rooted in the big ideological struggles of the late 1980s and early 1990s, and instead derives from the more recent experience of trying to implement policy over the last decade.

Thus, the influence of Erwin – so central to the big decisions of the period from 1990 to 2004, will decline, not least because of his new portfolio, public enterprises. Although important to the new emphasis on domestic industrial policy, it is still less important than it was because so much of the restructuring of state enterprises has been completed; only Transnet really remains, and the formidable Maria Ramos is firmly entrenched and in command there as the chief executive.

Loyal deputy

The deputy president, Phumzile Mlambo-Ngcuka, is typical of this shift – a woman without any strong factional support or great history in the ANC liberation movement, but with a reputation for competence and excellence. Her appointment was something of a surprise. Not because she is a woman – Mbeki's excellent record on this front I have already remarked on – but for his decision not to use the deputy presidency to satisfy a substantial political grouping within the ANC.

The favourite to succeed Jacob Zuma was his former wife, Nkosazana Dlamini-Zuma. But, not only did Mbeki turn elsewhere when he sacked Jacob Zuma in May 2005, he did not even find time to contact Dlamini-Zuma to inform her of his decision. Mbeki can be utterly ruthless at such times. According to a presidential advisor who was very close to the action at the time of the decision, Dlamini-Zuma 'literally cried, literally cried for days, she was so shocked'.

Bheki Khumalo, the former presidential spokesman, says that, when Jacob Zuma was in the position, the role of deputy president was very low-key – 'not a powerful position at all, with very little executive authority'. As the Constitution makes clear, the role of the deputy president is entirely for the president to determine. Whereas Zuma was confined to vague areas of government, such as the 'moral regeneration' campaign, Mlambo-Ngcuka has been tasked with some far more substantial domestic policy responsibilities – most notably leading the development of an integrated policy approach to the 'second economy'.

While the role of the deputy president would generally be unlikely to include any serious policy content, luck was on Mlambo-Ngcuka's side when she took office as the second in command. She came into office at a time when talks were going on about South Africa's economic growth pattern, which continues to exclude the majority of the population. In parliamentary responses to the 2005 State of the Nation speech, Mbeki referred to a 'developmental state', hinting that the government has a much bigger role to play in assisting the economy to grow in a way that will alleviate poverty for the majority of citizens. Mlambo-Ngcuka came into office as the matron of a shift in policy – the hastily termed Accelerated and Shared Growth Initiative of South Africa (ASGISA).

The programme aims to bridge the gap between formal and informal economy, respectively termed 'first' and 'second' economy by the president. The acronym, like many others in the country, is not the easiest, as finance minister Trevor Manuel was struggling with it in his 2005 Medium-Term Budget Policy Statement. Referring to ASGISA, Manuel said in his Budget speech: 'The deputy president [Mlambo-Ngcuka] calls this initiative Assss giiiii, asgiii … what …' The acronym became attached to Mlambo-Ngcuka, giving her both additional status and purpose.

The core objective is to halve poverty and unemployment by 2014. Through this programme, the government aims to attain 6 per cent economic growth, a 'shared economic growth'. The role of the deputy president in this substantial project is that of coordination and oversight.

The governance system

In addition to the cabinet itself, there are now 'cabinet clusters'. Mbeki likes systems, and the cluster system is one of his major reforms. There are five sectoral committees: social (chaired by health minister Manto Tshabalala-Msimang); economic, investment and employment (chaired by trade and industry minister Mandisi Mpahlwa); international relations, peace and security (chaired by foreign affairs minister Nkosazana Dlamini-Zuma); justice, crime and security (chaired by safety and security minister Charles Nqakula); and governance and administration (chaired by public service and administration minister Geraldine Fraser-Moleketi).

Cluster committees meet every two weeks, and ministers prioritize attendance. 'You can't miss those,' one advisor told me. They are very important locations of decision-making, less cumbersome than the full cabinet and with more detailed documentation. The cluster committees deal with political questions, as well as key questions of policy implementation. It is also the place where vibrant tussles between ministers and their directors-general occur. But the committees are not much smaller than the cabinet itself – the social sector committee, for example, has twenty cabinet ministers and eight deputies, and in some quarters there is ambivalence over its effectiveness.

Kader Asmal, when still in the cabinet, was not enthusiastic about the cluster committees in general, nor is Trevor Manuel, though most of the other cabinet members are more positive. Asmal made the point that the cluster committees are 'an attempt to strengthen "joined-up government", but unless the budget is allocated to the clusters – which it is not – then it can't be joined-up decision-making'.

In any case, it is very hard to make budget decisions in a committee with as many as twelve members where the debate is 'conditioned' by the position papers produced by the very able members of Manuel's staff. On this point, however, Manuel points to the importance of the ministerial budget committee – separate to the cluster committees – which, he says, he has introduced 'to diffuse the idea of a government within a government, or that I am special, and to encourage a sense of shared responsibility for budgetary decisions'.

The National Treasury: Government within a government

The department of finance – or 'National Treasury' as the Constitution names it – is often accused of being a government within a government. For a number of reasons this is true to a large extent, though Manuel tries to underplay it, citing the ministerial budget committee as an example of his inclusivity. But the department's technical expertise, the support of the president, and Manuel's own personality and character have combined to create the sense that it is a separate power centre.

Like Mbeki, Trevor Manuel exudes power. In 1995, I remember walking to the front of an SAA Boeing 747, which had just transported us from London, in time to see Manuel emerge from the first-class section and skip down the stairs to a waiting car. Although he still had the Mexican Zapata-like moustache then, he had already ditched the beard and was beginning to look the part of an international financier. Now even more so. He is a tall, broad-shouldered man who is ageing well, and he has learnt to look tough and elegant at the same time. Women find him very attractive. As Kader Asmal says, 'Trevor has an extremely physical presence, which is daunting.' Good suits help, of course. And Manuel is now one of the best-dressed men in South Africa. As I noted in a more frivolous piece in *GQ* (South Africa):

> Politics is about power, by definition. Power is exerted by individual men and women; what they choose to wear impacts on the exercise of their power. Clothes denote and amplify – or dilute – that power. But beyond this, collars are the real key to understanding the geography of political fashion here, with two major categories: the 'cutaway' collar and the non-cutaway, traditional, narrower collar. A cutaway collar broadens a man's shoulder and enlarges his chest, implying greater power, whilst creating space for a bigger tie-knot, which further multiplies the effect. Note those who favour such cutaway collars: Trevor Manuel, Tito Mboweni and Tony Leon. The two TMs are the two most powerfully attired politicians in South Africa and two of the five most powerful people in the country. They are fortunate that they are both tall, handsome men, on whose

significant frames a two or three-piece suit – and they both have the self-confidence to wear waistcoats when the weather and the occasion permits – looks magnificent, and both are well paid enough to afford good quality cloth. Significantly, they were the first black finance minister and reserve bank governor respectively. They had to win a war of perception and credibility, and persuade a sceptical audience that they were up to the task. Looking the part was half the battle won.

Similarly, Manuel has learnt to protect himself and to project power through numbers. Although his grasp of his subject is now superb, and he has a great capacity for thinking on his feet, he was not always so convincing. The first time I heard him speak was soon after I arrived in South Africa in February 1994, at an election rally in Cape Town. Manuel, who headed the ANC's economics team, was presenting their economic policies. What I saw and heard was a man who did not really fully understand what he was talking about. Though he manoeuvred his way around some of the issues raised with a mixture of charm and evasion, some of the questions from the floor exposed him. At moments he looked lonely and vulnerable. Perhaps experiences like this scarred him. Now, he never ever appears in public, or even in meetings, without at least five advisors and public servants alongside him.

When Manuel met with Bolivian president-elect Evo Morales in January 2006, he had no fewer than eight advisors, four on each side of him. It was an impressive display, enhanced by Manuel's deft welcoming line to Morales: 'Your victory is not just a victory for the poor in Bolivia, not just a victory for the poor in Latin America, but a victory for the poor of the whole world, and we salute your victory.'

In media briefings it is the same. If it is a difficult question, perhaps about the minutiae of policy or about a fact or figure, he will elegantly deflect it to one of his colleagues. In this way he not only spotlights 'Team Finance', but it is also damn good politics. It makes him look authoritative and secure, in sharp contrast with health minister Manto Tshabalala-Msimang, who will often appear in meetings or at press briefings alone, thus accentuating the image of an embattled, lonely figure.

When I ask Manuel who has been his greatest influence since he became minister of finance in 1996, he reveals his political *nous* immediately: 'Thabo Mbeki.' This is not brown-nosing; I am sure he means what he says.

According to Manuel, '[The president's] head understands economics and the tough policy choices.'

Erwin agrees: 'Mbeki is a trained economist, one of the best in the country.'

Says Manuel: 'Being in a job like this without the political air and ground cover would be impossible. [Mbeki] has never wavered in his support.'

The key event for Manuel, Mbeki and the post-1994 government was the switch in macroeconomic policy and strategy in 1996, from the RDP (the Reconstruction and Development Programme) – the mantra of the pre- and immediate post-1994 ANC – to the far more controversial approach of GEAR (Growth, Employment and Redistribution). It was *the* pivotal event – and a 'very tightly managed' change in policy, according to Erwin.

The date, 14 June 1996, is seared on Manuel's memory, as is Mbeki's comment when he gathered the press together that day in Tuynhuis, knowing that the left would interpret the shift as an adoption of neo-liberalism and Thatcherite economic principles. He quipped, 'So call me Maggie Thatcher.'

Manuel talks of 'psychological barriers', as well as actual exchange rate barriers. Before GEAR, the market had reacted negatively to his appointment as finance minister. The rand appeared to be heading towards free-fall and the finance team was battling against an 'amorphous market', as Manuel famously described it at the time.

Manuel, with his then deputy, Gill Marcus, and his then director-general, Maria Ramos, went to see Mbeki at his home. They were worried about breaking the 'psychological barrier of R4 to the dollar'. Manuel now laughs at the thought, as since then the rand has fallen to R13 to the dollar, and gone back up again. It was a precarious situation, but Mbeki analysed it in an 'avuncular way'; Mbeki teased out the issue to the point where Manuel came to appreciate 'the barriers of fear that can trap you'.

Mbeki has given Manuel what the latter calls a 'long mandate', so they do not meet often aside from at the usual cabinet and cabinet cluster meetings. Instead, Manuel draws on the resources of 'Team Finance', the staff at the National Treasury, which even his detractors admit are a highly skilled group of people. With Maria Ramos, his DG for many years, he formed a formidable team. Although 'they relied on each other', notes a close colleague, 'it was not a symbiotic relationship'. Ramos is more conservative than Manuel; she provided the technical competence, he the political direction. The Public

Finance Management Act, an internationally admired piece of legislation that imposes financial probity and sound procedure on the whole system of governance, was 'Maria's genius', adds the colleague. Together they recruited the very best minds from around the country.

There is resentment as well as admiration in various circles. An advisor to another cabinet minister once complained to me that finance only provides its memos the night before a cabinet meeting, so there is very little time to read them, and, therefore, less opportunity to engage with the finance people. The implication is that it is a deliberate tactic by the National Treasury.

I agree with Jeremy Cronin's view that Manuel is not only highly effective, but also that he cares deeply about the poor. There may be significant disputes among leftists like Cronin over whether or not Manuel has been too prudent at times and too concerned with economic stability, but Manuel's good faith and determination to create a strong, stable environment for real growth is accepted.

Given the precarious, roller-coaster ride of comparator economies during the same period, Manuel's accomplishments deserve proper recognition. He is now the longest-serving finance minister in the world. Continuity underpins his power; he has status and, with his victory in the ANC NEC ballot at the Stellenbosch conference, political strength in the wider party. Coming top of the five-yearly vote proved the depth of the organization's admiration for Manuel.

The 'tough choices' have been about withstanding pressure from the left. He has relished the challenge: 'It brings the smart street fighter out in him,' says one parliamentary colleague. And he will not give an inch, lest it be interpreted as weakness. So, when I ask Manuel who else's views interest and influence him, he offers up the name of one Brit – Will Hutton, whose latest book he is reading – and two American economists: Danny Rodrik at Harvard and Joe Stiglitz at Columbia.

What about locally? Pause for reflection; shake of the head. Long eulogy on the excellence of Team Finance. He is too clever to say, even off the record, whom he listens to outside the walls of finance. It's smart politics. And a sign of his toughness.

I interviewed Manuel the day after the UNDP's report had criticized South Africa's macroeconomic policy and, specifically, among a number of things, inflation targeting. When inflation targeting was introduced soon after the

1999 election in February 2000, the finance committee in parliament, chaired by the resilient ANC MP Barbara Hogan, held a meeting. The finance committee invited some outside experts to offer their views on the wisdom of inflation targeting. Maria Ramos and some of her staff also attended the meeting, and they went ballistic when their views were challenged during the ensuing discussion. Ramos called Manuel immediately afterwards. And Manuel called Mbeki.

The next day, the whole of the ANC component of the committee was ordered to Pretoria and given a dressing down by the president, which illustrates Manuel's power and its strategic application. It also illuminates the power balance between the executive and parliament, and the constraints imposed on parliament's capacity for effective oversight of the executive – a topic I return to in some depth in Chapter 4. As an exercise in intimidation, Manuel's ploy at least partly worked. Whenever the committee now heads towards a political hot potato, some of its members will start to worry about the consequences. On at least one occasion, ANC MP Ben Turok has screamed to a colleague: 'You will get us before the president again!'

Smooth government at the top?

The ministers are influential as well as important when it comes to their line functions. Being a minister is a multidimensional job: part leader, part manager, part strategist. To Kader Asmal, the 'sole job is to act as a dynamo. Micromanagement might be necessary sometimes, but where a minister is active and energetic, he or she can change the whole environment in a government department.'

Creating what Asmal calls *'elan'* or 'flair' in your area of government is a matter of conviction, and can help dispel the '4.30 p.m. syndrome' of the public service.

Working hard does make a difference. Those ministers whose legislation or policy is not thoroughly prepared are exposed in cabinet meetings, because Mbeki can see through them.

As in any organization, some employees are in a better personal space in which to work hard. While he was in cabinet, Asmal shared a ministerial house in Pretoria with Trevor Manuel, and without family to distract them, they would invariably work late into the evening, often into the small hours

– Asmal smoking merrily at the kitchen table, Manuel in the TV room. Some of their colleagues would not have such freedom, and their focus on work would not be so exclusive.

Because Thabo Mbeki is himself a manager and likes to stay abreast of the major developments within his government, there are some difficult managerial issues that still need to be resolved if political power is to be exercised smoothly and efficiently. Foremost among them is the number of people that report to the president. At a rough count, there are about forty-five: the cabinet ministers, the premiers, his immediate staff, and, in effect, the military chiefs of staff (he also appoints the directors-general, though they do not in any real or practical sense 'report' to him). It is almost certainly too many.

Accordingly, the department of public service and administration (DPSA) has flown a decidedly controversial kite: the creation of a two-tier system for the cabinet, with a senior tier of cabinet ministers chairing an increased number of cluster committees and reporting directly to the president, with the other ministers reporting to them.

It was, it should be emphasized, merely kite flying. Geraldine Fraser-Moleketi, minister of public service and administration, is well versed in the need to first test the waters in the ANC with this sort of proposal. The controversy lies in the hierarchy element in the organization. Paradoxically, although the ANC is very hierarchical in practice, it is always reluctant to extend the reach of the formal hierarchy structure unless it has no real choice. Unusually, the DPSA's proposal was referred to the law and governance group of the ANC, where most of the premiers and many of the cabinet sit, and was duly shot down. According to sources close to the DPSA, the idea is not dead and may well resurface in the coming year or two.

The DPSA is engaged in many of the most important structural govern-ance issues. There is a body of opinion within the ANC that believes the provincial layer of government should be abolished. To this group, rather than enhancing devolved government, the provinces are an unnecessary obstacle to such a process, standing as they do between national and local government.

The DPSA, which is inclined towards the 'abolish-the-provinces' view, has learnt the lessons of the two-tier cabinet proposal, and instead fed its thinking into the ANC's policy conference prior to its five-yearly national conference in Stellenbosch in December 2002. The advantage has been that, whenever it has wished to raise the subject, the DPSA has been able to 'root' the discussion in the ANC conference documents, thus providing a 'legitimizing' shield.

So there is still some major tinkering to be done at the top of government if it is to optimize its power and performance. What is clear is that, while cabinet is influential, there is a first-among-equals status accorded to the minister of finance. This is not unusual; it is the case in many governments. However, the effect is to give macroeconomics a central place in the policy firmament. Again, that may be neither unusual nor inappropriate. But the government within a government is a bastion that others find hard to challenge. Enhanced by the unyielding support of the president, Trevor Manuel has accumulated power and now exercises it with an assurance that is formidable to his opponents. He not only has power, but has learnt, like his boss, how to use it effectively and, at times, ruthlessly. As such, Manuel is South Africa's third most powerful man.

That, then, is the top quartet: Mbeki, Netshitenzhe and Manuel, and Mojanku Gumbi. Then, Phumzile Mlambo-Ngcuka, Alec Erwin and Essop Pahad jostle for position in the second group. A third group of favoured, loyal ministers and advisors, such as Geraldine Fraser-Moleketi, her husband Jabu Moleketi (a new face in the government, as deputy minister of finance, but for ten years previously minister of finance in Gauteng), Sydney Mufamadi, Thoko Didiza, Lindiwe Sisulu and Manne Dipico, are also top-twenty players, but they are regularly eclipsed by key figures from other sectors, especially business, and by one or two other individuals from various political power centres, such as COSATU – as I will explore in the Conclusion.

But to conclude with the cabinet: in parliamentary systems, as I noted at the outset of this chapter, the membership of the cabinet is drawn from and is accountable to parliament. Squeezed as it is by the far more powerful structures of the presidency and National Treasury (the 'government within a government') above and alongside, and by the growing technocratic capacity and expertise of the departments and their directors-general below, the cabinet's raw power is circumscribed.

Yet, because of the way in which Mbeki encourages his cabinet to operate, with time for serious political scrutiny of all issues, it thus serves as a political filter that permits other voices and opinions to seep into the process – from the ANC as a party, its alliance partners, business and civil society, and beyond.

Walter Bagehot described the role of cabinet in *The English Constitution* in 1867 thus:

> The efficient secret of the English constitution may be described as the close union, the nearly complete fusion, of the executive and the legislative powers ... A cabinet is a combining committee – a hyphen which joins, a buckle which fastens, the legislative part of the state to the executive part of the state. In its origins it belongs to the one, in its functions it belongs to the other.

Although the South African governance system, with its brilliant, overriding Constitution and Bill of Rights, now greatly differs from the British, it has retained the core element, which is that the cabinet is the primary executive authority and is accountable to parliament. Moreover, the legislature and the executive overlap in the cabinet – Bagehot's 'buckle'.

Because the former is so overshadowed by the latter, the cabinet is a crucial institutional receptacle of political power in the new South Africa. Having explored its role and influence, the next two chapters consider the two parts of the belt that join at the 'buckle': the public service and parliament.

3

The Public Service

Loyal Mandarins?

Special advisors

It was not even six o'clock in the morning when Sue Rabkin's cellphone buzzed and brought her to consciousness, her irritation only slightly mollified by the discovery that it was a text message from her husband, Pallo Jordan, the minister for arts and culture. A classic South African political marriage in so many complex ways, they used to spend half the time apart – Jordan in their Cape Town house, Rabkin in her Johannesburg home or travelling with 'her' minister, Mosiuoa Patrick 'Terror' Lekota.[1] Thankfully, a place back in the cabinet after five years in parliament (albeit heading various key political committees) has impelled Jordan to spend more time in the north.

Rabkin is a 'special advisor', an extraordinary job to have. Not much is known about this class of advisor attached to each minister. It is, to say the least, a multidimensional role. A mixture between bag carrier, personal confidant and political fixer, a typical advisor even has the chance to occasionally research and advise on policy issues. They will prepare cabinet memoranda, read all the other cabinet documents for the minister, prepare summaries, and provide comment and advice on positions to take and their implications.

In the overarching scheme of this book – which aims to distinguish two subcategories of political power, namely, importance and influence – special advisors are utterly 'unimportant': they are not part of the public service, their job titles are so vague as to be meaningless and their job security is almost entirely linked to that of their minister. But they are entirely indispensable. Every politician needs a trusty *handlanger*. And thus they are hugely influential.

The content of the special advisor's job varies from ministry to ministry; each minister is entitled to appoint two full-time special advisors. 'In my case,' says another special advisor, 'I do not carry bags, nor play any role in terms of "political fixing". The bulk of my involvement is on the side of research, policy advice and, lo and behold, fixing up the quality of inputs that come from the officials in the department, as well as speech writing for the minister.'

The international obligations of ministers are becoming massive as South Africa continues to play a leadership role in the international arena. So, many special advisors will also provide technical support when their minister takes on responsibility in one of these multilateral bodies.

But there is an even more important aspect of the role of special advisors, and the reason why they are regarded as 'political appointments', and that is in strengthening the link between the political agenda of the government – as represented by the cabinet ministers – and the public service, as implementers. 'So,' adds the special advisor, 'a key part of my job is to pre-emptively align departmental and party political policy positions – which is particularly important, given the long planning cycle in government and continuous exchanges between party political and government agendas.' The content of the job also shifts, depending on the relationship between the minister and his or her director-general. Advisors are often the first person a minister will turn to in a crisis.

I met Rabkin early one evening in Pretoria, on the same day she had been woken by Jordan's SMS, which, although it clearly charmed her, had also woken her early from her slumber. She still had to drive back to Johannesburg at the end of a long day at the side of 'her' minister. It's a hard job, Rabkin told me, because 'your schedule is the minister's schedule, and that is a very busy one'.

'I am an extra pair of eyes and ears,' Rabkin continued. 'I have no formal power, but you have access to the minister ... Advisors are the only people who don't have to knock.'

Though again, this may depend on the minister and the precise nature and history of his or her relationship with their special advisor; 'I can assure you I have to knock,' said another special advisor.

Another told me that 'most politicians and most ministers are unpleasant, and most of their staffers have a terrible time'. Rabkin is clearly not one of the discontented; her affection for her minister is evident. Despite the insecurity and the long hours, it is a very nice job because, she says, 'there is no admin!' I asked her why Lekota had wanted her as his special advisor.

Special advisors (as at February 2006)

Ministry	Special advisor
Agriculture and land affairs	Vacant
Arts and culture	Prof. Keorapetse Kgositsile
Communication	Vacant
Correctional services	Vacant
Defence	Sue Rabkin
Education	Martin Mulchay, Dr Teboho Moja
Environmental affairs and tourism	Dr Shaun Vorster
Finance	None
Foreign affairs	Yolisa Maya
Health	Ray Mabope
Home affairs	Mike Ramagoma
Housing	Sethe Moodley
Intelligence	None
Justice and constitutional development	None
Labour	None
Minerals and energy	Boy Mkalipi
Provincial and local government	Zam Titus
Public enterprises	Vacant
Public services and administration	Hanlie van Dyke-Roberts
Public works	Afzal Brey
Safety and security	Leslie Xinwa
Science and technology	None
Social development	Vukani Mthintso
Sport and recreation	None
Trade and industry	None
Transport	Dr Ian Phillips
Water affairs	Prof. Denis Goldberg

'I originally worked with him in the organizing department of the ANC. I had already been in the defence secretariat for five years [when he was appointed to the cabinet after the 1999 election]. He said he liked my political *nous*.'

Rabkin, like all special advisors, certainly has that. She is steeped in the ANC, knows its culture and traditions like the back of her hand, and is a wily, astute and very independent-minded observer of the movement's political patterns. She is also fantastically irreverent with her distinctive North London accent (where she was born and grew up). Those who know her will attest that any authentic record of a conversation with her will contain its fair share of asterisks. As a Londoner myself, it is always good to have a conversation with someone who applies the word 'wanker' with such acuity.

Rabkin, like many of her comrades who were exiled in London, has a somewhat schizophrenic attitude towards Britain. Although she finds the British civil service conservative, to my very great surprise she also speaks about it with reverence. She tells a story about how a group of South African civil servants were taken over to the UK by minister of public service and administration Zola Skweyiya, who had been in charge of the public service in the ANC before they took power in 1994. They met a man called Geoffrey Morgan, whose sole job was to oversee people's development in the civil service. His task was to spot talent and ensure that people were on the right career path.

Also, Rabkin adds, 'the British don't overcomplicate things'. In Mozambique, where she also spent time, merely obtaining a passport or bringing over a deck chair was a bureaucratic nightmare.

It is clear that Rabkin thinks that having a Mr Morgan, with that kind of expertise and focus, would enhance the South African public service. 'The skills accumulated by cadres in the ANC were political and organizational skills. The conditions under which we worked were not conducive to developing administrative skills. Anything written down could land in the hands of the enemy and result in arrest, and even death.'

The difficult business of how to exercise discretion where there is no obvious rule to apply – which is really a key part of being an effective administrator – was not part of the ANC exile curriculum.

Rabkin further expands the point and draws attention to a fascinating dislocation between what she believes is the broader outlook of many of the exiles and the MDM (Mass Democratic Movement) activists who generally had not been exposed to the educational opportunities of the exiles. She clearly means no disrespect towards the UDF, and indeed quotes Ruth First's exhortation that the exiles were 'not accountable' in the sense that their life in the shadows inevitably meant that the normal rules did not apply to their actions. Instead, credibility depends on your ability to represent people's views – something the UDF most emphatically did at home. Yet there are plenty of former exiles unlike Rabkin whose snobbery in relation to the UDF crowd is manifest.

The texture of these internal ANC cultural issues, which I will discuss in later chapters, has a significant impact on government, because in a very substantial sense the culture of government is now heavily infused by the culture of the ANC. This is not to say that state and party have fused, although that is a distinct possibility in the future, but that, because ANC members can now be found in all the various strata of government, their own traditions and idiosyncrasies affect the bureaucratic culture that is emerging – warts and all.

But it is skills, or lack of them, that is the major issue. It means that, in the words of one senior public servant, 'you often can't get to the problem. We spend a lot of time trying to sort out the system. There is workshop syndrome, which preserves the collective. It is useful but time-consuming.' Certainly the public service seems to be in a permanent workshop. Call any department and try to speak to a middle-to-senior public servant, and the response is invariably, 'Sorry, in a workshop,' or 'Away at a *bosberaad* [strategy meeting].'

'Capacity' in the public service

There is also a lack of understanding of how the government system works, even at middle and lower-senior managerial level. One senior public servant told me how, at a recent strategic planning workshop (there we go again!), a discussion about government had turned into a Politics 101 lecture. More than one manager did not understand the difference between the executive and parliament.

According to a well-placed source inside the department of public service and administration, there is a resistance to proper training despite the workshop culture – the more so the higher up the ladder you go. The source's view is that a lack of content skills is not the problem. Where hard skills are needed, he says they are generally there. There are plenty of experts. It is administrative and management capacity that is lacking, and, in many cases, adequate, ingrained processes and systems.

How often have you heard the phrase, 'The government is short of capacity,' or 'Lack of capacity is the main obstacle to implementation,' and wondered what exactly do they mean by 'capacity'? Well, the answer is simple: it is a euphemism. They mean that human capacity – as in people with sufficient experience and expertise – is lacking.

One of Thabo Mbeki's advisors once told me that 'the chief gets so angry at times when a letter is put in front of him and there is a stupid mistake in it. It drives him mad. He always asks for it to be redone.' One deputy director-general in a national department complains about how much time she has to spend redrafting memos and speeches, more often than not by people at director level. More experienced managers are constantly taken away from their core functions to meet the needs of others. The legacy of apartheid, especially in terms of the skills and education deficit for the majority community of the country, means that the period of transition is elongated. Therefore, this sort of practical obstacle is inevitable during a period of transition, but it is mightily distracting from the primary set of managerial responsibilities.

Super servants: The DGs

I interviewed Gilbert Lawrence, director-general in the office of the premier of the Western Cape, on the day after the elections in 2004. I arrived at his office directly from the Cape Town Independent Electoral Commission results centre. It was just after lunch, and finally the results were starting to pour in. Ignoring the overall figures, but looking instead at key voting districts, it became clear to me that the New National Party (NNP) was doing even worse than anticipated. Plainly, its former electorate did not approve of the NNP's proximity to the ANC.

I had just told a press conference at the results centre that it seemed clear to me that the NNP vote had collapsed. I offered Dr Lawrence the same view. My interview with him was to be off the record. His words may have been, but his broad smile was not. Lawrence was appointed to the position of the province's most senior bureaucrat in late 2002, a promotion from DG in the provincial department of health.

For Lawrence, after a long career in medicine and a short but interesting one in bureaucracy, life was about to get easier. For two years he had coped with the extraordinary situation of a two-party government that was, according to him, a 'collaboration and not a coalition'. As premier of the Western Cape, Marthinus van Schalkwyk had initially insisted (like his predecessor, Peter Marais) on Lawrence briefing him but not the ANC leader, Ebrahim Rasool, ahead of provincial cabinet meetings. According to Lawrence, this meant that the ANC was always playing 'catch-up' in the cabinet meeting itself, which wasted everyone's time. Van Schalkwyk, whom

Lawrence describes as 'an astute politician, always on guard', eventually relented, and Lawrence was allowed to brief Rasool as well.

One of the distinctive features of the South African governance system is the demarcation between the ministry and the department. Although the overall pedigree of South Africa's parliamentary system is Westminster, this curious distinction between ministry and department is not seen in White-hall. It is not clear what its origin is. Lawrence says that 'we have not really quite settled whether we are following a particular model. Should it be the "yes-minister" British model, or the American system – all in or out?' (In the USA, when the administration changes after a presidential election, the senior bureaucrats as well as all the Secretaries of State will go.)

The effect of the peculiar South African system is to create two centres of power: those around the minister and those in the department. Hence, the head of the department – the director-general – is an important figure. Just how influential the directors-general are, and whether in fact they enjoy more or less influence than the special ministerial advisors, is probably no longer a moot point. DGs are surely now in the ascendant. Indeed, says one special advisor, 'It is really silly to compare the DGs and special advisors. Advisors and, for that matter, ministers, do not control any resources. Special advisors have just their own knowledge, skills and only twenty-four hours in a day. Compare that with the staff and money that a DG can use to back up his policy work, not to mention the fact that they drive implementation ...'

In the first years of democracy, they were a jumble: a mixture of old guard, brand new guard – but essentially political appointees, rather than people appointed on merit – and a few odds and sods. Slowly, a rationalization has occurred. And, in a parallel pattern, an increasing solidarity among the DGs.

This trend clearly worries as much as it excites the DPSA. A core group of DGs is beginning to act in unison – a caucus within a caucus, so to speak. It is a fairly recent phenomenon that started about two to three years ago, according to most insiders.

'Under the pretence of managerialism,' says one DPSA source, '[the DGs] are staking a claim to a strong policy role for themselves.'

This is said with a mixture of anxiety and admiration, as it represents an even greater departure from the British civil service model, where the head of the department is very careful to stay clear of a policy-making role, sticking purely to implementation. Not long before the April 2004 general elections,

President Mbeki interviewed each of his twenty-six national DGs, and several admitted to 'the chief' that they harboured an interest in a career in politics. This is hardly surprising if one examines the background of a significant number of the current batch of DGs.

Linda Mti, DG of correctional services and national commissioner, is a former MK commissar, ANC MP and director-general of the National Intelligence Coordinating Committee (NICOC), a very important and influential body. He is a senior and high-flying deployment by the ANC into the bureaucracy, but someone who could easily return to the political side of the fence.

January Boy Masilela, DG at defence, is likewise and, unsurprisingly, a former MK operative. Similarly, Barry Gilder (home affairs, 2003–05) went into exile in 1976 and joined MK three years later. After a long career in ANC Intelligence, he joined the South African Secret Service (SASS) in 1995, and was appointed general manager, foreign offices. After sequential promotions, he was appointed as the deputy director-general operational services at the National Intelligence Agency (NIA) on 1 January 2000, before moving in May 2003 to be director-general of home affairs, in order to keep a close eye on the then minister of home affairs, IFP leader Mangosuthu Buthelezi.

To the surprise of many observers, Gilder swapped jobs with Mzuvukile Jeff Maqetuka – another ANC exile with a long career in intelligence – to become the intelligence coordinator at NICOC.

But while it is true that most incumbent DGs have an ANC background, it would be too simplistic to call them 'political appointees'. Some have become career public servants, and others are specialist professionals in their fields. Lesetja Kganyago, National Treasury (finance), is a case in point. Prior to 1994, he worked in the ANC economic policy department. Since the ANC came to power, he worked in both the department of finance and the Reserve Bank as a part of his grooming for the high office he now holds.

So, too, the former DG of agriculture, Bongiwe Njobe. Her parents were ANC in exile, but she has always specialized in agriculture and can be called a professional agriculturalist. However, her work has included working for the ANC in Tanzania, for the ANC Women's League and then, in 1995, in agricultural policy development for the ANC. She subsequently left to take up a senior executive position at SA Breweries.

Not all the DGs are ANC-aligned, however. Professor Itumeleng Mosala

(arts and culture) has a political history with AZAPO, though his appoint-
ment mirrors that of another AZAPO member who serves in the cabinet,
Mosibudi Mangena, the minister for science and technology. Advocate Rams
Ramashia, for a while DG at labour, also has an AZAPO background.

In contrast, there are some obvious non-party political specialists. Thami
Mseleku (education, then health) is a professional educationalist and, because
of his non-partisanship and competence, has attracted so much respect
from all sides of the political spectrum that the rumour mill has offered his
name as a possible premier of KwaZulu-Natal – acceptable as he would be
to both the ANC and the IFP.

Dr Crispian Olver (DG at environmental affairs and tourism) initially
worked in the department of provincial and local government as deputy
director-general, local government. Among his responsibilities was helping
to draft the White Paper on the new local government system, as well as its
legislative framework and implementation. He also coordinated the provision of municipal infrastructure, and maintained and regulated municipal
finances at a national level.

From July 1994 until June 1996 Olver worked in the national RDP office,
where he was in charge of development planning and local economic development. As such, he represents the nearest thing to a 'pure' public servant.
Although he was previously a medical practitioner, he has become a specialist in his area through his career in the public service.

Mpumi Mpofu, for a time DG at housing, but now DG at transport, is
armed with an honours degree in urban and regional planning, and also
has a postgraduate degree in town planning from the University of Coventry.
Just thirty-three years old, her curriculum vitae includes working for the
Coventry City Council, the London Docklands Development Corporation
and the London borough of Southwark. In 2004 she married Dali Mpofu,
the CEO of the South African Broadcasting Authority.

Clearly, the DGs are a central cog in the whole system of governance
with very significant influence and power. This power tends to increase the
longer an individual is in position. Alastair Ruiters, for example, was DG for
trade and industry for over five years (appointed in January 2000). He is a
strong personality with a firm grasp of policy detail (an Oxford University
PhD with five years' experience working in the engine room of trade and
industry – small business promotion and commercial regulation).

Current DGs (as at June 2006)

National departments	Director-general
Agriculture	Mr Masiphula Mbongwa
Arts and culture	Prof. Itumeleng Mosala
Communications	Ms Lyndall Shope-Mafole
Correctional services	Mr Linda Mti
Defence	Mr January Boy Masilela
Education	Mr Duncan Hindle
Environmental affairs and tourism	Ms Pamela Yako
Foreign affairs	Dr Ayanda Ntsaluba
Government Communication and Information Service (GCIS)	Mr Themba Maseko
Health	Mr Thamsanqa Mseleku
Home affairs	Mr Mzuvukile Jeff Maqetuka
Housing	Mr Itumeleng Kotsoane
Justice and correctional services	Adv. Menzi Simelane
Labour	Dr Mbuyisela Vanguard Mkosana
Land affairs	Mr Glen Thomas
Minerals and energy	Adv. Sandile Nogxina
Intelligence	Mr Manala Manzini
National Treasury	Mr Lesetja Kganyago
Provincial and local government	Ms Lindiwe Msengana-Ndlela
Public enterprises	Ms Portia Molefe
Public service and administration	Prof. Richard Levin
Public works	Dr Sean Phillips (Acting)
Science and technology	Dr Phil Mjwara
Safety and security	Mr Themba Mathe
Social development	Mr Vusimuzi Madonsela
Sport and recreation	Prof. Denver Hendricks
Trade and industry	Mr Tshediso Matona (Acting)
Transport	Ms Mpumi Mpofu
Water affairs and forestry	Mr Jabulani Sindane

Shadowing his very influential minister, Alec Erwin, Ruiters developed a powerful niche within the policy-making process. Erwin is a formidably strong personality and was comfortable with Ruiters, and was able to hold him in check where necessary.

It is self-evident that the personality, history and experience of the minister and his or her DG will have a huge impact on where the power lies between the two. As the veterans of the 1994 Mandela cabinet move on, it is likely that the balance of power will shift slightly but significantly towards the DGs. Thus, who they are and how they operate, given their personal histories and professional CVs, will be a decisive component in the capacity and power of the public service in the coming years.

However, a factor that may help keep a comfortable balance of power between the cabinet and the DGs, despite the growing power of the latter group, is the fact that several ministers have held their portfolios for longer than their DGs, given the high turnover of DGs in recent years.

Part of President Mbeki's purpose in conducting the interviews with the DGs was to try to find a better match between DGs and ministers. It is a pivotal relationship with a heavy dose of mutual dependency. Often – and increasingly so – the minister or MEC and the DG may be from the same political party (usually, of course, the ANC), and sometimes the DG may be more senior in the party, especially in the provinces, than the minister or MEC. In the Eastern Cape government a few years ago, the medical superintendent was censured by the DG of the health department, but not long after was appointed to the provincial cabinet as minister, and wasted no time in exacting his revenge on the public servant!

In the early post-1994 years, the ANC faced a number of DGs from the old government. Although they were able to remove some, the sunset clause in the Interim Constitution made it hard to do so, and some clung to their positions. One example was Rusty Evans, the DG of foreign affairs. It was clear that his views were out of kilter with those of the ANC.

A source in the department of foreign affairs told me that Evans, faced with a UN Assembly vote on the Cuban blockade, had advised his new minister that '[South Africa] should vote with the US in defence of the blockade, or at the very least abstain, in order to "protect South Africa's relationship with the USA"'.

Given that, of the 190 members of the UN, only Israel would vote with the USA, and in the context of Cuba's long-term support of the ANC during the struggle against apartheid, this was absurd, to put it mildly. Professor Peter Vale, a critical and independent academic voice on international affairs issues, criticized Evans, yet the deputy minister of foreign affairs, Aziz Pahad, defended him vigorously in public. In private, an admission was later made of the obvious: that the new ministers were almost entirely dependent on their DGs to run the government, whether they cared for them and their politics or not.

How much has changed? As the analysis of DGs shows, the make-up of the most senior public servants is completely different now. The current batch are highly skilled and very experienced people, and certainly at one with the ruling party. The question now is whether they are too close to the ANC. Will their own ambitions and proximity to the ruling party create obstacles for clear-sighted implementation? Will they want to dabble too much with policy matters?

Currently, unlike the rest of the public service, the DGs hold contract positions. There is now a move by them to change this: 'They want to have their cake and eat it,' according to a senior DPSA source. According to the source, the DPSA is nonetheless continuing to 'bounce around the idea that not only the DGs, but the entire senior management' be turned into an elite group that can be deployed 'as a strategic force'. The senior management service (SMS) dispensation actually provides for this, but hitherto has not been utilized very extensively for this purpose.

Dr Ayanda Ntsaluba, now DG of foreign affairs, is an interesting example of an elite civil servant being moved from one department to another. He worked both as an intern and later as medical officer at Umtata General Hospital, from January 1983 till September 1985. Following a period of detention and solitary confinement, he went into exile at the end of 1985, mainly in southern Africa – Zambia, Angola and Tanzania – as well as Uganda.

Following the watershed events of 1990, Dr Ntsaluba proceeded to study for his MSc (HFP) at the London School of Economics, culminating in his admission as a Fellow of the College of Obstetricians and Gynaecologists of South Africa in April 1993.

But his career in medicine was soon interrupted by his appointment in June 1995 as deputy director-general in the national department of health, responsible for policy and planning. He was part of the team that produced the ANC's health plan for the party's 1994 election manifesto, and a driving force behind the health White Paper, 'Towards a national health system'.

Like Kganyago at finance, this was a further example of forward planning by the ANC, for in June 1998 he was appointed as acting director-general for health, and confirmed as director-general in September 1998. But then, after five years, he was moved across to foreign affairs to fill the post of DG in September 2003, which had remained vacant for a lengthy period. One reason given by a ministerial insider is that 'Ntsaluba could cope with Dlamini-Zuma, a notoriously difficult minister, when at health he did so and, in fact, outlived her tenure there'.

Having noted this, however, an alternative rationale for Ntsaluba's sideways move should be kept in mind: not because it was a more sensible deployment of his expertise, but because he had seriously fallen out with the minister of health, Manto Tshabalala-Msimang over HIV/AIDS policy. Ntsaluba holds 'orthodox' views about the link between HIV and AIDS and, therefore, the best way to treat the virus; the minister no longer does.

Hierarchy and bureaucracy

Talk to anyone in government and the conversation soon becomes littered with acronyms, especially ones that include the letter 'D': DG (director-general), DDG (deputy director-general), CD (chief director) and D (director). This is the staple diet of this profession; these are the benchmarks of hierarchy and accomplishment, and therefore of power. Together, these four ranks constitute the SMS – nothing to do with text messaging, but the abbreviation for the senior management service. SMSers have different sorts of contracts and pretty attractive levels of pay.

Senior management service positions and basic salary scale

Hierarchy of positions	Approximate salary scale
Director-general (DG)	R800 000
Deputy director-general (DDG)	R640 000
Chief director, senior manager	R500 000
Director	R400 000
Deputy director (DD)	+R271 000
Assistant director	R133 000
Administrators; senior personnel	R90 000

As noted, the director-general is the head of department (HOD). Under the Public Finance Management Act (PFMA), he or she is the accounting officer for the department and carries considerable financial responsibility. At provincial level they are sometimes called superintendent general (SG). At provincial level, it gets very complicated. While all the DGs at national level are currently on the same rung, at provincial level some heads of department are SGs, while others are at deputy director-general (DDG) level because, for example, an education department in one province may have a budget of R40 billion, but, in another, just R40 million.

The relationship between provincial DGs and their opposite numbers in the national executive is also very important. As noted in Chapter 2, provincial ministers (or MECs – members of the executive council), meet with their national counterpart in a structure known as 'MINMEC'. A meeting of DGs shadows this – known as the 'Technical MINMEC'. These meetings take place roughly every six weeks, either in Pretoria or Cape Town, although they do try to rotate.

As part of their growing unity, the national and provincial DGs have formed a body called FOSAD, which, although it sounds like a new branch of Israeli intelligence, actually stands for Forum of South African DGs.

Transforming the public service

As for the general transformation of the public service, Geraldine Fraser-Moleketi, the minister of public service and administration, reported in her July 2003 Budget Speech to parliament that 37 per cent of the public service staff are African women. This represents a dramatic shift since 1994. The old public service was heavily skewed in favour of whites, as the following chart illustrates:

Figure 1: Racial representation within central public service, 1995[2]

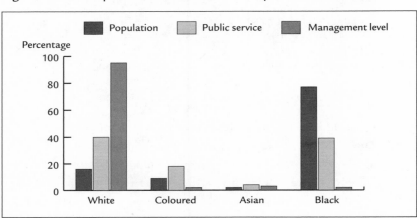

(Used with permission by the Human Sciences Research Council)

Figure 2 shows the current racial composition of the South African public service, which, read with Figure 3, depicts the more significant shift in the distribution of senior posts (as Vino Naidoo's analysis in the *State of the Nation Yearbook* notes). However, despite these gains, as Naidoo says: 'Although the ratio of white to black senior management demonstrates a sizeable shift in reversing senior marginalisation of black public servants under apartheid, the problem of management capacity remains.'[3]

Figure 2: Racial composition of the South African public service, 2003

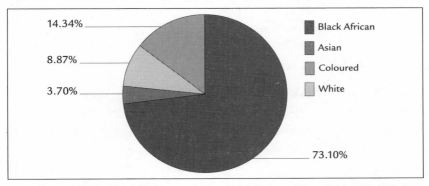

Source: Modified from absolute numbers presented by the public service commission in 2004
(Used with permission by the Human Sciences Research Council)

Figure 3: Senior managers by race and salary level

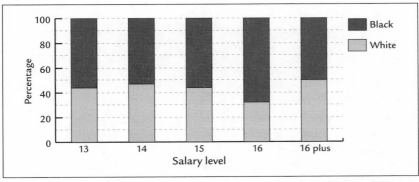

Source: Modified from DPSA 2000
(Used with permission by the Human Sciences Research Council)

Its own policy statement on the establishment of a senior management service in the public service[4] shows that the DPSA itself recognizes this:

The report and the ensuing debates confirmed the following persistent problems:

- High turnover rates in scarce occupations and problems in recruiting and retaining skilled senior personnel
- Poor levels of performance and skills among some senior staff, leading to inadequate service delivery
- Under-developed performance assessment systems, notwithstanding positive developments in introducing performance agreements
- Insufficient attention to training and development and nurturing a sustainable senior executive corps
- Little horizontal mobility due to rigidities in the employment framework and under-development of core leadership/managerial competencies.

This, in turn, needs to be set against the backdrop of the recommendations of the excellent 1998 report of the Presidential Review Commission, headed by Professor Vincent Maphai, which reached the following conclusions about the public service:

> The Commission concludes that, given the Government's stated national goals with respect to reconstruction and development, nation building, community empowerment and democratic consolidation, the role and functions of the public services have to be rethought fundamentally. We offer a framework for such a role. We believe 'in principle' too, that there is no justification for the massive number of public officials, *given the resources available and the priorities of government*. The present Government has retained, and added to, what has been essentially a public service characterised by 'separate development' duplication. This is simply unsustainable. Furthermore, the inability of the state to compete with private sector salaries may suggest the need for a smaller, professional, highly skilled and well-paid public service. In short, the cornerstone of the new public service should be *social need, capacity, and cost*.[5]

The report then went on to arrive at some crisp recommendations:

> **What is required, in the view of the Commission is a relatively small but highly motivated, focused and well-paid public service.** This can only happen if core functions are clarified and if public servants adhere strictly to the public service Code of Conduct. In addition, the Government will

need to seriously consider alternative service routes and outsourcing to other providers, particularly through creative and innovative partnerships with the private and community sectors.

In the light of this conception of the state, the question of **what the public service ought to do** would largely be shaped by **three** considerations:

> - Social need within the parameters of both cost and capacity;
> - The capacity of different agencies (national, provincial and local governments; private sector and non-governmental organisations);
> - The cost of state activities.

In light of the above, it is important to try and specify the specific yardsticks against which government performance should be measured. Or, in other words, **what should a professional civil service look like?**

Finally, this crucial section of the report invited an answer that encompassed a number of fundamental elements: promotion of leadership in government; a professional service ethos; setting of standards of public service performance; eliminating corruption; clarity about the distinction between an administrative role and the role of elected politicians. The report was damning of the failure to develop a clear vision or strategic direction.

That is why, when he took office in 1999, President Mbeki appointed a strong negotiator with a high work rate and a propensity for understanding bureaucratic detail to be minister of public service and administration. Geraldine Fraser-Moleketi is widely admired for all of these qualities, yet after several years in office (she has been DPSA minister since 1999) it is still hard to assess how far she has been able to develop the role and, therefore, the power of the public service.

The communist tax collector

People matter greatly to institutions. Institutions – any organization – are nothing without the people within them. It is people who shape the institution's vision, values and practice. Hence, it matters greatly to identify leadership. And, accordingly, the deployment of certain individuals to key posts in the public service is hugely significant.

Initially, as noted in the next chapter on parliament, the great majority of ANC leaders were put inside parliament – partly because it seemed the obvious and most convenient thing to do at the time, and partly because the Constitution had to be written and negotiated, so it was important to have them there. After two to three years, a massive brain drain commenced as ANC leaders were deployed in other fields.

Pravin Gordhan is archetypal of this process. He played a very central part in the constitutional committee, the key committee of the Constitutional Assembly, between 1994 and 1996, and also helped forge a new, powerful role for the parliamentary portfolio committee on constitutional affairs. The question for him was: What next?

As a dedicated communist, Gordhan was too far to the left for Mbeki's comfort to serve in his cabinet, but, equally, too sharp an operator not to have on your side. Mbeki found the perfect spot for him: the South African Revenue Service (SARS). At first glance, the sight of this communist pharmacist (his profession prior to 1994) at the helm of a tax collection service appears invidious. Yet, upon further examination, it makes perfect sense.

As Gordhan will explain in careful detail, the core strategy of SARS in recent years has been to maximize the collection of tax so as to ensure that government has all the income that it is entitled to receive from taxpayers. This has involved a dual strategy of stick and carrot. Carrots in the form of amnesty periods and creative advertising campaigns around the annual tax return date; sticks in the form of a much more ruthless approach to tax evasion.

On this, Gordhan talks the language of the brilliant strategist that he is: 'We can never have as much capacity as them, but my plan has been to ensure that we have the legal resources and capacity to show the wealthy, powerful people who want to evade their tax responsibilities that we mean business.'

The HQ of SARS near Brooklyn, Pretoria, bristles with pomp and high technology. It exudes authority and confidence, and asserts: 'Don't mess with us.' The public servants who work here look like they are proud to do so, and it is clear that there has been a trickle-down effect to local revenue offices. The shift in culture towards one of professionalism and integrity is striking; Gordhan deserves great credit. The figures are almost as impressive as the Brooklyn HQ. In 2005, SARS's tax collection shot above expectations, recording around R21.9 billion due to improved enforceability. The revenue-collecting body has been able to register more than 7000 new taxpayers in 2005; its improved collection procedure has seen the collection of 4.1 million outstanding returns. The growing amount of collected revenue may have to do with the burgeoning expenditure on luxury goods and cars, and not necessarily improved revenue collection methods. However, tax collection methods, particularly tightening loose ends on corporate tax collection methodology, have had tremendous impacts on the growth of revenue. SARS is clearly no longer a toothless body.

Had Gordhan stayed in parliament, he would still be exerting influence, but it would be heavily circumscribed by a combination of the prevailing political and system limitations. Had he left parliament to focus on his role in the South African Communist Party (SACP), where he is a long-standing member of the politburo, he would, like Blade Nzimande, general secretary of the SACP, have retained a voice and, again, some influence, but this time circumscribed by the ideological and intra-alliance constraints of this period.

So, given that he was temperamentally unsuited to business and ideologically inappropriate for cabinet (at least as far as the president is concerned), heading a state institution was an ideal place to go. At SARS, Gordhan is doing what he always wanted to do as a socialist: collecting tax from the rich to pay for the needs of the poor – and doing so effectively and efficiently.

Servants of the people?

It is sometimes said by critics both outside and inside the ANC alliance that the ANC is in office but not in power, in the sense that it continues to win handsome electoral victories, but that it is unable to convert its powerful mandate into powerful government. Such a critique is an oversimplification and therefore an overstatement, but it is not so far from the truth the further down you go on the public service ladder. A tough historical legacy, lack of proper management and administrative skills, and the pressures of transformation mean that the public service is important and influential for both positive and negative reasons.

A strong minister with ambition leads the DPSA. Mbeki originally installed Geraldine Fraser-Moleketi in the department after the 1999 elections because he believed that she would be uncompromising with the public sector unions. The state needed to reduce the vast army of people it employed. In some provinces, the wage bill accounted for over 90 per cent of the budget; a realignment of resources was needed to permit greater expenditure on infrastructure and capital.

To be fair to her, Fraser-Moleketi has never embraced a crude position on whittling down the numbers of the public service. She has always preferred the language of 'an appropriately sized public service'. Increasingly, she has actually raised the issue of growing the public service in the right places and of revisiting a wage bill that is not proportionately keeping up with the marketplace.

Yet, strangely, there is no single document that captures the vision of transformation in the public service; it would have to be pieced together from the various Budget Speeches of the minister in recent years. Nonetheless, no one can fault the energy and single-mindedness of Fraser-Moleketi, who will continue to be a huge influence on a range of public service–related issues, such as the national anti-corruption strategy. Her sense of commitment to her portfolio even extends to her own master's thesis, which she is writing in her spare time on this very subject.

In the coming years, a key test for Fraser-Moleketi will be how she deals with the growing potency of the DGs and, in particular, with a conundrum that has now emerged. On the one hand, there is a recognized need for power- ful leadership at the top of national government departments, with a flexible, highly skilled cadre of managers. There is a determination to ensure that the positions are sufficiently well paid so that not only will top-notch people be attracted to the public service, but they will remain there and not be lured into the private sector like Ramashia and, before him, the immensely talented Sipho Pityana (DG of labour from 1995 to 1999, and then foreign affairs from 1999 to 2002; he is now managing director of Laetoli Investments Corporate).

On the other hand, anxiety exists that they may be creating a Frankenstein's monster – that this 'potent cadre' DG will become, if not the tail, then the middle that wags the head. Public servants are supposed to be servants of the people. The paradox is that the best way of doing so is for the DGs to serve their political masters.

The theory reads as follows: people elect a parliament, which appoints an executive (the cabinet), which makes policy decisions that the government departments carry out. Too much political power – too much influence to add to their obvious importance – and the DGs could interfere with this structure in damaging ways.

Looked at from another perspective, DGs may act as essential guardians of a deeper public interest or, at least, as internal checks upon political excess. This is an adaptation of the 'Yes, Minister' approach – alluding to the hilarious British TV sitcom that dramatized the suave establishment civil servant protecting his hapless minister from harm – where, in order to protect the public service from silly political decisions, you need people at the top of the public service with enough expertise, and the power that derives from it, to be able to withstand the pressure from the elected politicians to carry out ill-considered instructions.

This is an appealing idea. But the fact that a skills weakness and management deficit still exist remains a cause for concern. Indeed, it seems that, in putting so much emphasis on getting the DG stratum right, the ANC has neglected to think through how best to get the right skills and talent at middle-management level (directors, deputy directors), where so many of the weaknesses still lie. Encouraged by the tone set by President Mbeki in recent years, senior public service management has become adept at making use of available competence. For example, the skills of many of the most 'competent white "old-guard" public servants from the old dispensation, especially Afrikaners, have been harnessed, and they are playing a very supportive role', according to one DPSA insider, who adds that 'the old homeland dispensation officials are much more problematic'.

There are two serious consequences for power that arise from ongoing weaknesses in the public service. First of all, it dilutes government's ability to deliver on its mandate, and therefore weakens it vis-à-vis other interest groups. Political power is a zero-sum game. If one person's power weakens, someone else's strengthens, and vice versa. Second, it therefore also weakens the public service's power in relation to the other parts of the executive, such as the cabinet. When either or both of these things happen, a simple question, posed by Sue Rabkin, deserves attention: 'Who benefits from weakness in the public service?'

On this suitably Socratic note, this modest review of the role and influence of the men and women who advise the politicians and implement their political choices concludes. We turn next to the institution that, at least in theory, they all account to, and that is parliament.

4

Parliament

The Good, the Bad and
the Simply Irrelevant

Hard work can be dangerous – and rewarding

Early summer in Cape Town, 1999, and well past midnight, Johnny de Lange was woken by a cat. He tried shouting at it, and his then wife Pam immediately knew something was very wrong. She turned on the light and asked him to speak again. His lips moved, but only a strange noise came out, as if, he jokes now, he was auditioning for a role as a whale in *Finding Nemo*.

But it was no laughing matter then. De Lange, an ANC MP and chairperson of the parliamentary committee on justice, was suffering a mild stroke, or TIA (transient ischaemic attack). The reason? Not, as some wags might claim, as a result of his bout of fisticuffs in the National Assembly chamber, for which he is widely and, in many quarters, fondly remembered.[1] But because of sheer hard work.

De Lange is in so many ways a walking contradiction. Most importantly, he contradicts the cynical assertion that parliament is a waste of time and money, that it does and achieves nothing. He is the complete antithesis of the commonly perceived lazy, good-for-nothing MP. De Lange wears his heart on his sleeve, whether he is playing cricket for the Spin Doctors' Cricket Club or debating a difficult amendment with the opposition in parliament. He has passion and compassion, roughly in equal measure. He scares some people, but he has an absolute heart of gold; he is soft putty in the hands of my little daughter, India Jane.

In the ten years between 1994 and his appointment to the executive in May 2004, De Lange's justice committee rewrote, often in painstaking detail, almost every single piece of legislation – over 120 of them – that came before his committee. There are lessons to be learnt from his personal experience. First, that if you work too hard and don't exercise enough, your health can be put at risk. Second, that there are MPs who work damned hard. Third, that hard work can be rewarded in politics. Fourth, and most importantly, that parliament does matter; parliament and its individual members have the potential to be very influential indeed. I say *potential* deliberately, because the potential remains largely unrealized. There are complex reasons for this, which, if there is to be a proper appreciation of the place of parliament in the political firmament, must be thoroughly understood – especially if citizens are to comprehend the role that their public representatives can, should or do play.

De Lange was a remarkable member of parliament, a truly great parliamentarian – in the Victorian sense. And I say 'Victorian' not with sly reference to De Lange's propensity for duelling, but because of the 'classic' role that he had forged for his bit of parliament in the creation of the law-making, assertive role of the committees. He has since been promoted to deputy minister of justice. Based on the criteria of hard work and dedication, there has not been a more deserving appointment.

In classical governance theory, the legislature (parliament) writes and passes the law; the executive (cabinet and the departments of state) executes the law by implementing it; and the judicial arm of government (the courts) enforces the law and oversees its compliance.

The same process might have been at least partially applied in the nineteenth century, but modern government practice does not begin to match the above theory anywhere in the world. As government has become more and more complex, and the responsibilities more and more far ranging, so the legislatures of the world have become less and less powerful.

Making law is only one part of the overall governance equation. Most real government power is exercised through executive action and, especially, budgetary and resource allocation decisions. The law sets the framework for this and remains very important, but, even there, such is the imbalance in resources between the two arms of government – executives tend to have all the expertise, and legislatures very little – that parliaments tend to follow the lead of the executive rather than the other way round. With the parallel emergence of strong political parties over the past fifty years, this trend has been further entrenched. A strong ruling party will operate to ensure that its membership in the legislature follows the line set by its membership in the executive – the cabinet ministers and president.

The new parliament

When parliament convened on 23 April 2004, eleven days after the elections, the first task of the National Assembly was a rather curious one – to remove Thabo Mbeki from among its membership. Not everyone knows this, but the president is not a member of parliament, even though, as the number one candidate on the ANC's list, he was the first person to be sworn in. It is a peculiarity of the South African system that, although the president heads cabinet, which is accountable to parliament, he or she ceases to be a member of parliament the moment the National Assembly elects him or her to be president.

So, as in 1999, Thabo Mbeki served as a member of the National Assembly for less than two hours. As he sat and watched the other 399 men and women being sworn in, Mbeki could look around him and reflect on how things had changed from the day ten years before when Nelson Mandela had passed through the same process.

FW de Klerk had sat opposite Mandela as leader of the largest opposition party, the National Party (NP). By the time of Mbeki's second electoral victory in 2004, the National Party was in its death throes, so, while the familiar, if unwelcome, faces of Tony Leon and Mangosuthu Buthelezi were still across the aisle, in order to see the NNP leader, Marthinus van Schalkwyk, Mbeki had to swivel and stretch his neck to look down the length of the National Assembly to that far corner of the seats where the smallest parties are crammed against the front line of the ANC backbenchers.

Mbeki's thoughts may have dwelt on the fact that the electorate had delivered an even more convincing victory for his party at the end of his first term of office than it had at the end of Mandela's term. Whether this was predominantly due to the failure of the opposition or the success of the governing party is a moot point. While analysts were still analysing the question, Mbeki could contemplate his own pivotal role in the campaign, which was to focus attention on the solid accomplishments of his government rather than its equally manifest failings.

Occasionally, his colleagues engaged Mbeki in conversation. His closer confidants, such as Essop Pahad, would come and sit down next to the boss. Others, less intimate, would stand and lean towards him. Mbeki would have noticed the massed ranks of his colleagues seated behind and alongside him, and he would have observed the changes from 1994. Many of the veterans and leading lights of the struggle years were gone, either dead or deployed elsewhere.

The 1994 ANC intake had been quite extraordinary in terms of its calibre; I doubt if there has ever been a more densely talented parliamentary party in the political history of the world. Essentially, the ANC put all its leaders and best people in parliament. It did not really know what else to do. As Mandela himself later admitted: 'Ours was not a planned entry into government. Except for the highest echelons, there was no planned deployment of cadres. We were disorganized, and behaved in a manner that could have endangered the revolution.'[2]

This disorganization was further reflected in the fact that not only was the ANC not schooled in the arcane ways of parliamentary process – unlike the experienced members of the Democratic Party (DP), whose seven MPs accordingly punched far above their weight during the early years – but parliament itself was neither equipped nor inclined to assist.

There are many stories of how new ANC MPs were treated with thinly disguised disdain by the old-guard secretariat of the National Assembly. For two years, the DP persistently outwitted the ruling party while it found its procedural feet. It took the Reverend Makhenkesi Stofile just as long to get to grips with how to organize a large parliamentary party – his reign as ANC chief whip was as chaotic as it was uncertain in its management.

Yet this was also a 'golden age' for parliament. There were two distinguishing features. First, the Constitutional Assembly, which, although technically a combined sitting of what was then the Senate and the National Assembly, in reality was constructed around the fulcrum of its constitutional committee. Its thirty-strong membership represented the intellectual crème de la crème of the ANC, and also of the opposition parties. Second, the quality of debate was remarkable, and it is hardly surprising, therefore, that such an internationally admired Constitution should have emerged from its work.

The engine room: Parliamentary committees

At the same time, a group of ANC MPs quickly realized that not only had they not been chosen to be part of Mandela's cabinet, but that the important and exciting task of writing the Constitution would not last forever. The job had to be completed, as indeed it was, by May Day 1996. Driven, ambitious and talented men and women, they realized that they had to create an alternative career path within parliament.

Hence the rapid evolution of the parliamentary committee system: the engine room of the new South African democratic parliament. Blade Nzimande, Pravin Gordhan, Gill Marcus and Johnny de Lange, to name but four pre-eminent examples, led the education, constitutional affairs, finance and justice committees into pastures new.

Strong – or *stronger* – parliaments have combated the international trend towards executive dominance, with the development of strong committee systems. In the wider public, not a lot is known about the committees and how they operate. They do not sound very sexy, and they do not attract television or radio coverage. But they are the real engine room of parliament.

The creation of a real committee system was the most exciting development in the evolution of the South African parliament since 1994, and at its best it is as strong as virtually any other parliament in the world. The committee system is underwritten by the Constitution, which is unusual but helpful. Sections 55–57 of the Constitution provide for the role of committees: parliament must create mechanisms to hold the executive to account; the committees have the authority to receive evidence and summon witnesses; they must facilitate public participation in the parliamentary process.

De Lange recalls that prior to the ANC taking power in 1994, they had little knowledge about parliament. Raymond Suttner had written about the potential role committees could play, but when fellow Western Cape ANC executive members Bulelani Ngcuka and De Lange were sent to investigate this, De Lange told Ngcuka, 'I'm buggered if I know anything about the running of parliament. I've been trying to burn it down, not make it work!'

They discovered that the old, apartheid-era committee system was a joke. The secretariat was tiny, with one clerk serving five committees. And the committees met in secret to rubber-stamp the executive's laws and policies. So, De Lange and Ngcuka (later a member of the Senate) took the tricameral parliament's rules, including those on committees, and 'removed all the obnoxious stuff'.

According to De Lange, it was the very first formal rule change proposed in the first democratic parliament of May 1994. Ironically, given his apparently pro-executive stance ever since, the ANC got Kader Asmal to propose the amendments, which included the opening up of the committee meetings.

Since then, the rules committee, and especially its subcommittees, has been very important in determining the style and character of the new parliament. As a consequence, a long-running and still unresolved contest for power within power has continued unabated between those MPs who want strong committees and the Speaker of Parliament (Frene Ginwala, until she was unceremoniously removed in May 2004), to whom committees represent an alternative, and competing, centre of power.

De Lange had often been at the forefront of the debate, usually with the support of most of his parliamentary colleagues, clashing with Ginwala over rule changes and budgetary authority questions.

It was, however, not an open-and-shut case. As Lawson Naidoo, at the time Ginwala's aide de combat and special advisor, says: 'The argument – De Lange's – is sound if applied to those committees that function well and properly, but many of the other committees functioned haphazardly, invariably without a long-term plan or strategy. Sometimes they wanted resources that could, in our view, have been better spent elsewhere. Many committees wanted to go on international study tours every year, often without producing proper reports, so it was impossible for us to see what institutional benefit accrued.'

Other committees argued for researchers who, Naidoo says, were really intended to be the chairperson's personal dogsbody and not a resource for the committee as a whole. When some committees ran to the private sector to cover the costs of study trips and researchers, obvious conflicts of interest arose, which attracted the further attention of Ginwala's office.

Naidoo's assessment is quite correct – he and Ginwala were right to be prudent. The problem was that it frustrated the hell out of those committees that were, like De Lange's, working well and working hard. Ginwala sought to regulate the manner in which committees functioned. Given her style and the way she operated, she got up many people's noses, thus undermining her goals.

De Lange and his allies got around Ginwala's obstruction by creating subcommittees of the rules committee, which were harder for her to control and which steadily revamped the procedures of parliament. Between 1996 and 1998 they were aided by an expert from Britain, Stephen Hardwick, who devoted himself to writing explanatory memos to the ANC, setting out how to use the procedures effectively. Parliament worked better as a result. Power rapidly shifted to the new committees.

As De Lange puts it now: 'The Speaker could not run forty committees.'

Whereas in the old, pre-1994 parliament, the Speaker had absolute power, the Speaker now had to share it, learning to work with and through the rules committee and other committees.

The two most expert scholars of the South African parliamentary system are Professor Christina Murray and Dr Lia Nijzink. According to them, the most important task of committees is to 'develop expertise, to gather information and to do the detailed work that must underpin properly informed decisions about public policy'.[3]

Committees are often surprisingly unpartisan, as MPs focus on the detail of legislation and policy analysis. The expertise of the group, as a whole, is essential in this regard, and the ability of MPs to work together, in an informed and productive manner, is a key component of a successful committee. Committees offer the public an opportunity to state their case to MPs through public hearings. These forums offer citizens a relatively non-partisan platform from which to engage legislators on the details of the law.

Public hearings concurrently offer MPs the opportunity to learn from civil society and to enrich their understanding of their work and its possible on-the-ground repercussions. Nijzink and Murray believe that 'committees can provide a forum for public participation, a source of expertise outside of the executive and less partisan [in a more] problem-orientated discussion'.[4]

In other words, not only can committees provide an aperture through which the public light can stream, but the effect is to help enable MPs to avoid a conflict with their colleagues in the executive part of government by pointing to the evidence from 'real life'. Ministers and their departments often rely heavily on expert opinion. Parliament – when it works well – creates a balancing exercise to be performed between this executive expertise and the expertise of non-governmental experts, as well as ordinary people. In this way, parliament's role is to mediate differences of opinion and, therefore, different voices of influence.

The powers granted to committees by the Constitution are considerable. According to Sections 56, 69 and 115 of the Constitution, the legislature and committees may:

- Summon any person to appear before them to give evidence under oath or affirmation, or to produce documents.
- Require any person or institution to report to them.
- Compel in terms of legislation or the rules and orders, any person or institution to comply with a summons or a request for a report.
- Receive petitions, representation or submissions from any interested persons or institutions.[5]

Murray and Nijzink note that committees often request particular persons or institutions to present work to them, but rarely use their powers to compel them to do so, as this is regarded as an instrument of last resort. Murray and Nijzink conclude that these powers indicate 'the complexity of the relationship between the legislature and its committees. [The Constitution] gives committees a degree of autonomy over their own affairs. However, committees have no formal decision-making power. Their mandate is limited by the terms of reference set by the Rules of the legislature. They advise the legislature on the matters that they have considered but do not take binding decisions.'[6]

Internally, committees need to develop their human and institutional capacity in order to fulfil their function within the legislative system. In this regard, the members of the committees and their support staff, and the ability of the group to understand and interpret their work within the context of the portfolio, are essential to fulfilling their mandate.

So, for the first time, the South African people could interact with their rulers through the public participation processes that these and other committees developed. Parliament as an institution was at the forefront of this, with a dedicated public education department headed for a time by the energetic Alf Karrim, who worked alongside the committees to develop public participation and outreach programmes. And some of the committees worked very hard too; previously a part-time rubber-stamp during the apartheid era, parliament became a full-time place of work.

Apart from De Lange's committee, Nzimande and Gordhan led on major policy reforms. Meanwhile, the much-maligned Tony Yengeni led a defence committee that contained experts such as Thenjiwe Mtintso and Ian Phillips, who were truly expert in military matters from their own experience in MK.

However much they tried, the old generals could not escape their specialist scrutiny. A major review of defence policy was conducted and a new vision developed, though not without hiccups along the way. At one point, Yengeni got fed up with the way the generals were speaking to him.

'We are the elected representatives of the people, so show some respect,' was the essence of what he said to them.

General George Meiring, a hangover from the previous era, was furious, and went straight to President Mandela. It was a delicate time, when Mandela was trying to shore up his strategy of national reconciliation.

'We did not realize then what we know now,' says a former advisor, 'that there was no way they could organize a coup.'

But the outcome was that Yengeni and his ANC colleagues were ordered in front of Mandela and given a thorough dressing-down.

The role of the committee chairperson is critical to the new parliament's well-being and relevance. There are twenty-six portfolio committees, one for each government portfolio. As De Lange says, 'This creates twenty-six political platforms for the opposition from which to launch attacks on the ANC.'

He then makes a very interesting point: 'The strength of the committee depends on the strength of the individual who is chairing it, and the hegemony of the committee, especially among the ruling party members. If you have a weak chairperson and committee, who is scared of the opposition, then he or she is more likely to close things down. But if you took on the issues, then the ANC can show that it has the ideas. People in the opposition realized it was not the plenary, where you can talk nonsense and get away with it. We knocked the socks off of them on the issues.'

He points to the fact that many of the early chairpersons – Gordhan, Nzimande, Suttner – were intellectual giants with a culture of open debate, confident in their own ideas and therefore willing to have robust discussions in their committees. The quality of the debates flourished, and, by osmosis, parliament prospered in such circumstances. As a chairperson, De Lange always encouraged a confident approach from the ANC members. 'Let us not be scared of them,' was his attitude. 'Let us draw the intellectual satisfaction of beating the other side on the merits and on the substance.'

Although he met with the ANC committee members separately as a group, De Lange claims that 'we never had set positions. We would first hear what the public had to say. While I had to make sure that I dealt with matters in accordance with ANC policy, I would also want to question and probe what came to us from the executive. I should add: our committee was strongly supported and encouraged in this approach by both our ministers during this period.'

This was not the attitude of all chairs, however. As another chairperson of similar parliamentary vintage explains: 'Some of my colleague chairs were concerned about defying "ANC policy". Some of them were not comfortable enough – it's got fuck-all to do with the ANC wanting to control – and they were not sufficiently *au fait* with ANC policy, and they would see what came from the executive as "approved", so they were not receptive to new ideas.'

The success of certain committee chairs was also premised on the strong working relationships that they forged with their respective ministers. This, in turn, depended on their political weight within the ANC. De Lange was fortunate. His minister, Dullah Omar, was an old friend; they went back a long way and trusted each other implicitly. De Lange had reasonable, but less frequent, contact with Penuell Maduna during the 1999–2004 parliament, but, says De Lange, Maduna always listened to the committee with an open mind and, if convinced, 'basically accepted our approach'.

Sea change

For the first few years, things were happening: parliament was an exciting and important place in the new political firmament. But then, imperceptibly at first, there was a sea change. From 1997, parliament entered a new phase, which one might, perhaps harshly, describe as a period of degradation, in the sense of 'downgrading' rather than ruin. Institutional momentum was lost as the ANC decided to redeploy large numbers of its most senior MPs. The switch in strategy was articulated in a document titled, 'The National Democratic Revolution – Is it Still on Track?' penned by the ever-influential Joel Netshitenzhe.

Pinpointing the need to transform institutional power, the document identified six 'areas of power': the Constitution, the legislatures, governance, state machinery, economic relations and the 'depth and content of the national debate'.

Overendowed with intellectual capital, the ANC leadership decided it had to disinvest from parliament and redeploy key individuals. Many of those who left were senior ANC politicians with considerable technical, political and leadership skills. Although De Lange stayed on to continue to till the fields of justice, Gordhan, for example, became head of SARS, and Marcus went on to the Reserve Bank. Others, most notably Cyril Ramaphosa, went into the private sector. His move reflected the other component of the strategic imperative, which was later articulated in the 1997 *Strategy and Tactics* document arising out of the ANC's fiftieth national conference in Mafikeng, namely to deploy ANC cadres to key positions within the untransformed centres of power, in order for them 'to fulfil the mandate of the organization'.

Armed with this resolution, the national working committee's (NWC) deployment committee went to work. By 2003, 186 of the 252-strong original class of 1994 had been redeployed to other areas. And not just the older, more established members of the party. A young star such as Nat Kekana, having climbed up the parliamentary ladder to become a committee chair, was taken to work for Telkom just a few months into the role. Many of those who were left behind were – to pick a relatively polite term – 'docile' in their level of performance – serving out their time, earning their pensions after years of selflessly serving the struggle.

As the above brief survey of the relevant ANC policy documents suggests, the ANC itself lacked the internal organization, capacity, resources and political will to plan and implement a cadre-deployment policy prior to the 1997 conference. This resulted in an over-concentration of senior ANC personnel in the National Assembly. In the period beginning 1996, the ANC's NEC, and after 1997, the deployment committee, located within the NWC, transferred many MPs from parliament to other branches of government (provincial and local), as well as to the civil service, private sector and government departments.

In 1994, 252 MPs represented the ANC in the National Assembly. In 1999, this number increased to 266. In 1999, 136 of the original 252 MPs elected to the National Assembly on the 1994 ANC ticket returned to parliament. By the end of the second parliament, in 2004, a total of 102 of those MPs elected in 1994 remained in parliament. If one removes from this group those MPs who sit in cabinet and who do not engage in the day-to-day proceedings of the legislature, the figure drops to 75.

The conscious redeployment of ANC cadres from the National Assembly caucus is evident in the increase of departures after cadre-deployment decisions were implemented within the ANC after the 1997 conference. Prior to 1997, 47 MPs left parliament. In the seven years since then, an additional 140 MPs have departed the National Assembly.

The final report of the ad hoc joint subcommittee on oversight and accountability noted in its recommendations that the 'expertise acquired during the first and second democratic parliaments will largely be lost over time as a new crop of MPs get elected into their seats. It is therefore critical to develop an institutional memory and allow parliamentarians to build upon this strong foundation.'[7]

The implications of the exodus of ANC MPs through redeployment will have additional implications for the development of an institutional memory and, by association, the effective functioning of the National Assembly.

The importance of parliamentary experience is underlined by the fact that, of the twenty-six ANC chairpersons of National Assembly portfolio committees, eighteen, or 70 per cent, have been in parliament since it commenced in 1994; twenty-one of the seventy-five MPs who have remained in parliament since 1994 have been portfolio committee chairpersons at one time or another. The nature and extent of these changes also illustrate the degree to which the parliamentary caucus of the ANC is subject to the decisions of the ANC's deployment committees and the party leadership.

The majority of outgoing MPs (excluding retired and deceased MPs) have continued their careers in ways that remain intimately linked to the state. Eighty-two of these former MPs remain in the pay of the taxpayer. This group of eighty-two is split evenly between those who work as civil servants in state institutions and government departments, and those who represent the ANC in other legislatures: the National Council of Provinces (NCOP), and provincial and local government. The transfer of legislative skills and experience to government departments and other legislatures is indicative of the ANC's decision to focus on delivery and to improve intergovernmental relations.

In line with the ANC's commitment to strengthen party structures, a further thirteen former MPs are now employed by the political parties that constitute the ANC caucus through the tripartite alliance (twelve ANC, one SACP). All of the deployments to local and provincial structures, as well as to party structures (possibly excluding Blade Nzimande, who became full-time secretary general of the SACP) would have been initiated, or at least vetted, by party leadership through deployment committees. Those MPs who have shifted from the national to provincial ANC lists in the 1999 elections would only have done so with the party's blessing. The same logic should be applied to the majority of those who have entered the civil service.

The four MPs who have resigned in disgrace (one after having been initially deployed to a diplomatic post in Mozambique) did so only after having been pressurized by the party leadership. The role of the party in effecting these resignations should be applauded. The remaining forty-eight MPs of whom I have records (excluding retired and deceased MPs) are now pursuing private interests.

It is likely, however, that some of these private appointments were made with the blessing of the ANC's leadership (for example, Max Sisulu and Cyril Ramaphosa remain ANC NEC members, while they pursue private business interests). Fourteen of these MPs are now in business, five are in academia, five joined the United Democratic Movement (UDM), four returned to their previous careers (lawyer, farmer, singer and traditional leader respectively), two have taken up positions with NGOs, and one is now the chief curator of the Robben Island Museum.

The Great Brain Drain

Underlining the 'brain-drain' effect from parliament to the executive, but also, significantly, signifying that to be a committee chair is a potential springboard to higher, executive office, twenty-six chairs have departed – a very high turnover in just two parliaments. Ten have gone into the cabinet or become deputy ministers.

The following lists detail the portfolio committee chairs of the National Assembly (excluding the NCOP) who have departed parliament.

LEFT PARLIAMENT:
- **Tony Yengeni**, chairperson of the joint standing committee on defence, 1994–1999. Former chief whip, resigned in disgrace from parliament in March 2003.
- **Pregs Govender**, chairperson of the joint standing committee on the status of women, 1996–2002, quit parliament for academia on 24 May 2002 (in protest over the arms deal and government inertia on AIDS).

- **Janet Love**, chairperson of the portfolio committee for agriculture, water affairs and forestry, 1994–99, is now an advisor to the minister of water affairs and forestry.
- **Mongane Wally Serote**, chairperson of the portfolio committee on arts, culture, language, science and technology, 1994–2002, left parliament on 7 May 2002 to take up a position as CEO of the Freedom Park Trust.
- **Saki Macozoma**, chairperson of the portfolio committee for communications, 1994–96, quit parliament on 28 March 1996 to become CEO of Transnet, a post he left in February 2001 to concentrate on private business interests. He is currently CEO of New Africa Investments Limited (NAIL), chairman of financial institutions at Stanlib and Andisa, and a director of the Standard Bank of South Africa, the Standard Group, the Liberty Group, Murray & Roberts and Volkswagen SA. He is a major shareholder in and deputy chairman of Safika Holdings.
- **Samuel Moeti**, chairperson of the communications committee, 1996–99, left parliament after the 1999 elections. He is now district mayor of the Vhembe district in Limpopo.
- **Nat Kekana**, chairperson of the communications committee, 1999–2003, resigned from parliament in June 2003 to take up a position as group executive for regulatory and public policy at Telkom.
- **Pravin Gordhan**, chairperson of the constitutional committee, 1994–98, left parliament in March 1998 to become deputy commissioner of the South African Revenue Service. In 1999 he was appointed commissioner of the same organization.
- **Carl Niehaus**, chairperson of the portfolio committee on correctional services, 1994–96, left parliament to take up a position as South African ambassador to the Netherlands. He returned to South Africa to become the executive director of the National Institute of Crime Prevention and Reintegration of Offenders, a post he left in 2000 to become a director of Deloitte & Touche SA.
- **Limpho Hani**, chairperson of the portfolio committee on correctional services, 1997–99, resigned from parliament after the 1999 elections.
- **Blade Nzimande**, chairperson of the portfolio committee on education, 1994–99, resigned from parliament after the 1999 elections to become general secretary of the South African Communist Party.
- **Zingile Dingani**, chairperson of the joint standing committee on finance

for 1996, left parliament after the 1999 elections to become MEC for finance in the Free State.

- **Raymond Suttner**, chairperson of the committee on foreign affairs, 1994–96, left parliament in 1999 to become South African ambassador to Sweden. He is now a fellow of the Wits Institute for Social and Economic Research (WISER).
- **Ebrahim Ebrahim**, chairperson of the committee on foreign affairs, 1997–2002, quit parliament on 1 June 2002 to take up an appointment as advisor to the deputy president.
- **Sokhaya Abraham Nkomo**, chairperson of the health committee, 1996–2002, left parliament to become the South African high commissioner to Malaysia.
- **Mpho Scott**, chairperson of the home affairs committee in 2002, left parliament in January 2003 to take up a position as executive chairman of Africa Legends Energy, a BEE company that acquired a 25 per cent stake in Caltex SA. Scott is also a director of Univest, the BEE partner of Equity Aviation (49 per cent owned by Transnet), which was involved in a protracted dispute with baggage workers who went on strike for four months in 2004.
- **Titus Mafolo**, chairperson of the housing committee, 1994–97, left parliament to become political advisor to President Thabo Mbeki.
- **Marcell Golding**, chairperson of the committee on mineral and energy affairs, 1994–96, left parliament in February 1997 to become chairperson of Hosken Consolidated Investments. He is currently also acting CEO of e.tv.
- **Duma Nkosi**, chairperson of the mineral and energy affairs committee, 1997–2001, left parliament in 2001 to become executive mayor of the Ekurhuleni Municipality.
- **Sakhiwo Belot**, chairperson of the public enterprises committee, 2000–01, was appointed as the Free State MEC for tourism, environmental affairs and economic affairs.
- **Max Sisulu**, chairperson of the RDP committee, 1994–96, became chief whip of the majority party after the Reverend Makhenkesi Stofile's departure. He then left parliament in 1999 to become CEO of Denel, and is currently the director of corporate affairs at Sasol and a non-executive director of Harmony Gold.

- **Beatrice Marshoff**, chairperson of the RDP committee, 1997, left parliament in 2001 to become MEC for social development in the Free State. In 2004, Marshoff was appointed premier of the Free State.
- **Solomon Tsenoli**, chairperson of the RDP committee, 1998–99, left parliament after the 1999 elections to become MEC for local government and housing in the Free State.
- **Linda Mti**, chairperson of the safety and security committee, 1994–95, left parliament in 1996 to become the coordinator for intelligence (DG position) in the NIA. In 2001, he was appointed national commissioner of the department of correctional services.
- **Rapulane Molekane**, chairperson of the safety and security committee, 1996–99, left parliament after the 1999 elections to become consul-general in South Africa's embassy in Germany.
- **Edna Molewa** (née Sethema), chairperson of the trade and industry committee, 1994–95, left parliament at the end of 1995. She is now premier of the North West Province.
- **Rosemary Capa**, chairperson of the correctional services committee, 2000–01, was deployed to local government as a councillor after the local government elections.

TO CABINET OR DEPUTY MINISTERSHIPS:
- **Lindiwe Sisulu**, chairperson of the intelligence committee in 1995, was appointed deputy minister of home affairs in 1996, a position she held until May 2002, when she was promoted to minister of intelligence. In 2004, Sisulu was named minister of housing.
- **Mandisi Mpahlwa**, chairperson of the finance committee, 1997–99, was appointed deputy minister of finance in 1999. In 2004, Mpahlwa was promoted to the position of minister of trade and industry.
- **Nosiviwe Mapisa-Nqakula**, chairperson of the intelligence committee, 1996–2002, and former chief whip of the majority party, was appointed deputy minister of home affairs in May 2002. In 2004, Mapisa-Nqakula was appointed minister of home affairs.
- **Buyelwa Sonjica**, chairperson of the portfolio committee on water affairs and forestry, 1999–2003, was appointed deputy minister of arts, culture, science and technology in February 2003. Sonjica was appointed minister of water affairs and forestry in April 2004.

- **Peter Mokaba**, chairperson of the portfolio committee for environmental affairs and tourism, was appointed deputy minister of environmental affairs and tourism after the expulsion of Bantu Holomisa in 1996. His appointment as deputy minister was not renewed after 1999. He has since died.
- **Gill Marcus**, chairperson of the joint standing committee on finance, 1994–95, was appointed deputy minister of finance in 1996, a position she held until the 1999 elections, when she was redeployed to the South African Reserve Bank as deputy governor.
- **Manto Tshabalala-Msimang**, chairperson of the health committee, 1994–95, was appointed deputy minister of justice in 1996 after the dissolution of the Government of National Unity, a position she held until the 1999 elections, when she was appointed minister of health. She was reappointed in 2004.
- **Phumzile Mlambo-Ngcuka**, chairperson of the public service and administration committee, 1994–95, was appointed deputy minister of trade and industry in 1996. She was promoted to minister of mineral and energy affairs in 1999, and retained the position in 2004, until May 2005 when she succeeded Jacob Zuma as deputy president.
- **Elizabeth Hangana**, chairperson of the housing committee, 1998–2002, left parliament in 2002 to become MEC for housing in the Western Cape. In 2004 she was appointed deputy minister of provincial and local government.
- **Lulu Xingwana**, chairperson of the sport and recreation committee, 1994–99, and of the ad hoc joint committee on the status of women, 2002–04, was appointed deputy minister of mineral and energy affairs in 2004 and, in the June 2006 reshuffle, was promoted to minister of land affairs.
- **Johnny de Lange**, chairperson of the justice and constitutional affairs committee, 1994–2004, was appointed deputy minister of justice and constitutional affairs after the election in 2004.
- **Rob Davies**, chairperson of the trade and industry committee, 1996–2004, was appointed deputy minister of trade and industry after the election in 2004.

Within the ANC, it would appear that being a member of parliament is not perceived as being an end in itself. Instead, the party and, in some cases, individuals, use it as a 'stepping stone' to other positions within the state and the private sector. It would appear that parliament, as such, is not 'professionalizing'. It is hard to fault the strategy of deployment on one level, as clearly the ANC needed to spread its talent across all key parts of society and government. However, what it has failed to do is properly think through how to develop a new wave of capable, younger MPs.

The justice committee

In contrast to the overall changes in parliament, Johnny de Lange's former committee, the portfolio committee on justice and constitutional develop-ment, has been a model of relative stability over the first ten years of the functioning of parliament. The committee enjoyed consistency in the form of its chairperson, De Lange, who oversaw the work of the committee for a decade from its inception in 1994 until 2004.[8] Some stakeholders have criticized De Lange's management style, but the consistency of his leadership has allowed the committee to accrue an institutional memory and organ-izational culture that has worked in the interests of all represented there.

Party composition of justice committee

	1994	End of first parliament	1999	End of second parliament
ACDP	1	1	1	1
ANC	21	18	15	13
DP/DA	2	3	4	4
FF/VF	1	2	0	0
IFP	4	3	2	3
NP/NNP	7	9	3	2
PAC	1	0	1	1
FA	NA	NA	1	NA[9]
UCDP	NA	NA	1	1
UDM	NA	NA	2	1
Total	37	36	30	26

Of the thirty-seven MPs who sat on the committee at the beginning of 1994, twenty-one served the full five-year term, and a further two MPs served for four years. In the last three years of the committee's work, only four members left, compensated by four new members. The relatively high turnover of

MPs across committees during the first years of the first parliament is a result, in part, of parties weighing up priority portfolios relative to their constituencies. These decisions are especially tough for minority parties, which do not have the strength in numbers to assign MPs to every committee. As a result, opposition parties have to weigh up the merits of each portfolio and their human capital, and assign MPs to committees according to a kind of political cost-benefit analysis. In terms of declining representation, the assigning of ANC MPs to the committee has dropped significantly over the ten years.

Many of the twenty-one core committee members who sat throughout the five-year term were senior members of their parties, with experience in the law and of the transitional negotiations. Their collective experience and knowledge of the portfolio allowed for a stable, generally non-partisan and informed forum for discussion of legislation. The consistency of participation allowed the committee to develop skills and understanding among and between members over the full five-year term, which contributed to the accrual of institutional memory and an organizational culture that expedited high-quality legislation.

The close of the first parliament saw the exodus of twenty-four members of the committee; however, twelve were carried over to the second term, when a new thirty-member committee was established. Of these twelve MPs, six had participated in the committee since 1994, thus ensuring continuity and the transfer of skills and experience to the new committee. Fifteen of these thirty MPs sat in the committee throughout the second parliamentary term. Five of these fifteen MPs had served the committee for the full ten years.[10] The size of the committee shrank a little over the five years, with twenty-six MPs serving at the close of the second parliament.

The high number of members leaving the committee after the first term was in part a consequence of the drastic change in the opposition political landscape, with many NNP MPs (seven exits) not being re-elected back to parliament following a significant loss of support in the 1999 elections. The eighteen newcomers to the committee in the second parliament reflected the relative increase in support for the DP at the polls, as well as the UDM, United Christian Democratic Party (UCDP) and the Federal Alliance (FA), which had not existed in 1994.

Interestingly, floor-crossing did not overly affect the composition of the committee. The only impact was Sheila Camerer changing parties – from the NNP to the DA – but she did not vacate her seat. There has been a core group of MPs from both sides of the house who have accompanied De Lange during his long tenure.

This stability of membership has undoubtedly contributed greatly to the committee's effectiveness. De Lange's successor, Fatima Chohan, is an interesting example of a new breed of career politician. Then in her early thirties, she was redeployed from the Gauteng parliament in 1995, and as an attorney was grateful to be deployed by the whippery into the justice committee. As shrewd as she is charming, Chohan has proved to be an able understudy to De Lange since 1999, regularly deputizing for him.

SCOPA and the arms deal: Parliament and the bottom of the barrel

Chohan has enjoyed a wider influence in parliament, arising from her chairing of a special, ad hoc committee to investigate the oversight role of parliament – arguably its most important and vexing responsibility, as the huge furore over the standing committee on public accounts (SCOPA) revealed.

SCOPA is a vital committee, perhaps the most important sub-institution of parliament. The one good thing to emerge from the controversy was that the general public acquired at least some passing knowledge of the otherwise obscure concept of 'parliamentary oversight'. The expression was repeated time and again, as pundits in the media examined the ANC's reaction to parliament's response to South Africa's largest-ever procurement – five contracts with international companies totalling around R60 billion.

Although it is now an old story, there is more than a touch of the fable about it. Andrew Feinstein, the young ANC MP with a Cambridge University master's degree in economics, was generally regarded as a rising star. Although he only joined the ANC in the early 1990s and had no particular history of ANC activism, he had been elected to the Gauteng provincial legislature, after which he was redeployed to the National Assembly in 1996. Naturally, he was deployed to both the finance and the public accounts committees, and soon became a leading light on both. After 1999, he was elected to lead the ANC membership of SCOPA. Everything was going well for Feinstein; he was enjoying life in parliament, and, unlike many of his colleagues, felt in his 'naivety and idealism' (his words) that he was performing an important democratic role in SCOPA.

Then the bombshell dropped. A draft report from the Auditor-General arrived on his desk in mid-2000, raising some initial concerns about the process that had led to the Strategic Defence Procurement Package (to give it its full title). It was the duty of SCOPA to further examine the issues. This they did, calling evidence and considering the documents.

They published their own interim report in October 2000, an act that, with hindsight, represented a watershed moment for parliament. The report listed a series of concerns that SCOPA regarded as serious and deserving of a more intense investigation. Indeed, such was the complexity and possible depth of the wrongdoing, the committee, without objections from any party, recommended a multidisciplinary investigation involving the Auditor-General, the Public Protector, the National Director of Public Prosecutions and the Special Investigating Unit, headed by Judge Willem Heath.

With the end of the parliamentary term in sight, the ANC leadership was dozing and missed the import of the resolution. It went through by unanimous resolution in the National Assembly, much to the later chagrin of the chief whip, Tony Yengeni. When the ANC leadership finally woke up to the cat they had let out of the bag, they were horrified. There were too many skeletons in this particular cupboard.

One of the allegations was that defence minister Joe Modise had received a payment of US$10 million from British Aerospace (BAE). (In November 2003, Andrew Feinstein alleged on Swedish radio that, in fact, the payment by BAE and its consortium partner, SAAB, had amounted to $35 million, and had been made to the ANC.)

Over the Christmas holidays, frantic attempts were made to turn back the clock. After discussions on Christmas Day and the Day of Goodwill, Ginwala issued a statement saying that parliament had not really intended to appoint Judge Heath's team. At times, the ANC suffers from collective control-freak syndrome. Heath was far too independent, running around the country like a bull in a china shop, seizing files and computers here and making arrests there. Loved by the mainstream print media, his high profile had gone to his head. He had all but forgotten that he was heading an administrative tribunal established by statute as a part of the executive arm of government, a fact that partly saved the government. In late 2000, the Constitutional

Court had ruled that it was unconstitutional for a member of one arm of government, in this case the judiciary, to preside over a part of another arm of government, here the executive.

Feinstein continued to press his case, aware now that he was up against mighty political forces, which increased his determination but not his political prospects. On 22 January 2001, he was summoned to the chief whip's office where, to his great shock, he was sacked as convenor of the ANC group on SCOPA. Vincent Smith, a party apparatchik with a reputation as a political fixer, was appointed in his place.

In an exercise in pure political cynicism, Smith, with his sidekick Neo Masithela, filibustered SCOPA into the ground over the next twelve months. Tactically outmanoeuvred, neither Feinstein nor the chair of the committee, IFP MP Gavin Woods, was able to save the committee. It was politically neutered, its balls, so to speak, cut off by the ANC's determination to take full political control of the matter. In mid-year, Feinstein resigned to take a job at the South African investment bank Investec in London. It had been an appallingly stressful time for him and his family. Infamously, Essop Pahad had screamed at Feinstein, 'Who the fuck do you think you are?'

This is a summary of some of the main elements to the story, which demonstrates the absence of a culture of parliamentary oversight. As I have written elsewhere: 'The issue highlights the fundamental tension in many parliamentary systems of loyalty, while carrying out the parliamentary duties of oversight and accountability. It shows the weakness of individual MPs. More importantly, it shows the strength of the executive arm of government vis-à-vis the legislative. Far from the executive obediently carrying out the orders of the legislature, in fact, it is the legislature that is to all intents and purposes the subordinate institutional partner.'[11]

In contrast to the portfolio committee, whose oversight responsibilities have to compete with their law-making obligations, SCOPA is purely an oversight body. It is charged with the task of checking that public expenditure has occurred in the manner intended and with full value to the public. In this, its role interlocks with the constitutional mandate of the Auditor-General, one of the 'Chapter 9' constitutional watchdog institutions. That is why there is a strong case for trying to insulate SCOPA from the normal partisan pressures imposed by a competitive party political system.

The work of SCOPA is extremely technical, and the experience and expertise of MPs are therefore disproportionately valuable to this committee. Turnover of MPs on SCOPA has been exceptionally high over the ten years of its existence. The drop in total membership numbers and the continual shuffling of members have undermined the ability of the committee as an institution to accrue institutional memory and maintain a constant organizational culture.

The table below tracks the extent of the turnover of MPs as experienced by SCOPA. Total membership of the committee fluctuated wildly during the first five years, peaking at thirty-six in 1995, declining to twenty-six in 1997, and then rising again to thirty-five by the close of the first term. In 1996, two years into the committee's work, only thirteen of the original twenty-seven MPs assigned to the committee had enjoyed an uninterrupted stay. By the end of the first parliament's term, that number had dropped to six, although an additional six MPs have served four years.

Turnover of MPs

	1994	1995	1996	1997	1998	1999	1999 (2)	2000	2001	2002	2003
Membership	27	36	30	26	35	35	23	24	26	27	25
Exiting MPs*	7	12	13	2	11	26	0	11	5	6	0
New MPs**	27	15	7	7	0	0	14	1	13	7	4

* Exiting MP figures are taken from the end of each year.
** Figures for new MPs are taken from the beginning of each year.

Of the thirty-five MPs who served on SCOPA at the end of the first term of parliament, only nine returned for the second term. Of these nine MPs, only two (Barbara Hogan and Billy Nair of the ANC) had sat on the committee since 1994, and two others (Gavin Woods of the IFP and Laloo Chiba of the ANC) had sat for four years.

In the second term, turnover of MPs was again a characteristic of the committee. By the year-end of 2001, only twelve of the twenty-three original MPs remained on the committee, and further experience was lost when Barbara Hogan, who had served since 1995, departed (Nair, Chiba and Woods remained). Hogan returned to the committee in 2002.

By the end of the second parliament, only seven of the then twenty-five members of SCOPA had served the full five years on the committee. Of these seven, Chiba, Nair (both ANC) and Woods (IFP) had served a full ten years.

During the course of 2000, the arms deal and the subsequent investigation thereof dominated the profile of SCOPA. At this time, in an effort to extract the maximum political capital possible from the work of SCOPA, political parties packed the committee with party heavyweights, who had little or no experience of the work and spirit of the committee.

ANC out:
Felix Fankomo; Feinstein; Hogan; Serake Leeuw; Marshoff
ANC in:
Louisa Mabe; Neo Masithela (party whip); Percylia Mothoagae; Andries Nel (party whip)

DP out:
Brian Bell; Ian Davidson (both backbenchers)
DP in:
Nigel Bruce (former editor of *Finance Week*, senior MP); Nick Clelland-Stokes (rising star in the DP, parliamentary counsellor to Tony Leon at that time); Tertius Delport (former PW Botha cabinet member and senior member of the DP); Raenette Taljaard (rising star of the party, good technical skills)
(NNP at this stage functioning as part of the Democratic Alliance)

NNP out:
Pierre Rabie
NNP in:
François Beukman; Sheila Camerer (chairperson of party caucus); Pierre Uys (former MEC for local government in the Western Cape, and now MEC for health in the new Western Cape government)

IFP out:
G Bhengu
IFP in:
Sybil Seaton

UDM out:
S Naidoo

UDM in:
Bantu Holomisa (leader of the UDM)

Of these newcomers, Holomisa, Delport, Clelland-Stokes, Taljaard, Uys and Nel had left by the end of 2002.

The impact of the electoral system

One of the most important factors in assessing the power of parliament is to focus on the power of the individual MP. In the South African electoral system, with a 'pure' proportional representation (PR) system and no constituencies, the seat in parliament is 'owned' by the party and not the MP. This gives an obvious controlling power to the party managers, especially the chief whip. Whereas in a constituency-based system an MP can say, 'I am here representing the voters of X and Y, was voted in by them and am accountable to them,' they cannot say that in a PR system where the voters pick a party.

This effect is compounded by some of the socio-political and socio-economic realities of South Africa and its political class at this point in its history. MPs earn a good salary, but many are playing catch-up with their careers; many will have little or no pension provision; they are supporting a wider family or group of people; they have no other career to fall back on, and are too old to contemplate re-training. They need to hold on to their membership of parliament.

In the SCOPA/arms deal case, these factors played a role. Two of the more senior members of the ANC membership, Laloo Chiba and Billy Nair, have some political weight and prestige as former Robben Islanders, but not enough for them to feel secure about their positions in parliament. Neither is young; neither has a pension. Unlike Andrew Feinstein, neither is in a position to walk into a lucrative new career at a merchant bank. Initially they were as concerned about the way in which the executive had entered into the arms deal as Feinstein. But when the ante was upped, the pressure became too great, and they cracked. They abandoned Feinstein to his fate. Thus, the SCOPA story also illustrates the pre-eminent importance and influence of what are known as the 'ANC study groups', which just means the ANC membership group in any particular committee.

The chief whip

There are other key figures in parliament. First, the chief whip. If cabinet is the 'buckle', then the chief whip is the belt and braces. In parliamentary systems, chief whips are there to marshal the troops and maintain party discipline. The position generally tends to attract charismatic people with real political weight, who can use their stature to coerce recalcitrant individual MPs into line.

Thus, the first three chief whips were big names: Makhenkesi Stofile, Max Sisulu and Tony Yengeni. The incumbent chief whip, Mbulelo Goniwe, is a more junior figure in some respects, though with an esteemed ANC heritage. His predecessor, Nathi Nhleko, was a relatively short-lived experiment in picking a more youthful technocrat. Well-liked and approachable, Nhleko struggled to stamp his authority on his troops. In a sense, the chief whip has to be more than a bit of a bastard; Nhleko was and is far too nice. Goniwe's appointment shows that the ANC is confident that it has parliament – and more particularly, its own caucus – firmly under control.

Often, the deputy chief whip is an almost equally important figure, doing all the legwork and making significant decisions about who will answer which particular parliamentary question, who will make which speech in the House and in what sequence, and what the line will be. So it was that Geoff Doidge, in whom the British aide Stephen Hardwick invested a great deal, became a very influential deputy chief whip to both Sisulu and Yengeni. Doidge is now chair of chairs, which is another important position.

His replacement, Andries Nel, a suitably ingenious character who appears to revel in the chicanery of being a whip, is a classic political fixer who will probably go far. There is a whole team of whips in support, generally one for each committee.

In addition to the whippery, the leader of government business has a certain amount of power, though less so than the committee chairs and chief whips, which involves settling the government's programme, and negotiating priorities and sequencing with parliament and its committees. It is a cabinet position, but not a separate one; at present, Phumzile Mlambo-Ngcuka holds the position, as did her predecessor as deputy president, Jacob Zuma.

John Jeffrey (known universally as 'JJ') is another individual whose personality appears well suited to the nooks and crannies of parliamentary life. The parliamentary counsellor to the president involves a different sort of role: more a link man than an operator, he or she is the president's eyes and ears in parliament. It is, apparently, a key stepping stone for higher office. All of the previous incumbents have gone on to greater things: Essop Pahad, into the cabinet; Charles Nqakula, likewise; Willie Hofmeyr, to head the Special Investigating Unit in the DPP; Sue van der Merwe, to deputy minister of foreign affairs. The appointment of Manne Dipico, JJ's predecessor and the successful former premier of the Northern Cape, was an underwhelming surprise. Not to me: Dipico is assured of great things in the future.

All of these role players meet, with the presiding officers and the chair of the ANC caucus, in what is known as the political committee. The political committee was created after the *Sarafina II* controversy, when the ANC appeared to lose the plot in parliament and, amid chaotic scenes, tried to wrest control of the issue. It learnt a hard lesson – it is very difficult to impose an imperial decision from on high at the last minute; greater political coordination is needed at all times. When the next political hot potato came round, the political committee was ready and waiting, as Andrew Feinstein found to his cost.

Madam Speaker (again)

The Speaker of Parliament is more than just the titular head of the institution or its 'presiding officer'. Frene Ginwala had been a reluctant Madam Speaker. In her first interview after being unceremoniously removed from the position (against her wishes), she said that she had wanted to remain Speaker for another year or two, and then move on to become Speaker of the first Pan African Parliament.

She admitted that she hadn't wanted the job at first, and had rowed with President Mandela when he appointed her to the position. Clearly neither Mandela nor Deputy President Mbeki had wanted her where she wanted to be: in the cabinet.

'It confined me,' she says now, with regret. 'I had other plans for myself.'[12]

Ginwala had been persistently unable or unwilling to delegate properly. Many of her former colleagues feel that she was, in fact, very executive-minded, not least because she desperately would have liked to be a member of the cabinet. Said one ANC MP colleague: 'As a manager she was despotic, and resented the growth of the committee system, over which she had insufficient control and which thereby sapped power from the plenary, where she did have full control.'

Baleka Mbete, Ginwala's successor, is an artist and formerly Deputy Speaker, and is not known for her organizational skills. Speaker of

Parliament is a curious position for her. After her involvement in a maladministration incident in Mpumalanga, in which she'd unlawfully acquired a driver's licence, Mbete was sent into a sort of political holding pattern. The position of Deputy Speaker is generally considered inconsequential. With someone as forceful as Ginwala in the chair, there was little for Mbete to do but serve her time, as punishment for her misjudgment. The ANC is a forgiving organization, and now Mbete's career is back on track.

The National Council of Provinces

Last, the National Council of Provinces (NCOP), the second house of parliament, deserves a mention. Not, sadly, because it is either important or influential, but because it is neither, though Christina Murray, professor of Public Law at the University of Cape Town, might contest this statement, such is her admiration for its state-of-the-art institutional design.

There is scant evidence that the NCOP really matters. In Chapter 6, I refer to the recent case of the Anti-Terrorism Bill and COSATU's last-minute and successful attempt to stop the bill prior to the election. When COSATU realized that someone had inserted some new provisions dealing with industrial action after the bill had passed from the National Assembly Committee, they made representations to the NCOP, which duly removed the offending clauses. Whether COSATU and thereby the NCOP were wrong, as the relevant ministers would argue, or not, when the bill went back to the National Assembly, the NCOP's amendment was rejected by the National Assembly – which it is entitled to do with any law that is of purely 'national competence' (that is to say, not a law particular to the provinces).

The NCOP was conceptualized as a place for the articulation and protection of provincial interests. Legislation that has a provincial relevance – so-called Section 76 bills – has a more complex procedure: the National Assembly can only reject an NCOP amendment with a special majority. The fact that the National Assembly can still reject an NCOP amendment shows where the power lies.

The NCOP is a cleverly designed institution, but it has no political weight. Its past two chairpersons, Naledi Pandor and Mosiuoa Lekota, did little to change that, impatiently waiting for elevation to a position that really matters – namely the cabinet. Johnny de Lange says that, given the sparse human resources – just fifty-six permanent members – the NCOP must learn 'to focus more exclusively on Section 76 bills'. The current permanent chairperson, MJ Mahlangu, has a mountain to climb. If they don't reach the summit, then by 2009 the NCOP will be not so much a spent force than an ornate hot-air balloon that could never quite make it off the ground.

Quo vadis parliament?

The development of a viable committee system, led by people like Johnny de Lange, has given parliament a serious raison d'être. Laws can be rewritten, and depending on the character of the chairperson and his or her relationship with the minister, and with the ANC caucus in general, the committee can have a serious impact on policy. But the development of the committee system has not been even; for every strong committee, there is also a weak, ineffectual one. Very little institutional memory has been built up.

Thus, some commentators will be writing further obituaries for parliament. According to them, a huge majority and a weak and divided opposition will play into the hands of those in the executive who want a feeble, ineffectual parliament. Perhaps this will prove to be the case, but it need not be so. Wiser ANC politicians want the opposite to happen. They want to be kept on their toes. They know they have a big majority and that it gives them political space to move.

Parties with small majorities have cause for anxiety about oversight, lest it catch them out and further threaten their trembling grasp on power. The ANC need have no such worries. The only question is whether such maturity of outlook will prevail, or whether a complacent, lazy approach to its massive parliamentary majority will be the hallmark of its attitude to parliament in the years to come.

The disgraceful way in which the ANC handled parliament's oversight on the arms deal and its closing down of dissent within its membership of SCOPA not only set new standards in political cynicism, but degraded a hitherto effective and efficient committee. That was the parliamentary low point of the last twelve years. Now committees will need to show that they are made of sterner stuff. It also means that the ANC study groups will have to show that they have independent minds and are willing and prepared to stand up to the executive. They need to develop the sort of institutional oversight culture that Chohan longs for in order to counterbalance the inherent constraints imposed by a strong executive culture in the ANC, and the fact that individual MPs have very little power, due to South Africa's current electoral system.

Now, when Mbeki looks behind him in parliament, he will notice many new faces, the new, younger intake of MPs, as well as an odd assortment of refugees from virtually every other political party in the country. The ANC has become a very broad church indeed. As parliament enters a new phase, much will depend on whether the new MPs will turn out to be a fresh breed of professionals who are there on merit, and not because of a debt of loyalty owed to them from the struggle days.

If this is to happen, mentorship will be required from the small but potentially significant core of the ANC 'A-Team' who have survived since 1994, such as Yunus Carrim, Patekile Holomisa and Barbara Hogan, to name but three; as well as the middle tier of MPs, young but experienced, such as Chohan. Because of them and the dedicated work of committees such as the justice committee, parliament still matters, though it could and should matter a lot more.

5

The ANC

Heart of the Body Politic

The South African parliament that I have just explored is a mass of contradictions. One of them is architectural. The site of parliament is grand and full of colonial resonance. The clean white pillars of the former Senate building catch the bright sunlight as you walk up Government Avenue to the parliamentary precinct in the morning.

On the right, halfway up, there is an entrance for the public. Once inside, the Victorian gloom descends as you walk down dark wood-panelled corridors with patterned green carpets to the central lobby. This area is the meeting place between the two houses of parliament. Carry on left, and you proceed quickly through to the modern design of the National Assembly. Turn right, and you double back to what is now the National Council of Provinces, and was once the Senate.

But the most interesting room is right there, in front of your nose: the Old Assembly Chamber. It is modelled almost directly on the House of Commons in Westminster. Cramped benches face each other across a divide that is no more than ten feet. Green leather seats and old wooden tables, and a massive high chair at the head of the room, fill this chamber. This is where the constitutional committee met during the epic sittings that produced South Africa's magnificent Constitution. Now, it is where the ANC caucus meets every Thursday morning at ten.

It's quite a squeeze these days. The ANC has 279 seats in the National Assembly, and 36 out of 54 permanent seats in the NCOP; it won 70 per cent of the votes in the 2004 general election, and therefore 70 per cent of the seats in the National Assembly. But in September 2005, 14 MPs 'crossed the floor' to the ANC, effectively increasing its majority to 73 per cent in the National Assembly. The ANC has a total of 329 representations out of a combined 454 seats in both houses (the National Assembly and the NCOP). This number does not include four 'special' delegates that each provincial legislature is entitled to in the NCOP, in addition to six permanent seats for each provincial legislature.

Although the caucus's importance and influence are underplayed, both politically and in terms of the ANC constitution, its main relevance derives from the fact that this is now the one place, apart from the five-yearly national conference, where the government and executive elite has to rub shoulders with the 'infantry'. ANC leaders claim that they work closely with local activists and officials in the local parties, but the truth is that your average ANC backbench MP very seldom spends time in the company of those in the cabinet.

Although not every cabinet minister will attend every caucus meeting, the idea is that they should be there, and often they are. On certain issues, they are exposed to mainstream backbench thinking in all its great diversity. And, if astute, the speakers will often be careful to frame their comments in terms of 'their constituency' or the 'grassroots', indicating their connection to the people they represent.

This is a tug on the collective conscience of the cabinet, and, as a tactic, is the most potent available to the backbencher. The ANC's culture is such that it still yearns to remain a grassroots, mass-mobilized party. So, a key 'trigger' phrase will contain such words as 'my constituency', or 'back home, the general feeling among the community or the membership is …'

Given that the seat they occupy is owned not by them but by the party, it is about the only ammunition they really have. One of the problems with South Africa's parliament is that, although it looks like Westminster, especially on the inside, it is nothing like Westminster in its social culture.

Most of the backbench MPs live in one or other of the ghastly parliamentary complexes in Cape Town, in Acacia Park or Pelican Park. Coaches are provided at the start and end of each day to ferry the 'infantry' in and out, while the ministers are swept away in limousines to their ministerial homes or the private second homes they have bought. This underpins the notion of two classes of MP with very different lives.

The intention with the MPs was very deliberate: to create a 'normal' nine-to-five working day – especially to accommodate the many women MPs with after-hours parental responsibilities. Unlike in Westminster, MPs do not dilly-dally after the end of the sitting, and there are no evening sessions during which MPs can gather in bars. Whereas the House of Commons has more than thirty different bars, each with specific rules about who can and can't enter, the National Assembly has just one, and it is seldom occupied.

Anthony Sampson reports in the latest edition of *Anatomy of Britain* that 'many members insisted that the social life in the evening, in the tearoom and the bars, allowed ministers to mingle casually with the other members. Ministers are obliged to mix with the "poor bloody infantry", said [Labour MP] Chris Mullin.'[1]

In South Africa, there is no such culture and no such opportunity.

There are, therefore, serious limitations on the power of the caucus, many of which reflect the same political constraints that were discussed in relation to MPs in the previous chapter. Moreover, whenever the caucus has looked like taking on a more assertive role, the executive of the ANC has come down hard.

This was particularly apparent during the period when Thabang Makwetla (now premier of Mpumalanga) was chair of caucus, between 1996 and 2001. Makwetla is a loyal Mbekite and a political 'enforcer, like Essop Pahad', according to a former ANC MP. So, if a discussion ever looked as if it might get out of hand, either Makwetla, unprompted, would bring a halt to the proceedings, or else Pahad would pass him a note, and the discussion would soon stop.

Despite the ingrained tradition of debate within the ANC as a move-ment, this tradition is prone to exception – especially in a body such as the parliamentary caucus, which is not formally a constitutional entity (in terms of the ANC's constitution). Thus, when the executive is in trenchant mood, there are no questions or debate at all. After South Africa led the invasion of Lesotho in 1998, Mbeki returned from overseas in time for a meeting of caucus. He rose, and basically said, 'These were the reasons, this is why it was done; there is no time for questions,' even though many ANC MPs had lots of questions they wanted answered.

On another occasion, Mbeki presented a bizarre paper in which he blamed the CIA for the growth of HIV/AIDS. At the end of the speech, as one ANC MP recalls, 'Sixty per cent of the caucus cheered, and the rest of us sat there in stunned silence. There was no debate on the issue and no debate in caucus on any of the controversial issues, such as the arms deal.'

The former editor of the *Mail & Guardian*, Howard Barrell, then the newspaper's political editor, was in parliament that day. Minutes after the caucus had finished, several ANC MPs contacted him in shock to tell him about Mbeki's remarkable outburst. Barrell included a detailed description of what had taken place in his column the following Friday, so specific and accurate that the ANC parliamentary leadership concluded that the Old Assembly Chamber had been bugged, and promptly ordered a 'sweep' of the room. But nothing was found.

During this period, many ANC members of parliament became disillusioned; many considered resigning. Some, like leading gender activist and head of the high-profile parliamentary standing committee on the quality of life and status of women, Pregs Govender, did. To her, and to others, being a backbench MP returned a decreasing level of power.

The bottom line is that the caucus is a formidable setting in which to challenge the executive. As was noted earlier, the cabinet represents a 'buckle' that joins parliament with the executive and thereby 'fuses' the two arms of government. The practical, political effect of this – an inbuilt structural flaw in all parliamentary systems – is that the system requires backbench MPs to exercise oversight over their more senior colleagues.

In the caucus room itself, to reduce the political equation down to its core sum, this means a backbencher standing up in front of over 300 people and challenging the minister or the cabinet, people who by definition hold more power than the backbencher in the party. Put in these terms, it is hardly surprising that it happens very seldom. This is not to say that there is *no* debate.

The former National Party MP Manie Schoeman, upon whose jaw Johnny de Lange landed his famous punch, later crossed the floor to the ANC. After attending his first ANC caucus, Schoeman sought out a former NP colleague and said, in an awestruck voice, 'It's true! They really do talk and debate!'

Formal structures

Where, then, does the real power lie in the ANC? Its national executive committee is its formal seat of greatest authority. The NEC election is the most important election at the national conference, which takes place every five years. The fact that the ANC decided to make the national conference a five-yearly event has in and of itself reduced the power of the wider membership. Although the national conference can influence policy issues (see Trevor Manuel's concern about getting a clear mandate on macro-economic policy at Mafikeng in Chapter 2, for example) and is therefore important, its influence beyond and between the actual meetings is limited. Its importance lies in its rallying role.

As a journalist, I flew up early one morning to attend the Mafikeng conference in 1997. My aeroplane from Cape Town was delayed; I was anxious that I was going to miss President Mandela's speech (or the 'President's Report', as it is called). I drove like a maniac through the rolling countryside of the North West Province, arriving in its hot and dusty capital almost an hour after what was supposed to have been the starting time of his speech. Perhaps I could still catch the last part. I need not have worried: it started late and proceeded for an Olympian seven hours!

The press is handed copies of the speech. As everyone knows, Mandela delivers his speeches at a speed that can best be described as stately. This speech was over a hundred pages long. After about an hour we made some calculations based on his current rate of progress, and worked out that we would be there until midnight.

After three hours, there was a break for lunch. Behind the scenes, colleagues were trying to persuade Mandela to have the report 'taken as read'. Typically, he refused, agreeing only to skip some of the more boring passages. What he didn't skip was powerful stuff, attack after attack on the various opponents of the ANC. As he launched into a tirade against the media, I teased editors Moegsien Williams of the *Cape Times* and Shaun Johnson of the *Sunday Independent*, with whom I was sitting.

Two hours later it was their turn to tease me, wagging their fingers in mock admonishment as Mandela delivered a vicious assault on 'certain NGOs'. I later discovered that Frank Chikane, director-general in Thabo Mbeki's office, had written this passage (Mbeki himself had written most of the rest of the mammoth report). For some reason, Chikane chose to home in on one particular donor and one specific part of its donation portfolio in South Africa, which just happened to be the part that was at that time funding my programme at Idasa. It was quite an uncomfortable moment. But, when one saw it in the overall context of the speech, which represented a scattergun attack on everything and everyone, aimed at rallying the troops and creating unity in the movement, it was easier to take.

The main media focus of the Mafikeng conference was Winnie Mandela. In what turned out to be 'Winnie's Last Stand', she had threatened to contest one of the leadership positions. The internal election process was being handled for the ANC by an NGO, the Electoral Institute of Southern Africa, headed by Dren Nupen. When the moment for nominations came, Nupen was required to walk across the stage carrying an envelope that contained the verdict on whether Winnie was standing or not.

Glamorous and very blonde, Nupen, in a surprisingly short black skirt and stilettos, crisply tap-tapped through the silence that filled the vast hall. Time came to a standstill, awaiting Winnie's decision: she had decided to withdraw. Meanwhile, I suspect, the 'carefully crafted' resolution on the economy was being, well, carefully crafted. The Winnie show was probably a carefully stage-managed diversion from the real politics off-stage, Dren's stilettos and all.

Stellenbosch in December 2002 proved less tense. By then, the policies were either cemented or, where they were not, for example on issues such as the basic income grant, they had been neutered in the crucial 'pre-conference policy conference' held in October. The dramatic equivalent to the Dren Nupen moment was when Nelson Mandela chose, for some inexplicable reason, to arrive late, just as Thabo Mbeki was reaching the climax of his President's Report. This is how I reported it in my *Mail & Guardian* column that week:

> I felt bad for Thabo. So I think did many people. Though most of the delegates in the hall were too busy ululating their praise song for Nelson Mandela to have time to contemplate the feelings of their current President. The facts are straightforward: there was fog at Umtata; Mandela's plane left late and so he arrived at the opening plenary session of the ANC's national conference late.
>
> But the consequences were more complex and poignantly so. Mbeki was approaching the end of a two-hour speech. He had just added an unscripted phrase to a line about how opponents' attempts to sow dis-unity would be defeated – 'as will be demonstrated during this national conference' – that attracted the largest cheer of a hitherto coolly received speech. A sense of momentum was gathering that housed the possibility of a powerful climax.
>
> But the moment – the possibility – was stolen, eclipsed by Mandela's

regally shuffled journey to a seat at the front of the stage. It was pure theatre, more Ibsen than French Farce, as the timing was, in the words of one very senior ANC official afterwards, 'absolutely disastrous, a protocol nightmare'.

On the one hand, the speech of a President should not be interrupted in such a manner by **anyone**. By anyone. But Mandela is not, of course, **anyone**. Hence the decision, discussed in huddled fashion by a small group of ANC national executive committee (NEC) members on the stage, sanctioned by national chairperson Terror Lekota and communicated for final approval to Mbeki at the podium on a slip of paper, that Mandela should enter the vast auditorium.

The warmth of his greeting was telling – and for Mbeki inevitably and, surely, hurtfully so. He was entitled to be hurt and furious. Advised as he should have been of the proximity of the end of the speech, Mandela should have recognised the effect that his entrance would have and ordered his chauffeur to drive around the block.

After his speech had drifted quietly to a close, Mbeki brooked no ululation of his own, milked no applause, but in an act of contrasting utter simplicity, took his seat and fiddled with his now redundant speaking notes, as behind him NEC members jostled to embrace Mandela. No one approached him; it was as if he was not there. Even the three big screens above the crowd focused on Mandela, as if it was he that had just completed the President's Political Report.

I have rarely seen such a painful scene of loneliness played out so publicly in politics. In emblematic fashion, it captured so much of the essence of Mbeki's leadership style: the cold and detached intellect, the serious, calculating demeanour, and the unapproachably aloof personality.

I mention this incident because the national conferences of political parties are inevitably theatrical, and theatre is an important part of normal political life. At Stellenbosch, the real drama was in the election of the NEC.

In the build-up to the conference, the left had been taking a real hammering from Mbeki's people. Dumisani Makhaye, a provincial minister in KwaZulu-Natal and heir apparent to Peter Mokaba's old role of public hatchet man for the left, had been attacking both the 'ultra-left' and, more specifically, members of the SACP and COSATU. A list had been prepared and circulated of people who were 'too communist'; delegates were to vote for other candidates.

But the plan did not work – certainly not completely. The depth of historical support and enduring crossovers between the ANC membership and COSATU and the SACP make it impossible to 'blacklist' the left in this way. COSATU leaders had chosen not to stand for the NEC in any case; they had taken the strategic decision to stay outside, so 'we can be more critical without fear of being disciplined', as one office-bearer told me at the time.

As the primary constitutional structure within the ANC, the NEC matters a great deal. When it convenes, there is a sense of history; the full broad church of the ANC and its divergent ideological traditions (more on that below) are all represented. Doing well in the NEC elections is important and allows someone like Cyril Ramaphosa, who has essentially been out of the political game since 1996, to sustain not just his connection, but his standing – both his *locus* (the right to be there and to speak) and his status. Examining the membership of the ANC NEC provides, therefore, all manner of clues as to the direction and orientation of the party.

Look and note who is in the 'top 20': in first place, Trevor Manuel, his reward not just for his stewardship of the economy, a stable backdrop for the growing number of black businessmen in the ANC, but also his willingness to accept invitations by branches and, where necessary and congenial, imbibe the odd late-night whisky or two; Cyril Ramaphosa in second place; the balance between the old guard and the new: Winnie Mandela, Kader Asmal, Frene Ginwala and Pallo Jordan from the old guard; Thoko Didiza (a very high-ranking number four), Phumzile Mlambo-Ngcuka and Geraldine Fraser-Moleketi from the new.

Not many votes, however, separate the 'top 10'. Interestingly, the ANC, which is always uncomfortable with individual popularity and prefers to accentuate the 'collective', does not publish the votes attained by the NEC election victors – only the order.

Since 1994, the NEC has been remarkably stable in its membership. Out of sixty NEC members elected in the 1997 Mafikeng conference, forty-three were re-elected at the 51st national conference held in Stellenbosch in 2002 – a 71 per cent retention. There are currently seventeen new names on the NEC list since the 1997 national conference. Out of the seventeen new names that appear on the list, about six places were vacant because serving members had passed away due to various illnesses (Joe Modise, Steve Tshwete, Alfred Nzo, Peter Mokaba, Dumisani Makhaye and Dullah Omar). Of the new names that were directly elected to the NEC in 2002, at the Stellenbosch conference, about three have previously served in the council, either as ANC provincial chairpersons or ex-officio members. While some members have left for the private sector, most of them still retain their membership of the NEC, probably pursuant to the ANC's redeployment strategy: to groom strong representation in the higher echelons of the private sector.

The NEC only meets four or five times a year, so, although it is the most important structure, its influence is constrained by the infrequency of its meetings, and by its size and political character.

Its relationship with its main subcommittee, the national working committee (NWC), is crucial to understanding how power operates in the ANC. The NWC generally meets every Monday at Luthuli House in Johannesburg, and comprises fifteen members, plus the national office-bearers: president (Thabo Mbeki), deputy president (Jacob Zuma), national chairperson (Mosiuoa Patrick Lekota), secretary general (Kgalema Motlanthe), deputy secretary general (Sankie Mthembi-Mahanyele), treasurer general (Mendi Msimang), and the presidents of the Youth League (Fikile Mbalula) and Women's League (Nosiviwe Mapisa-Nqakula). ANC spin doctor supreme, head of the ANC president's office, Smuts Ngonyama, attends ex-officio.

The NWC has been largely stable as well. The current NWC membership, fifteen elected members, has been able to retain eight members from the previous body; thus, more than 50 per cent of its membership. In terms of its ethnic composition (if that can be said), twelve out of fifteen elected members of the NWC are Nguni, with three from minority groups. The national chairperson of the ANC, Mosiuoa Lekota, has rejected the idea that important positions in the party are reserved for the Nguni people.

In the build-up towards the 2002 Stellenbosch conference, the newspapers were punting the idea that 'disgruntled members' within the ANC were putting forward Lekota for the deputy president of the ANC because he is Sotho-speaking. The ANC retaliated in style, as usual, lamenting the 'nameless and shameless' who were behind the campaign and whose sentiments were 'alien' to the ANC.[2] Dissatisfaction about the so-called Nguni domination in key government positions and in the ANC is not without merit, even within the ANC itself. After winning the ANC national chairmanship in the 1997 Mafikeng conference, Lekota pronounced his election a victory for the Sotho-speaking people.

A seminal example of the power relations between the NEC and the NWC occurred at the first NEC after the ANC victory in April 2004. Held, as usual, at Gallagher Estate outside Johannesburg on 8 and 9 May, the main agenda item was a discussion to mandate the cabinet's proposed *lekgotla* (strategic planning meeting), scheduled for the following Tuesday and Wednesday, 11 and 12 May.

ANC NEC members, buoyed by the spirit of togetherness a successful election can deliver, waited expectantly as Joel Netshitenzhe began, on behalf of the NWC, to present a paper on the strategic way forward. The paper, someone noted, was marked 'secret', and had been distributed to a chosen few. The rest had to manage as best they could, creating an inequality in understanding and debate.

This sort of tactical machination is common currency. The NWC contains fourteen members of the cabinet (just over half of the cabinet). It tends to reflect the attitudes and policy positions of the ANC in government rather than the ANC as a party (even though neither Alec Erwin nor Trevor Manuel, the lynchpin policy axis within the cabinet, are members). This raises a fundamental question about the ANC in government: Is the ANC in control of government, or is government in control of the ANC? Where does the power lie in this relationship?

COSATU sources recall a particular bilateral meeting with the ANC over privatization at a time when strikes and other manifestations of serious conflict were occurring. Jeff Radebe, now minister of transport and veteran member of the ANC's NEC, made a substantial presentation about the privatization plan.

At the end, the ANC delegation, which was composed entirely of members of cabinet, basically turned to COSATU and, to COSATU's great surprise, said: 'The ANC does not have a position on privatization. The government is wallowing in PowerPoint, but the ANC does not have a position!'

Culture and history, and
the modernization of the ANC

The words and flavour of the language of many of the ANC's most important policy documents, such as its 1997 'Strategy and Tactics' document, are very notable. Jeremy Cronin, deputy secretary general of the SACP, says it is 'common for these documents to talk the language of Lenin, which is an attempt to rediscover ANC language of old, so as to combat the criticism of privatization, for example, from outside'.

However, it does help recover ideological coherence – a reminder that the party remains a party of the left, which is what the debate inside the ANC has been about since the mid-1980s and, to some, for much longer. As Cronin points out, it is impossible to imagine Tony Blair's New Labour Party publishing a document titled *Strategy and Tactics*, which is one of the favourite phrases of the left.

Treatment Action Campaign leader Zackie Achmat also contends that at times the ANC has a 'Stalinist mode of thinking; Essop Pahad was in Prague in 1968. There is a clash of culture between the historical, institutional memory of the ANC and the apparatus of governance it has created, which is ironic to say the least. The Constitution, for example, attempts to decentralize power and to disperse it across a wide range of institutions, including particularly the "Chapter 9" institutions – the Human Rights Commission, the Public Protector, the Gender Commission, and so on.'

Achmat notes succinctly that 'the ANC is highly centrist. This derives from the needs of the underground struggle and is influenced by forms of patriarchy and gerontocracy.'

Gerontocracy: a lovely word, and an accurate one. Patriarchy and gerontocracy are strong institutional instincts within the ANC, although, to Thabo Mbeki's great credit, his commitment to putting women into leadership positions, especially in cabinet, is changing this. But the way in which hierarchy, and therefore age, influences the way in which decisions are taken in the ANC should not be underestimated in any analysis of the way power operates inside the 'movement'.

But things are changing, and pretty fast. The old generation of Oliver Tambo, Walter Sisulu and Govan Mbeki is almost completely gone. The next generation, led of course by Thabo Mbeki, is fading fast – not only is Mbeki's term of office as president of both the ANC and the country coming to an end, but the key individuals who made the same journey will be moving on if they have not already done so – Kader Asmal, Alec Erwin, Jeff Radebe, Ronnie Kasrils, Zola Skweyiya: it is hard to imagine any of them being in a post-2009 cabinet.

A new generation is moving in: Phumzile Mlambo-Ngcuka, Thoko Didiza, Saki Macozoma, Manne Dipico, to name but a small sample. The question is, who will bridge the transition? Which is very probably another way of asking the even bigger question: Who will be the next president (both of the ANC after its December 2007 national conference, and, thence, the country after the 2009 general election)?

Regardless of who leads the ANC and the generational shift in leading personnel, certain fundamental traditions will remain, ingrained in the culture and practice of the ANC. To the outsider, they appear impenetrable or, at best, outdated. For example, there is a very strong tradition within the ANC of debating things carefully internally first. 'It is messy, it can be very slow, but that is the way it is done,' explains John Jeffrey, Jacob Zuma's former close advisor and parliamentary counsellor (and now parliamentary counsellor to the president).

'The tradition,' says Raymond Suttner, a veteran ANC activist and academic, 'is to deal with your issues inside the organization.'

He cites what happened to Jeremy Cronin when, in 2002, he gave an interview to an Irish academic, Helen Sheehan, and chose to criticize what, in a compelling phrase, he called the 'Zanufication' of the ANC.[3] Cronin was forced to apologize shortly afterwards, and did so with tail between his legs.

To the uninitiated, this simply appears to be old-style concealment and paranoia. While it is true that part of its historical rationale was the need to maintain disciplined secrecy against the apartheid-government enemy, it goes beyond that: the ANC way is to debate comprehensively, and robustly, behind closed doors.

So, too, when Fikile Mbalula, president of the ANC Youth League, made some intemperate public comments about Zimbabwe and how government policy should support Robert Mugabe more, not less, without having first raised the points inside ANC structures. Alec Erwin told me: 'No one will say anything to these young comrades at first. But there will come a time in the next few months, when someone like Pallo Jordan, with his rapier tongue in the NEC, will put him firmly in his place over this.'

This is the first grand tradition: one of a respect for process (out of which the culture of politics as a whole derives, as mentioned at the end of the Introduction) and for 'the structures' – an admirable sense that individuals are not above the collective parts of the party.

The second grand tradition is far more complex. Sitting in his capacious office on the eighteenth floor of 120 Plein Street – the ghastly, totalitarian-era building that ministers use when they are in Cape Town for parliament – minister for intelligence Ronnie Kasrils waxes lyrical about the ANC's hybrid ideological tradition.

'Put simply,' he says, 'it's about the relationship between class and race. As to the balance between the two, there are key divides and cleavages historically. The trade unions and the SACP, with their Marxist, socialist influence, as an agent for class change. On the other side, there is the instinct towards African nationalism. The ANC emerges from this as a broad-based movement.'

Because minister of intelligence is high up in the hierarchy, Kasrils gets a corner office, enjoying spectacular views of both Table Mountain and, across the city, Robben Island. How rich and delicious the irony: of this descendant of what Jeremy Cronin calls the 'East European Jewish socialist tradition ... which is a very important influence on South Africa and culture in South Africa'[4] eloquently preaching about the ANC's role in South African history from the office that was once Prime Minister BJ Vorster's!

The socio-economic conditions of nineteenth-century South Africa, Kasrils argues, with a pronounced industrial revolution and the growth of the mining sector, meant that a class consciousness arose, which was the primary ideological driver within the ANC during the early decades of its life. But, as Kasrils then explains, the advent of an explicitly racist state in the mid-twentieth century meant that it was natural and inevitable that a black Africanist response would emerge and then compete for hegemony within the ANC. Since then, the two ideological traditions have jostled for primacy.

It is a very complex subject that deserves and certainly requires a full treatise, for which there is no room here. But, the key to understanding the ANC's finessing of the tension between the two great impulses is leadership. Mandela and Mbeki, Kasrils maintains, are both in their own way classic examples of what is required.

'Look at Mbeki's speeches,' urges Kasrils, 'and there you will find the "code-breaker", for Mbeki is the class–race prism. His analysis always takes account of both and crosses the divide between them to a greater or lesser extent.' Whereas Mandela was more 'intuitive' in his resolution of the tension between the two, Mbeki is 'more analytical'.

Thus, Kasrils claims, Mandela was more prone to *subjective* responses to people and situations; in contrast, Mbeki, despite perceptions, does not take things personally and wants to be challenged in an *objective* sense. Mbeki is fond of asking his ultimate Socratic question: 'Will the centre hold?' The triumph of Mbeki and Mandela has been to ensure that the ANC's fundamental division between its race-orientated African nationalist tradition and its class-based Marxist tendency has been balanced sufficiently for the party to retain a sense of equilibrium.

I have digressed into these areas not because they necessarily help to explain how power is exerted, but because they provide the backdrop against which all the major power plays are made, whether it be a macroeconomic policy switch or the battle for the succession. Both are considered in the context of the ANC-led alliance as a whole in the next chapter.

On the organizational side, the ANC is also in a state of flux. The driving force behind the changes is Thabo Mbeki and, perhaps with even more in-fluence over their direction, the ANC's secretary general Kgalema Motlanthe. Motlanthe could still be the next president of South Africa. Thus, he deserves careful attention, not least because he is not a well-known public figure. Verging on the reclusive, he makes Thabo Mbeki and Joel Netshitenzhe look like celebrity models in comparison. But, mirroring the tradition of the ANC described above, Motlanthe is very well known *inside* the ANC.

I will never forget the reception that greeted his election to the position of secretary general at the ANC national conference in Mafikeng in 1997. It was the biggest celebration of an otherwise rather taut week. It was as if, at last, with all the tension of the behind-the-scenes angst about the shift to GEAR and the more public display of collective anxiety over Winnie, Motlanthe's election could release the pent-up tension of a thousand people stuffed into a baking sports hall. When the result was announced, he was carried from the back by a group of supporters. It took another fifteen minutes for him to reach the stage, struggle songs filling the air. There could be no doubting the popularity of this election.

The son of a miner, Motlanthe was secretary general of the National Union of Mineworkers (NUM), where he built his political base. There is a persuasive neatness about Motlanthe's CV; the seventh year of every decade appears especially significant: for ten years, from 1977 to 1987, he was imprisoned on Robben Island; from 1987 to 1997, he was secretary general of NUM; since 1997, when he succeeded Cyril Ramaphosa, he has been secretary general of the ANC, whose next national conference is in 2007 ... at which point he will be fifty-eight, three years older than Mbeki when he became ANC president in 1997.

Motlanthe appears a little older than his years, partly because his hair is now greying, but mainly because he has a soft voice and is a gentle man, possessing an almost old-school politeness, with an engaging smile. There is a paternal aspect to him that is endearing. Yet he is also tough and, at times, remarkably candid.

His secretary general reports both to the Stellenbosch national conference and to the national general council (NGC) – a mini-national conference that takes place halfway between national conferences; the most recent in Tshwane in July 2005 – were both notable for their candour and forthrightness. No secretary general of Blair's New Labour would dare to be too honest about the party's problems in public. For example, in his report to the 2005 NGC, Motlanthe offered this incisive critique of the problems facing the ANC at branch level:[5]

> The picture of our branches is very uneven. In general, across all provinces, the best-organised branches are in the minority, with the vast majority functioning according to the basic minimum of constitutional requirements. In many of our branches there are no sustainable political programmes and community campaigns. They are conflict-ridden and unstable and in many instances fraught with fights over leadership positions, selection and deployment of councillors, tendering and control of projects and recruitment of membership in order to serve factional or selfish interests.
>
> In many cases, the reasons for division and the resulting lack of coherent and consistent branch organisation are not rooted in ideological differences. Rather, these problems rest primarily on the preoccupation on the part of public representatives with securing access to and control over public resources. This in turn leads to tensions between cadres

deployed in ANC structures and those in government and undermines
the effectiveness of our public representatives.

Like Mbeki, Motlanthe is known to have strong views on corruption and
little tolerance for the politics of personal enrichment. His analysis strikes
at a root cause of the extent to which the ruling party is used as a vehicle for
personal enrichment and commercial opportunity through state resources.

This is not the place to assess the degree to which corruption is a growing
problem in and for the new South Africa. Suffice it to say that the experience
in many other countries demonstrates the dangers of the links between state
and party. Nor is this the place for me to further promote our campaign at
Idasa for transparency around political donations.

At the moment there is absolute secrecy – donors are free to give as much
as they like however often they like, in complete secrecy without any regulation. Though he has not said so publicly, Motlanthe has come to recognize
the disadvantages that weigh as heavily on the scales as the advantages. Secrecy
enables donors with malign intentions to seek to exert undue influence on
policy and on tendering decisions with the impunity that secrecy provides.

On the other hand, the ANC is a very expensive ship to keep afloat. It relies
heavily on wealthy and private donors. Some of those are the usual corporate
suspects, but, when the ANC is really short of money, as it always is in the
run-up to election campaigns that routinely cost in the region of R120 million
or more, it sends the begging bowl around to the Comrades in Business, such
as Tokyo Sexwale, Cyril Ramaphosa, Patrice Motsepe and Ntatho Motlana.
According to one Luthuli House source, it is less of a begging bowl and
more of a knife-at-the-throat approach: 'We have created the conditions for
you to be so wealthy, so you owe us; write a cheque for R2 million please.'
Perhaps not surprisingly, according to the source, these individuals are
beginning to weary of these unrelenting demands upon their wallets.

Motlanthe has also been very frank in public about declining membership[6] and activism, and rigorous in his assessment of the need for reform.
In a paper titled 'Discussion Document: the organizational design of the
ANC "a case for internal renewal": an abridged version',[7] the following
ideas, believed to be Motlanthe and Mbeki's, were advanced:

> The 1994 elections and the final adoption of a new constitution for South
> Africa in 1996 marked a historic watershed in the struggle for freedom as

led by the ANC ... This new opportunity represented by a democratic dispensation involving, among others, the holding of democratic elections and a democratic parliament, raised the need to re-fashion the ANC's design in order to take full advantage of these new vistas ... This fundamental change in the mission of the ANC, from an extra-parliamentary movement seeking the forceful overthrow of the apartheid regime, to a political party that is part of a normalized political dispensation seeking to rebuild the socio-economic life of South Africa's former oppressed majority, once again implied that the ANC had to redesign itself to function optimally for the attainment of the new mission ... The most critical weakness of our party constituent structures at all levels is that they do not address the optimal mobilization of the motive forces for change. Secondly, our structures do not speak to the centres of power of our transformation. These two factors constitute the ANC's soft under-belly today ... The first generic recommendation encompasses ANC leadership organs at all levels, namely that the executives of the ANC at all levels from branch to province, must be structured in accordance with their responsibility to intervene and provide leadership to all centres of power, viz. the state, civil society, the economy, the battle of ideas and the continental and global arena.

In addition, the report encompasses the need for modernization in relation to internal elections:

The ANC needs to reform its election and selection processes in order to restore sanity within the ranks and to reduce the contemporary commotion and factionalism ... In this regard, we should learn from parties with a social conscience such as ourselves, for example the Swedish Social Democratic Party approach where in the election of the party leadership organs, the party conference elects a permanent Electoral Commission, which takes charge of the election process in the run-up and including at the next conference.

And, last, on the question of the role of individual members and 'cadres':

The legacy of the pre-1990 period has proved difficult to sustain under the new conditions, because the material conditions which were responsible for the movement to have at its disposal thousands of loyal, disciplined, dedicated, devoted and determined cadres have altered. The challenge the organization faces is how we continue to prepare for future human resources needs in circumstances where cadres now enjoy a relative degree of economic independence from the organization and in planning their lives.

This is an impressive agenda for change. It demonstrates that the ANC has at its helm leaders who are not shying away from the challenge, but that the ANC's capacity and, therefore, its power remains uncertain. A political party depends, for its power, not just on votes, but also on human resources and organizational capacity. The paradox is that, while the ANC looks certain to dominate electoral politics for the foreseeable future, as a party it could continue to weaken, especially in relation to these other centres of power – business, civil society and, especially, government.

Let us end where we began, with a crucial point to grasp: The ANC is central to all things political in South Africa. But the ANC as an organization is not the same thing as the ANC in government. Of course there is an overlap, and the former remains the predominant route into the latter. But the balance of power lies with the latter.

Thus, with a bitterly divisive battle for the succession raging and testing the cohesiveness of the organization in terms of ethnicity and ideology, 2006/07 represents an interesting moment in its history. On the one hand, it recognizes the need for organizational change, and yet it is desperate not to lose the ethos and values of its days as a liberation movement.

Indeed, despite these 'modernizing' influences, a 'movement', not a 'party', is how many in the ANC still prefer to see it; a grand coalition that covers the whole of the centre and centre-left ground of South African politics, in partnership with its two great alliance partners, COSATU and the SACP – a pivotal subject, to which I now turn.

6

The Alliance

Fatal Attraction?

COSATU: Mass influence

It took just one call to halt a major piece of legislation. Such can be the influence of COSATU. The head of its parliamentary office, Neil Coleman, called his boss, Zwelinzima Vavi, the general secretary of COSATU. Then Vavi made the call – in this case, to the cabinet minister concerned, Charles Nqakula. The legislation was the Anti-Terrorism Bill; the date, February 2004.

Both elements of this story are crucial to its analytical value. The context was international. After the events of 11 September 2001 and the attack on the World Trade Center in New York, governments around the world were compelled to pass new legislation increasing their powers to 'deal with potential terrorists'. Many countries did so with thinly disguised zeal, seeing it as a chance to strengthen the state's powers and to roll back the human rights protections so painstakingly acquired by activists over the past half-century. An interesting and little-known fact is that South Africa had already begun its move towards legal reform before 9/11, prompted in part by the small but ongoing threat of the far right, as well as the bombing campaign in Cape Town between 1999 and 2000 (which was linked, though never conclusively, with an organization called People Against Gangsterism and Drugs (PAGAD)).

The bill continued to move slowly, even after 11 September. By 2003, it was stuck in the National Assembly. A myriad organizations had made submissions, expressing a variety of concerns. More than 100 submissions were made and more than 50 organizations/entities were invited to make presentations before the safety and security committee. COSATU was one of them. As usual, its parliamentary office, set up in 1996 and headed since then with skill and dedication by Neil Coleman, had made a formal submission. Since 1995, COSATU has made over 250 submissions to parliamentary committees and government departments – it is an extraordinary record. What is so telling about it is its range, which reflects the wider, more profound point about COSATU – that it is far more than a trade union organization. By this, I mean that it takes a far wider view of its political role than most trade union umbrella entities around the world, which tend to restrict themselves to matters that directly affect their affiliates or, at most, their affiliate members.

COSATU goes beyond this. It takes on any matter that affects the working class – again broadly defined to include not just those who work, or who have worked, but those who are unemployed, which in modern South Africa means eight million extra people. This broad approach is sometimes described as 'transformative trade unionism' – meaning, in the words of political economist Fiona Tregenna, herself a former member of Coleman's team in parliament, 'active and independent, but politically engaged; with "shopfloor" issues being taken up in tandem with a broader agenda of transforming the basic structure of the economy and society. Recognizing that power is located not just in the state apparatus but in various nodes, COSATU identified a range of sites of struggle in which to engage in a multi-pronged approach'.[1]

This is COSATU's inherent strength as an organization. Its monumental mandate – self-created – drives it into every nook and cranny of politics. The Anti-Terrorism Bill is a good example of its approach. Why get involved? Coleman gives three reasons. First, there was a labour issue relating to limit-ations to the right to strike in the case of workers in 'essential services'. But, second and more importantly, it raised major human rights issues; COSATU is concerned to protect an environment that is conducive to human rights. COSATU is mindful of the fact that, when you pass a law, you are legislating not just for the present government, which may be human rights-friendly, but for future governments, which may not be. COSATU has watched with increasing interest and concern how the rights of workers have been harmed by President Robert Mugabe's thuggish regime in Zimbabwe.

The third reason is a first cousin to the first two: 'It is not beyond the realms of possibility that certain laws could be used against the left.' *Even by this government*, are the words that Coleman does not say, but which are ineluctably implied. Coleman is too smart to come out and say it. He is a veteran of alliance politics – as hard a school as it is possible to imagine. He is a person who is both young and a veteran. He is as much a part of the political furniture as a favourite armchair. Coleman has been with COSATU for seventeen years, yet he still appears youthful. This is due in part to his wiry, slight physique; he looks after his health carefully. I first set eyes on him as Mbhazima (Sam) Shilowa, then the COSATU general secretary, strode into the lobby of the Old National Assembly during the final negotiations on the Constitution. Coleman, a step behind Shilowa, but wearing an identical red COSATU T-shirt and cap, was the key advisor during those intense negotiations. With Zwelinzima Vavi, then the deputy secretary general, matching Shilowa's heavyweight boxer's stature, Coleman was like a terrier scuttling around, buttressing his leaders' positions with supporting material and arguments. Friends say that although he has mellowed in the years that have followed, he is no less sharp in his analysis and strategic thinking.

Coleman's team in the parliamentary office is talented and has proved to be a useful training ground for younger protégés. Oupa Bodibe, for example, joined the office in around 1997 as a relatively raw young activist, but left in 2000 as a skilful lobbyist, steeped in the new parliamentary and political process, to become a valued and influential advisor within the general secretary's office. (He has now moved on further to lead COSATU's economic policy think tank, NALEDI (National Labour and Economic Development Institute).)

Bodibe is an adept tactician, as I discovered working with him during the long years when we fought for a strong access to information law (1995–2000). He represented COSATU on the Open Democracy Campaign Group (whose role in lobbying for the passage of a strong access to information law is described in Chapter 1) and realized early on the importance of fleshing out the constitutional right to access privately held information, as well as information held by the state. He saw the extension of the right as valuable in both a general and a specific, union-related sense. With so much of the traditional state now controlled, through privatization and contracting-out, by the private sector, modern human rights, such as the right to access information, need to extend into the private sector if the notion of public accountability is to be meaningful.

The parliamentary office has been prolific. *Accelerating Transformation* outlined COSATU's engagement with policy and legislative processes during the period of the first democratic parliament, 1994–99.[2] In the appendix, it cites well over 100 submissions made on policies and draft bills, ranging from the Budget and tax issues, to pensions, water and health policy, and immigration, across more than twenty government departments. It is a very impressive publication. The introduction boasts that 'COSATU has established a significant presence on a wide range of policy and legislative processes. The voice of organized workers has consistently been raised on virtually all key social, economic and labour questions.'

The publication was followed in 2001 with a two-inch-thick lever-arch file containing all of the actual submissions. It is an important historical document, demonstrating the direct effect of COSATU's lobbying. Cross-referenced to the table at the end of *Accelerating Transformation*, in which one column summarizes COSATU's proposals and another the response/impact, it is possible to see the gains that organized labour has secured in defence of its interests – what the document calls the 'major breakthroughs as well as the serious setbacks'.

Because of their wide mandate, the parliamentary office has much ground to cover. With the Anti-Terrorism Bill, they missed a beat. Substantially amended, and mostly to their satisfaction, the parliamentary office overlooked a last-minute set of additions that were added to the bill just before it was passed by the National Assembly and then passed on to the National Council of Provinces, where the problematic amendments were challenged by COSATU. According to a later memorandum of the central executive committee (CEC) – COSATU's equivalent of the ANC's own national executive committee (NEC) – which sat between 23 and 25 February 2004, its concerns were summarized as follows: the bill has 'the effect of including unprotected strikes. That is, strikes where workers do not first try mediation or give adequate notice, in the definition of terrorist activity.'

In addition, the bill listed certain sectors as 'essential services', so that any attempt to disrupt them, including strikes, could be labelled 'terrorist activity'. In both cases, the CEC took the view that 'this returns us to the days of apartheid'.

No one can satisfactorily explain how the new provisions crept into the bill at the last minute. That in itself is an intriguing indicator of how 'hidden hands' – a public servant, perhaps, or an order from a minister or his or her special advisor – can secretly disturb the open process of parliament.

If COSATU, with its relatively extensive capacity for monitoring, and its alliance connections, can be caught off-guard, what chance does everyone else have? COSATU's leadership was appalled. Already engaged with the Anti-Terrorism Bill, the last-minute amendments raised it to a 'life-and-death issue', according to Coleman. His office leapt into action. Argument was presented first in an urgent submission to the NCOP committee, and then in an internal paper, dated 20 February 2004. The issue was raised in the alliance – which, in formal terms, means that it was raised at the regular meeting of the three general secretaries. The CEC memo provides a neat exposition of the political armoury available to COSATU; it deserves full quotation:

> Legal advice on the so-called Protection of Constitutional Democracy Against Terrorists and Related Activities Bill suggests that it constitutes a massive attack to the constitutionally guaranteed right to strike ... If the Bill is rammed through in the current form, the CEC decided that COSATU must use everything in its power to protect our hard-won constitutional rights to strike. It adopted a programme that includes:
> - Requesting an urgent intervention by President Thabo Mbeki and ANC Secretary General Kgalema Motlanthe. Letters requesting this intervention have been dispatched and discussions are under way.
> - COSATU will immediately submit a Section 77 notice to NEDLAC, stating its intention to go on a protected national general strike if its demands are not met through the mediation process.
> - COSATU will instruct its lawyers to prepare a Constitutional Court challenge. This would be the first time COSATU has had to take the government to the Court to protect workers' rights.
> - We will file a complaint with the International Labour Organisation (ILO) since the Bill undermines not only our own Constitution, but also several ILO conventions to which South Africa is a signatory.
> - We will mobilise the ICFTU and all our sister unions to use everything in their power to put pressure on our government.

As a 'textbook' menu of lobbying choices, nothing could be more exemplary or illustrative. The document should be added to Politics 101 classes throughout the country. There is the internal – in this case the ANC tripartite alliance – route. There is the democratic institution route (in this case, NEDLAC), but with the direct suggestion of strike action. There is the legal route – taking advantage of the rule of law and a progressive Bill of Rights. There is the external pressure, making use of COSATU's high standing in the international labour world. It also demonstrates the range of COSATU's political options and, thereby, its latent power.

The NCOP responded – a rare example of it acting in an important and relevant fashion – and its committee made a number of amendments, which were then cursorily ignored when the bill returned to the National Assembly. Because this was national legislation, the National Assembly could ignore the NCOP. Suddenly there was a crisis. And hence the phone call to Minister Nqakula.

COSATU was horrified to discover that Nqakula, a diligent man, was unaware of the amendments that had so enraged them. A former general secretary of the SACP and currently its national chairperson, Nqakula shared COSATU's concerns. He in turn made some calls of his own, one of them to Manne Dipico, the premier of the Northern Cape. The call to Dipico, however, had nothing to do with the Northern Cape, but everything to do with the upcoming election.

Dipico had been put in charge of the ANC's 2004 general election campaign. He was horrified by the news. COSATU's active involvement in the campaign was critical to his unfolding strategy, which was less Saatchi & Saatchi and more samp and boerewors. He had decided that, in the absence of the massive budgets of 1994 and 1999, getting close to the people was going to be the organizing theme of his campaign. COSATU were essential for this: he needed their networks, their organizational capacity and logistics, their leaders and their vigorous participation in nearly all campaign activities. The more he thought about it, the more horrified he became. More calls were made. President Mbeki was consulted. The bill was halted.

Power and numbers

This story, as deeply illustrative of COSATU's influence as it is, needs to be looked at in a wider context. It must be recognized that, skilful and industrious though it is, the parliamentary office is just one of a number of entry points for COSATU. Moreover, although it has embraced the techniques and tactics of modern-day political lobbying, it is not the sole engine for the federation's power. There is a 'bread and butter' dimension to COSATU's work that can be seen most obviously in the wage-bargaining and other non-wage-related employment and sectoral negotiations by its affiliates, especially in the workplace. Beyond, it runs campaigns against job losses, squaring up to business as well as government as The Employer, and therefore The Class Enemy. The notion of class struggle is still a driving imperative. Asked about SATAWU's strike action in protest of Transnet's restructuring plans in March 2006, the union's general secretary, Randall Howard, gave the following response to the *Sunday Times*:[3]

> Q: Why have you run to Minister Erwin now? I thought you'd agreed to a mediation process?
>
> A: That's because management fucked it up. They came to the meeting on March 4, which was the first day of the mediation process, and informed us that they had signed a sale agreement transferring Metrorail to the Department of Transport, but we've never discussed that issue. There was an agreement in principle, yes. But we're not going to take that kind of arrogance where, at some point, when you feel you've had enough consultation, you just move out and implement. Workers didn't struggle for that in this country.
>
> Q: What's your sticking point?
>
> A: Unilateralism. That's what the whole dispute is about.
>
> Q: And the fact that you're afraid workers' benefits and jobs will be endangered?
>
> A: It's not about fear, it's about rights.
>
> Q: Aren't these protected by the Labour Relations Act?
>
> A: If you're talking about a transfer process then you've got a cushion for 12 months. But that's not good enough. We want a five-year job guarantee.
>
> Q: Why should they get a five-year job guarantee?
>
> A: Why should they be unemployed? Why should they be retrenched?
>
> Q: Everyone else faces that possibility.
>
> A: That's why we have to fight capitalism. Do you think we must accept what in your view is normal? Retrenchment is normal, job losses are normal?

Many middle-class South Africans despair of what they regard as a 'strike mentality', a view that was further encouraged by the unruly violence that accompanied the security workers' strike and marches in May 2006. It is important to understand that 'policy engagement and mass action have been seen as complementary rather than distinct strategies. For example, strikes and demonstrations being strategically combined with detailed alternative economic proposals in the contestation of macroeconomic policy. There is a saying in COSATU that "you cannot win at the negotiating table what you have not already won on the street".'4

While it may be true that government has developed the ability to shut its ears to the clamour from outside – often saying 'we want solutions, not protest' – such a dual strategy serves to remind those on the other side of the negotiating table that there are numbers and potential social unrest to take into account.

It is in its relationship to the ANC in government that the most telling political equation is calculated. Both COSATU and the SACP, but especially COSATU, are scarred by a definitive event that continues to cast a long shadow over the tripartite alliance. That event was the decision taken in 1996 to abandon the Reconstruction and Development Programme (RDP) and replace it with the neo-liberal Growth, Employment and Redistribution (GEAR) policy.

I spoke with many COSATU and SACP leaders in preparation for this chapter, both on and off the record. Either way, three themes cropped up in almost exactly equal measure in their analysis of the relationships within the tripartite alliance. The first is the switch to GEAR: it was the watershed of all watersheds. The second is the explanation of the justification for remaining within the alliance, a topic on which I will dwell in the concluding part of this chapter. The third is the scraping-the-bottom-of-the-barrel disputes of 2002, when the alliance came as close as it ever has to breaking up – so far. Aptly, these three form a triangle within which the tripartite alliance continues to busily cohabit; the triangle sets parameters on the interrelationship and the power and influence of each of the partners. This is why any discussion about the strength of the alliance and the relative power of each partner must refer to the historical period. The power ebbs and flows. With the Anti-Terrorism Bill, COSATU had a huge bargaining chip: the election campaign, as is acknowledged by all the main players. Once again, in the lead-up to the March 2006 local government elections, COSATU's bargaining power increased and it could apply pressure with greater confidence. In 2001–02, under attack from right-wing forces within the ANC, COSATU was far weaker; it was subject to a concerted, coordinated assault to test its power – and it survived.

'Ultra-left' critics regard this ebb and flow as a sick ritual in which, inexorably, COSATU is duped. Dale McKinley, for example, likened the relationship of COSATU and the SACP with the ANC to that of a dancing couple. Observing it from the outside, the dance appears to be a partnership, and a beautiful one at that. As such, according to McKinley, the SACP and COSATU leadership can point to themselves in the ANC's embrace, gliding across the dance floor, and claim the 'embrace' and 'partnership' as real and existing and fruitful.

But McKinley asserts that the dance is a mirage, that the partnership is a hoax, and that, in fact, unbeknown to the observer, the senior partner (ANC) is leading the other in the dance, forcing them to 'toe the line'.[5] COSATU and the SACP have more influence and power than this imagery, vivid as it is, portrays. Although COSATU membership has dropped slightly, from 1.8 million to 1.7 million between 2000 and 2003, its capacity to mobilize in numbers gives it power; similarly, 'a demobilization of mass-based popular movements in itself shifts the balance of forces unfavourably, which may further limit the scope for transformation'.[6] Says Coleman: 'The mass support is not only about numbers, but our traditions of organization and our strategic positioning – at the point of production and the more general factor that the working class in South Africa remains more strategic and coherent than in other societies.'

This organizational capacity can be traced back to the troubled 1980s. Coleman recalls that COSATU was a key strategic force during the years leading up to the CODESA negotiations, combining mass action with a negotiating capacity 'par excellence'. 'Negotiating skills,' says Coleman, 'are our bread and butter.' COSATU's influence, as the Anti-Terrorism Bill memo reflects, is still based on this combination – the threat of mobilization, combined with the capacity to negotiate skilfully based on quality research and argument. Whether it is the COSATU parliamentary office's submissions to parliamentary committees, or the economic analysis of the policy unit headed by the widely respected Neva Makgetla, who even receives invitations to present papers to the president's policy unit, the level of professionalism is striking.

COSATU affiliates

Union	General secretary	Membership
CEPPWAWU: Chemical, Energy, Paper, Printing, Wood and Allied Workers Union	Welile Nolingo	67 162
CWU: Communication Workers Union	Macvicar Dyasopu	29 320
FAWU: Food and Allied Workers Union	Katishi Masemola	85 069
DENOSA: Democratic Nursing Organization of South Africa	Thembeka Gwagwa	72 000
MUSA: Musicians Union of South Africa	Oupa Lebogo	700
NEHAWU: National Education Health and Allied Workers Union	Fikile Majola	234 607
NUM: National Union of Mine Workers	Gwede Mantashe	299 509
NUMSA: National Union of Metalworkers of South Africa	Silumko Nondwangu	174 212
PAWE: Performing Arts Workers' Equity	Kagiso Senkge	365
POPCRU: Police and Prisons Civil Rights Union	Abbey Witbooi	91 000
SAAPAWU: South African Agricultural, Plantation and Allied Workers Union	Danny Boy Masemola	21 966
SACCAWU: South African Commercial, Catering and Allied Workers Union	Bones Skulu	107 553
SADNU: South African Democratic Nurses Union	Freddie Mohai	8 680
SACTWU: South African Clothing and Textile Workers Union	Ebrahim Patel	110 216
SADTU: South African Democratic Teachers Union	Thulas Nxesi	214 865
SAFPU: South African Football Players Union	Sipho Ndzuzo	198
SAMA: South African Medical Association	Dr Aquina Thulare	4 224
SAMWU: South African Municipal Workers Union	Roger Ronnie	114 127
SASAWU: South African State and Allied Workers Union	Mthimkhulu Mashiya	144 127
SASBO: The Finance Union	Shaun Oelschig	58 656
SATAWU: South African Transport and Allied Workers Union	Randall Howard	79 325

COSATU has 1.7 million members, spread across twenty-one affiliates. In terms of its leadership and its structures, what you see is pretty much what you get. There is a national congress that meets every three years, a central committee that meets between congresses, and a central executive committee that meets three times a year. In between, decisions are taken by the office-bearers' collective, which comprises the national president and two deputy presidents, the treasurer, general secretary and deputy general secretary. There are regional replicas of this structure and seven main departments: secretariat, organizing, international, communications, education, parliament and policy.

The 'other' comrades: The SACP

The SACP has around 30 000 cadre members. It is a number that may surprise quite a few people. All are paid-up members; many are active, both in the party and in the ANC – there is a large crossover. An ANC leader once told me: 'Thank god for the communists. Without them we would fall apart. They work hard and are very committed. As I say, without their energy, many of the structures would cease to operate.'

The crossover extends to COSATU, too. Many of the party's cadres are shop stewards. It is a relationship that the general secretary of the SACP, Blade Nzimande, is keen to deepen, and tries to do with 'methodical engagement', according to his deputy, Jeremy Cronin. Is there a communist party in the world that still has such an influential hand on the tiller of political power – at least in a major nation, which, because of its regional power, South Africa is? Brazil, perhaps. Indeed, this description of President Lula da Silva's cabinet has the flavour of South Africa's own:

> The government's top positions are meted out to an ecumenical mix, some appointments based on ability, others on the settlement of political obligations. Most have arrived from the left. Chief of Staff Jose Dirceu once went into exile in Cuba, where he underwent both guerrilla training and the facial camouflage of plastic surgery; he has hung a photo of Fidel and himself behind his desk. Marina Silva, the environment minister, grew up in a family of Amazon rubber tappers; her nearest neighbors were a two-hour walk away, and she saw her first electric light at age 5 during a trip downriver for medical care. But on the economic side,

Lula's choices have been decidedly more conservative. Henrique Meirelles, president of the central bank, used to be the head of global banking at FleetBoston Financial. Luiz Furlan, the minister of development, industry and commerce, was a millionaire poultry exporter. Finance minister Antonio Palocci, while a *petista* and an ex-Trotskyite, is a dedicated convert to fiscal orthodoxy.[7]

COSATU is a formidably proportioned giant; in contrast, the SACP is 'small but perfectly formed'. Is there a rivalry between the two partners? Well, put it this way: when I told a contact in the SACP that I would likely put them in the same chapter as COSATU, he said, 'Fair enough, that's the way I would do it.' But when I told someone from COSATU, their reaction revealed the way in which *they* think the power balance swings: 'Hmph. Hanging onto our coat-tails again, are they?'

The influence of the two alliance partners is a fluctuating commodity that swings as wildly up and down as the stock exchange. At the point of the transition to democracy in 1994, there was a delicately balanced cocktail of naivety and realism within COSATU. Coleman again: 'As early as 1993, there was a paper kicking around in which it was predicted that the old centres of power' – meaning the 'old establishment' mix of white-owned capital, the National Party and old-guard institutions and public servants – 'would resist post the 1994 election. This was not a distrust of the ANC, but a realization that there would be obstacles. The naivety was that we thought we would be fighting the resistance hand-in-hand with the ANC.' In a graphic phrase, he adds: 'As a result, our forces – meaning the democratic movement as a whole – were confined to barracks.'

It was at this point that the ANC leadership took advantage. In the dead of night, and with as much subterfuge as it is possible to muster in politics – only about three or four people knew the full extent of the shift in policy and its timing – in essence, the ANC screwed its alliance partners. The greatest policy shift in the history of the ANC, and neither COSATU nor the SACP were informed, let alone consulted. As with individual human relations, there is always a seismic moment when you discover the hidden truth about someone.

This was the moment for COSATU and the ANC. Had they been playing poker, the ANC would not have blinked. As Coleman says, 'The forces were confined to barracks' – such was the brutal, ruthless incision of the switchblade. Remember Maria Ramos's message from her political master? 'GEAR is non-negotiable.' This was a tumultuous first: nothing had ever been non-negotiable in the alliance before. As a result, the power and influence of COSATU and the SACP have been fundamentally circumscribed ever since. In politics, such a defeat scars you; it is virtually impossible to recover. Carry on, yes; retrieve some lost ground, maybe; fully recover, almost certainly not.

As Tregenna states: 'The major setback for the working class has been the failure of the ANC government to fundamentally transform the structure of the South African economy. Notwithstanding changes here and there, there is a strong continuity in the accumulation trajectory before and after political democratization. The majority of people are still excluded from ownership or control of assets. This essentially capitalist accumulation path has not resolved the systemic structural crisis of underdevelopment, nor can it do so.'[8] Part of the political strategy of GEAR was to be able to face down the left, especially COSATU.

Echoing the perspective offered by William Gumede in his book *Thabo Mbeki and the Battle for the Soul of the ANC*, political analyst Ralph Mathekga asks:

Did the ANC deliberately circumvent COSATU and the SACP in its shift from the RDP to GEAR? Well, flaunting political arrogance in the faces of one's allies is one thing, but inability to sell a major policy shift is quite another. The ANC was able to put on an arrogant face during the shift to GEAR. But this may also amount to a strategy to eclipse the dilemma that the party was actually under. It would have been an embarrassing exercise for the ANC to turn around – against the backdrop of sheer poverty, inequalities and rising unemployment – and engage with SACP and COSATU on the justifications for a shift from the RDP. Under pressure from the international financial community, the ANC played both the dumb and 'we did our part' cards, while at the same time partly convincing itself that GEAR's success will ultimately exonerate the party's seemingly reluctant shift to GEAR. Alas, things did not happen as planned. GEAR failed to deliver what was promised and the SACP and COSATU observed from the sidelines. GEAR is totally disconnected from envisioned transformation.

A calculation of the attitude of COSATU's leadership at the time was fundamental to the ANC's strategy. Shilowa asked of his colleagues: 'Do we call the workers out to the streets on the proposed levels of Budget deficit?' Even though the idea that GEAR could be broken down through immediate negotiation proved to be a grand self-delusion, few of COSATU or the SACP's leadership would with hindsight have done things differently. However, some of them now realize that a court challenge should have been undertaken for failing to take GEAR through NEDLAC. It is, in these circumstances, remarkable that COSATU's morale was not sucked dry. If anything, it has rallied, especially since the days of 2002, when organizational incoherence was tested by the threat posed by the right wing of the ANC.

That period is now viewed as a second watershed. Whether psychologically this has been imposed onto history in order to eclipse the pain of the first – the shift to GEAR – or whether it is objectively justified is a moot point. As I mention in the previous chapter on the ANC and its national conference in Stellenbosch in December 2002, there was a deliberate attempt 'to eliminate us,' according to an SACP leader. 'The message went out that some of us were "too communist". A list [of names] was circulated, but it did not work.'

Why not? Because around a third of the delegates to the national conference were members of both the SACP and ANC. The crossover benefits flow both ways, it would seem, and although he dropped a few places in the NEC list, Blade Nzimande was re-elected, as were Jeremy Cronin and Phillip Dexter (SACP treasurer). The COSATU leadership, in contrast, chose to withdraw from the contest in order to be able to adopt a more independent stance against the onslaught from the right of the ANC (although a small number of affiliate/regional leaders did stand unsuccessfully). Says one COSATU leader: '*They* have never been able to smash us.'

The 'ultra-left' badge

The ANC NEC document in Spring 2001 that formalized the attempt to isolate the 'ultra-left' can now be seen as a clear strategy by the ANC to force the issue of whether the SACP and COSATU should remain within the alliance. At the time, although it was clear from sources and from the general deportment of those involved in the tripartite bilateral meetings that things were bad, it is clear now that they were very bad indeed.

When you talk to leaders of COSATU and the SACP, it is evident from what they say that, contrary to the determinedly stoical public and even private statements at the time, a split had been a real possibility. It was, therefore, a test of political strength and willpower. For the ordinary citizen looking in, these divisions and factions within the left are baffling. What, for example, people ask, is the 'ultra-left'? What does the term mean? SACP deputy general secretary, Jeremy Cronin, provides this lengthy yet neat definition:

> The defining feature of ultra-leftism is its excessive **exaggeration** of **subjective** factors. The subjective feelings of militancy of a small group of revolutionaries; or the deep anger and impatience felt by large masses of workers and poor; or the attractiveness of an immediate advance to socialism – important, understandable and, in many cases, even admirable subjective feelings of this kind are assumed to mean that the **desirable** is also, more or less, **immediately possible**. This is why Lenin, appropriately, referred to this tendency as 'infantile'. He writes, for instance, of the ultra-left tendency in Germany in 1920:
>
> > *It is obvious that the 'Lefts' in Germany have mistaken their desire, their politico-ideological attitude, for objective reality. That is a most dangerous mistake for revolutionaries to make.* (Lenin, '"Left-wing" communism – an infantile disorder', *Selected Works*, p. 541)
>
> The excessive subjectivism of the ultra-left also expresses itself in the ways in which it tends to explain away reverses or difficulties. These, too, are excessively subjectivised – leaders are 'sell-outs' and 'traitors', the masses are 'misled', or suffering from a 'false consciousness'. These accusations may, or may not have some relevance, but ultra-leftism tends to evoke them all too hastily. The flipside of this excessive subjectivism is that ultra-leftism tends to underrate or even ignore the objective factors within a given situation. The real and potential impediments to a rapid advance are discounted. The strength of opposition forces and the dangers of counter-revolution are neglected. The objective weaknesses of progressive classes and strata are themselves also characteristically ignored. The conflation of what is desirable with what is possible results in adventurism, a tendency to voluntarism, the advocacy of reckless leaps

forward, based on sheer willpower, which can result in serious defeat and disaster. As a consequence of all of this, ultra-leftism tends not to understand revolution as process. Everything is immediate, all-or-nothing, victory or sell-out. This, in turn, results in many of the zig-zags that are so often a feature of ultra-leftism, bouts of excessive optimism, followed by depression and the predictable accusations of betrayal and sell-out. Lenin writes of this tendency that it *'easily goes to revolutionary extremes, but (it is) incapable of perseverance, organisation, discipline and steadfastness'* (p. 520). Because of its exaggeration of the immediate, ultra-leftism tends, also, to greatly exaggerate tactics at the expense of strategies. Tactics are elevated into strategies, and even principles. For instance, ultra-leftism often rejects compromises on principle. Participation in parliamentary democracy is sometimes rejected, for all time, and the tactics of a general strike or an insurrectionary seizure of power are counter-posed to any other approach, and turned into timeless strategies if not principles. The ultra-left approach is also often characterised by what Lenin neatly described as the 'tactics of sheer negation'. We see signs of this in our own current reality (anti-globalisation, anti-NEPAD, anti-ANC government). All of these characteristics of ultra-leftism result in a general inability to appreciate or participate in the often long-haul of organisational building and the concomitant need to work patiently, resolve secondary contradictions, and manage the complexity of mass movements, alliances and broad fronts. As a result, the organisational practices of ultra-leftism are typically characterised by factionalism and the propensity to endless splitting and fragmentation (which is why, incidentally, the 2002 ANC S&T Preface attempt to present the ultra-left as a vast South African conspiracy with global tentacles is not only factually incorrect, but simply bizarre). Another related feature of ultra-leftism's inability to build organisation is a propensity to enter into a parasitic relationship with established organisations, institutions and campaigns, using the tactics of entryism. These are the characteristic features of the ultra-left tendency. We have tried to show that these features are interconnected and mutually reinforcing. In real life, of course, ultra-leftism will manifest itself in many varieties, and with varying degrees of 'purity'.[9]

The real division in the broad left – or what Cronin calls 'two broad lefts' – is between those that are clear that the future of the left is outside of the alliance – the 'ultra-left' – and those that see it as still within the movement.

For a simple breakdown of the left, this is as clear and straightforward a way to understand it – and it is not simplistic. There may be divisions and factions within the ultra-left – and indeed a defining feature of the far left is its apparent infinite capacity, wherever it may be in the world, to find ways to argue and create disunity – but the one thing that links all its members is that they think the ANC is a 'sell-out'.

In contrast, COSATU and the SACP have not given up on the ANC. Not by a long shot. They still believe that the fight for the heart and soul of the ANC, which has been a fifty-year fight, continues unabated and unresolved. The root core calculation – and this is where there is a marked commonality of language across the SACP and COSATU leaderships – is that the objective realities of the world mean that 'the best crack at thoroughgoing social transformation is a very substantial majority, and one that gravitates around the ANC', according to an alliance leader.

As this book went to press, this strategy – and the decades-old partnerships that it underpins – was being tested as never before. Both the SACP and COSATU, but especially the former, were publicly speaking about 'going it alone'. A historic discussion document, a special May 2006 edition of *Bua Komanisi*, the SACP's in-house journal, invited discussion about the possibility of fighting the 2009 general election as a separate political party.

For some of the more prudent tacticians on the left, 'social transformation' is the new code expression for 'socialism'. Thus, says another, 'the contest is for the trajectory and character of the ANC, and that for a left that is serious about a social transformation process, the best chance lies with a "majority project"'. Part of the calculation is that, outside of the alliance, there would be a danger that the ANC could go off the rails. There is a defensive origin in COSATU's adherence to the tripartite alliance – at the very least it gets COSATU a hearing; at best, full consideration of its position.

FRELIMO, the ruling party in Mozambique, is cited as a progressive party that lost its way, partly because it did not have strong ties with the trade unions. This was the view that prevailed during the 2001–02 slump in ANC–tripartite alliance relations, as it had before. This time, neither COSATU nor the SACP leadership blinked. Instead, both organizations came back strongly at the ANC. In a remarkable paper prepared by COSATU ahead of a crisis bilateral meeting with the ANC in February 2002, it took the fight to the ANC, arguing that the ANC had effectively lost the plot.

At the start of the paper, COSATU asserts that 'it is difficult to establish what the ANC's theoretical perspective is on important elements of the transition ... perspectives on key national issues relating to the transition often appear to emanate from government, or even a government department, rather than from the ANC'.[10]

Decoded for the man or woman in the street, what this means is that COSATU is teasing the ANC, accusing it of lacking intellectual integrity and of having been duped by the technocrats in government. The footnote is even better: 'Differences on policy, while often presented as clear differences between COSATU and the ANC, are usually differences with government or government departments. ANC policies tend to be closer to ours, or undefined. On issues such as privatization, economic policy, industrial policy, etc., the ANC either has no clear policy or there are significant disagreements with government – this policy confusion has emerged in alliance meetings.'[11]

Idasa analyst Ralph Mathekga again: 'Unlike the ANC in power, the SACP and COSATU produce more discussion papers than the ANC. Why? While the ANC as a governing party does not have a higher standard of proof to justify its policy decision-making – it only has to declare any policy shift a "practical" move – the left has to start by de-scrambling policies so as to then provide alternatives. Since coming into office, the ANC has somehow retreated from any discourse that requires deeper analysis. Policy decisions have been reduced to technical shifts. A shift from RDP to GEAR was treated by the ANC as if it was equivalent to changing a mortgage bond from one bank to another, with the aim to capitalize on a 2 per cent interest cut. A shift from GEAR to ASGISA (the Accelerated and Shared Growth Initiative for South Africa) – following implicit acceptance that GEAR has too many shortfalls – is also punted as a "medium-term" intervention strategy and not a major policy shift. COSATU and the SACP are fully aware of the ANC's evasive manoeuvres. The SACP and COSATU may rightfully claim to understand the ANC more than the ANC understands itself.'

The alliance partners' strategy during the rest of 2002 worked. The ANC was largely ground down during the various meetings that took place during the year, culminating in the Stellenbosch conference at the end of the year at which the left and its project of contestation lived on – greatly weakened, yes, from years of battering by Mbeki and his followers, but still alive and kicking. The reality is that the wider constituency of the ANC, and its political centre, outside of government, is essentially left-of-centre. There are serious contradictions within the ANC, particularly expressed in the differences between ANC positions outside of government (progressive) and inside government (conservative). This fundamental contradiction is deepening, and was clearly expressed at the ANC's 2005 national general council, when major disputes around the 'modernization' of the ANC and 'reform' of labour market regulation brought the ANC and its alliance partners into sharp divergence of opinion.

The years 2001–02 were therefore a litmus test for the SACP and COSATU. But they passed the test and, as a result, their influence, once heading firmly downwards, has been revitalized. What now, and of the future? After the April 2004 elections, there was the warm, fuzzy afterglow of the election results. This is partly because of a genuine gratitude within the ANC about the role that COSATU, and Zwelinzima Vavi in particular, had played in the campaign, and partly because of policy shifts.

Interestingly, in the 2006 local government elections, the ANC was markedly less reliant on COSATU for its organizing capabilities. They apparently relied instead on a traditional modern-day, 'pure party' campaign strategy, using the party leaders to stage *imbizos* and roadshows, and the media as their main channel of communication to the wider electorate, rather than the mass rallies and house-to-house visits of yesteryear.

Thus, the influence that COSATU exerts at election time through its mobilization leverage may be in decline. The efforts of COSATU to assist the electoral campaign – by using its members to go out into communities – have shrunk significantly, mainly as a direct result of the reservations of some affiliates. And their efforts to campaign for the ANC within its own ranks are minimal. Except for the customary visit of Vavi or Willie Madisha to the Cape or KwaZulu-Natal, the evidence of the 2006 local government elections suggests that the leadership is no longer well disposed towards expending its political capital on helping the ANC win elections. This may be because of a recalculation of the cost-benefit analysis of the alliance. Or, it may represent a serious miscalculation: if assisting the ANC at election time represented one of the alliance's biggest bargaining chips, then discarding it may be an example of cutting off one's nose to spite one's face.

Alliance sceptics

There are plenty of 'alliance sceptics' inside the broad labour-left church who would welcome the former. One such is Sahra Ryklief, who heads the respected Labour Research Service, which has a long-established track record of solid research and training in wage and other workplace-related matters. She suggests that 'the only thing the ANC really needs COSATU to do at election time is to shut up and let election campaigning proceed. Is this real power, or an acknowledgement of nuisance value? If so, can the ANC withstand the vexation? Can COSATU risk causing it or, alternatively, risk forsaking the influence that comes from being a nuisance?'

Defenders of the alliance, however, point to the record of direct policy influence. Though the two alliance partners were screwed on GEAR, *Accelerating Change* charts the many victories for the left before and after the shift in macroeconomic policy, pivoting around one of the most progressive labour law regimes in the world. They point also to the extension of child support, the shift away from privatization and the shift in the fiscal stance.

'Whatever Trevor [Manuel]'s bluster,' says a source in COSATU, 'and he can bluster as much as he wants, we are achieving direct results.' To Ryklief, the only way to evaluate the alliance is by identifying specific gains. Political influence, she argues, must be a matter of concrete achievement: 'Has the alliance led, and will it continue to lead, to greater influence of the left in and outside government? Or, more importantly, has it led, or will it lead to, a thoroughgoing social transformation? If not, it would merely be the creation of majority consent to be governed badly, would it not?'

Both critics and defenders of the alliance point to what they call the 'five lost years' between 1996 and 2001, when social expenditure finally returned to its 1995 level. Both point the finger of blame at the ANC in government. The cost of this period of fiscal austerity was a high degree of social conflict and the running down of the public sector. Asks Coleman: 'And in whose interest?' He points to two main beneficiaries: the domestic financial sector, and international capital. And not the domestic private sector in the general sense; small and medium business was almost crippled by the high interest rates that were a key part of the GEAR strategy.

The idea that international investment would fill the gap was, says Coleman, 'lunatic'. In this context, he suggests, it is clear that those people who support the DA continue to drive economic policy. And, in turn, that there is a lack of strategic cohesion within the ANC. Coleman argues that GEAR was initially defended on the basis that '[it was] the most effective way of implementing the RDP, and only later was it presented as it is now, as a "stabilization strategy".'

So, having learnt of the limitation of their power back in 1996, having regathered strength by holding their strategic nerve during the second litmus test of 2001–02, and having provided invaluable support for the ANC election campaign in 2004, both COSATU and the SACP began Mbeki's second term of office feeling confident. A fresh feeling of quiet confidence about their own political power project, which is to influence the historical course of the ANC and to steer it left once again, emerged. But the plan was blown off course by the events surrounding the battle for the succession, notwithstanding the significant fights at the ANC's 2005 NGC and 'the defeat of conservative forces at the NGC', as one COSATU leader claimed in a conversation we had.

The Zuma effect

The period leading up to the ANC's 2007 national conference, and the election of someone to succeed Mbeki as leader of the ANC – and almost certainly thereafter the presidency of the country – was always going to be rough. Quite how rough, few of us could accurately have foreseen. The year 2005 was especially rough: the Shaik trial, which was as much about the integrity of then Deputy President Jacob Zuma as it was about Schabir Shaik, threw South African politics into a cauldron of frothing uncertainty. By the end of the year, a senior alliance leader was moved to make the following remarkable private suggestion to me: 'If JZ is convicted, it will provoke a reaction equivalent to the assassination of Chris Hani.' I do not believe that JZ was being compared with Hani, or even the circumstances surrounding Hani's death. Hani's murder was the work of white, right-wing fascists; however carefully orchestrated, there was clearly a respectable case to bring against Zuma. Rather, it was about the possible popular reaction. Depending on the precise date of the corruption trial, by the time this book is published, the accuracy or otherwise of the prediction will likely be known.

As I write, a new phase in ANC–COSATU/SACP relations has commenced, ostensibly pivoted around Jacob Zuma. Although the outcome of the divisions that have emerged in the alliance over the future career of Zuma and, specifically, his prospects of succeeding Mbeki as both president of the ANC and the country, are unknown, what is clear now is the extent to which the Zuma matter impacted on the intra-alliance relationships, especially in 2005, and especially during the important ANC NGC, held in Pretoria at the end of June 2005.

The NGC is important because it falls halfway between each national conference and represents a staging post in the monitoring of progress on national conference resolutions. Given that the ANC chooses to hold national conferences only every five years, it is an opportunity that has to be grabbed. Hence, the 2005 NGC saw two very significant kites being flown. The first concerned a possible organizational redesign (part of the 'modernization' process discussed in the previous chapter). The second, a policy document, mainly penned by Jabu Moleketi, invited the idea that there should be some retreat on the system of labour market regulation that was introduced during the Mandela administration and which the alliance regards as one of its greatest victories.

To the alliance partners, both sets of ideas were anathema. As a COSATU leadership insider puts it, 'the "modernization" proposals were about taking power away from the branches and diminishing internal democracy, and were thrown out along with the labour market policy paper'. But for the Zuma issue, the resistance might not have been so concerted and the ANC's response not so accommodating. 'JZ gave people the courage to be stronger on the issues of policy ... sometimes in the past, people have been too afraid to resist; the NGC represented a collapse of that fear and, therefore, a sea change in the centre of gravity.'

Certainly, insiders confirm that the NEC of the ANC had never before been so divided – on any issue – as on Zuma, with the knock-on effect that it proved harder for the leadership to drive consensus on policy issues, such as the modernization and labour market policies. Thabo Mbeki read the mood, recognizing that the NGC faced a rebellion, and ended the council with a very conciliatory speech. The question arises whether ANC–alliance politics is a zero-sum game or not. If the ANC is split and weakened, is that necessarily good news for the alliance partners? If one's stock is down, is the other's necessarily up? As a COSATU leadership figure admitted to me,

'The JZ issue has been quite damaging to the movement as a whole and to the left in particular.' At the forthcoming COSATU congress, in September 2006, the union will be compelled to resolve the deep-lying differences surrounding its approach to the Zuma matter and its relationship with the ANC leadership.

The ostensibly 'blind' support of Jacob Zuma by both the COSATU and SACP leadership – Vavi spoke in March 2005 of an unstoppable 'tsunami' of support for Zuma – attracted criticism from both inside and outside the left; affiliates criticized Vavi for adopting what was at that point an un-mandated position. Until the Zuma issue surfaced, COSATU and the SACP were strong and clear on matters of corruption; their shows of support for Zuma, including the establishment of a legal support fund, undermined the credibility of their anti-corruption stance.

In August 2005, when its central committee resolution called for both the withdrawal of the charges of corruption and the need for a 'political solution' to the crisis, it was rightly interpreted by many commentators, and by middle-class opinion, not only as unrealistic, but violating the principle of the separation of powers. In essence, COSATU was calling for executive interference with the judicial process – the very thing that they had railed against in relation to Zuma. The hidden logic was this: to correct a wrong, another wrong must be perpetrated. COSATU insiders privately question the wisdom of the tactics. But they justify it thus: Zuma is the victim of a political campaign; he has not been treated fairly; he will not get a fair trial – and so the charges should be withdrawn. The August 2005 central committee statement speaks of the 'concerted, politically-inspired campaign to destroy the deputy president'.[12] Moreover, they point to the democratic culture of the confederation: the majority of affiliates, with the wholehearted support of their membership, had called for the central committee to adopt this stance. There was – and at the time of writing, still is – considerable anger about the way in which it is perceived Zuma had been treated. So, the central committee of COSATU had little choice but to take this stance.

However, the rape charges introduced a new phase. Vavi's statement at the time that Zuma was charged, in late 2005, was far more circumspect. Inside COSATU there was a full recognition that this charge represented the 'end of the road for JZ', as one insider remarked. Even if acquitted, the smear would remain forever. The charge, so offensive to the ANC–alliance's long-held commitment to the rights of women, enabled the ANC's NEC to temporarily paper over its cracks and again close ranks around Mbeki. The centre of gravity had shifted – but only for a short while. As a fraught year came to a close, major policy decisions were railroaded through against the wishes of the alliance partners. First, a demarcation dispute involving the community of Khutsong – whereby it would become part of the North West Province instead of Gauteng, against the wishes of the great majority of its citizens – was confirmed by cabinet, without any further consultation.

Shortly afterwards, cabinet, in equally decisive manner, confirmed the decision to proceed with the R20-billion 'Gautrain' project – despite the profound reservations of the alliance partners. As 2006 began, the talk from within the alliance leadership was once again one of betrayal; one COSATU insider told me that 'like with any bully, there is a tendency to bluster and threaten ... for us the question is, is it a new phase or just a bluff?' At the twentieth-anniversary COSATU rally in Durban in November (prior to the rape charge), in an attempt to curry further favour, Jacob Zuma told the assembled crowd that 'the alliance must drive government'.

With Zuma down and almost out with the rape charges, the ANC in government was reasserting its ascendancy over policy and politics. Zuma's acquittal in the rape case tilted the balance of power back again. He emerged, deeply wounded, but determined to pursue a campaign for retributive justice and the ultimate prize: the presidency.

Conclusion: Pissing inside or outside the tent?

Both alliance partners are blessed with extraordinary leadership. Zwelinzima Vavi is an awesome operator: strong, clear, hotheaded but controlled, indefatigable. Whereas with Mbhazima Shilowa, his predecessor, one detected a soft underbelly, with Vavi one senses there is only steely resolve. This comes across clearly in his public positioning. As he himself once told senior colleagues, 'We have got to display a necessary level of arrogance, given the hostile class interests stacked against us; we cannot afford to vacillate on our core issues.' Blade Nzimande is equally astute, with a colossal intellect and a calm, measured sense of political strategy. Neither man can be written off; both will remain key forces of influence within the ANC alliance and, therefore, throughout South African politics for the foreseeable future.

Neither can be bought off, such is the depth of their independent core. One of the most famous political idioms is Lyndon Johnson's, when he referred to an opponent as someone whom he would rather have inside the tent, pissing out, than outside pissing in. Mbeki has drawn as many of them into the tent as he safely can – from the left and the right. This is where Essop Pahad probably has the greatest impact – calculating who the weak ones are: those who can be co-opted, and those who cannot. Jeff Radebe, for instance, previously a SACP central committee member (as was Pahad himself), was co-opted through his appointment as minister of public enterprises, the very ministry that was responsible for privatization.

Mbhazima Shilowa's redeployment from COSATU is a further example of the compromising of the left leadership. As premier of Gauteng, Shilowa inherited, and has had to implement, a very austere, centre-right basket of policies in the guise of Egoli 2000 – including the laying-off of council workers and the nourishment of public–private partnerships – although he has nonetheless won the respect of the broad alliance in the province, and united previously fractured forces. Shilowa also implemented progressive programmes on certain issues such as HIV/AIDS, and is likely to be a very significant player in South African politics for the foreseeable future, with connections and credibility in a wide range of networks.

Meanwhile, the SACP got rid of Essop Pahad and Jeff Radebe in their 2000 national conference elections; Geraldine Fraser-Moleketi, who had been deputy chair, did not even make it to the central committee. The ones that remain outside should take it as a compliment as much as anything else. And – let me be clear – the ones that are 'in' the tent may have been sucked in, but it does not mean they are not talented: the two Moleketis, Kasrils and Charles Nqakula are all people of talent and integrity. There is even more talent that has not succumbed, though they remain inside the bigger tent.

There are many political actors who exert influence in the new South Africa; it is a relatively pluralist political society – which is one of its strengths and one of the reasons for feeling confident about the future. What distinguishes COSATU and the SACP from the rest? The answers are the alliance and the entry points it provides to people to the ANC and to government (as the story at the beginning of this chapter illustrates); a partnership with history; a 'special relationship'.

Another answer is the 'red telephone', as Sahra Ryklief calls it, adding: 'But in how many instances has this red telephone just been a "toy telephone"? There was the abandonment of the RDP; now there is the accelerated growth strategy, where COSATU is also clamouring about the lack of full consultation and has raised substantive objections to the absence of a coherent development strategy. Then there are the looming labour law amendments. And how many other examples are there of the toy telephone that the leadership is silent over, because of the sheer humiliation of admitting to it?'

So, to return to the tent analogy: COSATU and the SACP find themselves outside the inner tent, but inside the outer tent, trapped, so to speak, against the flysheet ('Pissing on ourselves?' inquires Ryklief). It's a tricky position. Yet, for the seasoned political gymnasts of the COSATU and SACP leadership, the alliance with the ANC represents more of an opportunity than a threat where, like a lengthy marriage, the dividends of inside influence outweigh the habitual frustration of reproach and resentment and the occasional ritual humiliation. Divorce is always an option. But staying together is the safer option. And it may even be the right thing to do.

A fantasy left cabinet

Appointing an alternative cabinet, comprising only SACP and COSATU leaders and key individuals, plus one or two other related odds and sods, is a device for me to illustrate the range of talent and its potential influence. This helps me justify what otherwise might seem like a frivolous exercise in the context of a very serious issue – the ongoing contest for the ideological heart and soul of the ANC. As in Fantasy Football, you can select your own team. Here is mine – one that is every bit as talented as Mbeki's cabinet, and perhaps even more so:

- Zwelinzima Vavi: President, naturally.
- Willie Madisha: Deputy president and minister of intelligence services.

- Pravin Gordhan: Minister of finance. The pharmacist/activist/ communist-turned-tax-collector is currently the director of the South African Revenue Service and relishing the role. He would be an excellent finance minister, such is his natural brilliance and acuity in both economics and politics. Neva Makgetla would be his deputy, with special responsibility for industrial policy, public works and tourism, which I have added to the portfolio because its current attachment to environmental affairs is both awkward and irrational – invariably there are inherent tensions between tourism and the environment. It would be better to have those tensions resolved at cabinet level between full ministers than within the departmental confines, as at present.
- Ebrahim Patel: Minister of trade. Patel has a breadth of knowledge and experience on trade policy issues and international economic politics – including membership of the governing body of the International Labour Organisation (ILO), and experience of the World Trade Organization (WTO).
- Blade Nzimande: Minister of foreign affairs. Although Vavi has excellent international connections, he would pay less attention to foreign relations than Mbeki. Nzimande, like all true Marxists, retains an innately internationalist perspective, and has the wit, charm and knowledge to fulfil the role with distinction.
- Gwede Mantashe: Minister of minerals and energy. As general secretary of the National Union of Mineworkers (NUM), he knows the terrain, so to speak, and is well respected by all the major stakeholders – he would not 'scare the cattle', meaning Anglo et al., and including the ANC. According to one knowledgeable union source, he is 'probably Mbeki's top man in the union leadership and has been strategically placed'.
- Jeremy Cronin: Minister of education. The part-time poet would have an opportunity to spread his zest for knowledge and thinking to a crucial portfolio.
- Godfrey Oliphant: Minister of labour. Former mineworker leader, COSATU deputy president, and chair of the labour portfolio committee in parliament. Leading member of the SACP.

- Phillip Dexter: Minister of public enterprises. As in real life, with Alec Erwin currently in the post, this is a crucial portfolio. To develop a new approach to the role of the state and private capital, removed from the old black-and-white ruts of the privatization vs nationalization debate, and, therefore, an ideal place for the politically savvy and persuasive Dexter.
- Rob Davies: Telecommunications. Currently deputy minister of trade and industry, Davies's dedication to his task deserves promotion.
- Joel Netshitenzhe: Minister of health. Netshitenzhe was crucial to the government's shift in attitude and policy on HIV/AIDS treatment – so, a chance for clear leadership in the fight against the pandemic. Moreover, the cabinet as a whole would be greatly enhanced by his intellectual presence and experience at the heart of government.
- Neil Coleman: Minister of social development. An opportunity to turn his thinking on the basic income grant and people's budgeting, to name but two of the big projects that Coleman holds close to his heart, into reality.
- Yunus Carrim: Minister of provincial affairs and local government. Although I would prefer to use this deeply thoughtful man in a more prominent position, after several years at the helm of the parliamentary portfolio committee on provincial affairs and local government, it would be a waste not to use his knowledge of the portfolio.
- Tony Ehrenreich: Minister of public services and administration. With a strong record of speaking out against corruption and in support of whistleblowers, the charismatic Western Cape COSATU secretary general would certainly stir things up in this pivotal portfolio.
- Dumisa Ntsebeza: minister of justice and constitutional affairs. The charismatic, fiercely independent former head of investigations at the Truth and Reconciliation Commission (TRC) is now in private practice at the Cape Town bar.

Charles Nqakula could stay in his current position – at safety and security (or 'human security' as I would rename it) – along with Sydney Mufamadi.

Both past or present Communist Party central committee members can remain in the cabinet, but with Carrim taking his current post, Mufamadi would need to move to home affairs, to which I would add the correctional services portfolio. I would promote Jabu Moleketi, another former politburo member, to the cabinet as minister of defence – a real test of his ability to control the budget bullshitters.

Adopting the Mbeki approach to inclusivity, would this 'dream' COSATU/SACP cabinet include any other 'pure' ANC members? The three most prominent members of the current cabinet – Mbeki, Manuel and Erwin – would have to go: the ideological differences and the history of political contestation would make their inclusion impossible, for obvious reasons. Pallo Jordan (not an SACP member, but a dyed-in-the-wool socialist intellectual all the same) would be an important thinker to keep at the cabinet table and in his current position at arts and culture, but with science and technology merged into the portfolio. The talented and widely respected Thoko Didiza could be retained and shifted to transport; and Mosiuoa Lekota to a newly merged agriculture and land affairs portfolio (he was diplomatic and persuasive with the farmers when he was premier of the Free State).

The rest would have to go. As a specialist deputy minister for HIV/AIDS, ANC member and TAC leader Zackie Achmat would be invited to join the government.

With sport reduced to a deputy ministership under arts, culture, science and technology, and public works merged into the National Treasury, and cutting the job of the minister in the presidency altogether, along with the other adjustments mentioned in passing above, the cabinet is reduced from a bulky twenty-eight (including the president and deputy president) to a much more manageable twenty-three. So, come the revolution … It's fun, Fantasy Politics, my version. Fantasy Politics, their version, is the limbo land of being inside the tent while trying to piss inwards, which is at best a rather messy exercise. COSATU and the SACP exert influence, all right. But is it as much as their leadership thinks they do, or would they be better off walking out?

7

The Opposition

Blind Leading the Blind

As I caught the lift up to the Democratic Alliance election campaign head-quarters in Sandton in March 2004, I saw reflected in the mirror the shirt I had chosen to wear that morning. It was a *guayabera*, one of my favourite Cuban shirts. What had earlier in the day seemed like a sensible choice for my interview with the long-standing, proudly Communist Party member Raymond Suttner, now seemed like a tactical own goal. James Selfe, the chairman of the DA, had on more than one occasion accused me in the press of being a communist; my choice of shirt would do little to dispel the idea. Not that I minded the accusation, or even for one second regarded it as a slur, but his reasoning was tenuous, to say the least.

In 1994, while working with the ANC's Western Cape election campaign, I wrote a few articles for the independent, socialist *Morning Star* newspaper in London, which had somehow survived the end of the Cold War, as well as the end of its financial support from the Soviet Union. I admired its capacity for survival against all odds, and so, when the *Guardian* and *The Times* declined to even look at a couple of articles on the election that I had written, and did so with a curt snootiness, I called the *Morning Star* and offered to send them the occasional piece gratis (I knew they had no money).

I was oblivious to the fact that all the big newspapers already had at least two correspondents, and probably at least two stringers as well, so the last thing they wanted was unsolicited copy from a wannabe freelance commentator.

The *Morning Star*, however, accepted willingly, and I ended up filing regularly for them during the final dramatic days of the campaign. I think they rather liked having a de facto 'South Africa correspondent', and I certainly enjoyed pretending to be one. It was certainly worth seeing the look on the face of the correspondent from the *Daily Telegraph* at Mandela's inauguration when he asked me which paper I was with.

'What, the *Daily Star*?' he asked with a sneer, referring to the downmarket tabloid.

'No, the *Morning Star*,' I repeated.

'Good god,' he said, visibly taken aback. 'They've got a chap out here, have they?'

'Yes, of course,' I said.

He actually looked as impressed as he did surprised.

But back to Sandton, March 2004, five weeks from polling day, and the purpose of this chapter – to weigh up the political importance and influence of the main opposition political parties in South Africa, and who is important and influential within them.

My brief digression is not entirely immaterial: it hints at one of the most important shifts in South African politics in recent years. Though they would deny it themselves, I refer to the Democratic Party's marked move to the right. To Selfe, the fact that I had written for the *Morning Star* meant I was a communist. Therefore, he had once reasoned in a newspaper article, my employer, Idasa, was pro-ANC. This stark, simplistic, black-and-white reasoning is emblematic of the paradox of modern-day liberalism – at least of the sort practised by parties such as the DA. It is an inherent 'illiberalism'. They might as well say, 'We respect your right to hold any view, provided it is the same as ours, and providing you are not a communist.'

President Mbeki made a similar point, far more elegantly, in parliament in his June 2004 Budget vote debate, when he said: '[T]he Hon Leon says, "We desperately need in our country a plurality of views and true intellectual and moral independence from the ruling party." This conclusion is based on an assessment of what is happening in the country with which we disagree. Indeed if we had the time, we could demonstrate quite easily that what the Hon Leon believes is desperately needed is precisely what characterizes public discourse in our country. Of course it may be that when he speaks of a desperate need for a plurality of views, he is calling on everybody to differ with and oppose the ruling party, regardless of the merits of the propositions of this ruling party. This amounts to arguing that to agree with what is patently correct is to suppress the plurality of views.'

Conservative liberals

When I say the 'Democratic Party' has moved to the right, I do so deliberately. The 'old' DP had evolved from the Progressive Federal Party (PFP), which had, with Helen Suzman at the forefront, been such a thorn in the side of the National Party during the final decade of apartheid. In those days, the DP's liberal credentials were generally impeccable. Tony Leon proudly acknowledges that his first 'real job' was as a campaign worker fighting for Helen Suzman's seat in Houghton.

But in the quest to differentiate themselves from the ANC, and as the ANC greedily consumed the middle ground of South African politics post-1994, the DP relocated towards the remaining space to the right. They further emphasized free market economics by contesting labour market regulation and other collective rights' policies, and focused on crime and corruption in an attempt to win support away from the ANC.

Tony Leon, a fine public speaker with a sharp wit but a harsh, unforgiving tone, was elected as the leader of the DP shortly after the 1994 general elections. His party had just seven seats in parliament, but they were filled with experienced men and women who knew parliament well.

As noted in Chapter 4, they knew how to extract the maximum from parliament in procedural terms. Colin Eglin, Ken Andrew (who was the first chairman of the important standing committee on public accounts), Dene Smuts and Mike Ellis, to name but four, individually and collectively punched above their weight. Certainly, for a party with less than 2 per cent of the vote, they attracted far more than 2 per cent of the headlines, largely because of the strong links they enjoyed with the English-language press and many of the parliamentary press corps.

This merry band of seven worked tirelessly, fought hard but fair, and contributed a great deal to politics during the initial period. Though their view might have changed since, in the light of subsequent events, many ANC politicians regarded people such as Eglin, Andrew and Smuts with considerable respect. Thus, they were able to exert influence in the Constitution-making process, where they won substantial concessions over issues such as the property rights provision and the institutional layout of the new governance system, as well as in the fast-expanding parliamentary committees. But, under the leadership of the ambitious Leon, they yearned for more. Politics is about the acquisition of power, so I should hardly blame them. But blame them I do.

Arguably, democratic politics benefits from having a range of ideological positions articulated. A clear voice of liberalism – individual rights, checks and balances on state power, an emphasis on freedom of expression and minority rights – is as important a voice as any. But it may not be a voice with wide appeal, and, from a political marketing point of view, may have a built-in glass ceiling. Perhaps sensing this, Leon searched for a more expansive strategy. He found a willing ally and a perfect mechanic for the upscaling in a young man called Ryan Coetzee.

Coetzee's ascendance to power within the DA is worth contemplating. His gumption and *chutzpah* is manifest in how he managed to assume the role of chief party strategist. Coetzee was initially hired as an intern in James Selfe's office during the first parliament (he was, at the time, active in the DP Youth structures), where he became increasingly irritated with what he perceived to be the 'debating society' character of the DP, inherited from the small and idealistic PFP, and believed he knew how to transform it into a 'real political party'.

He consequently drafted a memo to Tony Leon identifying the 'malaise' within the party, and offered his services as the man to sort it out. Leon recognized the potential of the upstart intern (then barely twenty-five years old) and hired him on the spot. His influence and power within the party have grown ever since. He now holds the position of CEO.

Coetzee is one of the more controversial figures of modern South African politics, along with people such as Manto Tshabalala-Msimang, Coetzee's leader Tony Leon, Mangosuthu Buthelezi, Essop Pahad and Thabo Mbeki, who have all, in different ways, been 'demonized' by the press. Though he might not like it, this represents exalted company for a young man in his early thirties. He has been vilified in the press as a Machiavellian presence behind the Leon throne.

Certainly, Coetzee has always been as much a strategist as a spin doctor. What he has offered is an understanding of the mechanics of electoral politics – for example, opinion polling – that few in this country can claim. In such a role he has exerted substantial influence over Tony Leon, and thereby opposition politics, from an improbably young age.

Of course, the excesses of youth have cost the DA dearly at times. The marriage with the NNP was a disaster. The 'Fight Back' slogan in the 2000 local government elections was effective, but only in attracting the most *gatvol* voters, while at the same time offending the biggest available market. Indeed, that slogan did the most to add to the demon-like image of Coetzee. 'Fight Back' was interpreted by the ANC to the electorate as 'Fight Black'. Tony Yengeni, then a key ANC campaign coordinator, came up with the counter slogan during a brainstorming session, and within twenty-four hours it was up on lampposts across the country. A subsequent legal challenge by the DP was upheld by a court of law, and the ANC was required to take the offending posters down ... but the damage was done and the moniker has stuck to the DP/DA, much to their chagrin.

Coetzee looks more like the manager of a rock band than a political campaigner. When I meet him in Sandton at the DA's election HQ, he is dressed as he usually is, in trainers, a T-shirt and a hooded sports top. In England he could be mistaken for a 'chav' – the contemporary word for disenchanted youth. As I walk in, both Coetzee and a member of the DA research team, Gareth van Onselen, son of the eminent Wits historian Charles van Onselen, are pacing up and down, cellphones pressed to their ears. One is doing a live radio interview, the other is listening to a phone-in programme on Radio 702 in which senior DA MP Douglas Gibson is mauling Avril Harding, national secretary and now chief whip of the Independent Democrats (ID).

Coetzee shows me around. Much to my relief, Selfe is out, though he has got his jibe in nonetheless. He has placed a huge cardboard cheque for R200 000 from iron-ore mining company Kumba on prominent display in Coetzee's office in reference to Idasa's campaign for transparency in private donations to political parties, which included a groundbreaking legal action against the DA, the ANC, the NNP and the IFP. The campaign had not been well received by any of the parties. Tony Leon showered obscenities on me in the business-class lounge at Cape Town airport soon after we had launched the application in late November 2003.

The parties were concerned that any requirement to openly disclose donations would have a chilling effect on private donations, in particular to opposition parties. But, to our delight, the opposite was happening. The corporations were coming out, agreeing with the principle of transparency that we were promoting, and also saying that now that everything was transparent, they could donate for the first time. Kumba was the tenth company that had announced such a policy. I should be paid a commission, I teased Coetzee, as we laughed at the cardboard-cheque jest.

The best way to view an opposition party is through the lens of an election campaign. That is when you see the warts and all, both the best and the worst. Coetzee is a live wire, sharp, confident, funny, as lithe in conversation as he once was on a cricket field (until the culinary exigencies of being in parliament after the 2004 elections began to take a serious toll). Like Johnny de Lange, Coetzee is a regular player for the Spin Doctors' Cricket Club (as are his colleagues Gareth van Onselen and Anthony Hazell), which I had formed with Lawson Naidoo in 1997.

Ironically, Coetzee's prowess as a batsman came to our attention when he turned out for 'the State' in our annual derby match in 2001 – he made a half-century that day. In fact, he makes fifty more often than he doesn't, in addition to being one of the finest amateur cover points I have played with. We signed him up immediately. Initially De Lange complained gently about the presence of the DA *spinmeister*, but, interestingly, the two are now comrades-in-arms on the field of play. There exists, I think, mutual respect for the competitive, never-say-die attitude they share towards the game. Both are as combative on the sporting field as they are in politics. The only argument we ever have with the umpires or opposition originates with either one or both of them. Something about the character of politics and politicians breeds such competitive, combative attitudes to life.

'An election campaign,' says Coetzee, 'is a very intense form of normal life.'

It is an interestingly worded statement. Coetzee means 'normal political life', but it subtly contradicts his private, oft-expressed view that there is more to life than politics. In 2001, Coetzee had tried to take a step back from politics to pursue what he claims to be his real interest, literature. He completed a part-time master's degree at UCT, but eventually succumbed to Leon's calls to return to the fold.

A second attempt to leave South African politics occurred in 2003, when he left to work with a New York–based political analysis and lobbying consultancy, which the DA engaged on occasion. Although Coetzee refuses to explain why he left, other sources have told me that he resigned after just six months because of his concerns about the ethical approach of his new employers.

Coetzee says that the DA's election campaign structure mirrors its normal structure. James Selfe is chairman of the campaign and chairperson of the Federal Council. He is a hard-nosed politician with a wealth of experience.

To Marthinus van Schalkwyk, the leader who took the NP into and then out of a coalition with the DA, Selfe represents much of what is wrong with the DA.

'The moment when I knew that I must part company with the DA was when, in 2001, Selfe said to me, "What is bad for the country is good for the DA."'

Greg Krumbock is a de facto executive director – apparently very much a hands-on manager. His official title is 'national executive director'. Krumbock, who in Coetzee's words is a 'non-politician politician', is pivotal. And in 2004, Coetzee was 'strategy and message', and still is, despite the grand job title – CEO – he now has. Nick Clelland-Stokes was the head of media relations and a small research team for the 2004 elections.

Leon's role is limited to two aspects: articulating the message, and money (i.e., speaking to potential donors and persuading them to part with it). Van Onselen now runs Leon's office, Russell Crystal the leader's events, with James Lorimer responsible for Leon's communications with the media.

Another minor functionary, David Maynier, who used to head Leon's office, has been sidelined to do the menial task of cold-calling for corporate donations. All men. And all white. The facts speak for themselves: here is a party run by a group of people of almost identical sociology – the same gender, the same ethnicity, the same class, the same schools, the same outlook on life. 'Groupthink' is inevitable. Take the three most influential figures in the party: Leon, Selfe and Coetzee. Two studied at the University of Cape Town, the other at Wits; all three went to prominent schools (Leon at Kearsney College, Botha's Hill, KwaZulu-Natal, Selfe at Bishops in Cape Town and Coetzee at Rondebosch).

The most influential woman in the DA is Helen Zille, who emerged from the chaos of a hung council in Cape Town following the March 2006 municipal elections with a precarious DA-led coalition. Of the 210 seats available in the city council, the DA won 90, the ANC 81, and the ID 23. The remaining seats were split between smaller opposition parties.

Zille is a woman of integrity and with a long record of work in the townships of Cape Town, such as Khayelitsha. That she has taken the trouble to learn how to speak Xhosa sets her apart; how many other white members of her party can speak an African language? In the intense period that followed her election to the position of executive mayor of Cape Town on 15 March

2005, with 106 votes against 103 (the combined votes of the ANC and the ID, with one member of either party breaking ranks to vote for Zille), she was portrayed as 'Godzille' and appeared to revel in the tough-talking image.

Rather than setting herself apart from the style and tone of her leader, Tony Leon, she contrived to sound like a chip off the old block. At the time of writing, her fragile coalition was just about holding together. But with the floor-crossing window in September 2007 on the horizon, there is every possibility that the ANC will be able to cherry-pick some of the councillors from the smaller parties, such as the African Muslim Party or the United Democratic Movement, who allied themselves with the DA. Thus, her window of opportunity may be as short-lived as it is likely to be troubled and controversial. Nonetheless, it represents an opportunity not just for the DA to build a governance heartland, but for Zille to break free from the 'boys' club' that runs the DA to reorientate its image and its way of doing politics.

Holding executive power in government gives her that chance. While she will need to remain disciplined to the DA's strictly enforced hierarchy, it will be far harder for Leon, Selfe and Coetzee to rein her in. I gained an insight into their true attitude to her when, in 2005, she was removed as DA representative from a multiparty committee that had been formed to look at the issue of party political donations and the funding of parties, which Idasa was convening. Zille had proved to be a thoughtful, constructive member of the committee, able to see the bigger picture. But the night before one meeting, Zille notified us that she would not be coming to the meeting. She was curt and tight-lipped about the matter, and clearly unhappy. An hour later, a call came from David Maynier, informing us that he would be replacing Zille, with words to this effect: she is far too weak and accommodating to represent our interests in such an important matter; I will be handling it from now on, and the leadership has given me complete authority. Zille is not to be involved at all in future.

In this respect it is worth considering the fate of another of the DA's most talented women. Even though she was the youngest member of the National Assembly in the 1999 parliament, Raenette Taljaard's considerable intellect and hard work meant that for a time she was not only a noteworthy irritant to the government on a whole range of issues, including trade policy and the arms deal, but the leading intellect within her party.

But her relationship with Leon staggered and eventually fell. They had several rows, which diminished her direct influence to the point where her position was untenable. The deeply ambitious Taljaard was embittered by what happened. It was abundantly clear that Leon could not cope with her challenging intellect; he wants 'yes-men' – literally – around him. Not surprisingly, Taljaard is now cynical about both party and politics in general, even though she commanded the respect of senior ANC ministers such as Trevor Manuel and Alec Erwin for her eagerness to play the ball and not the man and to engage seriously with the issues. Hers is a regrettable and unnecessary loss both for the DA and for parliament.

Taljaard is not the only talented young DA MP to drop out. Nick Clelland-Stokes left parliament at the end of the second democratic parliament in 2004. This was a surprise to many who considered him to be the heir-in-waiting, or at least an ascendant power within the party. His departure, to backpack through South America and South-East Asia with his new wife, is indicative of the strains imposed on MPs and young MPs in particular. Clelland-Stokes was just twenty-six when initially elected to parliament, and he toiled through many of his youthful years for the cause of the DA. In the end it seems simply to have burnt him out.

The veteran MP Dene Smuts is still highly regarded in the party, but she is less influential in parliament than she was, having adopted Leon's aggressive, adversarial approach to politics, which has lost her the respect she formerly enjoyed with the ANC during the first post-1994 parliament.

A deserter from the NNP, Sheila Camerer is respected in the DA for her hard work and because of her fund-raising abilities. 'She goes to lots of parties and knows lots of rich people,' says a senior DA source. Certainly, I can vouch for this. She is a zealot when it comes to accepting invitations to parties held by diplomats and the like.

But back to my meeting with Coetzee. By the time he has sung Krumbock's praises for several minutes, I am keen to meet the former accountant and property developer.

'But he is not keen to meet you,' says Coetzee. 'He thinks you might skewer him in one of your columns.'

I persist, and at the end of my long conversation with Coetzee, I am taken to Krumbock's office, where he sits behind a large desk covered in charts and spreadsheets. Krumbock looks nervous, and offers a rather damp handshake. He insists that Coetzee stay to monitor the conversation. But the softly spoken, fortysomething Capetonian is impressive as he describes how he first got involved in politics at sixteen, when the PFP had contested a by-election against the infamous Nat, LAPA Munnik, in Durbanville in 1976.

Krumbock is still good at fighting the NNP. Apparently he was the one who caught them out in 2001 when they were fiddling the membership numbers within the merged party. The NNP was paying people to join so as to increase their representation in decision-making bodies. This precipitated the end of the merger. Once Krumbock realized what was happening, says Coetzee, they decided to 'stop being such bloody liberals: these people [were] trying to take us over!'

Coetzee says he then had probably his biggest fight with Leon, trying to persuade him to get rid of Peter Marais. 'Tony,' says Coetzee, 'only makes up his mind at the last minute, but when he does – and I have heard this said of Tony Blair – he is fully committed.'

Krumbock, it would seem, is the numbers man: part manager (running the logistics), part accountant (deploying and overseeing the money) and part strategist (deploying the resources in line with a carefully tuned political strategy). Krumbock is routinely 'smuggled' into parliament by the DA via the NCOP. Although a Capetonian by birth and disposition, he has represented both Mpumalanga and KwaZulu-Natal in the NCOP. This state of affairs is indicative of how some of the political parties perceive the NCOP with contempt.

Krumbock's role in ferreting about for the party means that he is almost never in the provincial chamber, he sits on no committees and plays no part in the legislative agenda of the party in the house. This manoeuvre is largely meant to spare the party the burden of paying a political staffer a decent salary. This way the state pays for one of the key political players in the DA. Unappealing though this is, it does at least show a certain ingenuity in the face of scarce resources.

Self-delusions of grandeur

The 2004 general election was an acid test for the DA. Not only did the party need to consolidate its position as the number one opposition party, which they succeeded in doing, but they had to demonstrate that they have the capacity to break through the glass ceiling of South African opposition politics – the inability to win over ANC voters. They failed and are still recovering from the concussion caused by banging their collective head on a ceiling that is proving to be lower than their worst fears – around 12 per cent.

Coetzee gives me a full briefing on their strategy to win black votes, on the basis that I will not write about it before the 2004 election. Although he says he does not agree that South African elections are 'racial censuses', this is how he interprets the DA's challenge. The DA, Coetzee says, has three things in its favour: 'Access to money, coherent positions and identity, and good leadership – someone who can articulate the offer to the voters in a credible way.'

Referring to Peter Mandelson's long-term approach to rebuilding Labour in Britain in the late 1980s, Coetzee says that the DA has a long-term strategy based on shifting identities: 'The task is to create an intersection of the party's identity with the personal identity of the voter.'

In August 1999, Coetzee made a presentation to the DA's Federal Council, in which he outlined his vision for the strategy: first to take over the NNP, then to begin to challenge the ANC by showing it could win some of its voters over in 2004. Coetzee described it as a 'staging-post election'. By 2009, according to Coetzee's vision, the ANC would win less than 50 per cent of the vote.

National election results, 1994–2004 (adapted from IEC election reports)

Largest political parties	1994 election results %	1999 election results %	2004 election results %
ANC	62.65	66.35	69.68
DP (later to be the DA)	1.73	9.56	12.37
NNP	20.39	6.87	1.65
IFP	10.54	8.58	6.97
Total share of the vote	95.31	91.36	91.67

The only section of this strategy that looked on track after the 2004 elections was the NNP part. Decimated, the NNP won less than 2 per cent of the vote in April 2004, while the DA put clear blue water between it and the other opposition parties. Ultimately, though, it was disappointed in its 12 per cent showing.

When I'd seen him in March, Coetzee had '[hoped] for 20 per cent, but would settle for 18 per cent'. He took me through his figures, summoning a spreadsheet with the flick of a button. He defined a black voter market for the DA: 22 per cent of black people in four provinces: Gauteng, KwaZulu-Natal, Limpopo and Mpumalanga. He was not saying that the DA would win 22 per cent of the vote, but that the DA's unique and sophisticated tracking system had established that 22 per cent of black voters in those provinces have the DA as either their first or second choice. Most of them were lower–middle-class black people. Coetzee described them as 'aspirant'. The black middle-middle class and those wealthier were firmly anti-DA, he conceded. After all, they were doing very well under ANC rule.

The DA has resources, both cash and human, which no other opposition party has. They spent around R40 million on their 2004 campaign, not much less than the ANC, and vastly more than any other opposition party. And yet the money produced only 12 per cent of the vote, as well as a lot of disappoint-ment in the party. Behind the public facade, they felt a deep depression about once again having their collective head banged against the glass ceiling.

Because the DA has the capacity, it can make the noise, and thereby influence the tone and tenor of South African politics. In this sense, politics is not just about pure power, because the DA is clearly a long way away from being elected to government. But it is about how you can steer the agenda and challenge the ruling party, creating what leading political scientist Adam Habib calls 'a healthy uncertainty' in the political game.

Scarce resources

But one of the most worrying features of opposition politics in South Africa is the lack of capacity to build effective campaigns. Wander around the offices of the other opposition parties, and you will be horrified to discover the paucity of skilled, experienced individuals working for the leaders of the smaller parties. Most of the talent, both expertise and experience, has been oligopolized by the ANC and the DA. The others are left with the scraps, or they have to beg, borrow or steal where they can. There is little knowledge of how to design, implement or analyse opinion polls and focus groups, which are vital for developing a targeted campaign.

The DA has Coetzee; the ANC has built up the capacity internally, having retained US pollster Stan Greenberg on every election from 1994 onwards. The ability to retain someone like Greenberg is what sets the ANC apart. At one point in the 1990s, Greenberg was the retained pollster for the heads of state of Britain (Blair), Germany (Schroeder), the USA (Clinton), South Africa (Mandela) and Israel (Ehud Barak). The other political parties in South Africa, with the exception of the DA, could not afford his airfare, let alone his fees. Instead, a political scientist such as Lawrie Schlemmer will be sought out and persuaded to share his insights. Young people with enthusiasm but precious little experience find themselves doing remarkably high-level jobs.

The UDM is but one example of many. For most of the period between 1999 and 2004, the UDM had to manage in parliament with one person doing four jobs: Hennie Lombard was researcher, speechwriter, strategist and media liaison officer. Eventually, a second researcher and a media spokesperson were hired. Luckily, Lombard is energetic, innovative and very dedicated.

But, even so, there is only so much one man can do. MPs have to fill the gaps; hence, it is common for an MP also to be in charge of media relations or research. A leader such as Bantu Holomisa of the UDM lacks the support staff to turn ideas into operational practice. The Independent Democrats (ID), launched and led with great flair by the charismatic Patricia de Lille, faced similar challenges in the run-up to the 2004 elections, as they contended with difficult choices on strategy and focus.

As an example of how smaller parties have to innovate and how individuals can rise from nowhere to be in positions of influence, take Brent Meersman. An experienced theatre manager who has worked with Pieter-Dirk Uys, Meersman volunteered to work with the ID because he wanted a break from his usual routine, admired De Lille and wanted to see if the organizational skills, honed over his years in the theatre, could be usefully applied to politics. They could. With six months to go before Election Day, De Lille took a gamble and appointed him her campaign manager.

Meersman reflects now: 'I suppose I wanted an adventure. Well, I certainly got one; it was a roller-coaster ride! But we achieved what we wanted in terms of getting the brand out there and running a campaign with integrity.'

With not much more than R500 000 to play with, Meersman had to be innovative, and employed some tricks from his previous life.

'We had to make a lot of things up as we went along, and on a very limited budget.'

He took out adverts in the classified sections, for example under Births:

'We are pleased to announce the arrival of a new force in South African politics – Patricia de Lille's Independent Democrats!' In a generally dull and unimaginative campaign, Meersman injected some creativity: De Lille arrived for one media event astride the motorcycle of Lennit Max, the ID's candidate for premier of the Western Cape. At their main election rally in the Good Hope Centre in Cape Town, Meersman hired a wheelchair dance troup. His organizational zeal became central to the party's operations for a time, before Meersman ended his escapade into party politics and returned to the *other* world of theatre.

Something similar happened in 2006. After another two press officers in as many years, an eccentric writer, Steven Otter, turned up on the ID doorstep, having just spent a year writing a book on living – as a white person – in a shack in Khayelitsha, and ended up as its media officer. At the same time, a former NNP councillor from KwaZulu-Natal, named Haniff Hoosein, came for a meeting with the leadership in Cape Town and, according to an insider, 'made a couple of critical comments, to which De Lille said, "fine, stay and run the campaign then".' This entirely ad hoc, haphazard way of recruiting key staff sums up the great problems facing the smaller parties as they try to build organizational capacity.

Meanwhile, a bright young environmentalist, Lance Greyling, began as head of De Lille's office at the launch of the ID in July 2003, but became more influential as the campaign unfolded in terms of developing policy ideas. He found himself at number four on their candidates' list, and is now an MP in the National Assembly. It seems clear that power in the ID will continue to pivot around De Lille. Those who are close to her will have influence; those who are not will remain out of the loop.

At her best, De Lille is a compelling and persuasive, as well as charismatic, political personality. As Helen Zille fought desperately to put together a viable majority coalition in Cape Town after the 2006 municipal elections, it was not expected that the IDs would side with the ANC. Indeed, they had told the electorate as much during the campaign. Yet, on Tuesday 14 March, two weeks after the election and the night before the crucial council vote that would determine whether or not Zille had succeeded, De Lille called together her party caucus. Eyes afire, she was at her most passionate; despite rumours in the preceding days, few of the assembled inner ID core believed that the party would side with the ANC. But De Lille was clear in her mind:

the right thing to do was to vote against the DA coalition – to vote for transformation, not against it.

It was a powerful argument, though it went totally against the promise made during the campaign, that if the council was 'hung', the ID would not vote to allow ANC Mayor Nomaindia Mfeketo to hold on to power. It was a particularly rousing performance; few of her colleagues could resist De Lille's rhetoric. Only one, Greyling – ironically, one of the party's leading proponents of a more explicit social democratic ideological positioning – voted against the decision to ally with the ANC. As De Lille spoke, a colleague turned to Greyling and whispered, 'This deal was done a long time ago.'

The story is illustrative of De Lille's complex and, at times, ambiguous relationship with the ANC. De Lille is an intuitive leader, who relies on her gut instincts more than anything else. At times she is a thorn in the ANC's side, raising awkward allegations of corruption, such as in the arms deal. At others, there is an inevitable synergy of attitudes – De Lille, as much as any MP I have ever seen, has an innate ability to decipher every political issue in terms of what it means for the poorest members of society. So, naturally, she often finds common cause with the ANC in parliament.

As I noted earlier, every political leader has a *handlanger*. Like a toddler with a security blanket, the political *handlanger* is a necessary sop and sponge for all the tension that goes with the job. And there is nothing either disreputable or degrading about the role. Politics can be spiteful and demanding; the *handlanger* is the trusted confidant, the one person whom the leader can sound out, seek counsel from and trust.

The *handlanger* has the power of access – much like the special advisor to a minister described in Chapter 3 – but no particular importance: they are entirely reliant on the leader for their share of power; without the leader they are nothing. De Lille's *handlanger* is Avril Harding, a Cape Town businessman who, for the past few years, has worked with De Lille as her special advisor in parliament, and is now national secretary for the ID and chief whip in the new parliamentary party.

Like De Lille, Harding was a PAC activist before. He will have to learn the parliamentary ropes fast if De Lille's new party is to prove anything more than the latest flash in the party political pan. From a standing start as a brand new party launched less than a year before polling day, and wisely choosing to run an essentially uni-dimensional campaign based on De Lille's reputation and media-darling appeal, the party did reasonably well to muster 250 000-plus votes. The media and many analysts said it was a 'good result', even though it represented less than 2 per cent of the vote – less than half the 5 per cent target De Lille had hoped for.

Such is the reality of opposition politics in South Africa. As the ANC increased its percentage of the vote to almost 70 per cent, so the opposition further weakened. Proclaiming 1.8 per cent as a 'good result' could be seen as clutching at straws.

Behind the problem of lack of expertise and human capacity is the problem of funding. Politics in South Africa is expensive, due to a complex electoral market, with diversification of urban and rural, and many different languages, in a geographically large country. Pursuant to Section 236 of the Constitution, there is a public funding scheme, whereby around R80 million of taxpayers' money is distributed to those parties represented in parliament on the basis of a 90:10 formula – 90 per cent according to their proportions in parliament (which, increasingly, benefits the ANC, who has the lion's share) and 10 per cent equally among all the parties. The ANC and the DA are recipients of large amounts in corporate donations – though the precise identity of the donors and the amounts remain a secret. But it is clear from the estimates compiled by Idasa, which show the gap between the amounts received from public funding and probable election expenditure, that all the parties are very reliant on corporate donations.

Raising donations, however, is an immense challenge for the smaller parties. Rather than give cash, companies will often provide support in kind. In the run-up to the 2004 elections, for example, a Johannesburg publishing house gave the ID a night's free use of its printing press to print campaign posters. In the 2006 municipal elections, the ID was so short of cash that individual MPs were all but required to make personal donations of up to R100 000 to cover the R1.8-million campaign expenses debt. De Lille herself contributed R300 000. All of this is unacceptable. The funding regime for multiparty democracy in South Africa is in urgent need of reform.

Strange bedfellows

Inkatha is a particularly interesting party in South African politics, mainly because of its peculiarity. It does not conform to many political rules, and in attempting to categorize it, is about as slippery as a seal in a rainstorm. When you examine a picture of the parliamentary caucus, it is hard to detect what links all of the members, such is its eclectic diversity. It is certainly not linked by ideology, although the party has always had free-market economics at its centre, as well as profound interest in traditional leadership and federalism (with a distinct nod of the head towards Zulu nationalism).

Following its disappointing showing in the April 2004 poll, when its vote dropped from 8.58 per cent in 1999 to 6.97 per cent, the IFP lost power in its heartland of KwaZulu-Natal, and its omnipotent leader, Mangosuthu Buthelezi, lost his place in the national cabinet. Mbeki cheekily offered seats to two of his colleagues, Musa Zondi and Vincent Ngema, who were ordered by Buthelezi not to accept. Relations with the ANC were described as being at an all-time low, but the implications of this were not, at the time of writing, clear or easy to predict. Deprived of power and direct influence in both the national and provincial governments, Inkatha's future appears gloomy. In the 2006 municipal elections, it lost control of twenty authorities in KwaZulu-Natal and, despite continuing to control marginally more authorities than the ANC, there is no hiding the fact that the IFP is steadily losing its grip on its political heartland.

Inkatha is not a normal political party, because to all intents and purposes it exists as a support vehicle for Buthelezi. He once said: 'I am the tree under which you shelter.' Each and every senior member draws his or, very occasionally, her strength from the relationship with Buthelezi, who is masterful at maintaining multiple relations. According to one IFP MP, Buthelezi is forever writing notes to his colleagues. Virtually everything starts and ends with him. It is a key part of his strategy for political survival. Like a good rose garden, political power has to be maintained. In the case of the IFP, divide and rule is its leader's principal method.

Hence, the IFP is overly dependent on its leader for its strength. While Buthelezi has a strong constitution, born in 1928 he is now in his late seventies, and his energy is waning. Beyond Buthelezi, there is no clarity about what the party stands for. At the height of his powers, it was relatively easy to discern a clear preference for a free-market economy, combined with a social conservatism and a predilection for a federal system of governance, which would serve the notion of a Zulu nation-state. But, as former IFP stalwart MP Gavin Woods was to find, any suggestion that the party's public identity was in decline alongside that of its leader would be met with denial and defiance.

Woods had become well known for his dedicated and principled chairmanship of the standing committee on public accounts (SCOPA) during the height of the arms deal furore (see Chapter 4). In his November 2004 internal paper, 'The IFP – Crisis of Identity and of Public Support', Woods argued that 'strong leadership-driven parties will often fail if such parties' identity lack moral and policy substance'. In the September 2005 floor-crossing window, Woods left the IFP to help set up the National Democratic Convention (NADECO), which duly won a modest twenty-five council seats in the 2006 local government elections.

Jonathan Oates, a communications expert from the UK Liberal Party, who has since returned to Britain, fondly recalls his first meeting with Buthelezi. On the day he arrived in South Africa, he was told to make his way immediately to a national council meeting in Ulundi. He arrived halfway through the morning session, and was briefly introduced to Buthelezi, who was sitting in the row in front of him.

A Mr Tang, a South African businessman who was involved with the IFP, was making a presentation on the electoral strategy that he thought the IFP should adopt in the forthcoming 1999 elections. The Taiwanese community in KwaZulu-Natal, specifically in Ladysmith and Newcastle, where they form a considerable industrial class, has financially supported the IFP since their days as a Bantustan organization.

Halfway through Tang's presentation, plainly impatient and irritated by what he was hearing, Buthelezi turned to Oates and said, 'Mr Oates, when he finishes, I would like you to present a critique of his presentation.'

Oates had been in South Africa for just thirty-six hours, but he knew one thing: 'Saying no was not an option when responding to a request from Buthelezi.' To his credit, Oates got through it, and over the next two years worked with people such as the Reverend Musa Zondi to modernize the party's ability to communicate and make the most of its media relations. While it could still do far more to articulate its positions on many issues, the IFP's presence in the media now extends beyond its leader.

Zondi represents the modern wing of the party. A thoughtful and rather gentle man, he has commanded the respect of the ANC as Inkatha's principal negotiator in recent years. The two parties operate an ad hoc, three-by-three approach to resolving their tangles. Three senior members of each party will get together to thrash out the differences, and Zondi has tended to head the IFP trio.

For some in the IFP he is too congenial in his relations with the ANC, and also not strong enough. According to a person who is close to the leader, Zondi is 'intelligent and articulate, but is he strong enough? In Inkatha you need to have balls. Buthelezi makes his balls felt.'

Zondi himself is always careful to downplay any talk of him being Buthelezi's successor. Such talk is the kiss of death.

Otherwise, the only person with power in Inkatha is its national organizer, Albert Mncwango, who derives his power from his lineage. He is said to be an Nduma of the Zulu clan of which King Goodwill Zwelethini is the head, though on closer inquiry it turns out that 'Nduma' is more of a nickname, which arose from an internal IFP joke some years back. Zwelethini is generally regarded as weak; Mncwango makes up for it. To describe him as commander-in-chief of the Zulu nation, which has well-marshalled structures and a hierarchy, as some do, may be something of an overstatement; to another IFP insider he 'is influential in areas where King Zwelethini resides, but this is not due to any particular lineage'. Someone who knows IFP politics well describes him as a 'conservative radical from the Zulu rural heartland'.

As an MP, Mncwango causes a lot of trouble and has an ambiguous relationship with the IFP's veteran chief whip, Koos van der Merwe, because, unlike the other MPs, he has the power to resist Van der Merwe's varied techniques at making the MPs beholden to him, including lending them money. The IFP stood by Mncwango when, in 2004, he was convicted for raping his then-girlfriend at gunpoint in September 2000 and sentenced to ten years' imprisonment. Senior figures such as Musa Zondi publicly expressed their belief in his innocence and – shades of Jacob Zuma – blamed his political opponents for manipulating the criminal justice system. Mncwango's conviction was overturned on appeal in mid-2005, allowing him to resume his political career.

The identity of Buthelezi's *handlanger* is as curious as the party itself, but in the crazy world of Inkatha, politics has its own weird logic. Because of the need to balance competing forces against each other in order to neuter them, Buthelezi needs to keep his own immediate advisors out of the political equation; they need to be utterly loyal and devoted to him, which Mario Ambrosini is.

I met with Ambrosini in his large office in 120 Plein Street, the ugly tower block that houses government ministers and their staff when parliament is sitting. At the time of our meeting, Ambrosini was controversially employed as special advisor, as he was for the whole period during which Buthelezi was minister of home affairs. Thus, he enjoyed a double influence.

Ambrosini is a lawyer, and whatever one can say about his hubris or eccentricity, he is clever. I once described him in a column as 'a wannabe constitutional lawyer'. He had the deputy director-general of home affairs write a letter in response, setting out his legal credentials. Now that we are on speaking terms, he told me how he first got involved with Buthelezi. Ambrosini, who is Italian but with an American passport, had acquired the position of protégé of an older American constitutional law expert, named Blaustein.

'I wrote to him,' recalls Ambrosini, 'and he took me on board; we were a perfect match.' Blaustein then introduced him to Buthelezi.

Ambrosini may be suitably quixotic for Inkatha, but he does conform to the *handlanger* rule: he draws his power and influence solely from his boss. Without Buthelezi, he is nothing. Therefore, to double-cross his leader would be entirely self-defeating. He would have no other home to go to – at least not within Inkatha. At the time of writing, the future of Ambrosini, much like the future of Inkatha, is clouded with uncertainty. Albert Mncwango is just as clever as Ambrosini, and has competed for power with him for years. '[Mncwango] uses Mario,' says one insider, 'and Mario thinks he uses [Mncwango].'

Marginal(ized) voices

Given the circumstances in which most of the opposition parties find themselves operating, it is hard to say that they exert much influence in South Africa. Certainly they exert less power than in political systems where rotations of power tend to occur. But South Africa's electoral system of 'pure' proportional representation, which serves to limit the power of the backbench MP, does ensure that every vote counts. Therefore smaller parties are represented; they have a voice in parliament, and with a free press eager to report on opposition activity, it means they are not irrelevant.

However, as I note in the chapter on civil society, the ANC tends to take greater heed of serious-minded and well-presented policy advocacy from the activist NGO sector than of opposition parties. Yet they cannot be totally ignored. Indeed, both the IFP and the NNP have been able to exert some influence simply by being needed as coalition partners in recent years. The demise of the IFP–ANC relationship has eliminated some of that. Having wriggled out of the 'cobraesque' tangle with the DP, the NNP chose to die a gentler death within the warm but suffocating embrace of the ANC.

In very small ways, and not through any innate power of its own, AZAPO exerts some influence by virtue of its presence at the cabinet table in the form of Mosibudi Mangena, now the minister for science and technology. He is their only MP in parliament.

The opposition is fortunate that the ANC had agreed not to have a threshold for representation. In many proportional representation systems, parties have to beat a 5 per cent threshold before their representation kicks in. In fact, according to Kader Asmal, the ANC had insisted on no threshold as part of its outlook on inclusivity and national reconciliation. If the threshold rule applied to South Africa, there would be just three parties in parliament: the ANC, the DA and the IFP (as the table on page 173 shows, the biggest parties have commanded over 90 per cent of the share of the vote in each of the three elections since 1994). The smaller ones would not exist. That they are represented in parliament gives them a platform to build upon.

The ID, for example, may be encouraged by the fact that they have seven seats in the National Assembly, exactly the same number as the DP had in the 1994–99 parliament. As noted above, the DP was able to make a disproportionate amount of noise – something that De Lille's media appeal will also promote. The ID will also note the fact that, although the DA created a springboard, all it has served to do since is to propel the party hard into the glass ceiling that constrains the power of the opposition.

The ANC now dominates the middle ground of South African politics, and a large amount of ground either side of it, especially to the left. There is precious little ideological room to manoeuvre. The DA has moved to the empty space to the right of the ANC, but it does not appear to be rooted in especially fertile ground for growth. Hence, I agree with the analysis of up-and-coming analyst Jonathan Faull of Idasa, in an edition of *ePolitics* in 2005:

> The power matrix of dominant party rule deals opposition parties a tricky strategic hand: with the ANC dominating the centre, centre-right and centre-left, and working the 'talk left, act right' rhetorical slight-of-hand with impunity, the ability of opposition parties to define themselves as distinctly different from the ruling party is increasingly difficult. Consequently parties outside of the ruling party nexus are forced to take up positions to the extreme left or right of the dominant party to define their difference and appeal to voters. At the same time the ascendance of the ruling party has to become the focus of the opposition, and decisions have to be made as to whether 'constructive engagement' with the ruling party will extract political influence from the inside through a discourse of dialogue and consensus, or whether the interests of opposition constituents and the fortunes of the party are better served by 'facing up' to the dominant party from without, while trying to encourage influence on policy through an assertion of difference as an 'alternative government'. The NNP has explicitly thrown in their lot with the ANC; AZAPO and the UDM appear to be walking a bit of a tightrope between engaging the ANC through the structures of government, and criticising from the outside; while the DA wholeheartedly defines itself as a critical opposition, across the house and in all legislatures. The IFP is dabbling in both streams, while the ID's political strategy remains open to interpretation. On the part of the ANC, disunity among opposition parties is obviously a political boon, moreover cooperative governance is in line with the ANC's policy of working with 'like-minded parties' in the realisation of the 'transformation' of South African society; the inclusion of opposition parties within the executive is also characteristic of the emerging tradition of cooperative and consensus-seeking governance initially enforced through the provisions of the interim constitution in the form of the then-Government of National Unity.[1]

The real influence from the left comes from within the tripartite alliance. This is the opposition that matters and the challenge that is sporadically emerging, but with arguably increasing venom from social movements (see Chapter 10).

So, in conclusion, as far as the power matrix is concerned, the opposition parties are even less influential than they are important. In a competitive multiparty democracy, this should not be so. But, given the monopoly of credibility and legitimacy that the ANC still enjoys as the 'party of liberation', it may simply be a matter of waiting for that effect to slowly wear off.

But the ANC promises to be more adept at sustaining this image than other liberation movements one could name. It could be a very long wait. This is the first of three factors that will need to change to alter the party-political balance of forces. The second is that, until the one party with any serious capacity – the DA – changes both its leader and its strategy, it will be unable to exert any serious influence on politics in South Africa. Last, for as long as the other opposition parties survive on a range of advisors and technicians that can best be described as eclectic, nothing will change. Until serious strategic capacity is built into the other opposition parties to enable them to compete with the ANC for the votes of 'middle' South Africa – offering new ideas and an alternative vision for government – their influence and power will be strictly limited.

8

Spin Doctors and the Media

More Spinned Against than Spinning?

A great spin doctor will let you realize that you have been 'spun' only aeons afterwards. Like morphine taking over your senses, you slowly become aware that you've been duped or distracted from the scent. When it's skilfully done, it can even be quite pleasant.

Bheki Khumalo was the president's spin doctor from 1999 to 2005. While I was writing Chapter 1, on the presidency, I was sidetracked into re-reading several of the letters Mbeki posts online in his weekly 'Letter from the President'. Who writes these letters, I wondered yet again. Does Mbeki really write all of them? I phoned Khumalo: 'Bheki, a simple question. Who writes the president's weekly online letter?'

'He does,' Bheki said. 'Every single word of every single one.'

'Are you serious?' I asked, incredulous. 'Does he really?'

Like any high-quality spin doctor, Khumalo immediately sensed that, although I had asked a question that could be answered with a simple yes or no, I needed more. He provided the 'colour' without further prompting.

'He writes [the letters] by himself, usually at his house, late at night, maybe between one and two in the morning on Wednesday nights. Earlier, he will have his staff there looking things up for him on the Internet. You know, the cooks and those sorts of staff. There's a lot of multiskilling going on there!'

It's a brilliant story, because Bheki has conjured up a wonderful and irresistible picture in my mind. The president at home, slaving over his computer late at night, the loyal domestic staff happy to turn their hands to something else to be useful to their hard-working, thoughtful boss.

As an afterthought, and with this chapter in mind, I ask Khumalo: 'Bheki, what's your best bit of spin-doctoring recently? I need a story for my chapter on the media.' The truthful answer would be, 'About sixty seconds ago with you, you idiot!' But Khumalo, no doubt chuckling quietly to himself, requests time to think it over, and instead launches into a short monologue about how Mbeki hates spin and always rejects any ideas for clever media tricks. As *Mail & Guardian* editor Ferial Haffajee says, Khumalo is 'very good at making Thabo Mbeki more "human"'.

In 2000, I wrote a long piece for the South African edition of *GQ* magazine about spin doctors, profiling one of South Africa's most able examples, my former colleague at Idasa, Sipho Ngwema, who for several years did a superb job for Bulelani Ngcuka while he was head of the Scorpions. Headlined 'Trust Me, I'm a Spin Doctor', the piece included pen portraits of 'the new South African spin doctors'. The Khumalo pen portrait reads: 'Richly praised by insiders, Khumalo is now benefiting from having the "right product" to sell after some difficult years trying to sell the unsellable – Kader Asmal's predecessor as minister for education, Professor Sibusiso Bengu.' As one of his parliamentary colleagues told me, 'Kader loves to be centre stage and loves to be in the media.'

Of the others I wrote about in the piece, Parks Mankahlana, who was Mandela's director of communications, died of an AIDS-related illness soon after. He had remained in the post after Mbeki became president, but was on sick leave a great deal. The *GQ* piece was published with photos of Mankahlana, veteran political journalist Pippa Green, then deputy editor of the *Financial Mail*, and me having dinner at a Cape Town restaurant. When I asked Mankahlana if he would be down in Cape Town at any point in the near future, he said, 'Invite me for dinner and I will come down specially. I am fond of Cape Town.'

It was poignant; clearly he wanted a chance to say goodbye to the city. Although he had once been caught out lying for Mandela, misleading the media about the time and place of Mandela's wedding, he was still highly respected.

That was one occasion when the spin doctor became the story. Ryan Coetzee, whose influence in the Democratic Alliance I consider in Chapter 7, is now a member of parliament for the DA. Spin doctors rarely succeed in combining public office with being a spin doctor, as it is too easy to break one of the golden rules of spin-doctoring: don't *be* the story (or even part of it). Although I did not mention them in the *GQ* piece, the other two government spin doctors who are well thought of by the press are Thabo Masebe, who is Mbhazima Shilowa's spokesman as premier of Gauteng, and Logan Wort, Trevor Manuel's spokesman.

Until a fallout with Blade Nzimande prompted his departure to work for the Cape Town–based development NGO, the Programme for Land and Agrarian Studies (PLAAS), at the University of the Western Cape, in mid-2005, the SACP had one of the best spin doctors in the business, Mazibuko Jara. His leaving is a pity, because it is rare to find the left so clearly and meticulously represented by a spokesman. In his public statements on behalf of the party, Jara invariably found a balance between rigorous independence and nuanced criticism of the ANC.

Dr Murphy Morobe fills the crucial position of director of communications in the presidency. As I noted earlier, the position lay unfilled for a number of years for reasons that are far from clear, but which appear to be partly due to the failure of the director-general at the presidency, Dr Frank Chikane, to find a suitable candidate, and partly because Khumalo's success in the role obviated the need to move faster. Morobe is a gentleman in every sense of the word; like the man he has to work with closely – Joel Netshitenzhe, head of government communications (GCIS) – Morobe seems almost too nice for the hard end of politics and the smoke and mirrors of spin-doctoring. Perhaps more importantly, there must be a question mark over whether he will be able to handle his principal, Thabo Mbeki, with the robustness required. Clearly, given that Mr Mbeki is president, this is no easy task, as Khumalo and Netshitenzhe found in the case of Mbeki's controversial public stance on HIV/AIDS.

Trust me, I'm a spin doctor

I had ended the *GQ* piece with a quote from Tony Heard, the former *Cape Times* editor who had 'spun' for Asmal when he had been minister of water affairs in Mandela's cabinet, and who had, in media coverage terms, turned water into wine. Heard, who is now special advisor to Essop Pahad, minister in the presidency, told me: 'You can't surf if there's no wave.' Trust a spin doctor to deliver such a neat soundbite. And this, indeed, was the problem that faced Bheki Khumalo when he arrived in the presidency in 1999. In fact, it was a double-jointed, interlocking problem: Khumalo's principal – as spin doctors refer to their boss, in this case the president – was in the middle of a major crisis relating to HIV and AIDS and his apparent refutation of the link between the two. Part of the problem was that, in this case, the principal, Mbeki, eschews spin. Ironically, given that his ideological detractors regard him as a disciple of the watered-down 'Third Way' version of social democracy – all spin and no substance – and a companion therefore to Tony Blair, Mbeki's approach to media relations and presentation generally could hardly be more different from New Labour's obsession with the media.

Khumalo, aged thirty-three when he joined the president's office, was young and relatively junior for his new job. He was also one of those people who tend to look a little more youthful than they are. However, he was experienced in his profession: from the mid-1980s he had been the senior media officer for the UDF in the Transvaal. And, prior to moving to the presidency, had been Kader Asmal's spokesperson at water affairs.

Nonetheless, naturally, the new position represented a major challenge; his friends told him he was crazy to take it on. Luckily, he had people such as Tony Heard around whom he could consult and, even more importantly, Joel Netshitenzhe's weight to support him in his attempts to guide the president into slowly taking a different approach to the HIV/AIDS issue.

Mbeki and Netshitenzhe share more than one characteristic. Ironically, given his job, Netshitenzhe is not much fonder of spin than Mbeki. But Netshitenzhe is a strategist, and he knew that Mbeki's stubborn insistence on his essentially dissident approach to the HIV theory was costing the government a lot in terms of credibility, especially abroad, and that things had to change.

Khumalo now regards the outcome of this process as a 'defining moment' of Mbeki's first term as president. Today Khumalo looks back from his capacious new Midrand office as executive director of corporate affairs at Siemens with the equanimity that the passage of time provides: 'Wherever we went, for five and a half years, people would hound us about the president's views on HIV/AIDS. The media would always put him on the spot. Like the infamous occasion at the Press Club in Washington, DC. It was always like going into a lion's den. We had to try to shift it away from the media's terrain onto ours. This became the biggest thing we had to work on: how do we emphasize the government line – that South Africa has the biggest and most comprehensive anti-HIV programme in the world!'

As another member of the president's team put it later: 'The challenge for us was to persuade the chief: "Mr President, it's a strong message. Please forget about your personal view. Don't let the media provoke you."'

Politely, humbly, Netshitenzhe and Khumalo chipped away at Mbeki: please, Mr President, stay away from the science. In the end, they prevailed; the president disengaged from the debate. The process ended with the famous cabinet statement of 17 April 2002, drafted with his usual care by Netshitenzhe. There has not been a blip on this issue for some time, not since the *Time* magazine interview in September 2000, when Mbeki was quoted as saying, 'I do not know anyone who has died of AIDS.'

Heard explains that Mbeki did not have any close friends who had died of an AIDS-related illness, and so he was just being literal in his response. But it was a crass thing to say. As with Zimbabwe, as discussed in Chapter 1, so it is with HIV/AIDS: there is a resolute determination not to allow a media clamour to drive his policy-making. Or, in Heard's words, part of the issue is Mbeki's 'utter determination not to be knocked off course from the objective, which is a rollout that will work *in practice*'.

How sad, however, how unfortunate, that the president of the country with one of the highest rates of HIV infection in the world is now effectively muzzled from speaking about the subject. This is not to blame Netshitenzhe or Khumalo. On the contrary: they did what they had to do. Rather, how regrettable that this is a president who, like King Lear, is apparently blind to the harm that his personal obsession with the issue is doing to his reputation, to his government's health policy and to the patient community. With great regret, I am forced to conclude that there is no way back now: Mbeki's legacy, for all his other immense achievements, will always be seriously blighted by his quixotic preoccupation with the linkage between HIV and AIDS – a failure of communication and a failure of politics.

Both Morobe and Heard nowadays emphasize the new presidential line – at least the message that is communicated by them, if not their principals: comprehensive treatment rollout; most extensive implementation programme in Africa; R12 billion over the next three years; 90 per cent awareness; need for condom use.

Murphy Morobe is more of an incile than an exile. He was a leading light in the UDF, and famously escaped from police custody with Valli Moosa and Vusi Khanyile after months in detention, to seek political asylum in the US embassy (an extremely embarrassing event for the apartheid government). Another interesting fact about Morobe is that he holds a master's degree in public administration from the Woodrow Wilson Public Policy Institute at Princeton University, making him, on paper, one of the most highly qualified public servants in the country.

Prior to coming to the presidency, Morobe headed the Financial and Fiscal Commission (FFC), a body established by Section 220 of the Constitution to help navigate the balance between national and provincial budget-making, in itself therefore an important institution.

Given Morobe's education and his history as an activist in the UDF, 'in some instances', he says, he 'was described as "sidelined"'. He, and not I, brings this up in the interview. So perhaps it is a subject he feels the need to address because, on the contrary, the FFC position put him 'at the very heart of the reconstruction of the new institutional landscape, where I had access to all the players'. Part of his office-holding in the UDF was as 'publicity secretary', appealing to a broad community, something that Morobe emphasized would be at the centre of his role in the presidency when I interviewed him shortly after he took up the position in 2004. 'My understanding,' said Morobe, 'is that one of the reasons it is said that the president is "out of touch" is that there is so much coverage of his international engagements. But, for each international engagement, there are five to ten times the number of local engagements – with working groups, church groups, and so on.'

The edict that 'the president must be out of touch no more' had come from the national working committee of the ANC; momentum for a new approach – a 'more strategic view of the role of *imbizos*', in Morobe's words – grew with the success of the April 2004 general election campaign, in which Mbeki spent a lot of time visiting local communities. Morobe indicated that he wanted to see more of this: 'We need to create the right settings.'

In developing an appropriate media strategy, Morobe emphasizes the fact that you 'have to understand the style of the principal. There is no point in trying to make him something that he is not. Ordinary people appreciate a person who is genuine, not "spin-doctored". The president is a person with strong views and is not going to accept a plan that tries to present him as something that he is not. The media strategy has to allow for that.'

In fact, argues Morobe, contrary to the media-encouraged perception, Mbeki was neither the 'aloof' figure during the campaign nor in the *imbizos* subsequently organized by the presidential public participation unit.

Given his talents, there can be little doubt that Morobe will continue to play a very influential role in South Africa for the foreseeable future – whether it is in his current position or, perhaps more likely, elsewhere in government in the next administration.

Opposition spin

It is common practice for political parties to lobby the media by stealth, and to seek to influence the public agenda. The DA has far more experience and expertise than the other minority parties. DA researchers are often required to write bogus letters to the newspapers supporting this position or that, or attacking the government. This is regular practice, and a number of fictional people, for a number of parties, are regular contributors to the letters pages of newspapers. One NNP spin doctor – Rob Spaull, who moved with Marthinus van Schalkwyk to be his director of media at the department of environmental affairs and tourism – was on at least one occasion bold enough to use the pseudonym Dr R Tate (as in 'rotate'; as in 'spin doctor').

A good example of this stealth is the DA's response to one of Ronald Suresh Roberts's (a former advisor to Kader Asmal) regular attacks on 'Lance Corporal' Tony Leon (as Roberts likes to call him). Roberts had dug up some of Leon's writing when he served a military rag as a conscript in the SADF. Ryan Coetzee went ballistic and insisted that all the DA researchers draft letters to the editor on the matter, attacking Roberts. DA researcher James Myburgh was tasked with writing the 'official response', which appeared as a 'right to reply' Op-Ed under the name of DA MP Nick Clelland-Stokes. The following week, four letters appeared from 'members of the public' as lead letters in the letters pages of the *Financial Mail*, along with Myburgh/Clelland-Stokes's Op-Ed. The depth and extent of the response from 'the public' led the editor to address the issue in her weekly editorial column – all in all, a good harvest for the DA's spin machine!

The editors

How influential is the media with government? For a while Mbeki was so disgruntled with the press coverage he received in the South African press, he stopped reading the local papers. But he has taken them up again now. *Business Day* is the most influential daily newspaper in the country, as its readership cuts across elites in both the political and corporate spheres, and because its economics is so close to that of the president and his minister of finance (a theme I return to below). Staffers in the president's policy unit will carefully read opinion pieces written by policy analysts from 'reputable institutes such as the Human Sciences Research Council (HSRC) and Idasa' (according to one senior manager there), on the grounds that it may shape public opinion around a particular issue. The most influential newspapers for him are *Business Day*, the *Financial Mail* and the *Mail & Guardian*.

Like Mbeki, who has the *Financial Times* delivered to his home and regards it as 'the best newspaper in the world', Goolam Aboobaker, operational head of the presidential policy unit, reads *The Economist* whenever he can. The *Sunday Times*'s sheer readership numbers mean that it is influential, and its editor, Mondli Makhanya, is highly regarded in the presidency. So is his successor at the *Mail & Guardian*, Ferial Haffajee. Makhanya had managed to retrieve the reputation of the paper after a period under the editorship of Phillip van Niekerk and Howard Barrell, when its perceived obsession with sensational anti-government stories and, in the latter's case, vitriolic attacks on Mbeki, led to the government boycotting the paper from an advertising perspective.

As one of his peers says, 'Makhanya may not be the greatest journalist in the world, but he may turn out to be a great editor.'

The ambitious Haffajee's clear-minded intelligence means that, even though the presidency suspects that, as a possible ANC supporter, she is to the left of the party, she is still respected. *City Press* is the most obviously pro-government newspaper, and its new editor, Mathatha Tsedu, is close to the president, and good friends with Joel Netshitenzhe.

Nonetheless, its political coverage is now better than any other newspaper, with Tsedu devoting more space to it than any other broadsheet or tabloid, and its points of emphasis provide useful insights into the way that the political establishment is viewing a particular issue and the likely balance of forces on any given topic. He also has very steady judgment when under pressure – a vital quality for an editor.

Because they assume that the *Sowetan* is read by their typical voters, its coverage of issues is heeded by the presidency, but as its fortunes have dipped in recent years, so its influence has declined in the face of fierce competition from real tabloids, such as the *Daily Sun*. The *Sowetan*'s former editor, John Dludlu, was 'very tight' with Joel Netshitenzhe, and well respected as a serious-minded journalist. But the *Sowetan*'s owners, Johnnic Communications, decided that his more cerebral approach was unsuited to the market that the *Sowetan* was competing in, and he moved to be head of corporate communications at the massive government parastatal, Transnet. Barney Mthombothi, whom most media insiders put high on their list of respected editors, now edits another Johnnic-owned publication, the weekly finance magazine *Financial Mail*. In many respects, he conforms to the stereotype of the wise-old-owl, seasoned, professional editor. His editorial line is as balanced as it is nuanced, and he is also a former political editor.

With Tsedu, Haffajee, Makhanya and Mthombothi installed at some of the most influential newspapers, South African editorship may be in a healthier position than it has been for some time. None of them are push-overs. All are intellectually strong and independent-minded, prepared to criticize the government and the ANC where necessary, but acutely aware of the nuances and depth of the challenges the party faces, particularly with social transformation.

In contrast, the largest newspaper group, the Independent Newspaper Group, has withered on the vine, as its owner has cut budgets and forced its editors to manage with a minimum number of journalists. Also, its policy of pooling political journalists to write for the group rather than for individual titles has failed to work in practice under the management of first Zubeida Jaffer and then John Battersby. The latest head of political reporting is the immensely capable Angela Quintal, who has been reporting on politics and parliament since the early 1990s and is in my view one of the very best, if not the best, political journalists in the country, and it will be interesting to see if she can succeed where they have failed.

Quintal says that one of the constraints on powerful political journalism is the inexperience of most political editors. At a minimum, she argues, a political editor should have 'covered parliament, the courts at some point in their career, and in addition to having several years of political reporting under their belt, should also be conversant in issues of political economy'.

Few of the current batch of political editors match this criteria. For example, the latest political editor of the *Mail & Guardian*, Rapule Tabane, is under thirty, and Karima Brown at *Business Day* is only in her early thirties (although she was a very accomplished executive producer of SAfm's influential morning news programme, *AM Live*, for several years). Although it continues to break groundbreaking political stories, particularly concerning corruption, for a weekly the *Mail & Guardian*'s political team needs to be much stronger. Brown's political coverage is courageous and often passionate – but although strong views are a key part of a good political editor's make-up, prudent exercise of judgment is no less essential on finely balanced, breaking political stories. Nonetheless, there is much to admire about her Op-Ed pieces, especially on public ethics and political corruption.

The gallery

Sadly, good political reporters are few and far between. Some, like Haffajee, have moved swiftly upstairs into what is known within the South African media as 'mahogany row' (a reference to the polished wooden doors of management offices). *City Press*'s Mpumelelo Mkhabela is the most talented political reporter in parliament. Brendan Boyle, now with the *Sunday Times*, after many years with Reuters, is a political journalist of the old school – meticulous about detail and sourcing – along with other veterans such as Wyndham Hartley of *Business Day*. Similarly, Carol Paton at the *Financial Mail* combines strong technique with a good range of sources to produce reliable and consistent coverage of complex political stories. Willem Jordaan of *Die Burger* (of the Naspers Group) is probably the best of the Afrikaans political reporters.

Certainly after the tensions of the late 1990s, the relationship between the print media and the government, and Mbeki in particular, has stabilized. There were justified frustrations on both sides. Mbeki and his people can be terribly secretive; Haffajee maintains that, since Mbeki became president, people have become much more cautious about speaking on the record, especially on intra-party issues: 'Things have changed; people don't talk so easily,' Haffajee says. 'So many of the stories that my political journalists write are full of unnamed sources, which is a nightmare for me as editor.'

She regards this attitude as self-defeating.

From the government perspective, they rightly complain about the 'juniorization' of the newsrooms and the failure to report accurately. Some of the personal criticism of Mbeki was way over the top. Howard Barrell ran a full-page editorial early in his editorship of the *Mail & Guardian*. Under the banner headline: 'Is this man fit to rule?' he compared Mbeki to Stalin, and later approved a story about Mbeki being physically short, 'like Napoleon', and therefore prone to 'short-man syndrome'. This was madness: Stalin was a mass murderer. I thought the 'short-man story' was an April Fool's joke, but it wasn't. Mbeki was entitled to be incensed; who would not have been?

'Although [the electronic media] often gets a raw deal,' according to Haffajee, 'the SABC is enormously influential, and not just because of its size. They also have a fine team in place ... now.'

Haffajee offered this view at a time when Pippa Green was still head of radio news, controlling a large team and making decisions about the news priorities for news programmes across the country. Green is one of the most astute and well-connected journalists in the country, as Haffajee points out: 'Green put a mega-amount of information out there. It may not be sexy, but it is influence of a different kind. Lots of policy stuff, which she gets from government.'

Green is part of the Establishment. Her husband, Alan Hirsch, is economics specialist in the president's policy unit, and Green has impeccable contacts in the ANC. For a time in 2000 she was acting communications director for finance minister Trevor Manuel. Vuyo Mvoko, the SABC's former political editor, is a hugely talented journalist with an impeccably independent outlook. He always wears the look of a man under great stress – understaffed, and with pressure from above and below. The SABC has not been a happy place to work for many years, especially in political coverage.

Protecting Mbeki

Neither Green nor Mvoko had, at least at the time of writing (in June 2006), been replaced. The head of radio news, Solly Phetoe, now covers the responsibilities of news editor. Snuki Zikalala is widely held to be one of the most influential figures at the SABC in terms of its political coverage and editorial stance. After a stint as a senior spin doctor in the department of labour, Zikalala rejoined the SABC in April 2004 as managing director of news and current affairs. The question of the independence of the SABC is not an issue I have space to explore here and I reach no judgment on the claims that are frequently made that Zikalala is, in effect, a political commissar determined to ensure that the public broadcaster's political coverage is favourable to the ANC in government.[1] However, in the final stages of the editing of this book, I did encounter an example of editorial decision-making that undermined my own confidence in the SABC's political independence. Independent filmmaker Ben Cashdan and well-known Joburg talk show host Redi Direko had won a commission to produce a biographical documentary on President Mbeki as a part of the SABC's 'unauthorised series' in autumn 2006, which included programmes on Judge Edwin Cameron and Independent Democrats' leader Patricia de Lille. Instead of the single thirty-minute programme that had been planned for each of the other subjects, the SABC decided that Mbeki deserved two. Interviews were conducted with veteran political journalist Allister Sparks and with *City Press* editor Mathatha Tsedu, and several more were lined up with prominent ANC politicians. Joel Netshitenzhe, head of Mbeki's presidential policy unit and the GCIS, was one of those lined up, but he suddenly withdrew from his interview, as did the others.

Netshitenzhe contacted Direko and told her that she was a young woman with a good future and she was risking throwing it all away by producing the programme. Direko was incensed, as well as upset, by this threat. The SABC's response was revealing. It decided to reduce the commission to one programme on the dubious basis that it thought it might come under government pressure after the first programme and be forced to pull the second part. Ironically, in the event, 'Part 1' was pulled just hours before its scheduled slot on SABC3 on 17 May 2006.

In the days that followed, a public spat between the SABC and the two producers ensued. The SABC at first claimed that the film had been pulled for unspecified 'scheduling' reasons. A week later, SABC CEO Dali Mpofu was forced to offer a different view, claiming that it was done on the advice of SABC lawyers, fearing that it was defamatory. Mpofu, who is an advocate, joined the SABC in 2005. Prior to that, he was the executive director for corporate affairs at the Allied Electronics Group (Altron), the technology, multimedia and telecommunications company. Mpofu joined the Altron Group in 2000, where he spearheaded the group's internal BEE charter, Altron Transformation Vision.[2]

I saw the film at various stages during its production. My own legal opinion is that it is not defamatory of Mbeki – far from it; it offers a very balanced account of his life, posing important and interesting questions about his politics and ideology, and allowing the viewer to draw conclusions from the primary source material and from the incisive analysis of Tsedu and Sparks. Tsedu had come to Cashdan's Johannesburg house two nights after the film was scheduled to be aired and, having viewed it, reached the same conclusion as me. The following Sunday, 21 June 2006, his newspaper, *City Press*, splashed the story on its front page – another example of Tsedu's independent judgment.

The anchors

The most influential other electronic journalists are the talk show hosts and news anchors. The most consistent talk show host, and possibly the best overall broadcaster in the country, is Tim Modise, now on 702/Cape Talk. I think of him as an alternative Mandela: a unifying force, a man of integrity, and for racist whites 'an acceptable black'. It is an exhausting, unrelenting role, and he fulfils it with grace and diligence. But he is also brave, taking on all the tough political issues and persistently steering the public discourse in fresh and constructive directions. Another talk show host, Vuyo Mbuli, who replaced Modise on SAfm's morning talk show, was unable to fill Modise's shoes with quite the same level of authority and, in autumn 2006, was replaced with the feistier Xolani Gwala.

The most capable English-speaking news anchors are curiously all called John. John Perlman, who anchors the very influential breakfast show *AM Live* on SAfm, is empathetically open-minded and knowledgeable; John Robbie (on the 702 breakfast show), charismatic and feisty; and John Maytham (on Cape Talk, afternoon drive-time), intelligent and sharp-witted. All have a good grasp of politics, and it is an absolute pleasure to be interviewed live by all three of them, especially Maytham – though his 'reach' on Cape Talk is far smaller than that of SAfm and 702.

Probably the most incisive interviewer, however, is Sally Burdett, now happily restored to the electronic media as a news presenter on e.tv, having 'rested' for a while at *Fairlady* magazine after several years at SAfm, many spent rising in the early hours to host *AM Live* (originally alongside John Maytham).

In 2001, after the bizarre 'plot' allegations around Cyril Ramaphosa, Mathews Phosa and Tokyo Sexwale, the late Steve Tshwete was called to give evidence to the parliamentary committee on safety and security. The chairperson, Mluleki George, gave him a pathetically soft ride, and Tshwete was basically permitted to give an ex–post facto justification for the whole episode, which he had announced during an interview broadcast on television news. A member of the opposition asked him if he had consulted with the president before making the extraordinary statement about the three ANC leaders, and Tshwete replied in the negative. I found this totally unbelievable, and a few minutes after the end of the meeting, said as much in a live interview on SAfm's lunchtime news programme, which Burdett was anchoring. Quick as a flash, she followed up: 'Are you saying that Minister Tshwete lied to parliament?'

It was exactly the right question, and I was exactly where I did not want to be – in a corner. Even though I thought that Tshwete had done exactly that, I did not want to say so on national radio. It was not in Idasa's interests to start accusing senior cabinet ministers of lying, certainly not without having thought through the strategic implications. So, I did what Peter Mandelson trained us to do in the late 1980s with a hostile Tory press in Britain, namely, if you don't like the question, answer another one, which I duly did.

Commentators

Goolam Aboobaker confirms that attention is paid to the media in the presidency. On the subject of commentators, the presidency is frustrated by what a source there describes as a 'dearth of black analysts'. Intriguingly, the source maintains that certain black journalists and commentators who criticize the ANC get promoted quicker, because the media is desperate to have these names on their pages, regardless of the quality of the analysis.

The source points to Justice Malala, editor of the now-defunct *ThisDay*, and Xolela Mangcu, the *Business Day* columnist who appears to court controversy wherever he goes, as examples of this species. Mangcu is a fairly rare breed: a black liberal democratic intellectual. Sipho Seepe, the political scientist, is another, and was reviled for his relentless attacks on Mbeki when he was a columnist on the *Mail & Guardian* under Howard Barrell's editorship.

In contrast, Steven Friedman's thoughtful and careful analysis is respected, as is his successor as head of the Centre for Policy Studies, Chris Landsberg, even though he 'can blow hot and cold' and has a well-earned reputation for 'spreading himself too thinly'. Adam Habib of the HSRC is probably the most incisive left-of-centre commentator, able to balance the need for authoritative, academic research analysis with sharp, accessible commentary.

The latest self-styled 'independent political analyst' is a man called Aubrey Matshiqi, a former spokesperson with the Gauteng government. He crops up everywhere, but after an initial period where his analysis did not inspire great confidence in any quarter, least of all the presidency, he has matured. In international relations, the presidency admires Professor John Stremlau of Wits University, who wrote regularly for *Business Day* before he left South Africa in February 2006 to take up a senior position in the Carter Center, the foundation headed by former US president Jimmy Carter.

My colleague at Idasa, Judith February, now listed in both of the prominent 'little books' – the *Financial Mail's Little Black Book* of influential black people and *Leading Women of South Africa* (published by the *Mail & Guardian* and MTN) – has developed a strong media profile as a political commentator. February is always willing to offer contextualized political analysis and is especially good on television.

Some pressure groups have also begun to realize the importance of the media. At Idasa I have always prioritized the media and instilled into my staff the importance of providing accurate, balanced data and comment. The media needs that, and democratic debate needs expert input. But the media also needs a reliable service, and it seems that there are few commentators or NGOs that can be counted on to be reliable – hence the fact that some appear to attract all the coverage.

The Treatment Action Campaign, which I rate as the most effective lobby group of the new South Africa, has also gone out of its way to serve the media. Nathan Geffen, the TAC's media liaison officer, has noted that media relations have always been a part of the organization's advocacy strategy:

'We make a point of always trying to be available to the media, and trying to answer their questions, no matter how long it requires,' he says. 'No matter whether we have to spend hours discussing with one journalist a particular issue, it's worth it because journalists are the key to obviously disseminating accurate information to the public.'[3]

Media ownership

As my former colleague, Sean Jacobs, points out in his fascinating doctoral thesis on the media and democratic politics in South Africa, the TAC has skilfully been developing a 'media-friendly' image,[4] although, as he points out, the TAC has certain advantages over other NGOs. For one, the TAC can frame its issue as one of health rather than economics, thus avoiding a 'subversive' or 'left-wing' tag because of the organization's social diversity (although in his interview with me, the TAC's Zackie Achmat lamented their failure to attract middle-class professionals as public representatives of their campaign); and second, because their spokespeople, Achmat and Mark Heywood, are 'well-educated, articulate members of the middle class'.

Jacobs's main thesis contends that 'in post-apartheid South Africa, media overwhelmingly serve the imperatives of factions in government that favour market-driven solutions to questions of inequality and poverty in South Africa at the expense of more interventionist models, as well as those of capital, both South African and international'.

But Jacobs adds a significant rejoinder: '[Yet] the media can also have a combative relationship with the state or capital, and have frequently been marshalled to do just that by forces opposing the direction of economic reform. As such, media is a potent and often ambivalent power centre in post-apartheid South Africa that must be understood on its own terms.'[5]

The trends in media consumption in South Africa, as in any other society, run parallel to income and literacy levels. Radio and TV are the media that reach the majority of the population, with tabloid magazines and semi-tabloid newspapers such as the *Sowetan* and *Daily Sun* trailing at a distance. South Africa's 'broadsheets', *Business Day* and *Mail & Guardian*, take the smallest share of the market, correlating with the limited number of high-end, middle-class people likely to enjoy the editorial pedigree of these papers.

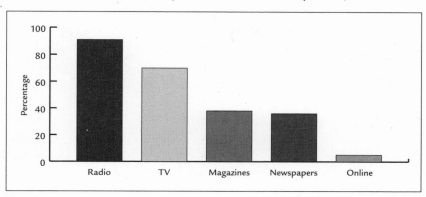

Source: www.omdmedia.co.za, adapted from Statistics SA

Ownership patterns clearly impact on the ideological approach of the media and, thereby, on the media's relations with government. Aside from small community outlets, important though they are, and the public broadcaster (the SABC), the mainstream media is a profit-making industry. People forget that. As Jacobs points out, Tony O'Reilly has essentially asset-stripped the South African part of his operation of its intellectual capital – its journalists – in order to protect profits.

Ownership	Published newspapers
Independent News and Media (South Africa) Ltd: owned by Tony O'Reilly	*Star, Cape Argus, Cape Times, Daily News, Mercury, Pretoria News, Business Report* and *Daily Voice*
Johnnic Communications: owned by black business groups, trade unions, and National Empowerment Consortium	*Sunday Times, Sowetan, Business Day, Sunday World, Daily Dispatch, Financial Mail, Herald, Weekend Post, Algoa Sun, Ilizwi* and *Our Times*
Naspers (Nasionale Media), which owns Media24	*Die Burger, Beeld, Volksblad, Daily Sun, Rapport, City Press* and *Sunday Sun*
Caxton and CTP Publishers and Printers: 38% owned by Johnnic Communications	*Citizen*, and 30 regional community newspapers
Mail & Guardian Limited: owned by Trevor Ncube	*Mail & Guardian*

I met with Mathatha Tsedu in 2003, when he was still editor of the *Sunday Times*, to explain Idasa's intention to sue the four main political parties to assert the public's right to know about their private donations. Tsedu said he would definitely cover the issue – and he did – because it was of great importance from a socio-equality point of view. Yet it was also a strong political story, and so would get past the 'bean counters', who were concerned that his desire to cover the 'real' South Africa was going to drive wealthy readers and advertisers away. Tsedu clearly felt trapped by the commercial reality of his industry.

So, in conclusion, the media does matter. Despite the tensions between the media and government, and all of government's frequent protestations about the media, there is, in fact, a substantial coalescence of interests. If Sean Jacobs is only half right – and I am confident that he is at least that – then the mainstream media in South Africa are influential not just because government does in fact care what is said about it, but because the media is such a useful ally to its macroeconomic approach.

9

The Judges

Politics on the Bench

My phone call was on another subject altogether. So I was shocked by the outpouring that came, unsolicited, from the other end of the telephone. This particular High Court judge, well known for his persistent high spirits, was *gatvol*: 'We are facing a crisis. Judges with a non-racial view of life are few and far between. It's an appalling mixture of black populists and white judges imprisoned in the past.' This comment echoed another made by the respected legal affairs journalist, Carmel Rickard, as early as 1999: 'Most members of the judiciary now fall into one of two camps, each with a distinct collection of political baggage; one had strong connections with the previous government and its philosophy, the other with the present regime'.[1] It is the seam that runs underneath the bench and which, like the San Andreas fault line, persistently threatens to engulf the structure on the surface. The Cape High Court, for example, has suffered a series of earth-shaking tremors.

When Judge John Hlophe was appointed as judge president in May 2000, few would have predicted that such an apparently affable man would stir up such passions. In November 2004, Hlophe penned an explosive report submitted to the minister of justice, Brigitte Mabandla, which was leaked, and was broken in a dramatic front-page splash by talented young *City Press* reporter, Mpumelelo Mkhabela.[2] The report lists alleged racist incidents that Hlophe witnessed or had fallen victim to since his appointment as judge president. Hlophe accused white judges of practising exclusion, at times subtly, at times more directly. In one of its most robust passages, Hlophe wrote:

> I believe that [the] Cape Bar is very reactionary, it does not welcome black judges. I would even say it despises black judges. It is my sub-mission that this is a calculated attempt to undermine the intellect and talent of black judges, in particular by some white legal practitioners

who clearly want to keep the Bench as white as possible. As long as these racial practices continue, we will never be able to transform the judiciary.[3]

A High Court division is like a small firm; in the Cape division, there are twenty-eight permanent judges and five acting judges.[4] A well-run division should be like a team, with the various judges working in cooperation for the greater good. The judge president is crucial in this regard, leading and managing the division. He or she also decides who will sit on each case; in the allocation of cases, the judge president is highly influential. Hlophe's report shredded the morale and cohesion of the Cape division. This is not to bash Hlophe just for the sake of it. The Cape bench, with some progressive exceptions, along with the Cape bar, is a very tight, conservative club that deserves a shake-up. Indeed, the same can probably be said of the bar and the bench countrywide.[5]

The problem with Hlophe's report was that it painted a far too simplistic and crudely drawn map of the state of race relations in the division and, in so doing, turned many of the more progressive judges and advocates against him. In part, too, Hlophe seemed to use the opportunity to 'name and shame' some of his colleagues at both the bench and at the bar – including Jeremy Gauntlett SC, Judge Dennis van Reenen and, notably, his deputy, Jeanette Traverso, with whom relations had soured substantially over the past year. In 'naming and shaming', Hlophe broke the unwritten rule of the bar and the bench: he spoke outside 'the club'. It was not that there was not legitimacy or truth in the report, but rather the way in which a confidential report had found its way into headline news that set the proverbial cat among the pigeons.

Perhaps Hlophe was further emboldened by the ANC's 'January 8 statement' in 2005, in which President Mbeki talked about changing the 'collective mindset' of the judiciary and the need for transformation within its ranks.[6] Mbeki was entirely correct in his assertions on transformation, although the statement is still interpreted by many as a part of an orchestrated attempt by the ANC to 'control the judiciary'.[7] But it is not that simple.

Hlophe was one of a number of appointments to judge president made in the late 1990s and early 2000s, when President Mbeki made it clear that it was crucial to install black leadership at the head of the various divisions. Many excellent appointments have been made in other divisions – for example,

Judge President Bernard Ngoepe in the Transvaal Provincial Division. Intriguingly, the justice minister at the time of Hlophe's appointment, Penuell Maduna, did not support his appointment, at least privately, doubting his ability, and advised several Cape judges accordingly, suggesting that the acting judge president, Edwin King, be persuaded to stay on. King was hardly popular himself, and so some of the more vociferous judges began to lobby Maduna and other members of the Judicial Service Commission (JSC) to appoint someone, knowing that it might well be Hlophe.

The allegations made by Hlophe are still to be fully addressed as they were not tackled by either the then chief justice, Arthur Chaskalson, or subsequently by his successor, Pius Langa. Neither of the two elder statesmen of the court have had the stomach for this fight – Chaskalson was on his way out, and Langa finds the hanging out of dirty legal laundry in public too unbecoming of the profession. Transformation is a messy and unforgiving business and spares no individual and no institution. Both the bench and the bar should brace themselves for further turbulence over the next few years in what will be a necessary but bumpy ride.

Transformation of the judiciary

Legal fraternities – and I speak from direct personal experience – tend to be conservative in outlook and ruthless in defence of their personal professional self-interest. The bar is a club, with hidden conventions that you break at your peril; the pressure to conform is intense. I remember interviewing the then minister for justice, the late Dullah Omar, in 1994. The main topic of the interview was the Truth and Reconciliation Commission (TRC), which was soon to begin its dramatic hearings. Omar, with his old friend Johnny de Lange as chair of the parliamentary portfolio committee on justice, in guiding the TRC Act towards the statute book, had sought to find a balance between justice and reconciliation. Whether or not they have been successful is a hotly contested, moot point.

I had my own ulterior motive for conducting the interview. At the end of my sabbatical year, I was eager to remain in South Africa. I was searching for suitable employment opportunities. As a qualified barrister with seven years' experience at the London bar, I investigated the possibility of practising in South Africa, but discovered that it would be necessary to re-qualify from scratch. There was apparently no reciprocal qualifications scheme such as the British one that permitted many exiled South Africans to enter and flourish at the British bar. At the end of my interview with Omar, I raised the issue and asked him what it would take to change the rules to permit someone like myself to practise at, for example, the Cape bar. Omar raised an eyebrow, paused for thought, and then with a wry smile said: 'If you could convince me that such a change would help make the Cape Town bar less elitist and would help break up their monopoly of power over the legal profession, then I'll consider changing the rules.' Omar's manner was usually lugubrious in the extreme, but as he developed his point that day, his habitually monotone voice rose and he became positively animated.

Transforming the bar is vital to transforming the bench, because, although the Constitutional Court has thrown a wider net, in general judges are selected from the ranks of the practising legal profession. There are currently 1871 advocates in the country. The race and gender statistics for the General Council Bar appear as follows:[8]

	White		African		Coloured		Indian		Total
	male	female	male	female	male	female	male	female	
Sr Counsel	281	10	7	–	7	1	16	2	324
5 years and more	670	89	58	8	9	4	37	8	883
Under 5 years	215	69	115	27	15	11	33	28	513
Non-contributing	68	38	21	5	8	5	4	2	151
Total	1 234	206	201	40	39	21	90	40	1 871

In South Africa, there has been substantial debate on whether the pace of transformation is too slow, whether white candidates have been overlooked for appointments to the bench, and whether adequate measures are being taken to facilitate the entry of black and female candidates. This debate has in recent years taken place against the heated backdrop of the package of laws government has been seeking to pass on the transformation of the judiciary. Speaking during the debate on the president's State of the Nation speech in February 2003, and taking his lead from the president's own comments, the bill's chief proponent, Johnny de Lange, then the chair of the parliamentary portfolio committee on justice and constitutional affairs, and now deputy minister of justice, told the National Assembly that, historically, the South African legal profession was overwhelmingly white and male, and that 'this distortion in the legal profession has largely been responsible for the distortion on the bench'.

The slow pace of transformation of the legal profession in turn delays progress on the bench. This is the first contextual factor that needs to be taken into account when assessing progress in transforming the judiciary to the point where it will enjoy the comprehensive legitimacy that comes with full representivity. The baseline for measuring progress was 27 April 1994. At that time, according to the department of justice, there were 165 judges, of whom 160 were white men. Critics of transformation need to take this factor into account as well.

In late March 2006, Chief Justice Langa briefed the parliamentary portfolio committee on justice and constitutional affairs. He told the committee that the numbers were still 'pitiful' in terms of the gender imbalance: of the 218 judges, 184 are men, 115 are white and 102 of those are white men, with 13 white women. Of the 102 black judges, 82 are men and 21 women. How you view these statistics really depends on whether you are someone who regards the glass as half full or half empty. Clearly there is still a long way to go, as the chief justice conceded to the committee. But, from a very low base, there had been a dramatic increase – for example, the proportion of white men had in twelve years more than halved from 97 per cent to 47 per cent.

Racial transformation of the judiciary as at 2004 is shown below (note that, at the time of going to print, hardly anything has changed in terms of the figures provided by the chief justice to parliament in March 2006).

The Constitutional Court has led the way. The first Constitutional Court, appointed in 1994, comprised four (broad) black people (three African, and one Indian), and seven white people. Of the eleven, only two were women. Now, the court comprises eight (broad) black people (seven African and one Indian) – a reversal of the proportions from 1994 – but reflecting the wider problem in the legal profession, still with just three women. As to magistrates, Langa reported that of the 1 833 magistrates, 1 288 were men and 545 women; 893 were white, and just over half, 940, black.

Thus, addressing racial and gender imbalances in respect of a particular appointment at a particular court should constitute a powerful factor in

Racial transformation of the judiciary, 2004[9]

COURT	WM	WF	BM	BF	CM	CF	IM	IF
Supreme Court of Appeal	16	1	2	–	–	–	1	–
Northern Cape	2	1	1	–	1	–	–	–
Eastern Cape	12	–	2	1	–	–	2	–
Cape of Good Hope	16	4	4	–	3	–	–	–
Free State	11	–	2	–	–	–	–	1
Transvaal	42	4	13	3	1	–	4	–
Natal	13	1	7	–	2	1	2	–
Bophuthatswana	1	–	1	2	–	–	–	–
Transkei	2	1	3	1	–	–	–	–
Ciskei	2	–	1	–	1	–	–	–
Constitutional Court	6	1	2	1	–	–	1	–
Land Claims Court – acting	–	–	–	–	–	–	–	–
Labour Court	5	1	2	–	–	–	1	1
Venda	–	–	2	–	–	–	–	–
Total	128	14	42	8	8	1	11	2

Key: WM: white male; WF: white female; BM: black male; BF: black female; CM: coloured male; CF: coloured female; IM: Indian male; IF: Indian female

the appointment process. The assertions in the 'Hlophe racism report' should therefore not be looked at in a vacuum, nor be allowed to degenerate into the politics of personality. By doing so, the real questions related to transformation of the bar and bench become obscured. Thus far, nothing particularly constructive has come out of the very public debate on the issue. On all sides of the divide there has been a level of recklessness – beginning with responses surrounding the ANC's 8 January 2005 statement. The debate is more complex than the un-nuanced assertion by some that the judiciary is being wholly undermined, and it is about more than saying the country needs more black judges. It should rather also be about creating a change in the way in which justice is dispensed and the way in which citizens experience justice. The carelessness of words on the part of politicians and law practitioners, and not the act of transformation itself, threatens to undermine the confidence that ordinary citizens have in the judiciary and the system as a whole.

How does one frame a discussion on transformation of the judiciary that is constructive and gives meaning to constitutional values? The debate needs to go further than the transformation of the bench and changing its composition – important as that is. What sort of access do women have to the profession? If the level of female representation on the bench is low, why is that so? How is it possible to offer serious incentives to successful black lawyers to make themselves available for positions on the bench? What contribution can be made to increase the pool of black candidates at law schools and as young entrants into the profession? Is there a need to support young black advocates who find start-up costs at the bar prohibitive? For real transformation, which deepens democratic development, there needs to be wise and measured leadership – not only from the bench, the bar and legal academics, but especially from politicians – despite the temptation to score political points. The conversation is too important and the stakes too high to be hijacked by alternative agendas.

The power of the judges

Institutional and social transformation, especially on the scale of the new South Africa, encourages volatility. What is perhaps more surprising is that of the three branches of government, it is the judiciary, more so than the executive, and certainly more so than the legislature, that appears more precarious. This diminishes the power of the judiciary as an institution and undermines its authority and power. All other things being equal, what power do judges have? Or, to put the same question slightly differently, what is the nature of the relationship between judges and politics? In a groundbreaking 1977 book titled *The Politics of the Judiciary*, London School of Economics professor John Griffith made the argument that judges cannot act neutrally, but are compelled to act politically. It caused massive controversy in Britain at the time, similar to the controversy that, at the time of writing, is raging in South Africa on the issue of the accountability of judges. Griffith explained the political role of judges neatly, describing

> the judiciary as one of the principal organs of a democratic society without whom government could be carried on only with great difficulty. The essence of their function is the maintenance of law and order and the judges are seen as a mediating influence. Democracy requires that some group of persons acts as an arbiter of power and the individual ... Judges then, in this view, are an essential part of government but exist to operate as a part of democratic organization. They take their place alongside the other two great institutions of the executive and Parliament,

more passive than they, but indispensable. No doubt there is something of a dilemma in the judiciary's position as both upholders of law and order and protectors of the individual against a powerful executive. But this is explained in terms of checks and balances or countervailing power and so what might be an inherent contradiction dissolves in a cloud of words which nevertheless, be it noted, defines the function of the judiciary in *political* terms.[10]

In the classical exposition of the three branches of government, laws are made by the legislature (parliament), executed by the executive (cabinet and departments of state), and interpreted and enforced by the judiciary. But it is not quite so simple. In Chapter 4, I noted how, in practice, the driving force of legislation is in most cases the executive. There is a degree of overlap in functions as well as powers – an effect that is accentuated in 'Westminster' systems of government, where members of the executive (ministers) are also members of the legislature. In Britain itself, the overlap extends to the third branch of government in that the House of Lords has a dual function: it operates as the second house of parliament (equivalent to the National Council of Provinces in South Africa), and its judicial committee is the highest court in the land.

Thus, members of the House of Lords' judicial committee – referred to as 'Law Lords' – are often called on to interpret or enforce laws that they themselves have had a hand in writing. This is not the case in South Africa. The judicial arm of government is separate from the executive and legislative arms, at least in terms of membership. The overlaps come in different forms. The most obvious is in the selection of judges, where the Judicial Service Commission, whose role is considered in further detail below, offers recommendations to the president, who then actually makes the appointment.

So, back to this question: What, precisely, is the nature of the political influence of judges? Although South Africa's legal system is now a hybrid in terms of origin, derivations and instincts, with traces of Roman-Dutch Law, common law and, now, constitutional law, its common law tradition of judicial precedent creating jurisprudence is central. So, first of all, therefore, judges make a law whenever a judgment sets a precedent and establishes a new legal principle or doctrine. Second, there is the question of statutory interpretation. As Griffith put it:

Statute law cannot be a perfect instrument. A statute or one section of a statute may be made to deal with some particular subject – perhaps with immigration, or drugs, or housing or education – but a situation arises where doubt is cast on the meaning of the words of the statute. Does the situation fall within words or not? The judges must then decide how to interpret the statute and by so doing they define its meaning. Not only therefore do they 'make law' through the development of the common law. They also do so by this process of statutory interpretation.[11]

Third, judges resolve disputes between parties. Sometimes the parties are private parties. But, sometimes, one of the parties is the state. The growth of what lawyers call 'administrative' or 'public' law is one of the most important developments in law of the past thirty years. When lawyers talk about a matter 'going on review', the 'review' they are talking about is 'judicial review', which, in turn, is shorthand for a jurisprudential concept that is still in its infancy – namely, the idea that the executive power of the state can be subjected to scrutiny by judges because the executive has exceeded its authority and acted *ultra vires*, or else on the basis of one or both of two other legal doctrines: natural fairness and unreasonableness.

In other words, if an executive agency reaches a decision 'illegally', or without proper regard to due process of law or procedural fairness – such as not permitting a directly affected stakeholder a right to a hearing – and/or reaches a decision that is beyond the bounds of reasonableness to the point of being 'irrational', then it may be overturned by a court upon application by a party whose rights have been adversely affected.

Judicial review as the core element of administrative or public law goes hand in hand with the parallel dramatic development of constitutional law. Not only have more and more countries adopted constitutions over the same period, but invariably the state is a party to a constitutional dispute. This is where the judicial wheels hit the tar road of democratic politics. In a constitutional democracy, such as South Africa's, the Constitutional Court – as the 'apex' court (leaving aside the current tussle between the Constitutional Court and the Supreme Court of Appeal on which of these courts should, structurally, be the country's 'apex' court) – has supreme authority, as guardian of the Constitution. As Section 167 of the Constitution states, the Constitutional Court is the highest court in all constitutional matters, and 'a constitutional matter includes any issue involving the

interpretation, protection or enforcement of the Constitution'. It is, therefore, the most important institution in South Africa. Whether its political
influence matches its importance is a separate matter.

The Constitution itself is certainly influential as well as important: I
often joke that South Africans carry around the small printed version in their
breast pocket. And for lawyers and politicians this is not far from the truth,
especially in the early years after its adoption in 1996. In deciding constitutional matters, the Constitutional Court has to be careful to respect the
proper limits of its own authority. In one of its earlier judgments, the court
provided a succinct description of where the boundaries lie, pointing out
that rationality, as a minimum requirement for the exercise of public power,

> does not mean that the courts can or should substitute their opinions as
> to what is appropriate, for the opinions of those in whom the power has
> been vested. As long as the purpose sought to be achieved by the exercise
> of public power is within the authority of the functionary, and as long
> as the functionary's decision, viewed objectively, is rational, a court
> cannot interfere with the decision simply because it disagrees with it
> or considers that the power was exercised inappropriately.[12]

Notwithstanding these words of caution, judges must exercise a 'creative
function' – a phrase coined by Griffith, which I cannot better – and it is in
the exercise of this creativity that a court will determine the weight of its
own influence. Non-lawyers tend to regard the law as an applied science.
Apply the correct rule to the given situation and, like a computer spitting
out a processed response, the correct result will emerge. Not so. The law
is an art and not a science. Moreover, judges are human beings and not
computers. There is, therefore, a large degree of unpredictability in the
application of the law, which happens to be rather convenient for the legal
profession. If it were an automated system of neutral application, there would
be little need for judges and even less need for lawyers to argue the case. In
South Africa, it would seem as if the judiciary needs a healthy quotient of 'the
creative function', for courts are often approached to deal with issues where
politics has failed the citizenry. The 'Modderklip' case was one such example.[13]
Surprisingly enough, the Constitutional Court endorsed the judgment of
the (normally 'less creative') Supreme Court of Appeal (SCA) in this matter.

The Modderklip case is a critical case regarding the state's obligation to provide access to adequate housing (in a situation of mass eviction of unlawful occupiers from private land), as well as protecting the rights of the landowner. The previous judgments (in the High Court and the SCA) confirmed the state's duty to both the unlawful occupants and the landowner. Thus, the state was required to take reasonable steps to ensure that the landowner, Modderklip, was provided with effective relief when its land was illegally occupied. The prior judgments also confirmed that the state was under a duty to find accommodation for the squatters – approximately 40 000 of them – who had 'nowhere else to go', and would literally be left homeless if they were evicted.

On appeal before the Constitutional Court, the state argued, among other things, that because Modderklip's property rights had been infringed by *private individuals*, the state had not breached any of Modderklip's rights. The Constitutional Court rejected the state's arguments. The court found that it was unreasonable of the state to stand by and do nothing in circumstances where it was impossible for Modderklip to evict the occupiers because of the sheer magnitude of the invasion and the particular circumstances of the occupiers. As the SCA had done, the court held that the state should compensate Modderklip for the unlawful occupation of its property in violation of its rights. The compensation also ensured that the occupiers would continue to have accommodation until suitable alternatives were found, and thus the state was relieved of the task of having to immediately find alternative shelter for the affected group of people.

Apart from enforcing the state's duty to landowners in the case of large-scale illegal occupation, the case is important for its application of the principles established in the landmark 'Grootboom' decision (see below). While the court acknowledged that 'those charged with the provision of housing face immense problems', the legal principles applicable to a mass eviction situation, where it is known that the eviction will result in a community being left literally homeless, were restated and applied. By virtue of some agile legal gymnastics, a careful balancing act was conducted. Such cases show that judges, whether by default or design, are not only political actors, but products of their socio-political environment. Bold law (or the 'creative function') provides a degree of unpredictability that is necessary and sufficient to hold the executive to account, but also crucially to provide social stability where that may have been threatened.

There is one other way in which the judges may impact on politics, and that is through judicial commissions. When something very serious goes wrong in public life, a mark of its seriousness is the appointment of a commission of inquiry. When it is very serious, it will be deemed necessary to appoint a judge to head the commission. Recent examples in South Africa include the King Commission (headed by Judge Edwin King), which investigated the Hansie Cronjé cricket match-fixing scandal, the Khampepe Commission of Inquiry into the future of the Scorpions (headed by Judge Sisi Khampepe), and the Hefer Commission of Inquiry into the allegations against former Scorpions head Bulelani Ngcuka, in 2004 (headed by the retired Judge Joos Hefer).

In each of these examples, and in many others, the judiciary has been required to step into political minefields of varying degrees of danger. The rule of law is a necessary but not sufficient condition for democracy. It, in turn, needs independent, honest judges, who command not only the authority of their office, but public legitimacy. Given their 'creative function', who they are and where they come from is critical to the quality of the rule of law.

Choosing the judges: The importance of the Judicial Service Commission

Because of the authority and power judges wield, as well as the transformation imperative, the selection process for judges is crucial and deserves special attention. There used to be an advertising campaign in Britain that said, 'A dog is a present for life and not just for Christmas', in response to the large number of abandoned, unwanted dogs following the Christmas holiday. So, too, with judges, who enjoy extraordinary security of tenure – traditionally regarded as a necessary ingredient to encourage real independence for the judiciary.

Apart from impeachment – a seldom-used, unwieldy process – judges are generally appointed for life. One exception is the Constitutional Court: Section 176 of the Constitution states that the period of office is twelve years, or until he or she attains the age of seventy, whichever occurs first, except where an Act of Parliament extends the terms. The Judges' Remuneration and Conditions of Employment Act, 2001, has extended Constitutional Court judges' terms to fifteen years in situations where their twelve-year term has expired or they have reached the age of seventy before they have completed fifteen years' active service as a judge, provided they do not reach the age of seventy-five before this point.

Hence, the selection process is even more important. Prior to 1994, it was entirely secret. As the excellent legal journalist Carmel Rickard put it in a discussion paper, 'all the appointments were decided on behind closed doors; there was no prior scrutiny by the public or the profession and the result was a bench that was largely a mirror of the political establishment: virtually all male, all middle-class and largely Afrikaans-speaking'.

But the Interim Constitution introduced the principle of an open system through a constitutional body – the Judicial Service Commission.[14] The JSC is chaired by the chief justice, who is now also the president of the Constitutional Court (currently, Justice Pius Langa). There are in addition twenty-two other members – a rather bulky number that has, at times, made the decision-making process a little unwieldy – composed as follows:

JSC members (as at May 2006)

Chief Justice Pius Langa
Justice Craig Telfer Howie (President, Supreme Court of Appeal)
Judge President Bernard Makgabo Ngoepe
Minister Bridgette Silvia Mabandla (minister of justice)
Advocate Milton Seligson SC
Advocate Morumo Tsatsi Khabela Moorane SC
Mr Julian von Klemperer
Mr Silas Nkanunu
Professor Johann Neethling
Mr ML Mokoena
Mr Tsietsi Simon Setona
Advocate George Bizos SC
Advocate Kgomotso Moroka SC
Mr Johan Ernstzen
Mr Jonas Ben Sibanyoni
Mrs Lindiwe Hendricks (minister for water affairs and forestry)
Advocate Tshililo Michael Masutha
Mrs Sheila Camerer
Mr Jacobus Hercules van der Merwe
Dr Frik van Heerden
Dr Corné Mulder
Advocate Seth Nthai
Mr Mninwa Johannes Mahlangu

As is the case of each and every body created by the Constitution, the numbers were carefully chosen. The ruling party has a plurality voice on the JSC. That is to say, it does not have an explicit inbuilt majority, but with three of each of the MPs' and NCOP's allocations, plus the minister of justice and the four persons designated by the president, totalling eleven, the ruling party virtually has veto power. In addition, since the president appoints the two practising attorneys and the two practising advocates, it is highly likely that more than one of them will be a strong ANC sympathizer.

This is a controversial issue, but my own view is that, given the need to transform the judiciary and to introduce the idea of accountability and representivity into the bench, it is entirely appropriate that the majority voice should be a loud one in the JSC. Others have criticized the JSC for being ANC-dominated. What is clear is that the process of open interviews that the JSC follows has introduced a large element of accountability into the system. On the Constitutional Court website, the list of judges permits access not only to their CVs, but to a transcript of their JSC interview.[15] The JSC hearings make for splendid theatre. 'They should be on radio,' asserts Dennis Davis, a Cape Division High Court judge.

Attending the open interviews or reading the transcripts, one can see how the strengths and weaknesses of individual candidates were teased out. The first set of interviews for the inaugural Constitutional Court appointments were remarkable for their robustness. One of the best-known members of the court, Justice Albie Sachs, was subjected to an unrelenting cross-examination by Wim Trengove SC, one of the country's finest constitutional advocates, over Sachs's role in an ANC-appointed internal commission of inquiry into the death, after four months in detention, of ANC commander Thami Zulu:

TRENGOVE: I am not suggesting that Thami Zulu was abused in detention. But you said in your report that he entered confinement as a large, well-built, slightly overweight person. He came out gaunt, frail and almost unrecognizable and he died a week later. And you also reported that the panel investigating him concluded very early on, soon after his solitary confinement, that they did not have a case against him for being an enemy agent. Did those circumstances not call for a strong condemnation of his prolonged detention without trial?
SACHS: Well I felt so.
TRENGOVE: Well you did not say so. You said merely if your view was the

one reflected here as the one view, you said merely that it [the detention period] was too long. There is no condemnation at all, simply a view that it might have been too long.

SACHS: I think there are various passages if you look right through that indicate a condemnation, certainly of the period in solitary confinement and …

TRENGOVE: No, I am talking about the length of detention without trial. Is the principle not quite unacceptable that people should be detained for fourteen months without a trial?

SACHS: Yes it is and I thought so.

TRENGOVE: Should you not have said so that is was unacceptable under any circumstances?

SACHS: You know what I did not want was a minority report.

TRENGOVE: Why not? Why not, is the principle not sufficiently important?

SACHS: No, because a minority report in that context would have been weaker than a majority, a consensus report that actually raised the issue.

TRENGOVE: A consensus report that comes to no result, it says there are some views this way and other views that other way and we therefore let it be. Was that a satisfactory outcome?

SACHS: I think a three to one minority would have been more propitious, more favourable to continuing that kind of thing than the statement we had. But just remember this was not a question of published judgments that people are going to look at and find the sense and all the rest, this was a report to the National Executive Committee [of the ANC].

TRENGOVE: Did your own independence and integrity not demand that you put an unequivocal condemnation on record?

SACHS: The issue was not my independence but the issue was to ensure and to prove that and to prove that I was an honest person.

TRENGOVE: Should the issue not have been your independence?

SACHS: No. The issue at that stage was to ensure that ill-treatment of people did not manifest itself, did not continue.[16]

The cross-examination continued in this vein for several more minutes. Observing the JSC hearings at the time, you could have cut the tension in the air with a knife. As is well known, Sachs was targeted by the Pretoria regime when in exile in the 1960s and lost an arm when a bomb that was intended to kill him exploded as he took his morning jog towards the beach in Maputo. Sachs himself recorded the experience in his celebrated journal, *The Soft Vengeance of a Freedom Fighter*.

In Bloemfontein in October 1994, Sachs was fighting for his professional life, fighting to keep hold of his greatest dream – to serve as a member of the first Constitutional Court of a liberated new South Africa. The excerpt is illuminating not just because of the scrutiny faced by the first batch of Constitutional Court judges (four members of the current court remain as survivors of that first JSC set of interviews: Sachs, Pius Langa, Kate O'Regan and Yvonne Mokgoro), but because of the light it sheds upon what are possibly the two most important aspects of the court: the independence of its members and, second, its style in reaching decisions – in particular, its determination to pursue consensus as far as possible, which, in turn, has encouraged a politically pragmatic yet humane approach, of which Sachs is one of the leading proponents. (It is a subject that I return to below.)

The JSC is thus one of the most influential as well as important institutions in the new South Africa. The final Constitution adjusted the balance of power in the JSC in favour of a greater proportion of politicians. Nonetheless, it rarely fails to offer a similarly searching examination of the credentials of applicants.

In April 2006, for example, Letty Molopa SC was interviewed for one of two vacancies in the Transvaal Provincial Division. Former counsel to Nelson Mandela, George Bizos SC, an iconic figure on the JSC, as in the bar, began with a series of questions about a particular case that Molopa had been involved in. They were tough questions, implying that she was mistaken on the details of the case. In the words of one observing journalist, the cross-examination 'sapped her morale', and she never fully recovered.

Other members of the JSC took up the theme: Thabang Makwetla, the premier of Mpumalanga, and not a man who can be described as anything other than a die-hard ANC loyalist, pointed out the inadequacies of her application form, and then asked her what her weaknesses were. Senior advocate Kgomotso Moroka sought to retrieve the situation for her friend, a relationship she admitted to at the beginning of the interview. She asked leading questions about what could have caused Molopa to fill in the form so poorly (she had been persuaded to apply at the very last moment) and about her seniority among black women advocates (she is the second most senior), as well as about the grave difficulties that black women advocates face at the bar. 'What,' asked Moroka, 'do we have to do to make them appointable to the bench?'

Moroka is the most senior woman SC, so, as she completed her question, colleagues on either side of her – Marumo Moerane SC and Julian von Klemperer – ribbed her with whispered asides about her own decision to decline to apply – something she is often teased about. Molopa's reply was telling: 'It is in the nature of the work that women are given. You find attorneys saying that women can handle divorces or unopposed cases. As a result women can't sustain their practices and instead of going up, the numbers decline.' As noted earlier, the fact that the conveyor belt is so defective means that the bar is not yet able to deliver the candidates for the bench necessary to propel its transformation.

Yet, despite this fruitful line of discussion, another black woman member of the JSC, ANC MEC for local government in Gauteng, Qedani Mahlungu, returned to the earlier theme, and brutally: 'You appear to be a person who does not pay attention to details.' As one regular observer of the JSC said immediately afterwards, 'Only a black woman could have put it like that, given the context.' Notwithstanding this uncomfortable set of exchanges, the JSC recommended Molopa's appointment to the bench, subsequently confirmed by President Mbeki on 12 May 2006.

The elegant calm of the Vineyard Hotel in the leafy-green Cape Town suburb of Newlands, where the JSC now always conducts its hearings, belies the intensity of its proceedings. With light streaming in from large windows, it is a metaphor for the important transparency of its work. Despite, and perhaps because of, the large number of politicians that now sit on the JSC, it is a body that is never criticized by either government or opposition parties; it enjoys a legitimately high position in the new institutional hierarchy.

The political disposition
of the Constitutional Court

Justice Kate O'Regan's October 1994 JSC interview was not without its own moments of probing angst. In O'Regan's case, her membership of the ANC was questioned. Asked by a member of the JSC whether she was or had ever been a member of a political party, O'Regan confirmed that she was a member of the ANC, though in somewhat apologetic terms:

> I said I am very active in a lot of things, but I am not active as a member of the ANC but I am a member of the ANC, and I must say it is not on my CV. The simple reason for that is that when asked for my CV by a range of organizations I just printed it out and only subsequently thought it was something I should have disclosed.

O'Regan was then asked if she would retain her membership if appointed to the court, and she confirmed that she would resign. Pressed further on whether past membership of a political party is a factor that should count against her, she regrouped and replied:

> No, I do not think that active political membership, as long as it is in the past in a sense, is necessarily, as I say, something that should exclude you from membership [of] a court. I think that what you do have to be able to be sure of as members of the JSC I think is that people will be able to hear arguments, that they will listen to arguments ... I think that is the test and there are many people who have never been active in politics who would not be the sort of people who would listen to arguments and people who have been involved in politics who would, so I think that is the test.

This is a persuasive response. What matters most is intellectual independence and an ability to listen. Membership of a party may well be largely irrelevant to this issue, a point that the court itself later had to deal with when, in a desperate but futile bid to challenge President Mandela's decision to appoint an inquiry into South African rugby, then SARFU president Louis Luyt applied to have several of the members of the Constitutional Court recused on the grounds of their alleged party political partisanship.[17]

During the course of the application, it was stated that, in addition to O'Regan, Justices Langa, Mokgoro, Sachs and Yacoob had also been members of the ANC at various times. O'Regan has proved to be one of the most incisive interlocutors on the court, along with a more recent appointee, Sandile Ngcobo. Yet, it has not stopped regular carping about the court and its supposed 'ANC bias', both from arch-conservative commentators such as RW Johnson, who peddles Afro-pessimism with the reckless abandon of a drunken confetti thrower, and some more progressive and respected commentators such as Steven Friedman, who really should know better.

According to the analysis of a trio of highly reputable administrative lawyers – Justice (as he now is) Dennis Davis, leading constitutional advocate Gilbert Marcus SC and Witwatersrand University professor Jonathan Klaaren – in the 1999 *Annual Survey of SA Law*, neither Johnson nor Friedman troubled to conduct any analysis of the court's actual voting record, and, with regard to the latter:

> Friedman's claims about the record of the Constitutional Court over the past five years are demonstrably wrong. Had the necessary research been done, Friedman would have discovered that the Constitutional Court has frequently ruled against the 'executive' (Friedman's euphemism for the ANC).

The article then cites five important cases in which the court had ruled against the ANC-led government. Since then, the court has overruled the government on probably the most politically vexed and contentious issue of the decade: its policy towards HIV/AIDS. More decisive than party membership is the social and intellectual diversity of the composition of the Constitutional Court. Even as the extraordinary 'founder class' of the first Constitutional Court, which was appointed in late 1994, moves on one by one, this remains the case. Senior judges in the older democracies tend to come from similar social backgrounds and from the same professional breeding ground: legal practice. Few have experienced anything else.

Part of the beauty of social transformation is not only the racial component, but the social and intellectual component. Not unlike the first class of new members of parliament in 1994, the first batches of Constitutional Court judges have rich personal histories, and in many cases they too have professional and personal journeys scarred by apartheid. The deputy chief justice, Dikgang Moseneke, was imprisoned on Robben Island from the age of fifteen for ten years, but twenty-three years later found himself pulled from a lucrative career at the bar to head Telkom during a crucial period of transformation after 1994 (he also chaired the country's first big empowerment company, NAIL, during the same period of six years, until 2001).

Justice Zak Yacoob, who happens to be blind, was also a prominent activist, as was Justice Albie Sachs. All three played significant roles in the build-up to democratic transition in 1994. Moseneke, for instance, served on the technical committee that drafted the Interim Constitution of 1993. Despite the obstacles of apartheid, some of the black judges practised either as advocates, such as Justice Thembile Skweyiya, or as attorneys, such as Justice Tholie Madala. Some of the members of the court have sat as judges for many years, such as Justices Sandile Ngcobo and Bess Nkabinde, whereas others come from academic backgrounds, such as Justices Yvonne Mokgoro, Kate O'Regan, Albie Sachs and Johann van der Westhuizen. More comprehensive pen portraits can be found in Appendix B.

These are real people who have experienced real life. So, while they are enjoined to reach carefully reasoned decisions of impeccable jurisprudential quality, they can infuse their deliberations with a dose of humanity that is rare indeed and which is apparent from the way in which the court conducts itself, notwithstanding the dark green robes and the necessarily formal setting.

The political power of the Constitutional Court

It is important to recognize the inherently political dimension to the proceedings of the court. A central feature of a system based on a constitutional Bill of Rights is that the court, in protecting those rights, has the authority and therefore the power to reject law or policy created by the legislature or the executive. This constitutional 'dialogue' creates obvious and inevitable tensions.

When applying the Bill of Rights, the court has to decide how far it can intrude. The discourse is often cast in terms of two characteristics – deference and activism. The legal and scholarly debates are often cast within this frame of reference: a judgment of the court will be commended for its 'activist' stance or criticized for its 'deference', or vice versa, depending on where you sit. 'Deference' refers to the extent to which the court is willing – or otherwise – to second-guess the executive or legislature.

Wise courts are well aware of the fact that, although they are guardians of the Constitution, and therefore exercise an ultimate form of authority that trumps all else, they must also respect a different form of legitimacy that comes with popular election. Whereas parliament and, through it, the executive, is chosen by the electorate at election time and awarded a mandate to govern accordingly, judges are not elected. On the other hand, too much deference may dilute the Constitution. An appropriate regard for the democratic political process and the legitimacy of democratically elected representatives should not be confused with 'public opinion'.

As one legal commentator has noted, 'The Constitutional Court has itself made it clear that it will not shrink from the difficult questions presented by the open texture of the Constitution, and will not resort to head-counting as a reliable means of substantive reasoning.'[18] The footnote to this commentary refers to the court's early judgment that capital punishment offended the constitutional guarantee of the right to life and adds that:

> The court's stance is most famously discernible in S v Makwanyane 1995 (3) SA 391 (CC) para 88 where Chaskalson P stated: 'If public opinion were to be decisive, there would be no need for constitutional adjudication. The protection of rights could then be left to Parliament, which has a mandate from the public, and is answerable to the public for the way its mandate is exercised, but this would be a return to parliamentary sovereignty, and a retreat from the new legal order established by the 1993 [interim] Constitution ... the very reason for establishing the new legal order, and for vesting the power of judicial review of all legislation in our courts, was to protect the rights of minorities and others who cannot protect their rights adequately through the democratic process.

In contrast, a later (2002) case concerning 'floor-crossing' offered a very good example of deference to the legislature.[19] The background was the formation and subsequent split of the alliance between the Democratic Party, the New National Party and the Federal Alliance. Each had won seats in the 1999 general election, and was represented in the National Assembly. But by the time of the October 2000 local government elections, the Democratic Alliance had reconstituted itself as a new party. The political marriage was hasty and ill conceived. It was more of a hostile takeover than a coalition; more acquisition than merger.

The DP was after the NNP's coloured working-class voters in the Cape and disaffected opposition votes elsewhere in the country. The plan was to ruthlessly gobble up the NNP. But not for the first time, the DP got ahead of itself. The NNP realized what was happening and resisted. There was a cultural dimension to this: in a simplified version, the Afrikaners of the NNP were deeply resentful of the self-evident arrogance of the English-speaking DP, epitomized by its leader Tony Leon. In the end, divorce was inevitable: in November 2001, the NNP withdrew from the DA.

However, local government representatives who wanted to leave the DA were unable to do so without losing their seats. The NNP's leader, Marthinus van Schalkwyk, was by now having secret discussions with ANC chairperson, Mosiuoa Patrick Lekota, and the idea of a merger with the ruling party was gathering momentum. Seeing the advantages that could accrue to it, the ANC quickly drafted the laws, including a constitutional amendment that would permit both councillors and MPs to 'cross the floor' in fifteen-day periods during the second and fourth year after an election (in all three spheres of government: national, provincial and local). The age of 'windows of opportunity' – or 'windows of opportunism', as the cartoonist Zapiro brilliantly caricatured the process – was born.

The impact of the laws – subsequently deemed not unconstitutional by the court – has been as significant as it has been controversial. All the available evidence suggests that it is deeply unpopular with the general public. In total, over 1 100 public representatives have crossed the floor since the inception of floor-crossing in 2002. It has resulted in changes of administration in two provinces and in a plethora of municipalities.[20]

The pattern of floor-crossing over the total period has generally resulted in the strengthening of the ruling party's representation, to the detriment of the opposition. The coherency of opposition has not only been undermined by declining representation but by the further fragmentation of the opposition in legislatures. Opinion polls have shown consistently that the effects of floor-crossing do not channel public opinion. In other words, a 2 per cent shift towards a party through floor-crossing does not necessarily reflect a concurrent shift in voter intention towards that party.

History can make a case for serious distortions in representation relative to the will of the electorate: the NNP effectively came off a base of zero in the 2002 local government floor-crossing window, and finished with representation of over 340 councillors. Yet this 'increase' in representation coincided with the party's most precipitous decline in support, as evidenced in the 2004 election results. Moreover, the proliferation of small new opposition parties in all legislatures has not held up to public scrutiny. Of the five new parties formed in the National Assembly through the 2003 floor-crossing window, only one, the Independent Democrats, was returned to the legislature through the ballot box. Meanwhile, the ANC has indeed managed to cherry-pick its way to an overwhelming majority and has been the net beneficiary of floor-crossing, as the following table for the period 2005 indicates:

Political party	% total of defectors gained	% total of defectors lost	Difference
ANC	56%	0%	+56%
DA	8%	20%	-12%
UDM	0%	12%	-12%
IFP	0%	20%	-20%
ID	0%	8%	-8%
ACDP	0%	12%	-12%
Newly formed parties (post-defection parties)	36%	0%	+36%

The most respectable argument that can be made in favour of floor-crossing is that, if one week is a long time in politics, as the cliché goes, then five years is a lifetime and, in South African politics, an eternity. Allegiances shift, parties change, voters' attitudes adjust. This is all true. Ideally, a political system should be able to adjust too. But the South African electoral system is based on a simple system of proportional representation. Indeed, the Constitution requires that the election process must be one that 'results, in general, in proportional representation'.[21] In the current system, every vote counts towards a national tally. This encourages multiparty democracy, and with the absence of any sort of minimum threshold to entry to parliament, a party that can win 0.25 per cent of the overall vote (at the last election, around 80 000 votes), will acquire at least one seat in the National Assembly. In a very diverse society, there is considerable merit to this system. It means, however, that the seat in parliament is owned not by the individual MP, but by his or her party. No MP is directly elected. Each owes his or her presence in parliament to the fact that he or she was on their party's electoral list. To permit an individual MP to 'cross the floor' to another party would, at face value, appear to be both illogical and entirely contrary to both the letter and the spirit of the system and, therefore, the Constitution.

This was the scope of the arguments before the Constitutional Court. The United Democratic Movement, led by General Bantu Holomisa, challenged the constitutionality of the proposed laws. My own organization, Idasa, presented arguments as *amicus curiae* (friend of the court), but strongly against the concept of floor-crossing, which we believed would encourage opportunism and favour the bigger parties. All the evidence from elsewhere suggests that bigger parties, especially those in government, can offer all manner of inducements to persuade individuals to cross to them. Often the inducement is the promise of a decent place on the ANC's list for the next election. Given the weakness of opposition parties generally, and their downward trajectory and poor resources (discussed in Chapter 7), a choice between being, say, twelfth on the UDM's list and 200th on the ANC's, represents no choice to a career politician bent on securing a long-term future in politics. The ANC is far more likely to secure at least 50 per cent of the vote than the UDM is to secure 3 per cent.

So, we return to the Constitutional Court. Wim Trengove SC represented the government and, on his feet for almost a whole day, gave an extraordinary exhibition of advocacy. It was breathtaking and persuasive, as compelling for Trengove's eloquence as for his management of the court. Unlike the International Court of Justice, for example, the South African Constitutional Court does not sit quietly listening to the arguments. It intervenes – often, and vigorously; sometimes startlingly early.

In the Treatment Action Campaign hearing, the accomplished senior counsel representing the government, Marumo Moerane, faced an uphill battle. That was obvious from the word go. I was there, and I timed it: the first interruption to his submissions from the bench came just less than ninety seconds after he got to his feet. A weak advocate will be blown rapidly off course by the torrent of questions and sharp observations. Like commercial jets circling in the skies above Heathrow, the eleven justices queue in a holding pattern, waiting to land their next intervention. It is relentless.

Tall and wiry, Trengove has a sinewy resolve and a crisp yet reassuring manner. Confronted by a proposition from the bench with which he does not agree, he will pause momentarily, then lean forward slightly and urge repentance upon the transgressor: 'No, Justice So-and-So, that is not right; the correct way to look at this issue is as follows ...' And then, almost seamlessly, he is back on track, tacking constantly into a judicial wind, but never losing sight of his course and his ultimate destination.

Trengove can get away with this, because he commands the respect of the court. They know that he knows as much about constitutional law as they do, so they will accept his firm responses to their questions. It is a matter of nerve as much as of law. The exchanges can be thrilling, even to a non-lawyer. There is an element of drama, not least because the stakes are often very high, literally a matter of life and death, such as in the Soobramoney case, when the court had to decide whether the applicant was entitled to access to a very expensive kidney dialysis machine that might save his life.[22] The court decided that the decision to refuse the treatment was not an unconstitutional breach of his right to adequate health care, contained in Section 27 of the Bill of Rights. Mr Soobramoney died shortly after the court's decision.

In the floor-crossing case, the court reached a pragmatic decision, with one of its most narrowly drawn decisions. Although the case was politically controversial and evenly balanced legally, the arguments were not especially complex. Even so, the court took a surprising amount of time (two whole months) to reach such a narrow judgment on such an urgent matter. The judgment was delivered by 'The Court', meaning that there was complete consensus on the details of the decision, as well as the decision itself (quite often, judges will reach the same decision, but by different routes of legal reasoning, and will wish to express themselves accordingly in separate judgments, whereupon the judgments are issued in the name or names of the particular judges).

But, at the hearing, the court appeared anything but in consensus. Interpreting the disposition of a particular judge towards a particular argument can be an extremely treacherous exercise; it is just as likely that the judge who most ardently questions an advocate's submission is, in fact, merely shoring up his or her own view in support of the submission as against it.

Nonetheless, in the floor-crossing case, the disdainful tone of Justices Richard Goldstone and Johann Kriegler's interruptions suggested that they were ill-disposed towards the legislation. In their turn, both Justices Sandile Ngcobo and Kate O'Regan, sharp as pins, appeared sceptical of the logic of Trengove's submissions on behalf of the state, while Justices Yacoob and Sachs appeared far more at ease with both the reason for and the potential effect of the proposed laws. Sitting in the middle of the court, the then chief justice, Arthur Chaskalson, and his then deputy, Pius Langa, were as hard to read as ever. Despite this, the court reached a unanimous position, with a narrow reasoning (see below).

Insiders tell me that this outcome was testimony to the artful chairmanship of Chaskalson, who was desperate to avoid a split court on such a politically emotive subject. As I noted above in the context of Justice Sachs's original JSC interview, there is a strong streak of political pragmatism in the court, which has been one of its guiding lights during its first twelve years. The strong preference for consensus above conflict and division is, as I noted in the Introduction, a distinctive feature of the new South Africa, even where it may involve discomforting compromises. One critic, Alfred Cockrell, complained as early as 1996 that the court was prone to what he called a 'rainbow jurisprudence', characterized by finding consensus where there is none, 'denying the existence of deep conflict in the realm of substantive reasons, assuming ... that constitutional adjudication is all about normative harmony rather than normative discord'.[23]

Perhaps, too, Chief Justice Chaskalson and a critical mass of his colleagues had temporarily lost their appetite for overturning the government, the case coming as it did just one month after the controversial Treatment Action Campaign case against the government's refusal to provide pregnant HIV-positive mothers with the antiretroviral drug nevirapine.[24] In contrast to the more assertive and expansive mood of their TAC judgment, in the floor-crossing case, the judges took a dry and narrow approach, as evidenced by this excerpt from the judgment:

> Objection was also taken to the introduction of the system during the term of the legislatures. It was contended that the anti-defection provision might have affected the way voters cast their votes and that its repeal would thus infringe their rights under section 19 of the Constitution.

> The section provides:
> (1) Every citizen is free to make political choices, which includes the right-
>   (a) to form a political party;
>   (b) to participate in the activities of, or recruit members for, a political party; and
>   (c) to campaign for a political party or cause.

(2) Every citizen has the right to free, fair and regular elections for any legislative body established in terms of the Constitution.

(3) Every adult citizen has the right-

    (a) to vote in elections for any legislative body established in terms of the Constitution, and to do so in secret; and

    (b) to stand for public office and, if elected, to hold office.

None of the rights specified in section 19, seen on its own or collectively with others, is infringed by a repeal or amendment of the anti-defection provisions. The rights entrenched under section 19 are directed to elections, to voting and to participation in political activities. Between elections, however, voters have no control over the conduct of their representatives. They cannot dictate to them how they must vote in Parliament, nor do they have any legal right to insist that they conduct themselves or refrain from conducting themselves in a particular manner. The fact that political representatives may act inconsistently with their mandates is a risk in all electoral systems ... According to the evidence a number of parties campaigned on the basis that they would oppose the ANC in the National Assembly. That, however, could not preclude a party from changing its mind after the elections and forming an alliance with the ANC. Persons who voted for that party may feel betrayed by such a decision, but they cannot contend that the change infringed their rights under section 19. Their remedy comes at the time of the next election when they decide how to cast their votes.[25]

As I pointed out at the beginning of this chapter, judges are human beings, not automatons. A case such as the floor-crossing challenge could have been decided within the bounds of reasonableness in either direction. An intuitive appreciation of the issue, as much as legal rationality, could guide an individual judge towards one outcome ahead of another. Though my distaste for floor-crossing is undimmed, the court cannot be blamed for the inaccurate proposition that has been peddled ever since by those in favour of it, namely that the 'Constitutional Court approved floor-crossing'. It did no such thing. No more than any judge or jury has ever found a criminal defendant 'innocent'.

Criminal courts reach verdicts of 'not guilty'. Equally, Constitutional Courts reach decisions about the constitutionality of a particular law, policy or exercise of public or private power. In the UDM case, they found that the proposed laws permitting floor-crossing did not offend the Constitution and were not, therefore, unconstitutional. Indeed, I have no problem what-soever with a holistic approach to the epic task of protecting the Bill of Rights and building a powerful constitutional edifice with a matching social culture. Rome was not built overnight. Patience is a prerequisite.

My sense is that, under the stewardship of Chaskalson, and now Langa – a 'black Arthur' in the view of one judge, who adds that 'Langa has always regarded Chaskalson as something of a mentor; they are temperamentally and legally similar' – the court opted to take a prudent approach to the more political cases that came before it, anxious not so much to be deferential as to be gradualist in forging a careful, long-term strategy for the defence of the Constitution. In the words of one judge, 'Chaskalson's attitude was that "this court will not lift itself unaided; we can't go to war with the government".'

The Constitutional Court and socio-economic justice

A similar attitude can be detected in the approach to the fairly small number of cases to have reached the Constitutional Court concerning the inter-pretation or protection of the so-called 'socio-economic rights' enshrined within the Constitution – which include the right to adequate health care, food, water and social security, and the right to access to adequate housing and a basic education. Many people would either regard these rights as fundamental to a dignified human existence or, because of their own wealth, take them for granted. For the great majority of South Africans, however, they are conspicuous by their absence.

Yet, for lawyers and politicians everywhere, socio-economic rights remain controversial, partly because it is a relatively new area of law, and partly because it makes politicians in government nervous because of the way in which the International Covenant on Economic, Social and Cultural Rights frames the approach that governments should take in response to such rights, namely to 'progressively realize' them (the same phrase that appears in the South African Bill of Rights). The contrast with civil and political rights is very clear, and the real point is this: realizing socio-economic rights means redistributing resources from the rich to the poor. The United States has never ratified the International Covenant on Economic, Social and Cultural Rights (nor, in fact, has South Africa). In this sense, the South African Bill of Rights is one of the boldest in the world, and the way in which both the court and the government respond to the challenge continues to attract attention from all around the globe.

Three main socio-economic rights cases have reached the Constitutional Court – the Soobramoney case, mentioned above, the Treatment Action Campaign case in relation to the provision of nevirapine, and Grootboom, which dealt with the right to housing.[26] There are complex legal points involved and it is not possible to do justice to them here. The consensus position of the leading experts, such as University of Stellenbosch professor Sandra Liebenberg, is not so much one of dashed hopes, but of disappointment laced with optimism that the struggle is far from over:

> The Constitutional Court is carving out an important role for itself in the enforcement of socio-economic rights. In the first place, it has created the possibility of challenging state or private action that prevents or impairs access to socio-economic rights – the negative duty 'to respect' the rights. Secondly, the principles of reasonableness review provide the basis for challenging the state for not giving effect to the positive duties imposed by socio-economic rights. Thus social programmes can be challenged for being poorly coordinated, unreasonably implemented or for not providing short-term relief for those in desperate need … However, by rejecting the concept of minimum core obligations under Sections 26 and 27, the Court has limited the circumstances in which individuals can directly claim socio-economic goods and services from the state … While the Court has developed clear and useful criteria for a reasonable government programme to realise socio-economic rights, it is regrettable that it has unnecessarily limited the potential of these constitutional rights to contribute to a better quality of life for all.[27]

Grootboom concerned a homeless community that challenged their local municipality's refusal to provide them with temporary shelter. The court held that the state's failure to make proper provision for people in desperate need violated its obligation under Section 26(1) and (2) of the Constitution to 'take reasonable and other measures within its available resources' to provide access to adequate housing.

As one commentator, Theunis Roux, observed, 'At first blush, this decision appears to be a remarkable slap in the face of a government that has made great strides in a short time to redress the apartheid housing backlog. Closer examination of the reasons for the decision, however, reveals a diplomatically worded and respectful message to the political branches, overwhelmingly endorsing their efforts, even as the Court finds fault with aspects of the national housing programme.'[28]

Another commentator, Siri Gloppen, further illuminates: 'The Grootboom judgment was acclaimed among international academics for its creative and politically astute reasoning – carving out space for itself in the policy-making process without usurping the space for political decision-making. For prospective litigants it was, however, discouraging that the Constitutional Court had limited its role to that of policing the policy-making process rather than recognizing an enforceable individual right to shelter, or defining a minimum core of the right to be given absolute priority.'[29]

On gender equality, the scales appear to tip more favourably towards the court. Two of the leading constitutional law thinkers, Professor Christina Murray of UCT and her former colleague Saras Jagwanth (now at the United Nations), commend the court for the fact that 'In the interpretation and application of the equality guarantee, the Constitutional Court has high-lighted the central place of equality in the new South African order.'[30]

However, they also express disappointment about one decision that sheds some light on the possible future trajectory of the court, given the fact that its composition has changed significantly during the period 2002–05, as some of the first batch of judges retired. In the Jordan case, the court was faced with the constitutionality of provisions of the Sexual Offences Act, which criminalized sex work and the keeping of a brothel. In its decision, an unprecedented division of 6–5 split the court. Justice Sandile Ngcobo gave the majority judgment, which was supported by Justices Chaskalson, Kriegler, Madala, Du Plessis (acting judge) and Skweyiya (acting judge). While he reached the same outcome as the minority judgment penned by Justices O'Regan and Sachs, he preferred not to go as far as them.

While Ngcobo's reasoning led him to conclude that the law was unconstitutional, he found against the argument that part of the unconstitutionality was direct gender discrimination against women prostitutes. In contrast, the minority judgment, which was supported by Justices Langa,

Ackerman and Goldstone, adopted a more contextual approach. As Murray and Jagwanth put it:

> Given the contextual nature of the equality test, the reasoning of the majority in Jordan is surprisingly acontextual and ignores the larger gendered framework within which the prostitution takes place. There can be no doubt that the vast majority of sex workers are women. The economic and social reasons for this are well documented. Thus, under the equality provision, and the test laid down by the court itself, the differentiation in question clearly constitutes indirect gender discrimination.[31]

Of the above two groups of judges, three remain on the court from each side. (Justices Mokgoro and Yacoob were on leave at the time.) Three new judges have been appointed since: Moseneke, Bess Nkabinde and Van der Westhuizen. It may be premature to say so, but there may be a trend towards two main factions in the court: a socially conservative side, and a more radical, progressive one. On which side of the fence the new batch of judges falls, especially Deputy Chief Justice Moseneke, will be crucial for the orientation and depth of the court's future influence on power in South Africa.

It may also be possible to detect some sort of pattern in the appointments to the court in the post-1999 period. Certainly it is clear that at that point, Mbeki, newly installed as president, and encouraged by his increasingly influential legal advisor Mojanku Gumbi, injected some much-needed energy into the process of transforming the judiciary. Soon after, Sandile Ngcobo was appointed to the court ahead of Edwin Cameron, in a JSC shoot-out between the two in April 1999. Cameron had sat as an acting judge and was highly regarded. As I have already noted, Ngcobo is a strong presence on the court, with a sharp intellect, and was the stronger of the two candidates. Yet, the point may well be not so much that a stronger or equal black candidate was being preferred to a white candidate, as many assumed at the time, but that the relative conservatism of the candidate made him even more attractive to the highest powers in the land.

So, too, with the decision of the JSC, on three occasions, not to appoint Geoff Budlender to a permanent position on the Cape High Court. Budlender, a leading activist human rights lawyer at the Legal Resources

Centre, and a man once described to me by the head of Idasa, Paul Graham, as a 'national treasure', was overlooked not, I suggest, because of the colour of his skin, as many chose to think, but rather because he, like Cameron, would have brought a far more 'activist' outlook to the bench, especially on socio-economic rights.

Judicial independence vs judicial accountability: A zero-sum game?

So, if judges don't only 'say the law but make it', then accountability becomes almost as important as independence. It would seem that the *leitmotif* for South Africa, as it enters its second decade of democracy, is increasingly the unhealthy overlap between private business interests and the duties of public office. The principal mechanism that has been developed to counteract the potential conflicts of interest that arise between a 'public duty', held by a public office holder such as an MP or a public servant, and any 'private interest' that they may hold in a commercial entity, is transparency – disclosure of the detail of the private interest pursuant to a code of conduct, such as the parliamentary Code of Ethics.

The question that arises in the case of the judiciary is that, if MPs, members of the executive, senior public servants and even local government councillors have to disclose their financial interests, why should judges be exempt from having to do so? How can one argue that judges are immune to influence?

In 2006, allegations surfaced against Judge President Hlophe and a number of other judges precisely on this issue, indicating the influence that corporate interests may have on the judiciary. In late March 2006, *Noseweek* magazine revealed that Hlophe had been on a retainer for a prominent asset management company. In terms of the 'rules' (which is largely an honour-based system), judges are not permitted to receive additional remuneration while sitting – a way of excluding the contaminating influence of the private sector on the bench. It is only 'allowed' if the minister of justice gives express permission (albeit in secret). However, the granting of permission is rare. And for good reason: Hlophe, during the period of the alleged retainer, handed down a judgment in favour of Oasis Asset Management.

The proposals contained in the Judicial Service Commission Amendment Bill would mean that judges declare their financial interests in a register. It would also mean that judges would be 'subject' to a code of conduct and would be able to be 'disciplined' should they behave in a manner inconsistent with their office. Judges have resisted attempts at both discipline and disclosure of financial interests, saying that it may well interfere with their independence.

The debate on the independence of the judiciary versus its accountability, which raged in the latter part of 2005 and throughout most of 2006, was in some quarters seen as Johnny de Lange vs the Judges. The controversial package of laws introduced by government in an attempt to enhance the accountability of the judiciary and to spur on transformation was largely seen as the hard-nosed De Lange acting as the ministerial proxy. The laws attracted controversy, mainly because they required constitutional amendment. While most of the critics of the proposed bills approved of the general aims of their proposed laws, two areas ruffled even the most progressive legal feathers – the first being the need for constitutional amendment to bring about transformation and accountability within the judiciary; the second, what some saw as the blurring of the lines between accountability and independence.

Legal education for judges, the declaration of judges' financial interests, (including a code of conduct for judges incorporated in the legislation) and giving the minister of justice final say over the administration of the courts saw legal luminaries like George Bizos SC – an iconic and influential veteran legal figure due to his long-standing association with Nelson Mandela, as his advocate – and Arthur Chaskalson, now unfettered in retirement, weighing in on the debate. Caution, they urged: once you 'legislate' accountability, you run the risk of emasculating the judiciary, specifically when it comes to issues of administration and 'judging the judges'.

They and others argued that the separation of powers and the countervailing power of the courts are best preserved without a constitutional amendment and with a minimalist approach to legislating accountability. Government, in its bid to transform and balance power evenly, clearly thought otherwise. At the time of writing, the debate was evenly poised. President Mbeki, feigning surprise at the indignation that the draft bills had caused, had in early 2006 proposed a period of a few months' further reflection and public comment and debate, which was further extended after the July 2006 *lekgotla* had considered the issue.

As the issue of regulating judges' outside financial interests shows, there is a tightrope to be walked between too much independence and not enough accountability on the one side, and the reverse on the other. There are many who believe that formal sanctions will afford the government the opportunity to encroach on the independence of the judiciary. On the other hand, why does the public not have the right to know what financial interests judges have? Why should judges slip through the accountability net?

In answering these questions, an absolutist stance is best avoided, for the answer is probably a grey area. Somehow a balance needs to be found between ensuring the constitutional requirement of judicial independence, while at the same time recognizing the need to hold judges to account – a balance that is critical to the equilibrium of political power in the new South Africa.

Looking ahead: A force for change or status quo

The Constitutional Court is regularly referred to as being the Apex Court. 'Tip of the Iceberg' might be a more apt phrase. Glinting in the sun, it represents so much that is excellent about democratic power in the new South Africa. But beneath it lies the rest of the judiciary, struggling along – under-resourced, under-financed, under-transformed and riddled with squabbles – although, as the quality of the Constitutional Court deteriorates, so the stock of the Supreme Court of Appeal, for so long the embodiment of an old, white and discredited judiciary, rises; and so the balance of influence may move somewhat towards Bloemfontein (the SCA's institutional home).

The bar, too, needs to move with the times. It is striking that there is such a small pool of senior constitutional advocates to choose from. Most of them are white men – Wim Trengove, Gilbert Marcus and Jeremy Gauntlett being the three most pre-eminent – who enjoy an oligopoly of access to the Constitutional Court cases and, thereby, a disproportionate amount of influence on how the court hears arguments and develops its jurisprudence.

The most important person in the judiciary is, by definition, the chief justice. But Pius Langa may not be the most influential. For one, his term as chief justice will be short. He will be seventy in March 2009, and will retire at or before that time. Compared with his predecessor (four years, compared with eleven), his opportunity to craft the modus operandi and the jurisprudence of both his own court and the lower courts will be limited. Instead, the deputy chief justice – an odds-on favourite to succeed him in 2009 – will exert a growing influence.

Dikgang Moseneke is a truly remarkable man. His life's journey is astounding: arrested and sentenced to ten years in prison when he was just fifteen, he then spent a decade on Robben Island. On release, he broke through into the legal profession and took silk after just ten years, which is about as quick a journey to being a senior counsel as it is possible to take. As well as serving on the technical committee that drafted the Interim Constitution, Moseneke was also deputy chairperson of the Independent Electoral Commission during the founding democratic elections of 1994. He got his hands dirty at the coalface of democratic transition.

Though he was at pains to disguise their identity, in his 2002 JSC interview, Moseneke referred several times to 'unnamed people' who were pushing him to return to the law and, thereby, to the Constitutional Court bench. President Mbeki was one of those people. Mathatha Tsedu, then editor of the *Sunday Times*, who is not well-known for liberal sprinklings of unwarranted praise, licked his lips and waxed lyrical at the time: 'It is a great appointment that will introduce into the higher echelons of our judiciary a man whose commitment to justice and the courage of his convictions are truly beyond question.'[32] In 2009, Moseneke will be sixty-two, so he will have a full eight years as chief justice – assuming he is not plucked from that position for even greater public duty. There is something he has in common with another of the most influential people in South Africa. Like President Mbeki's legal advisor and right-hand woman, Mojanku Gumbi, Moseneke's political background is not ANC, but the PAC. Gumbi and Moseneke are also good friends. That Moseneke will push the same clear Africanist line as Gumbi and Mbeki should neither be doubted nor necessarily feared.

What is more significant is what, if any, ideological foundation this approach is built upon. On that front, Moseneke is something of an enigma. Unlike the rather shy and relatively diffident Chaskalson and Langa, Moseneke is suave and socially confident. As one judge put it, 'He is clever, arrogant, charming, traditional and very rich – he doesn't need the job and is, presumably, incorruptible.' He will have considerable clout when he becomes chief justice, not least because his network of connections is so good, spanning the commanding heights of the economy to the presidency and the grand professions. He is as truly emblematic of a new elite as it is possible to be, and like Gumbi and others of their political ilk, more confident in dealing with powerful white people.

The Constitutional Court is an institution that is not merely 'First World', but better. It is much admired throughout the world; its commitment to excellence, and the superb building on Constitution Hill in Johannesburg which it now occupies, are points of justifiable national pride. I would agree with those academic commentators who have concluded that, while the Constitutional Court, and the judiciary in general, has 'maintained its autonomy by not blindly deferring to the executive branch in various disputes, it has also reflected a healthy respect for the political processes of governance'.[33]

As noted, there are some critics who contend that the court has not been assertive enough in pushing the frontier of socio-economic rights. Others maintain that it has probably moved as fast as it can. It is by definition the most important institution in the country – as noted, in a constitutional democracy, the Constitutional Court is the ultimate arbiter and guardian of the Constitution – but although its judgments have been profoundly influential, they might still have been more so under bolder leadership. As noted, Chaskalson and Langa are both conservative – not politically, but as lawyers.

Overall, however, the Constitutional Court remains in reasonably good shape – both as a creator of jurisprudence and as protector of the Bill of Rights. The years 2004–06 represented a transition period for the court, as many of the brilliant first intake of 1994 retired (Chaskalson, Kriegler, Goldstone) or entered the final phase of the period of their tenure (Madala, O'Regan, Sachs, Mokgoro).

As the following table shows, by 2009 all of the class of 1994 will have left the court. One senior counsel who appears often before the Constitutional Court is nostalgic for its early days: 'It was a superstar court, with very few mediocre or poor judges; now, sadly, it is a mirror image of that balance, with only one superstar judge – O'Regan – and only three other good judges – Ngcobo, Moseneke and Yacoob. It has gone from being one of the best courts in the world to one that is good at best and pedestrian at worst.'

Constitutional Court judges – tenure[34]

Judge	Date of birth	Age at 31/12/06	Date of appointment	End of tenure
Langa	Mar-39	67 yrs, 9 mths	Oct-94	Sept 2009
Madala	Jul-37	69 yrs, 5 mths	Oct-94	July 2009
Mokgoro	Oct-50	56 yrs, 2 mths	Oct-94	Sept 2009
Moseneke	Dec-47	59 yrs	Oct-02	Jan 2017
Ngcobo	Mar-53	53 yrs, 9 mths	Apr-99	July 2011
Nkabinde	1959	47 yrs	Feb-06	Feb 2021
O'Regan	Sep-57	49 yrs, 3 mths	Oct-94	Sept 2009
Sachs	Jan-35	71 yrs, 11 mths	Oct-94	Sept 2009
Skweyiya	Jun-39	67 yrs, 6 mths	Oct-03	June 2014
Van der Westhuizen	May-52	54 yrs, 7 mths	Feb-04	Feb 2016
Yacoob	Mar-48	58 yrs, 9 mths	Feb-98	Jan 2013

Two recent appointments, Thembile Skweyiya and Johann van der Westhuizen, have raised the eyebrows of many experts. Few expect them to be bold and assertive; instead, they are expected to be far more cautious in responding to constitutional challenges to government law and policy. The appointments that the JSC makes when replacing O'Regan, Sachs and Mokgoro will be crucial to the future trajectory of the Constitutional Court, and will determine the balance of power on the court for the next generation. By the time Moseneke becomes chief justice in 2009, only two of the ten other judges he joined in 2002 will still be on the court: Sandile Ngcobo and Zak Yacoob.

Ngcobo is more of a 'traditionalist' than Moseneke. In the phrase of one senior advocate, who cites Ngcobo's dissenting judgment in the Bhe case, where he was far less harsh than the majority opinion of the court on African customary law, he is a cultural conservative.[35] But the jury is out on precisely how conservative or radical Moseneke is.

One political analyst, Ralph Mathekga of Idasa, has 'reservations about the equation of a black judge with "progressive" judgments. This correlation, that black judges are more likely to deliver progressive judgments, seems to go unquestioned, and I think it should be questioned. I think there will be an emergence of black judges who do not buy in, and they may end up being labelled "Clarence Thomas".'

Nonetheless, Mathekga believes that Moseneke's court will be distinctive and potentially radical: 'As I see it, Moseneke has rejected a purely liberal perspective on equality (negative liberty, as we know it), for example, and will continue to argue for a more radical, "SA-focused" outlook of what the right to equality entails.'

So far his judgments on the court, although as elegant as the man himself, have offered few substantial pointers as to the direction he will lead the court. Moseneke may be more conservative than he seems. One member of the Advocates for Transformation (AFT) group in Pretoria told me that this had disappointed them when he made a speech in early 2006, in essence inviting them 'to hold your horses; accept gradual change at the bar'. He is, to the same AFT member, 'an innately conservative man; a Pretoria *boykie*'. Certainly, Moseneke likes to be in with the new establishment crowd, crisscrossing the social pathways of contemporary political and corporate power networks. Whether in time the 'Moseneke Court' comes to be regarded as bold or conservative remains to be seen, but certainly, whatever its direction, given the turnover during the current period and the respective personalities of the three chief justices, it will be far more 'his' court than either Chaskalson's or Langa's.

Finally, back to John Griffith, whose own conclusion in *The Politics of the Judiciary* was as follows: 'The judges define the public interest, inevitably, from the viewpoint of their own class. And the public interest, so defined, is by a natural, not an artificial, coincidence, the interest of others in authority, whether in government, in the City or in the church.'[36] The new diversity of the judiciary, both racial and social, does not necessarily mean a decisively more progressive exercise of judicial power in the long term. The gradualist prudence of the first decade of the Constitutional Court may yet ossify into something far more deferential and risk-averse. Or, with Moseneke's hand on the tiller, it may yet choose to navigate more adventurous waters.

Certainly the conclusion for South Africa now is decidedly different than for Griffith and 1970s Britain. It is not yet the case that there is a single, homogeneous judicial class whose interests accord and overlap with that of a broader establishment. But, soon to be led by such an establishment man, and with more and more judges taking advantage of lax rules that permit them to hold corporate financial interests, it may soon enough come to be so. Though it has stepped very cautiously at times, the Constitutional Court is a powerful counterweight in the overall balance of forces in South Africa. Only vigorous intellectual health, legitimate independence and public integrity can ensure that the judges continue to play an influential, as well as important, part in the country's future democratic life.

10

Civil Society

Touching a Raw Nerve

The first question a reader is entitled to ask at this point is: 'What the hell is "civil society?"' I remember the owner of the garage where I used to have my car serviced saying that experts on radio were always banging on about 'civil society', but he had no idea what they were talking about. It's a fair question, and one that is more easily answered in the negative than the positive; it is easier to describe what civil society is not than what it is.

Civil society is not government, in all its shapes and forms. It is non-governmental (hence the acronym 'NGO': non-governmental organization). It applies to the bigger, organized civil society organizations. Nor is it the private sector, as a for-profit company is not part of civil society. Hence, in my opinion, the media, except for its non-profit alternative media outlets, is not part of civil society. Lest we forget, most newspapers and radio stations are there to make money for their shareholders. And the public broadcaster is by definition part of the state.

Thus, civil society is All the Rest: the Church, the trade unions (although in this country, the major umbrella organization, COSATU, enjoys a special link with the ruling party, which means that they get separate treatment), the human rights pressure groups, the policy think tanks, the charitable trusts, the voluntary associations and the myriad different community organizations that exist. Some academics would then go on to distinguish between organized civil society and the rest. Certainly, when one refers to civil society, one does not mean individual citizens acting in relation to their own, individual interests.

Since politics is in practice often a contest for the public space, the fact that there are many such CSOs (civil society organizations) in South Africa, a country with an enviously rich history of civil society organization and activism, is terribly important for understanding the power relations that exist in society. The strength of civil society – its freedom to organize, to raise money, to lobby and to express itself, as well as its institutional capacity, including its intellectual and material resources – is often cited as a key indicator of the well-being of a democracy. Clearly, the stronger the civil society sector, the more likely that power can be diffused over a wide range of sectors, and the less chance for monopolies or oligopolies of political power to grow and exercise power indiscriminately.

As noted by a 2003 Idasa study[1] on the state of civil society in South Africa, conducted on behalf of the innovative Centre for Civil Society (CCS) in Durban (civil society even has its own civil society organizations to study itself), modern definitions of civil society emerged through the thought experiments of the philosophers Hobbes and Locke. Locke made the significant step of distinguishing the state from society, in which the separation of state and society led not to disaster but salvation. A community with an adequate consciousness of its own rights and enough confidence to challenge authority could tame the political powers that traditionally threatened and devoured human beings' 'natural rights'.

As the Idasa study notes:[2]

After the first democratic elections in 1994 the role of civil society changed dramatically vis-à-vis the state and society in South Africa. The 1994 election victory led to the expectation of a shared path forward for development, especially since many of the leaders of the anti-apartheid struggle moved to positions of power in the new ANC-led government. This resulted in a dearth in civil society leadership, which left civil society organisations weak and at times unresponsive. Many civil society stake-holders had close ties to the new government and, trusting their comrades to deliver on their promises, they saw a less obvious role for themselves as watchdogs. Deep loyalty to the anti-apartheid movement also kept voices of criticism at bay, as the ANC policy of a unified front prevailed.

Some CSOs adapted and flourished; others didn't and withered on the vine.

It is a large and diverse sector. Another recent study,[3] conducted in 2002 by the Graduate School of Public and Development Management at the University of the Witwatersrand, found that the non-profit sector employs around 650 000 workers, a substantial number of the employed population. In addition, the work equivalent to that of 317 000 workers, worth around

R5.1 billion, was done by 1.5 million unpaid volunteers. The proportion of work done by volunteers is greater, the study found, than in twenty-eight developed countries. These are serious numbers. While the sector cannot mobilize as powerfully as it did at the height of the struggle against apartheid, nor as rapidly or in such numbers as in India, it still represents a potentially powerful counterbalance to state and corporate power.

Changing civil society:
The new social movements

The Idasa civil society study concluded that, despite low levels of confidence in their own advocacy skills, civil society organizations feel that their policy-making inputs do contribute to government's decision-making in a measurable way. CSOs are learning more sophisticated advocacy techniques, as well as the need for varied strategy and tactics; a Plan B is essential! While parliament has at times proved fertile ground for lobbying, and some NGOs in particular have established a strong bridgehead in parliament, most are realizing that the key time to influence government is while it is making up its mind. Thus, interaction with the executive arm of government in the policy-design phase is crucial.

Unlike parliament, where one knows the rules and the members, the executive represents an opaque and shadowy world. Whereas parliament has to honour certain rules to grant and facilitate public participation, as noted in Chapter 4, the executive has far greater scope to ignore pressure groups and other CSOs. The Idasa study concluded that, in order to interact with policy-makers, CSOs need information, and often it is not available and government is unwilling to share. A study[4] conducted by the Open Democracy Advice Centre revealed that, although government tended to be more responsive to NGOs than other requesters, the overall level of responsiveness of the executive was very poor. Over 50 per cent of requests were ignored, despite the legal requirement to respond inside thirty days.

Partly as a response to what they perceive to be the closed-mindedness of government, new formations of civil society have emerged, typically referred to as 'new social movements'. What exactly constitutes a 'social movement' is an even more vexed debate than the one around the definition of civil society. The precise definition of social movements is elusive. The boundaries between a social movement and a football club, an independent religion, a vigilante group, trade union, political party or NGO remain fuzzy.[5]

Ebrahim Fakir, a former member of my staff at Idasa, suggests that 'the social movements are movements that organize themselves and mobilize their associational networks to challenge and resist the actions of the local State, which they conceive of as limiting citizens' access to public goods and services on a mass scale, and for a reasonable cost, or no cost at all in the case of the indigent and the poor. In addition these social movements see the local State as complicit in the implementation of neo-liberal programmes of privatization of public utilities, precisely those that are able to deliver the public goods and services that allow for the assertion of citizenship and the rights that accrue to citizenship.' For the purpose of this book and its deliberation about who controls power now, the social movements that are important and perhaps influential arise from a perceived gap that has apparently emerged on the left of the political spectrum and, in related fashion, as a response to the government's macroeconomic policies (specifically its approach to privatization and the provision of local services).

As Fakir writes in a recent, insightful paper on social movements: 'The "new social movements" did not emerge from a vacuum. There are two distinct, yet contradictory, interrelated and interdependent threads that underlie the phenomenon. The first is the state's adoption of certain policies and the effect these have had on communities. The second related issue is the negative effects of corporate globalisation and the linkages between social actors and activists and those in other countries confronting similar challenges ...'[6]

Trevor Ngwane is perhaps the most influential figure in the new social movements. Once an ANC councillor in Johannesburg, he broke ranks in 1997 once 'the mood changed within the ANC caucus: robust debates became muted; decisions were taken away from councillors, and we were discouraged from participating in local community forums. There were issues we couldn't discuss.'[7] Ngwane became more widely known as a result of a brilliant and esoteric short film made by Ben Cashdan, called *Two Trevors*.

The film followed Trevor Ngwane and Trevor Manuel as they attended, respectively, the World Trade Organization meeting in Washington, DC in December 1999, and the simultaneous anti-globalization protest. Manuel hated the film; Ngwane loved it. Certainly it captured the apparently profound dislocation between the ANC government's position and that of the new formations that were springing up: the Anti-Privatization Forum (APF), the Soweto Electricity Crisis Committee (SECC), the Western Cape Anti-Eviction Campaign (WECAEC), the Landless People's Movement (LPM) and the Anti-Eviction Campaign, to name but a few.

Aside from Ngwane, some of the social movements' most prominent member activists are Ashwin Desai, Durban Institute for Technology; George Dor, Jubilee South, veteran anti-globalization academic and activist; Professor Dennis Brutus; Professor Patrick Bond, who is based at the University of the Witwatersrand; Salim Vally, Wits Education Policy Unit; Dale McKinley, Anti-Privatization Forum, who was expelled some years ago from the SACP; Ahmed Veriava and Prishani Naidoo, Indi Media SA; Andile Mngxitama, Landless People's Movement; Anne Eveleth, also LPM; and Peter van Heusden, Anti-Eviction Campaign, Cape Town.

The backdrop to these trends is the emergence of some very compelling data on the hardships imposed on people as a result of privatization:

> Approximately ten million cut-offs have occurred because people have been unable to pay their bills. About two million people have been victims of rates and rent-evictions from their houses for the non-payment of rates [and because of an inability to do so] … more than 20 000 households per month have their electricity and water cut off … the Department of Provincial and Local Government reports that more than 296 000 disconnections of electricity and 133 000 of water took place in the last quarter of 2001, most of which would have been low-income households.[8]

Thus, the 'new social movements' are protests against the heterodoxy of the government's approach to the state. So, what this discussion about the power and influence of civil society boils down to is the future of the left – its strategy and tactics, as well as its ideology. Do the social movements matter? Are they more than a passing nuisance to those in government? Do they do more than prick consciences? Are they listened to at all?

When someone in power takes the trouble to give something a 'bad' label, it usually means that at the very least you have attracted attention. So, when in mid-2002 the phrase 'ultra-left' was hauled out, having first appeared in an internal ANC National Executive document believed to have been written in its original form by Joel Netshitenzhe, it was seen by the left as a provocative attempt to isolate them. But it depended on what one meant by 'the left'. For, as I looked into the issue at the time, assuming this to be high-handed and clumsy Mbekism at work, I changed my opinion, and realized that the main beneficiaries were the left *inside* the ANC rather than the left outside of it. In other words, by labelling the social movements' leaders 'ultra-left', the SACP and COSATU appeared more 'respectable' and sensible, and thus more likely to be listened to. This fits in not just with the predominant strategy of the SACP and COSATU, as discussed in Chapter 6, but also with the approach of the presidency, which is far more interested in technical solutions to problems than wild exclamations of ideology and harsh indictments of policy.

Goolam Aboobaker, deputy director-general in the presidency, responsible for the day-to-day running of the policy unit, disagrees. He says he 'does not know the name of the director of the Landless People's Movement. These social movements are not really taken seriously here, mainly because the issues they deal with don't appear to be the key challenges confronting the country. For example, how should we see the land question? Is it part of the agrarian question? Or in South Africa, is it an issue of urban land for houses? They don't appear to have an intellectual engagement with questions like these, so to us it does not appear to be a serious engagement.'

The Anti-Privatization Forum does not have a 'nuanced view', in Aboobaker's opinion. He cites a story involving a supper at ANC veteran activist Phyllis Naidoo's house several years ago. Aboobaker collected an old communist mentor, Old Man (AK) Docrat, to take to the supper. When he arrived, Docrat immediately went on the offensive: 'How do you explain this privatization thing?' According to Aboobaker, Naidoo shot back immediately: 'Why must you and I subsidize South African Airways when they run at a loss? You don't fly. I don't want to subsidize something that is mainly used by rich people.'

The left is less left than those at the heart of government may think; and those at the heart of government are far less right than those on the far-left think. Some of the key advisors to the president, including the vastly influential Joel Netshitenzhe, remain in my view committed to social transformation and social democracy. They have the obligation to deliver it; those outside have the luxury of being able to demand solutions that may or may not be viable, whether politically, legally, or economically, given the global climate and the constraints it imposes.

Somewhere between the heart of government and the left sit the ANC's alliance partners, the SACP and COSATU. It is about as comfortable a spot as sitting on top of the Table Mountain cable car in a howling southeaster: the view is certainly captivating, but there is a long way to fall, the grip is precarious and the stakes fairly high. It is deeply ideological territory and highly contested terrain. While I have views, some of which I choose to express in my columns in the *Mail & Guardian*, this is not the place to comment. What is important for my current purpose is the contestation of power and influence, not the objective or subjective rights and wrongs of the ideology of the combatants. On this, it is clear that at the moment the ANC in government feels confident that it can ignore the demands of the 'new social movements'. Though their numbers and activism may be gathering momentum, they are not yet powerful enough to greatly worry the new establishment – though that could soon change.

There is one recent additional development on the civil society scene – the launch of a 'new UDF'. The UDF was one of the key social mobilizations against apartheid. Many government and ANC–alliance leaders grew up within the UDF and came to lead it, as has been noted at various points throughout this book. It became the frontispiece for the internal resistance movement in the 1980s. So to launch a 'new UDF' is both bold and cheeky, but not entirely surprising. In the first place, there is a deficit in grassroots involvement in politics. Coupled with poor institutional development, the possibilities for ordinary communities to influence the political process – except through periodic voting – are slim, whether this limitation is perceived or real.

For example, Trevor Ngwane contested the 2005 local government elections under the banner of the Operation Khanyisa Movement (OKM). The OKM, while largely a distinct political party, has strong relationships with the Anti-Privatization Forum, and was constituted after extensive consultation with them. In addition, while small, there is significant overlap in the leadership and membership of the social movements and the OKM. While that is the case, there is also substantial disagreement among them, about whether elections should, in the first place, be contested. Hardly surprisingly, the OKM fared dismally in the local government elections.

Part of the new UDF's problem, as is the case with the new social movements as with certain other sectors of 'civil society' that purport to speak for the poor or their membership or 'constituency', is that they are not always as representative as they claim to be. Sometimes the depth of penetration in the particular community is not sufficient to ensure that theirs are the same interests as those of the people they so earnestly seek to represent. As Fakir writes, 'Civil society's limitations lie not in its lack of energy or independence but in its shallow reach: participation remains beyond many citizens who lack the resources to combine to act on their right ... civil society, while vigorous, is unable to extend its reach to society's grassroots.'[9]

This is the dilemma of representative democracy, where political parties are the principal channels through which popular opinion is conveyed. In developed democracies, ordinary citizens have their voices represented through pressure groups, sometimes in the form of lobby firms or single-issue groups. In those societies, the term 'civil society' refers to a broader public engagement, made possible by higher rates of literacy.

Thus, citizens are more conversant with the detail of policy issues, and hence they can track political events and attempt to intervene through organized bodies. While South African civil society organizations are making strides in advancing political education and citizens' awareness, many of these efforts are undermined by low levels of literacy. Therefore, the UDF-style model is a reasonable response to the social constraints; it aims to build solidarity outside political parties, or organized institutions, to create a parallel system of political engagement. A debate now continues as to the UDF's value and future; after an initial buzz, it appears to be fizzling out.

Viva TAC!

One civil society movement has matured way beyond this. The Treatment Action Campaign is the most successful new civil society entity that has emerged on the scene since 1994, and combines elements of the new social movements with more traditional policy and human rights NGO models. Headed by the award-winning activist Zackie Achmat, it has taken on the government in one of the most contentious areas, HIV/AIDS, and not only survived, but won many victories, including a momentous one in the Constitutional Court in July 2002 in which the government was ordered to immediately implement the rollout of antiretroviral drugs for pregnant mothers.

As noted in Chapter 9, the case was one of three very influential socio-economic rights cases that have come before the Constitutional Court during its first ten years, as well as compelling a major U-turn for government. It also demonstrates both the possibilities and the constraints for civil society in seeking to enforce socio-economic rights in the Constitution: 'The TAC case illustrates that strong organisations will be able to use the jurisprudence of reasonableness review to make strategic gains in challenging social programmes that are not responsive to the needs of the poor. However, the Court's rejection of the notion of minimum core obligations will make it very difficult for individuals living in extreme poverty to use litigation as a strategy to get immediate relief. There is also a danger that the state will fail to prioritise the basic socio-economic needs of vulnerable groups without the Court affirming this constitutional obligation.'[10]

The TAC is unique in one important respect: it is the only civil society organization that manages successfully to combine high-quality policy work and a litigation capacity with social mobilization. This multidimensional approach to their campaigning gives them both credibility and strength in numbers.

Zackie Achmat himself reflects the multidimensionality of his organization. He has an activist, ANC background, and the professional training, including legal expertise, to help guide the tricky strategic decisions he and the TAC have faced in recent years. Rightly, he is now widely regarded as South Africa's leading campaigner or lobbyist. The *Financial Mail* named Achmat as their 'Politician of the Decade' in their special supplement to commemorate ten years of democracy in April 2004. And he was nominated for the Nobel Peace Prize a year later. If you were to ask twenty random people who work in the civil society sector to nominate the most effective campaigner, I very much doubt that another name would be put forward.

The TAC has 10 000 registered members, and can and does muster the numbers for any occasion. I have been in meetings called to discuss issues which might appear tangential to the TAC's core concern (for example the arms deal), and, having accepted the invitation, the TAC will be represented by twenty people, most of them young and black, all wearing the now famous purple '+ve' T-shirt. The strategic importance of this is that it has become increasingly hard for government to dismiss the TAC as being non-representative, as it tries to do with other policy-orientated NGOs. The most common defence mechanism of the ANC is to challenge the credibility of NGOs by attacking their links with communities and ordinary people.

There has been a manifest failure on the part of the state in recognizing that, as Ebrahim Fakir puts it, 'civil society is fluid and dynamic, fragmented ... diverse, messy, complex and sometimes contradictory. Indeed, aspects of civil society activism have in some instances [such as some of the service delivery protests or the subversive attempts by the Boeremag] proved to be troublingly "uncivil".'

Very few of the leading NGOs in South Africa are membership organizations, unlike their equivalents in Europe or North America. Whereas Amnesty International, for example, can claim to speak on behalf of the approximately one million members it has around the world, my own organization, Idasa, even though it is the largest non-profit democracy organization on the African continent, does not have a membership to fall back on. We have to rely on the quality of our work instead of claiming to represent some nebulous 'public interest'.

Bruising encounters

I learnt this lesson the hard way. Months after joining Idasa in 1995 to set up its first parliamentary monitoring programme, I constructed a questionnaire to put to MPs, asking about their educational background and other biographical details, as well as their outside financial interests. It was quite a long questionnaire, with about 100 questions set out in a large, rather grandly appointed booklet. With the benefit of hindsight, I realize that it could have been more tactfully presented, but I did not anticipate the furore it would cause, especially within the governing party, who actually caucused on the issue to prepare a concerted, retaliatory response.

The chief whip sent around a circular suggesting – though not ordering – ANC MPs to ignore the questionnaire. Although about 100 of the ANC MPs ignored his advice, another 100-plus presumably took it, as we heard nothing from them, which undermined the purpose of the survey, which was to gather comprehensive information about the new parliament to disseminate to the public.

But I had contravened what I soon learnt was a golden rule of South African politics: consultation. Before you think about doing anything, consult. Before you take any actual step, consult. And, as you do it, consult again! Failing to 'consult' is the greatest sin in politics in this country. If you consult properly, you can get away with many other sins of omission. If you fail to consult, even the most anodyne action will invariably wilfully be given the most sinister interpretation.

Having committed the crime of non-consultation concerning the MPs' questionnaire, I was invited, along with my then boss, Mamphela Ramphele (later vice-chancellor at the University of Cape Town and subsequently managing director at the World Bank) and her boss, the head of Idasa, Wilmot James, to a meeting with the ANC chief whip, the Reverend Makhenkesi Stofile (now the minister for sport and recreation). Also present were the chair of the ANC caucus, Baleka Mbete (now Speaker of the National Assembly) and the ANC deputy president of the Senate, Bulelani Ngcuka. It was a fairly heavyweight reception party. In my naivety, I was baffled; all we were doing was asking a few simple questions of the nation's public representatives. We hadn't even said anything about them yet!

The meeting began with an exchange that I will remember until my dying day. Ramphele is a powerful woman, with a hugely independent personality and great drive. She had been a leading activist during the 1980s as a medical doctor, and previously in the 1970s as a close associate of Steve Biko. Despite her activist pedigree and her international reputation, her refusal to be formally part of the ANC movement meant that, despite Nelson Mandela's great fondness for her, the ruling party's view of her was ambivalent at best.

As we sat down to begin the meeting, Stofile opened with a coruscatingly brutal question: 'So, Mamphela, from under which stone have you crawled to bother us now?'

I caught and then avoided James's eye as Ramphele considered her options for what seemed an eternity. Then, with an ear-piercing laugh, she broke the silence. Big, backslapping embraces all round, and the meeting began. Why had we taken it upon ourselves to ask these questions? On whose behalf were we asking them?

'In the public interest,' James said.

'Well, who are you to determine that?' was the gist of Stofile's response.

And then the dagger to the heart: 'We were elected. Who do you represent? We report to the electorate, who do you report to?'

There is really no satisfactory answer to that question. So when Stofile, sensing blood, continued his cross-examination by asking me whom I reported to, I answered, 'To Dr Ramphele.' And then, to whom does she report? 'To Dr James.' And he reports to? 'The board of Idasa.' And them? Umm, I was running out of time and room to manoeuvre. 'To God.' It seemed the only thing to say to a reverend politician closing in for the kill! My attempt at a joke distracted the hound, but we were spared further humiliation and were then permitted to leave the headmaster's study, tails between our legs.

This was not the only subject in my ANC 101 course. A day later I was invited onto an evening radio programme on SAfm called *Microphone-in* to discuss the issue. An ANC MP, Johnny de Lange (now deputy minister of justice), was the other guest. It was an hour-and-a-half-long show, with just the two of us, and listeners were invited to call in. Things were proceeding smoothly enough and, despite his rumbustious manner, I felt I was handling De Lange with a reasonable degree of comfort.

Then, after a couple of callers had phoned in offering support for Idasa's right to pose the questions to MPs, I noticed the name written on the piece of paper. The call screener had put it in front of the presenter, Nigel Murphy (the SABC had not yet acquired the modern technology whereby the presenter has a computer screen to receive information from his or her producer). 'Cyril Ramaphosa', it read. I blinked. And swallowed. I was tired, and had misread it. No, it still said Cyril Ramaphosa. Perhaps there was another Cyril Ramaphosa, I thought. There wasn't, or if there was, this was not him. It was *the* Cyril Ramaphosa. Unlike me, Murphy could barely contain his excitement, waxing sycophantic about how good it was to have the ANC secretary general on his programme.

This ANC legend then proceeded to try to kick me all around the studio, though, being Cyril, he did it in a terribly courteous fashion, so much so that it was almost a pleasure. I was suitably deferential in return, and the next caller was summoned. 'Tony Yengeni'.

Oh, god, I thought, this is getting worse. Lighting another cigarette in triumph, Murphy was positively delirious; at that point in the programme's history, he had probably never had two black people phone in consecutively, never mind that they were such senior members of the ANC. I had met Mr Yengeni only once, when he was chairman of the joint standing committee on defence. I had managed to obtain an appointment to inform him of our research plans for the rapidly developing parliamentary committee system. He had been anything but friendly, and the conversation had quickly turned to MPs' pay. Looking back, with all that we now know about Mr Yengeni's predilection for luxurious 4x4s, what he had said then is rather poignant. We need to be well paid, Yengeni told me.

We were in his office, and I waited for him to put forward the classic argument – with which I happen to agree – that public representatives should be well paid so as to reduce the risk that they will be tempted to accept a bribe or other financial inducement. But this was not his argument. Instead, he said that, as the chairman of a committee, he needed to receive and entertain important dignitaries from overseas, and it was necessary for him to have plenty of money with which to buy the appropriate suits and ties. As it happens, I would be the last person to complain about his attitude, but it was nonetheless a curious thing to say.

On the radio programme, Yengeni was typically grumpy and brusque in his observations. This was not really how he preferred to spend a Wednesday evening. Trying to put Richard Calland in his place was really a bit beneath him. Not so the next two 'listeners' who called in: Blade Nzimande, MP and chair of the education portfolio committee, and Carl Niehaus, MP and chair of the correctional services portfolio committee. Murphy now looked like the cat that had not just eaten the cream, but the whole cow. Thrilled to bits, he glowed a puce shade of pink, and I was beginning to dislike him for it. De Lange was doing a good job pretending not to be surprised at what was happening. I did not know him well enough at the time to recognize his carefully framed expression of mock innocence, which he usually reserves for Sheila Camerer, the opposition MP who was a long-term member of the justice committee, or an umpire who has turned down an ambitious appeal for a wicket off his bowling.

Nzimande was both delicate and skilful in his probing, like a neuro-surgeon carefully inserting a scalpel. In my determination not to be intimidated by this roll-call of ANC glitterati – did they really not have anything better to do? – I had used up nearly all my emotional resources.

At one point, as my mind drifted back for some reason to my previous life in London, I consoled myself with the thought that this was still a lot less stressful than appearing as a barrister in front of the criminal court of appeal. Nonetheless, nearly exhausted, I almost lost it completely with Niehaus, I suspect to his not-inconsiderable satisfaction. Were it not for the fact that he seems to greet everyone with the same mischievous grin, I could be forgiven for thinking that in my case it is bestowed with a fond recollection of my discomfort that night in June 1995.

I felt great relief, therefore, when the programme finally ended. De Lange and I were both ill-tempered by then, and we ended with an unfortunate misunderstanding between us over something I had said, and as the programme's signature tune began to play, Murphy's attempts to thank us both were overlaid by the curses his guests were exchanging. It was not the most dignified way to conclude such a formative experience, but, happily, after a period of mistrust, my relationship with De Lange, whom I admire very much, was restored.

Of the four ANC MPs who called in that night, one is now more than civil to me, a second is positively friendly, and a third is a very helpful and often supportive contact. The identity of the fourth, who is none of these things, is probably obvious. About a year after the programme, one of the three confirmed what I already knew: that it had been an organized attempt to try to publicly hammer Idasa and me. The individual was gracious enough to concede that the attempt had largely failed.

What was surprising was not that they had called in – arranging for 'your people' to call in to a radio phone-in is a common tactic the world over – but that such eminent people had been deployed to do so, and in such numbers. Four was overkill; even to the least enlightened listener, it would have been obvious that it was a set-up. Moreover, what did this say about the insecurity of the ANC? As one of the last callers asked, 'Why was the ANC so touchy about this questionnaire and what did it have to hide?'

The next morning a relatively senior ANC MP telephoned me at my office to say that he had heard the programme. He thought it was pathetic the way the ANC had ganged up and tried to bully me, and he admired the way I had (largely) kept my cool and stuck to the arguments. Many years later, I am very happy to say that this telephone call meant far more to me than the caller will ever know, though I have tried to thank him since. 'Don't worry about it,' he said. 'Stick to your principles. What you are trying to do is the right thing.' Two other ANC MPs called during the course of the day, also expressing similar sentiments.

The wider point, which I hope justifies this personal anecdotal discursion, is this: the ANC is often more stung by criticism from those that it considers 'its own' than by its enemies. It tends to dismiss the criticism of the opposition parties, for example, with a contemptuous wave of its collective hand. The new social movements are labelled 'ultra-left' to isolate them and mark the fact that they are the 'other'. The closer to home the criticism, the more hurtful, apparently, and the more vicious the response and hence the very difficult moments experienced in relationships within the ANC tripartite alliance.

At the time of the anecdote, the ANC had still regarded Idasa as, if not within the tent, then certainly broadly within the camp. It had been a useful ally during the transition when Idasa had arranged the very first meetings between the ANC in exile and the Afrikaner nationalist establishment. Some historians even trace the start of the whole negotiation process back to a meeting arranged by Idasa in Dakar, Senegal, in 1987.

During the first democratic elections in 1994, Idasa had also provided important assistance with voter education and suchlike. But Wilmot James had introduced a new approach with the creation of a Public Information Centre, headed by Ramphele, which comprised three programmes, one of which was the Parliamentary Information and Monitoring Service (PIMS), which I was hired to develop and lead.

Support for me also came from an unlikely, but very powerful source: Professor Jakes Gerwel, President Mandela's chief of staff. I had always thought that it was a little surprising – and perhaps a little unwise – for the most powerful public servant in the country also to chair the country's most prominent democracy and governance think tank. But, hey, this is South Africa and anything is possible – and quite often entirely appropriately different.

During the controversy about the questionnaire, a senior group from the ANC had visited Gerwel in Tuynhuis, where the presidency is housed next to parliament, and beseeched him to use his power as chair of the board at Idasa to immediately halt the questionnaire. My source told me that Gerwel was furious. He told the delegation to 'piss off'. Not only was their approach to him inappropriate, he said, but they should not be so defensive about the questionnaire. I just wish Gerwel had communicated his support for me in some way, but I also realize that it would have been inappropriate for him to do so. In this way, his neutrality remained intact.

I deliberately conclude the chapter with this story, for two reasons. First, because it proves how important it is to have allies in high places, but, more significantly, because it shows how important it is to have people of integrity at the top. Gerwel, as everyone who knows him will attest, has such integrity. Every great leader needs people like him around them.

The second reason is that the whole story around the parliamentary questionnaire exemplifies the prevailing atmosphere of the greater part of the first years of democracy. It may be an illusion, or possibly self-delusion, but I sense that the period of greatest insecurity and unease is over, notwithstanding the hugely destabilizing internal ructions over the succession and Jacob Zuma. The ANC in government is coming to terms with its political power.

To an onlooker, the ANC's power was secured the very moment that the negotiations in the early 1990s confirmed that there would be a one person, one vote democratic election. But on the inside looking out, the view may well have appeared very different. Many obstacles stood in its path, there were many enemies with scores to settle, and the constraints on power, some of which are canvassed in the earlier chapters of this book and some of which I discuss in the Conclusion, were manifestly unsettling. If the phrase 'body politic' is apt because it denotes the idea that power is structured primarily in the interactions of human beings and not in inanimate institutions, then it is equally logical to apply to the ruling class the axiom that people tend to behave oddly when they feel insecure. In this respect, things have changed a great deal.

The ANC has won three elections in a row, the third even more emphatically than the first two. Despite their failings in government – principally in their apparent impotence in creating jobs and alleviating the harsh socio-economic inequalities that scar South Africa – the people appear both forgiving and loyal. Most of the more awkward political issues have been dealt with decisively. National reconciliation has been 'achieved'; the IFP has been 'defeated'; the Truth Commission passed without major mishap; most of the internal political scores have been settled one way or another (the Hefer Commission was the final hammering down of that); the commanding heights of the economy are stable and broadly on board; and the macroeconomic environment is stable (the ANC has proved itself far more responsible managers of the economy than its reckless apartheid predecessors).

Moreover, capacity is slowly being built up, in government and in most of the other places that matter, and 'their' people are spread around both government and other key 'centres of power'. Relations between government and media will always inherently and naturally include a certain 'edge', but that edge lacks the bitterness of the middle part of the first decade of democracy.

And though it is still at times painfully weak in communicating its strategy and rationale, the ANC in government is beginning to recognize and master the art of presenting its case, and doing so without appearing defensive and oversensitive. This is reflected in the increasing ease and openness with which government deals with other stakeholders. As I've said, perhaps this is a grand illusion; perhaps I am seeing only what I want to see. Or perhaps the succession battle will undermine this positive trend. Time will tell. But, truly, at this point I sense that the ANC is in power and no longer merely in office. Just as important is the sense that they know it, too, and that this distinction and its positive consequences on the general attitude towards governance are in all our interests.

Civil society – in all its many shapes and sizes – has a persuasive influence that helps to shape these attitudes. What certain civil society leaders say about those in power invariably has greater impact than the opposition parties. When Zackie Achmat describes President Mbeki as a 'coward' – as he did in the biographical documentary canned by the SABC (see pages 198–199) – or attacks the health minister's performance at an international conference on AIDS, it hurts. Thus, the relationship between those in government and civil society is neither linear nor homogeneous. Sometimes civil society organizations are supportive, facilitating processes that government could not; sometimes they are servile to the ruling party's interests. Other times they are more challenging. They complain publicly or sue the government; they mobilize people and prick the conscience of those in power, touching raw nerves.

The first decade marks a watershed in the use and application of political power. As the dust of a tumultuous and extended period of transition settles, and as the ANC's power is consolidated along with the democracy it fought for, it is a good moment to draw breath and contemplate the anatomy of power, both for the present and the future, and to search for the answer to the question, 'Who really holds the power now?'

Conclusion

Money and Power: The New Establishment

Public and private power: The congealing embrace

If there is one image that more than any other captures the essence – and confusion – of power in South Africa today, it is the photograph of murdered businessman Brett Kebble's coffin being carried into the memorial service at St George's Cathedral in Cape Town. Kebble, a white man, is carried by eight well-dressed black men, the majority of whom are leading members of the ANC Youth League. It would be pleasing to report that this image was one to add to the post-1994 litany of 'rainbow' images that adorned the Mandela era. In one sense it is. But in another, far more potent sense, it represents something very different: a congealing of elites, with a defiant crony-capitalist agenda. As the *Mail & Guardian* columnist John Matshikiza drolly put it: 'The entire ANC Youth League had their heads fashionably shaved so they could look snappy carrying out the coffin. It was one of those classic moments of "Please do not adjust your television set, the problem is actually reality itself."'[1]

Kebble had, to use the phrase of his father, 'flown too close to the sun'. The details of his business empire are still emerging at the time of writing. The full extent of what appears to have been a colossal corporate fraud is as uncertain as the identity of his assassins. It has been spoken of as South Africa's 'Enron'. It would be more apt to compare Kebble with Robert Maxwell – the émigré from Eastern Europe who built up a huge media empire in Britain only to die in mysterious circumstances in the Mediterranean Sea shortly before details of his theft of millions of pounds from his companies' own pension funds was exposed in November 1991.

It subsequently emerged that his complex labyrinth of companies, fully understood by him alone, were £400 million in debt. Maxwell had strong links with the British Labour Party and, according to revelations by, among others, the respected American journalist Seymour Hersh, was an agent for the Israeli secret service, Mossad. When Maxwell was buried at the Mount of Olives in Jerusalem, Israel's then prime minister, Yitzhak Shamir, said that 'He has done more for Israel than can today be said.'

President Mbeki did not attend Kebble's funeral service in Cape Town, but he did send one of his most trusted and senior lieutenants, Essop Pahad – a striking statement of Kebble's value and influence within the political elite. Pahad's speech included the following notable phrase: 'South Africa has lost a dedicated son.'[2] Pahad had spoken on the telephone with Kebble just hours before he was shot dead in his Mercedes while driving towards Melrose Arch in Johannesburg on the night of 27 September 2005. Kebble had pledged a R3 million donation to a museum project in Timbuktu, Mali, which is an important part of President Mbeki's African Renaissance project.[3]

The attendance list of the more than 1000 people packed into St George's Cathedral would make interesting reading – not a comprehensive 'who's who' by any means, but certainly a vivid sample of the eclectic mix that constitutes South Africa's contemporary establishment. Apart from Pahad, prominent ANC businessmen, such as Saki Macozoma and Tokyo Sexwale, were there, and Jacob Zuma's close confidant, former spy Mo Shaik, the brother of convicted fraudster Schabir Shaik.

There was old money and there was new money. Kebble spanned both. He was a businessman who speculated in politics. He also covered his bets. As noted above, he curried favour with President Mbeki. He also backed Jacob Zuma. In the Western Cape, he provided funds to different factions within the ANC, encouraging division. When the ANC Western Cape could not pay its bills in 2004, it was Kebble who gave it R500 000. He was also a major supporter of the ANC Youth League, providing R5 million in capital for Lembede Investment Holdings, its investment arm. As the investigative journal *Noseweek* commented in April 2004:

> [Kebble]'s played himself into a position of such influence that it evokes the image of a bloated spider poised in the centre of a very wide and intricate web. Situated strategically within his web are people who are themselves extremely well-connected. It is said with some authority that

he is probably the most influential white man in South Africa, if not the whole of Africa.[4]

In the light of later events and the ongoing inquiry, the *Noseweek* piece was perspicacious:

> But it begs the obvious question: where does he find all that money? It's an intriguing question because Kebble's companies (JCI, which is listed, JCI Gold, Consolidated Mining Management Services) are to all intents and purposes bankrupt. Over the past five years he and Roger have destroyed shareholder value in these companies on an epic scale. Kebble has managed to keep his companies afloat by tortuously complicated inter-company loans and share swops, employing skills more in keeping with a circus ringmaster than the mining magnate he pretends to be ... Meanwhile Brett continues to parade shamelessly as the enlightened face of South African capitalism.

Among Kebble's pallbearers were Lunga Ncwana, Andile Nkuhlu – in bright orange and lilac-striped ties, respectively – and Fikile Mbalula. Mbalula is the president of the ANC Youth League. Nkuhlu, who is also a member of its national executive committee, is a former chief director of the department of public enterprises, responsible for state restructuring, who resigned in mid-2002 after revelations that he had failed to disclose various gifts from Zama Resources, a company that had recently won a slice of the government's restructured forestry assets.

Over the years, Nkuhlu and Kebble had become close friends as well as business associates. After Kebble's death, Nkuhlu described Kebble as a 'great South African ... who broke much ground as a white', echoing his speech at the funeral in which he said that: 'In a country where what is black is still suspect, marginal and less credible, having Brett on your side made the world of difference.'[5]

As *Noseweek* also pointed out, Kebble 'uses the ANCYL as his passport into the charmed world of black empowerment'. Black economic empowerment is the new frontier for South African business. The important May 2006 SACP discussion paper *Bua Komanisi*[6] argues that 'since we are living in a capitalist society, and since we "need growth for development", then those who "control capital" will constitute, for better or worse, a central part of the advance-guard of the revolution'. The discussion document offers this view without any apparent sense of irony. Is this to be the Fabiani Revolution?[7] The discussion document does, however, proceed to a problem statement:

> Because of 'developed infrastructure, high levels of capital concentration, an increasingly dominant finance sector, and, in the past decade, transnationalisation of South African capital ... emerging black capital (at least the key faction most closely associated with the ANC and the state) tends not to be involved with an expansion of the national forces of production, including significant job creation. It is, rather, excessively compradorist and parasitic.'

This notion of the 'comprador' is an interesting and important one. According to one definition, the 'comprador bourgeoisie are non-capitalist bourgeoisie who owe their existence to imperialist capitalists but cannot function on their own as a capitalist class ... comprador bourgeoisie exist in developing countries and act in their own economic interests, often sacrificing national interests and the interests of their country's proletariat in order to do so'.[8] In other words, put crudely, 'compradors' are turncoats: people who lose sight of their revolutionary ideals, ensnared by the drive for personal profit.

The analysis in *Bua Komanisi* that follows is crucial to understanding the relationship of the new, younger, black capitalist class with both the state and with 'old money' in contemporary South Africa and, therefore, the curious interlocking elite interests that have formed since 1994:

> Its compradorism reflects its reliance on the patronage of established capital ... [it] has, typically, not accumulated its own capital through the unleashing of productive processes, but relies on special share deals, 'affirmative action', BEE quotas, fronting, privatization and trading on its one real piece of 'capital' (access to state power) to establish itself ... its parasitism is reflected in its reliance upon and symbiotic relation with the upper echelons of the state apparatus. It is state policies (BEE charters, with their ownership quotas and tender policies) that are driving the emergence of this class fraction, putting pressure on established capital to cut this emerging fraction 'a slice of the action' in order to remain in favour with the 'new political reality'.

I have provided this extended citation from the discussion document because I cannot easily improve on the analysis. It sums up the state of play very well. At the time of democratization in 1994, South Africa had a well-developed capitalist class. Economic sanctions and internal liberation movement pressure had squeezed it to the point where it was ready to push for political change, but it remained largely intact. Unlike other societies, there was little space into which a new capitalist class could move. It has had to develop on the back of the existing, established business class, developing entry points through people like Kebble and via the largely contrived opportunities created by government policy (e.g. tendering rules requiring BEE quotas and the like).

Naturally, this situation creates complex overlaps between public (state) and private power. As the *Bua Komanisi* document asserts, a major pillar of Mbekism (my use of the word, not theirs) is a 'powerful presidential centre ... in which the leading cadre is made up of a new political elite (state managers and technologically-inclined ministers) and (often overlapping with them) a new generation of black private sector BEE managers/capitalists'. This book has recorded the extent to which members of the political class have moved into business and sometimes back again. Often more than one hat is worn, giving rise to conflicts of interest so severe that, at its July 2006 meeting, the ANC's NEC was finally provoked into taking action.[9] *Bua Komanisi* goes on to speak of the *entanglement* of the two groups. It is the right word – a watchword, a central motif, for the New Establishment.

The new establishment

Monday 19 April 2004 saw the new establishment in all its glory. First World South Africa could be observed at its finest. The Independent Electoral Commission was having its resplendent celebration banquet. An interesting sight, though the most amusing part of my evening began in the bathroom, rarely the best place to start any conversation. So, when I bumped into Mandla Tisani, director of public affairs at Coca-Cola: Southern and East Africa, I chose to follow him out of the bathroom before introducing myself. Mr Tisani had been the second speaker that evening, and I had wondered why. He seemed out of place among the politicians and IEC officials.

The first speaker, naturally, had been Dr Brigalia Bam, the chairperson of the IEC. Parliament chose well when it appointed her to this position. She is calm authority personified: the perfect heir and antidote to her garrulous predecessor, Judge Johann Kriegler. I doubt if even Mangosuthu Buthelezi would not bow to her schoolmarm charm. She slipped up just once. 'At this election, the youth did something special ...' she began. But before she could complete the serendipitous thought, a wag at my table – the then head of the Human Sciences Research Council (another quango), Dr Mark Orkin, said: 'Yes, they didn't register to vote!' So, for the first time, the Ghost of Banquo raised his alarming head. The silent minority: the great unregistered. Why did the analysts (myself included) not raise this issue at the time of the (non) registration? Later, the analysis of non-registered voters appeared like an attempt to undermine the self-evidently emphatic victory of the African National Congress. A dispute about the precise figures remains unresolved, but up to seven million eligible voters may not have registered, the majority being potential first-time voters.

If this is so, it matters not a jot to the majority party. In fact, it far from undermines their victory. The ANC won 70 per cent of the 80 per cent of those people entitled to vote. If that fact tempers an exuberant celebration, what does it mean to the little parties? If, like the Democratic Alliance, you have won just 12 per cent of 80 per cent, it means you have the support of just one in ten of those entitled to vote. If you are the UDM, the Independent Democrats or the ACDP, it means you have acquired barely more than one in a hundred, which is a rather sobering thought.

Johann Kriegler, chair of the IEC in the 1994 elections, had been the third speaker at the IEC celebration; then Deputy President Jacob Zuma the fourth. Kriegler had been gracious and funny; Jacob Zuma, I thought at the time, urgently needs to find a new speechwriter. So why was Mr Coca-Cola the ham in this illustrious sandwich? I checked the menu, the invitation and the signage. Nada. I gazed at the big screen, and wondered why a sign pointing to the toilets had been placed so inelegantly high up, right alongside the screen. My eyes followed the arrow, and there it was. In a delicate pale white, the famous Coca-Cola insignia ingrained beneath the IEC logo on the long wall-hanging. I checked all the other wall-hangings, but this was the only place the logo appeared. Admirably understated and, but for the helpful toilet arrow, probably so discreet that few would have noticed it.

When I approached Mr Tisani, he jovially confirmed that Coca-Cola were the sponsors of the banquet as part of their overall support for the IEC. I asked how much they had donated, and Mr Tisani replied, 'We support democracy in the region by supporting electoral institutions, including the IEC, because we don't want to get into partisan funding.'

'Great.' I said. 'So how much did you give?'

'Well,' Tisani replied, 'that's not something we are going to publicize.'

'So it's secret funding,' I retorted.

'No,' said Tisani. 'It's just not for publication.'

'So it's a secret,' I repeated.

'No, it's just not for publication.'

It was clear that this could go on for some time. We both laughed. I tried a different tack: 'If you want to support democratic institutions in a non-partisan way, why are you sponsoring a banquet?'

'That's non-partisan as well,' Tisani said.

'Well,' I said, 'it ingratiates your company's brand in front of the political elite of this country, pretty much all of whom are gathered here.'

Mr Tisani shrugged. I told him that Idasa had recently sued the ANC and three other political parties to gain access to records of their private donations. I said I would see him in court. He said he would see me there too. We were both laughing. I was mostly joking. I hope he was too. Suing the ANC is one thing, Coca-Cola quite another!

We shook hands and I wandered off towards the exit. On the way, two young guys, arm in arm, swayed towards me. One was black, the other white. They seemed a bit 'tired and emotional' (to deploy the famous euphemism of the British satirical magazine *Private Eye*). They greeted me, and I paused to chat. We toasted the election. It transpired that they were in the private sector. I asked how business was. 'Hey man,' the black dude said, 'this democracy thing is just *great* for making money!' I scuttled off to find a quiet corner in which to write down this exchange. It was too good to be true; I feared that in the morning I would not trust my recollection.

An IEC source later told me that the banquet had cost R3 million. How the other half live …

So there we have it, the textured backdrop of the new South Africa: the ever-impressive sight of First World South Africa in all its glory, with its delicate but coy corporate sponsorship. Off-stage, a silent but substantial minority of mostly young people who choose not to vote. And an opposition in complete disarray and crisis, with an apparently chronic inability to tap into this latent but potential market of anti-ANC votes.

The IEC banquet was a showcase for the political elite, with its over-lapping circles of power and influence. The overlap between business and politics is especially important. Obvious examples of crossovers include Bridgette Radebe, millionaire chairperson of Mmaku Mining and wife of transport minister Jeff Radebe, sister to multimillionaire mining tycoon Patrice Motsepe, and sister-in-law of Johnnic chairman Cyril Ramaphosa. This unification of political and corporate elites is what the American Marxist sociologist William Robinson has termed the 'congealing of elites'.[10] As Connie Molusi, former CEO of Johncom, explained to me: 'In Mbeki's view of the transition, it was important to unite elites, because they are the people who could oppose the transition.' And: 'In mobilizing particularly the black elite and a sense of African nationalism at the economic level, it was just as clear that there would be an accommodation with white business.' Molusi's analysis is that Mbeki's intention with the creation of a black bourgeoisie is to '[create] a foundation for an African nationalist base, and [it] fits in quite neatly with his reform agenda throughout Africa'. Certainly, Mbeki is often accompanied on trips around Africa by the likes of Patrice Motsepe and Tokyo Sexwale.

In short, there is a New Establishment for the New South Africa, under-written by a New Network of Influence. Such networks are, by definition, amorphous. There is no list, no membership application form. Nor can one say that there is a formulaic list of characteristics; it is not a dating agency. Most of the network are black, but not exclusively so. Most are liberal democrats, though some are social democrats, and a few are democratic socialists. There are many very curious bedfellows. John Hlophe, the first black judge president of the Cape High Court, is in business with Braam Lategan, a former member of the bench with one of the worst records for hanging during the apartheid era.[11]

Unlike, say, the British Establishment, which Anthony Sampson described in the original *Anatomy of Britain*, there is no unifying ideology. Most are wealthy, but some are professionals with a middle-class income. Some are important because they hold important positions, but not all do; yet, all are influential by virtue of their membership of the network.

The network ranges 'from the chief justice to Bobby Godsell', in the words of Zackie Achmat, and has rapidly replaced the temporarily dominant network of liberal whites of the transition period. By this, I am referring to the elite group that gained ascendancy over the former Afrikaner elite once the transition became inevitable in the early 1990s. Indeed, the latter group's descent from power has been Icarus-like. 'Take Constand Viljoen,' says Achmat. '[He has gone from] being the second most powerful man in the country as head of the armed forces to having to beg for a "vry staat".' Although there are obvious exceptions to this rule, compared with the English-speaking white elite, Afrikaners have less economic power, and so have been moved aside. 'As a group, it is the old Afrikaans men who have lost the most power,' concludes Achmat, though as the case of Braam Lategan suggests, some have been resourceful as well as pragmatic in creating new opportunities alongside members of a new elite.

Godsell, the chairman and CEO of AngloGold, could easily be described as a member of the liberal white group, but he has survived, principally because, unlike someone such as Tony Trahar (the CEO of Anglo American plc), he not only is genuinely empathetic with the new political order but knows how to engage it and does so. The remainder have been eclipsed, although they still enjoy access to power, if not direct influence. I recall in mid-1999 discussing with the head of corporate affairs at the mining giant Billiton their need to jack up their lobbying capacity. Having conceded that Billiton were not properly up to speed with what was happening in parliament, the man then delivered a telling caveat: 'You know, the thing is, if we want real access to power, then our CEO [then, Brian Gilbertson] will simply call the president. And you know what? The president always takes the call.'

So, who's really in power?

With a man such as Thabo Mbeki in command, the presidency represents the cerebral epicentre of power: fittingly, given his Socratic disposition, the brain of the anatomy of South Africa. The nerve wires all emanate from here, with a network of influential people and forums, such as the presidential councils. In this context, the cabinet is largely overshadowed, though certain ministers and ministries, such as the government-within-a-government, the National Treasury, enjoy a special place and role in the anatomy. Although it continues to struggle with the challenge of using its power and authority, with grave capacity problems, parts of the public service, such as the new mandarin class of directors-general, and the ministerial special advisors, have serious influence over the way the body politic operates. Its patchiness, in performance and quality, means that it is open to undue outside influence, especially from business, and especially from those wishing to corrupt government.

What of the institutional counter-balances to this executive power? The rule of law is relatively strong, certainly in comparison to many developing countries; the judges are generally incorruptible, though the revelations concerning conflicts of interest and business interests held by some judges are worrisome. The Constitutional Court, though declining in quality, remains a bastion of enlightenment and intellectual authority; its judgments are by definition influential. How assertive it will be in the future will depend very much on one man – the current deputy president of the court, Dikgang Moseneke, who will likely commence a long reign as head of the court in 2009.

In contrast, parliament represents an even more uneven site of political power. Its place in the anatomy is far from assured, thanks to the feeble performance of many of its committees – though there are noble exceptions – and the strategic impotence of a chronically weak set of opposition parties. Thus, the far more influential 'alternative' sites of power reside within the ANC ruling alliance itself rather than outside of it. Though in a constant state of flux, the inherent tensions in the relationship between the ANC and its partners, COSATU and the SACP, mean that the most significant opposition voices are heard behind the closed doors of the alliance rather than in the open field of public discourse – though this tendency was in sharp reverse at the time of writing this Conclusion, catalysed by (though not caused by) the furore over Jacob Zuma.

The media has some influence, but rather as a mirror to, or servant of, the vested interests of business, such are the ownership patterns, with notably independent exceptions to the rule such as the *Mail & Guardian* newspaper. The growing influence of social movements has added lustre to the policy think tanks and non-governmental organizations, which punch way above their weight. South Africa enjoys a vivid, textured, pluralist civil society – again something that sets it apart from many emergent democracies.

Together with COSATU and the SACP, and the Churches, this vast array of civil society organizations represents the alternative chakra or energy centre of the anatomy of the new South Africa.

The vital organs of the new anatomy

Thus, the anatomy of power in South Africa is based on six vital 'organs': the presidency; the National Treasury; the ANC; transnational corporations and domestic big business itself; the new informal networks that crisscross the business–politics divide; and, last, civil society – the policy think tanks, to some extent, but especially COSATU and the new, emergent social movements.

These organs are held together by a complex matrix of arteries, muscles and bones. Like tendons and ligaments, there are some key institutions and individuals. First, the president himself, and his immediate team of advisors – each of whom enjoys significant levels of influence due to their proximity and access to the president. As noted in Chapter 1, of his immediate team, legal advisor Mojanku Gumbi is perhaps the single most influential, though her power is far less extensive than that of Joel Netshitenzhe, the second most powerful person in South Africa.

Essop Pahad's long-standing loyalty to Mbeki gives him a special influence, which might be waning as other advisors build up comparable service records, but remains substantial on key political choices. Pahad is a sort of de facto deputy president, though there are at least two members of the cabinet who are more influential than he, namely Trevor Manuel and Alec Erwin. Manuel heads the 'government within a government', the one department whose capacity far exceeds any other, and which is capable of exerting the power it holds. Erwin continues to hold a key portfolio in cabinet, but his influence lies in the axis with Manuel and the fact that he has been centrally involved in every major policy decision taken by government since 1994.

Thus, the batting order of political power is: Mbeki, Netshitenzhe, Manuel, Gumbi, Erwin, Pahad and, now, in 2006, the deputy president, Phumzile Mlambo-Ngcuka. Beyond these top seven, the picture becomes more complex, with parallel lines of influence running at dissecting angles from the epicentre. One line comprises big business. The other, the new intelligentsia. There are overlaps between the three groups: government, business and the intelligentsia. Some members of the black intelligentsia are 'in' with the president and/or the ANC leadership; the 'big' CEOs, some of whom, such as Patrice Motsepe, are members of the new intelligentsia. A third line is civil society, headed by COSATU leader Zwelinzima Vavi, which also consists of other skilled political campaigners, such as Zackie Achmat.

If business represents one leg of the new anatomy, and COSATU and progressive civil society the other – sometimes pulling in opposite directions, sometimes walking in step – then the new establishment represents the nervous system. And what of the ANC? The Constitution, with the Constitutional Court as its ultimate custodian, is the spine, but the ANC is the heart in South Africa's new anatomy, pumping blood and oxygen throughout the system. In his last edition of *Anatomy of Britain*, Sampson quotes Peter Mandelson, one of the key architects of New Labour, and Britain's 'father of spin', as saying: 'I do not think the government realizes the extent to which New Labour looks to many people like a huge and all-powerful establishment with its tentacles everywhere ...'

If this can be said of New Labour, with its clear but far less dominant majority in parliament and with a decidedly more dissident backbench, what can one say of the ANC? Surely, at the very least, exactly the same? Certainly, that is the media perception. But I suspect that it overstates the ANC's co-herence and power as a separate entity. And, as the analyses in Chapters 4 and 5 suggest, the key distinction is between the ANC in government and the ANC as an organization. The human heart contains a primary artery – the aorta, the body's main artery; the ANC in government is the equivalent in South Africa's anatomy.

Clearly, the overlap between the main decision-making forums of the ANC – especially its national working committee – and the most powerful figures in government is critical to the exercise of political power. But whether political power is homogeneous and subject to centralized control is a moot question. Zackie Achmat's overview is astute: 'The most important thing to remember about the new order is that it encompasses a wide range of cultures and ideologies in the operation of power. The reason the Eastern Cape is ungovernable is because of the old homeland bureaucrats. Equally, in the metropoles, there was an approach to decision-making that was based on every decision being made by Pretoria.' Thus, these old-style centralist tendencies – of the authoritarian apartheid regime – live on, accompanied now by a centralism of a different variety: that of the ANC's own tradition and culture, especially its exile history.

So there is a centrifugal tendency, but it is one that has to operate within the framework of the Constitution, with its various institutional checks and balances on power. There are other institutions that are very important, but not necessarily very influential. The Constitutional Court is the most obvious example. In theory the most powerful institution in the land, its influence over power is constrained by the fact that it exerts power only through the judgments that it hands down and, thereby, by the cases that reach it. Yet, the intriguing thing about institutional development, as I have emphasized in this book, is that institutions are composed of individual human beings.

Thus, the Constitutional Court is made up of eleven human beings. Another member of the liberal-left network, the court's president, Pius Langa, remains a powerful figure by virtue of his position, but is less connected to the new establishment network than some of his colleagues, such as Langa's deputy, Dikgang Moseneke, and Justice Sandile Ngcobo, who connect with a range of people, such as Njabulo Ndebele, the vice-chancellor of the University of Cape Town, Barney Pityana, the former head of the Human Rights Commission and now vice-chancellor of UNISA, as well as fellow judges in other divisions, such as the head of the Transvaal High Court, Bernard Ngoepe. Thus does the new intelligentsia network interweave with the institutional anatomy.

This is the first major question for the next few years: How will the new establishment network begin to cohere and exert a more coordinated form of political influence, and which ideological direction, if any, will it take? In particular, will it operate as a countervailing force to balance the naked aggression of South Africa's big capitalists? Or, as the evidence currently suggests, will it simply operate as a parallel or overlapping, complementary source of power? Following the buck usually makes sense in capitalist systems, and South Africa is no exception – monitoring the interplay between big business and government and the ruling party will continue to be the most useful stethoscope for listening to the heartbeat of power in the new South Africa.

Succession at the top

The second big issue for the next few years is The Succession: capital T, capital S. It was always going to be a rough period, but few would have anticipated quite how rough and how soon it would start. As Jacob Zuma's campaign to succeed Mbeki gathered momentum following his acquittal on rape charges in May 2006, so it seemed for a moment that Mbeki and his new establishment were losing control. No 'Mbekite' successor had emerged. And nor could they: Mbeki has neither the power nor the willingness to anoint a chosen successor. The ANC is simply too complex a beast to arrange such a thing.

There is an inherent awkwardness about the timetable. The ANC's next national conference is in late 2007, a full two years before the next election in 2009. At the conference, Mbeki is supposed to step down as president of the ANC. His successor in that position will be the ANC's candidate for president in 2009. This is not cast in stone, but it is as good as. It is a de facto, if not a de jure rule of ANC politics. The problem is that not only will the year preceding the conference be dominated by power play and talk, but once the successor is elected, in a sense he or she will become as important as the president himself. Certainly, the successor-in-waiting becomes an alternative and competing site of power. This creates discomfort for the incumbent president. Mbeki is unlikely to be attracted to the idea of being a lame-duck president for the last two years of his term.

As I completed this book, South Africa had entered a torrid period of uncertainty in contrast to the steady if unspectacular progress of its First World economy. An alternative scenario appeared on the horizon, one in which the New Establishment, the great beneficiaries of this stable economy, becomes increasingly anxious about the growing instability and its effect on the macroeconomic environment in which it has flourished. How the new establishment and, in particular, its capitalist cohort will react to the turbulence caused by the Zuma campaign will be telling. Either they will exert their power and insist that Mbeki quells the destabilizing contest for succession, or they will call for a change in the Constitution to permit Mbeki to stand again. It is not beyond the realm of possibility that Mbeki might engineer this scenario, and arrange for a 'stalking horse' to come forward to present an argument on why it would be in the national interest for him to return to power for a third term.

Such a scenario invites instability of a different order. The reaction of the right – Tony Leon's Democratic Alliance, et al. – and a nervous West will verge on the hysterical. The 'two-terms' rule, enshrined in most of the modern African constitutions, has become a benchmark for good governance and democratic commitment. Wherever leaders such as Sam Nujoma in Namibia, Balili Malusi in Malawi and Frederick Chiluba in Zambia have contemplated changing their respective constitutions to permit a third term, an outcry was heard both internally and externally. This is particularly and painfully ironic. In Britain, prime ministers can stand time and again, serving as many terms as they choose. That argument might be advanced to support the questioning and possible amendment of the Constitution.

Who, though, are Mbeki's likely successors? Hazardous though this exercise is, in my opinion, there are six possible candidates, or types of candidate. The first is a 'pure Mbekite' – someone chiselled from the same rock of pragmatism, with the same sort of African nationalist instincts and contemporary, 'modernizing' blend of conservative economics and left-of-centre social policy. While Joel Netshitenzhe may have the talent and virtually all of the necessary credentials, it is hard to see him overcoming what appears to be his genuine shyness and preference for the 'backroom'.

Interestingly, while Mbeki has put in place a strong layer of his own people in and around cabinet, it is hard to pick any of them as obvious candidates – part of the definition of this group is that they do not present any sort of rival leadership threat to Mbeki. Sydney Mufamadi, Charles Nqakula and Zola Skweyiya are the only male members of cabinet to fall in this category, yet none makes the pulses race. Outside of cabinet, but still within the ANC–Mbeki government fold, the only obvious candidates would be Reserve Bank governor-general Tito Mboweni and Gauteng premier Mbhazima Shilowa. Shilowa would be a dark horse but certainly one worth having a flutter on, if you are a betting man or woman. Mboweni, if he can summon sufficient support within the ANC, could be a very strong candidate indeed. He can tick many of the boxes.

The second and least likely type of successor is a woman. Now wouldn't that be something? A magnificent accomplishment for South Africa and a huge step forward for the continent, but still unlikely. As deputy president, Phumzile Mlambo-Ngcuka is well placed, but to be the next president she would have to win the election to be the ANC's president in 2007, and it is hard to see her summoning the broad coalition of support necessary within the broader organization. Thoko Didiza could be deputy president after 2009. Both are immensely talented, and far more sophisticated than Nkosazana Dlamini-Zuma, who has an abundance of raw intelligence, but is about as diplomatic as the proverbial bull in a china shop. I suspect that Mbeki rather likes her rough-edged, rough-diamond bullishness. But he will also recognize the folly that would be President Nkosazana. While Mbeki admires her strong Africanist tendencies, she lacks the composure and self-confidence of a Black Consciousness leader.

The third possibility is a compromise candidate, within which there are three subcategories. The first subcategory is an ANC insider-leader. With the reputation of the organization's deputy president, Jacob Zuma, so seriously tarnished, the position of secretary general is the most powerful after the presidency. Kgalema Motlanthe would, as I suggest in Chapter 5, have been in a strong position to mount a challenge, based on his inclusiveness and widespread popularity among a number of key ANC structures. But the wise money has moved away from backing him after he was implicated in the e-mail scandal that engulfed the ANC in the latter part of 2005, thus diluting confidence in his judgment.

The second 'compromise candidate' subcategory is Trevor Manuel. When I interviewed him, Manuel went out of his way to applaud the achievement of Paul Martin, who was, until he became prime minister of Canada in late 2003, the longest-serving finance minister in the world. Manuel now holds that title. His reference to Martin's accession to the ultimate prize may have been entirely unwitting, or perhaps a coded hint of his own ambitions. I believe that Manuel has the ambition and desire, as well as the experience and aptitude, to continue his ascent to the top of Disraeli's so-called 'greasy pole of politics'. I believe that Manuel has acquired a healthy appetite for power; the question is whether the fact that he is coloured and not black constitutes a glass ceiling. I am not convinced that it does. The NEC result in 2002 would bear this out.

While Mbeki might emotionally prefer to be succeeded by another black African, his intellectual determination to ensure that his economic project is not disturbed might lead him to conclude that Manuel would be the best person to protect his legacy. Moreover, if the turbulence of the succession battle gets worse, the new establishment will look for a compromise candidate that can satisfy a critical mass of opinion inside the ANC's electoral college, while encouraging external confidence and stability and thus protecting their own economic interests at the same time.

The third and final 'compromise candidate' subcategory is an ANC outsider. This is almost as unlikely as a woman successor. For this to happen, the individual would have to surge massively in the next two years, campaigning quietly yet strongly within the ANC alliance. They would need deep reservoirs of support within the ANC and its alliance. If they were not of Mbeki's ilk, it is likely that he would contain their move, or else try to squash it with the sort of manoeuvre that he employed with the 'plot allegations' against Ramaphosa, Sexwale and Phosa in 2002. All three of them remain big fishes inside the ANC, more so Ramaphosa and Sexwale, but especially Ramaphosa. There is no doubting his charisma, talent and leadership pedigree, but does he have the stomach for the fight? Has the corporate world softened or sharpened his political skills?

The sixth and last possibility is Jacob Zuma. His support is overstated; the question of incompetence is not. His most attractive characteristic, his geniality, is also his greatest weakness. Severely damaged by the rape charges and his bizarre evidence during the trial, which brought the ANC as well as Zuma into grave disrepute and prompted the establishment of an internal inquiry, the obstacle of the corruption trial also stands in his way.

A settled anatomy of South Africa?

There is sufficient uncertainty about The Succession to state that it will have an unpredictable, though potentially very substantial, impact on power over the next five years. As a factor, it adds to the final assessment: that while political power in the new South Africa remains in a state of flux, distinct new patterns are emerging, some of which are not so far removed from the old order. But I want to be clear about this: I am not saying that nothing has changed. On the contrary, on one level the country is unrecognizable from ten years ago.

Liberal democracy, with all its attendant civil and political rights and freedoms, is established. People are free to go where they please, with whomever they please. People can dissent in public; the press is free to publish what it likes, as are playwrights and filmmakers. There is vigorous interplay between civil society organizations, think tanks and the like, and government. There remains a sense that anything is possible, an atmosphere that continues to encourage what I see as a distinct South African characteristic: the entrepreneurial spirit and the quest for perfection.

For me, the contrasts between here and my old country, Britain, could not be greater. In Britain, it is a matter of shades of grey. Here, there is a cacophony of colour and texture. Get up in the morning in South Africa with a good idea and, with energy and a bit of luck, it will happen. In Britain, a lot of energy and a lot of luck might not be enough. There are entrenched interests and a culture of conservatism that promote slow evolutionary change, but nothing more exciting or radical.

But I must not run away with myself here. As I said in the Preface, while my intention is to present a vivid and positive account of political power in South Africa, I do not wish to do so through the rose-tinted spectacles of a Pollyanna. There are profound constraints on the freedom that the majority of South Africans can enjoy. Those constraints are the dire products of history. For as much as Tony Leon may wish the ANC to take responsibility for the present and to stop blaming apartheid, the truth is that its legacy is significant. The question is whether the structural alignments of contemporary South Africa promote change or the status quo.

As the new social movements strive to articulate the anger of the poor, challenges will be levelled at the status quo from both the soft and the hard left. COSATU expects to get a greater return for its partnership and influence in the next few years. If it does not, and if relations in the ANC alliance return to their nadir of 2002, perhaps prompted by an ugly succession battle, then there is a serious chance that it will recalculate the cost–benefit analysis of staying inside the alliance. A split to the left remains possible, though still unlikely. This is the other big question for the next period.

The harsh socio-economic realities of the 'two' South Africas, rich and poor, will continue to apply their relentless imperative – their *force majeure* – on the political elite. It is far from clear how it will respond. There are dangers if the trends of the first decade of democracy are sustained, with the equality gap continuing to widen and unemployment continuing to rise, and the vast majority of black people still impoverished.

The most dangerous trend would be an ugly combination of political centralism on the one hand, and an elite congealing of economic and political power on the other. 'Apartheid capitalism has given way to post-apartheid capitalism,' a left-wing academic says. 'Ownership and control of the commanding heights of the economy, the repressive apparatus of the state ... the army, police and judiciary, the civil service ... tertiary education and strategic research and development have remained substantially in the same hands as during the heyday of apartheid.'[12]

This Marxist analysis of power is valuable, because it prompts the idea that while much has changed on the surface and within the infrastructure of governance – built around the new Constitution – beneath it the same interest groups control real power, even though many of the faces have changed. *Plus ça change*. The more things change, the more they stay the same. In a way, therefore, the Quixotic challenge for the new establishment is to ensure that the more it changes, the more it really does change. In response, parallel developments – new networks of power inside the new establishments and new social movements in civil society outside of the establishment – will compete for hegemony. The one represents a new elite, with powerful vested interests in the current trajectory of politics and the economy. The other represents an excluded poor majority, with an increasingly angry determination to challenge the new establishment. Set within the elegant superstructure of a much-admired and much-vaunted new constitutional order, the most important institutions – parliament, NEDLAC and the Constitutional Court – will be the sites of a massive tussle for influence and power.

The outcome cannot be predicted for the following reasons: the lines are not yet clearly drawn; and there is a complex array of crossovers, creating intermingling interests and agendas. Some of the members of the new elite remain committed to social transformation – a new euphemism, in some quarters at least, for socialism. The most powerful capitalists – new and old – are installed within the new establishment and, although they are dominant, they are not yet hegemonic. There is a new anatomy of power in South Africa. Whether it is an anatomy that befits the 'New South Africa' and serves the majority is equally a matter of debate. A new establishment has formed, but its roots are shallow and its physiology largely untested. The power play has barely started. The battle for conclusive control of power has just begun. The new anatomy is anything but settled.

Appendix A

The Cabinet

Agriculture and land affairs: Lulu Xingwana

Lulu Xingwana is probably the most controversial person to have headed this department, which is charged with one of the thorniest policy issues in post-apartheid South Africa, namely the land question. Armed with a BSc degree from the University of the Witwatersrand and an MSc degree from the University of London, Xingwana joined agriculture in the latest cabinet reshuffle, following the death of public works minister Stella Sigcau in May 2006. Xingwana was promoted from deputy minister of minerals and energy to minister of agriculture and land affairs, a department which most thought was in the capable hands of Thoko Didiza, her predecessor.

Xingwana's appointment aroused mixed feelings, particularly from those who are cautious when it comes to the land question. For some, her appointment could signal the government's strong stance on the need to address the issue. She is known for her 'no-nonsense', robust approach: for instance, she referred to De Beers as a 'rich white cartel that was looting South Africa's diamonds'. Xingwana could provide the spark that agriculture and land affairs supposedly needs in order to accelerate progress in land restitution, or she could frustrate the good working relationship that Thoko Didiza had created among stakeholders around the land issue. In the eyes of opposition parties such as the Freedom Front Plus, Xingwana 'shoots from the hip', and may not be the best person for a sensitive portfolio such as agriculture and land affairs.

Arts and culture: Z Pallo Jordan

Pallo Jordan served the ANC as a spokesperson in exile under apartheid. He is highly regarded as one of the great contemporary intellectuals of the ANC. Interestingly, although he is generally regarded as a socialist, he has never joined the SACP, the traditional intellectual breeding ground of the alliance, due to his disregard for the Stalinist principles that used to guide the party.

The outspoken Jordan's relationship with the party and its leadership has, at times, frayed, and he was infamously detained by the ANC's security apparatus for six weeks in 1983. Since then he has risen consistently through the leadership ranks of the party. He was elected to the ANC's NEC in 1985 at the Kabwe conference, a position he has held ever since. In post-apartheid NEC elections, Jordan's popularity with the rank and file is evident: although it has dropped – in 1994 he was voted to the NEC in 2nd place, in 1997 in 3rd place (behind Ramaphosa and Asmal, respectively), and at Stellenbosch in 2002 in 10th position – he remains in the top echelon. He is also a member of the national working committee (NWC).

In 1994, Nelson Mandela appointed Jordan to the position of minister of posts, telecommunications and broadcasting. He was redeployed to the ministry of environmental affairs and tourism in the cabinet reshuffle arising out of the National Party's withdrawal from the GNU in 1996. In a move that was widely interpreted as a snub, Mbeki did not recall Jordan to cabinet in 1999. Jordan served as chairperson of parliament's foreign affairs portfolio committee from 2002 to 2004. His reappointment to cabinet in 2004 took many by surprise.

Jordan is regarded as a deep thinker with an excellent intellectual analytical framework. He has been accused by some of laziness and of lacking in management skills. Well known as a patron of the arts, it is thought that he will add value to what has generally been a low-profile ministry.

Communications: Ivy Matsepe-Casaburri

The president returned his incumbent minister of communications to her position in cabinet. Hailing from Kroonstad in the Free State, Ivy Matsepe-Casaburri cut her teeth with the ANC in exile. Since returning to the country, she has headed the SABC board in 1996, and was elected premier of the Free State in 1997. In 1999, Mbeki appointed her to her current portfolio. Interestingly, she has never served in parliament as a rank-and-file MP.

She was elected to the ANC NEC at the Mafikeng conference. She has not served in either the ANCWL or SACP leadership structures, and is not a member of the ANC NWC.

Matsepe-Casaburri's tenure as minister of communications has been plagued by a perceived lack of delivery, specifically relating to the licensing and rollout of a second national landline operator, and South Africa's inability to compete internationally regarding Internet bandwidth. She has been accused of meddling with internal matters relating to the running of the state broadcaster. In the wake of what was perceived to be a bold statement of intent by the president in nominating the premiers, many pundits predicted that non-performing and relatively elderly ministers, such as Stella Sigcau and Matsepe-Casaburri, would not return to cabinet.

Correctional services: Ngconde Balfour

Ngconde Balfour was deployed to parliament in 1997, where he served as a backbench MP until the end of the first parliament. In 1999 he was, surprisingly, nominated by Mbeki to the high-profile cabinet position of sports minister.

Balfour's tenure as sports minister ran hot and cold, with many sporting bodies accusing him of interference and an overly vigorous transformation policy, while praising his negotiating skills and pragmatism. But such is the prerogative of the sports minister, whose mandate remains vague, but whose actions impact on the fickle support of sports fans across the country.

Balfour began his political career in the Black Consciousness organization AZASCO (Azanian Student Convention) while a student at the University of Fort Hare. He later worked as a miner, before a ten-year stint as a school-teacher. He headed to Cape Town after joining the UDF to work as an employee of Archbishop Desmond Tutu. After the unbanning of liberation organizations, Balfour left to study further in Australia, before returning for a stint as director of rugby development within SARFU.

Since his deployment to parliament in 1997, Balfour has risen rapidly through formal governance structures, and was appointed to cabinet in 1999. In 2002 he was elected to the NEC of the party. His rise in popularity can be plotted on the ANC electoral lists, where he has gone up sixty-three places since 1999, to 8th on the National to National list.

The portfolio of correctional services is a tough job, more so given the inertia of the department under former IFP minister Ben Skosana. Balfour will be hard-pressed to deliver substantial change in the South African prisons sector, to improve the quality of rehabilitation, and to counter the widespread corruption and abuse of power highlighted by the Jali Commission. POPCRU, NICRO and other key stakeholders play an important role in shaping the sector. Balfour's negotiating skills and his ability to force through a much-needed tonic in paralysed bureaucracies bode well for the job.

Defence: Mosiuoa Lekota

Former UDF stalwart, Robben Island political prisoner, Delmas Treason Trialist and ANC national chairperson, Mosiuoa Lekota has returned to cabinet as defence minister, the portfolio he has held since 1999.

Lekota entered formal politics through the South African Students' Organization (SASO) in 1973, and became its leader in 1974. As a consequence of his political activities, he was jailed on Robben Island for six years. In 1983 he was elected national publicity secretary of the UDF, and was arrested again in 1985, and put on trial for his life in the so-called Delmas Treason Trial. He was acquitted, but had served four and a half years as a prisoner awaiting trial.

After the unbanning of the ANC, Lekota became active in formal ANC structures. He was elected to the ANC NEC in 1991, and initially chaired the Southern Natal regional party structure, before taking over the Northern Free State affiliate of the party. In 1994 he was elected premier of the Free State, and was later deployed to parliament as the first chairperson of the NCOP in 1997, amid infighting in the Free State party structures. In the same year he was elected as national chairperson of the ANC, sitting on the NEC and NWC as a consequence. In 1999 he was appointed to Mbeki's cabinet as minister of defence.

Lekota remains extremely popular with the rank and file of the party (though few of his peers on the NEC consider him to have been an effective chairperson of the organization). His portfolio complements his management and interpersonal skills; the appointment of hard-bargaining Mluleki George as deputy minister should suit the minister. Despite his ministerial position, he manages to get through a lot of work as national chairperson of the ANC, although a mild heart attack towards the end of 2005 forced him to slow down, further damaging his presidential prospects as a possible unifying, compromise candidate to succeed Mbeki.

Education: Naledi Pandor

Former NCOP chairperson Naledi Pandor was appointed minister of education by Mbeki to democratic South Africa's third cabinet in 2004. Pandor, born Naledi Matthews, was raised in one of the ANC's most famous families. Her grandfather was Professor ZK Matthews (organizer of the Kliptown conference) and her father is Joe Matthews (active in IFP politics since 1994, and a former deputy minister of safety and security).

Due to her family's political activities, she grew up predominantly in exile (in Lesotho, Botswana and Britain), returning to South Africa in 1989 to take up a lectureship position at UCT. She later moved into the university's administration, before being elected to parliament in 1994. She served the party as a whip, and later as deputy chief whip in the ANC caucus. During this time she also convened the education committee's subcommittee on higher education. In 1998 she was deployed to the NCOP as deputy chairperson of the Senate, and in 1999 was elected chairperson. Pandor was elected to the ANC NEC in 2002.

Pandor has hands-on experience of higher education in South Africa, both as a lecturer and senior administrator. This experience, as well as her understanding of the broader sector, will help her in the untidy task of merging and transforming South Africa's institutions of higher education, a necessary but unpopular mandate implemented by her predecessor Kader Asmal. Her working relationship with Enver Surty (former chief whip of the ANC in the NCOP) should help. The education portfolio is key to skills development and the long-term success of South Africa's economy, through the development of human and social capital. Education accounts for the highest proportion of government expenditure. Pandor will be under pressure to deliver in this high-profile portfolio.

Environmental affairs and tourism: Marthinus van Schalkwyk

The president nominated the New National Party leader, Marthinus van Schalkwyk, to the position of minister of environmental affairs and tourism after the ANC made good on its electoral agreement with the NNP regarding the 2004 general elections. He inherits a well-run and coordinated ministry from his predecessor Valli Moosa, who declined to run for re-election on the ANC lists. Moosa's deputy, Rejoice Mabudafhasi, has been retained, and will ensure some continuity.

Van Schalkwyk holds a degree in political science from the Rand Afrikaans University (RAU) – now the University of Johannesburg – and has lectured on the subject at both RAU and Stellenbosch University. He was elected to the last apartheid parliament in 1990, and returned to parliament in 1994, having coordinated the NP's media election campaign. In 2003 he left the National Assembly to take up the post of premier of the Western Cape, after the NNP had walked out of the Democratic Alliance.

Van Schalkwyk, who subsequently joined the ANC after the demise of the NNP in 2004, will need to perform well to maintain the profile and reputation his ministry accrued under the leadership of his predecessor.

Finance: Trevor Manuel

Trevor Manuel has been retained as minister of finance, the position he was appointed to in 1996, following the NP withdrawal from the GNU. Manuel remains extremely popular with business for his policies and implementation.

Manuel entered South African resistance politics with a bang in 1983, when he was elected at the age of twenty-five to the national executive of the UDF, also serving as the regional coordinator of the UDF in the Western Cape. During the 1980s he was repeatedly held in detention by security forces, accruing thirty-five months of detention without trial before 1990. After the unbanning of the ANC, Manuel worked full time for the party, and was elected to the NEC at the 1991 national conference. During the transition years, he headed up the ANC's department of economic planning.

In 1994, Mandela appointed Manuel as minister of trade and industry, a position he held until 1996, when he was redeployed to the finance ministry. He incurred the wrath of the ANC's alliance partners and progressive civil society organizations by implementing the growth, employment and redistribution economic stabilization policy in the early years of his tenure. Despite growing unemployment and misgivings among key constituencies regarding his performance, Manuel has remained extremely popular with the party's grassroots, especially in the Western Cape. In 1997 he was elected to the NEC in 7th place, and in 2002 he topped the list of NEC members nominated from the floor.

The appointment of Manuel's deputy, Jabu Moleketi, was widely expected, and many pundits predict that he will replace Manuel in the medium term. Moleketi previously served as MEC for finance in Gauteng, where he oversaw the implementation of innovative pro-business policies, such as the Blue IQ initiative. Manuel is now one of the longest-serving finance ministers in the world, and speculation is mounting that he will depart government to assume a position in a multilateral body, such as the World Trade Organisation (WTO).

Foreign affairs: Nkosazana Dlamini-Zuma

Dlamini-Zuma became active in politics through the Black Consciousness affiliate SASO during her years at the University of Zululand. She left the country to join the ANC in exile following the 1976 uprising, and was sent to the UK to study medicine, where she qualified as a medical doctor. In 1989, following years of work in Zambia, Swaziland and England, she was deployed to the ANC's health department in Lusaka.

She returned to South Africa after the unbanning of liberation organizations, and worked at the Medical Research Council in Durban from 1991 to 1994. During this time she was also active within ANC regional structures in Natal, and the national body of the ANCWL. In 1993 she was elected to the NEC of the ANCWL. In 1994 she was elected to the ANC's NEC (17th position – the second highest woman after Winnie Mandela). Her profile has continued to rise since the advent of democracy. In 1997 she was elected to the NEC in 12th place, and in 2002 in 3rd (only Manuel and Ramaphosa won more votes). She currently also sits on the ANC's NWC.

In 1994, Nelson Mandela appointed Dlamini-Zuma to the post of health minister, one of the toughest designations in cabinet. Her tenure was not without controversy, relating to the introduction of compulsory community service and internships in state hospitals for newly qualified doctors, the Virodene debacle and the *Sarafina II* scandal. In 1999, Mbeki appointed her minister of foreign affairs – a flagship portfolio considering his African aspirations and the centrality of the AU and NEPAD to his vision for the continent.

Health: Manto Tshabalala-Msimang

After obtaining a BA degree in 1961, Manto Tshabalala-Msimang left the country to study in exile. Between 1962 and 1980, she completed three medical degrees in Russia, Tanzania and Belgium. From 1979 to 1990 she worked full time for the ANC's department of health in Zambia. She returned to South Africa in 1990.

In 1994 Tshabalala-Msimang was elected to parliament from the ANC's lists. From 1994–1996, she served as the chairperson of the portfolio committee on health in the National Assembly. After the break-up of the GNU, Nelson Mandela appointed her as deputy minister of justice under Dullah Omar, a position she held until 1999, when Mbeki appointed her minister of health.

Within the ANC, Tshabalala-Msimang has emerged fairly quickly as a major player. In 1993 she was elected to the NEC of the ANCWL. She did not return to the ANCWL NEC at their 1997 national conference, but was re-elected to the executive in 2002. At the ANC's 2002 national congress, Tshabalala-Msimang was elected for the first time to the NEC of the organization (in 15th place). She also now serves on the ANC's NWC. Her rise in portfolio in the eyes of the rank and file is also evident in her jump up the ANC's electoral list. In 1999 she was elected to the National Assembly from 41st position on the National to National list; in 2004 she jumped twenty-nine places to 12th on the same list. Tshabalala-Msimang is married to ANC stalwart and long-standing ANC treasurer general Mendi Msimang. Msimang knows where all the financial skeletons reside – a position of power that may help explain the apparent political strength and durability of his wife in the controversial health portfolio – despite her poor reputation in the media and with AIDS activists generally.

Tshabalala-Msimang's tenure in the health portfolio has not been without controversy. She has fought a running battle with opposition parties, the media and AIDS activists, relating to her unorthodox and sometimes dissident views on the pandemic. Late last year the government committed itself to the rollout of antiretrovirals through the public health service – viewed by many as a climbdown by the minister and a victory for activist groups. Tshabalala-Msimang has won major concessions from pharmaceutical companies during her term in office, substantially reducing the cost of medicines in the public health service and ensuring the development of a generic drug industry in the country.

Home affairs: Nosiviwe Mapisa-Nqakula

Former exile and MK operative Nosiviwe Mapisa-Nqakula continues to track a rapid ascent through ANC structures. She underwent military training in Angola and the USSR and holds a teaching diploma from Bensonvale College in Sterkspruit, as well as psychology and management degrees from universities in Canada and the US. Mapisa-Nqakula is married to safety and security minister and SACP national chairperson Charles Nqakula.

In 1994 she was elected to parliament as a backbencher for the ANC. She served on the defence and intelligence committees. From 1996 to 2001, she served as portfolio committee chair of the intelligence committee. In 2001 she replaced Tony Yengeni as chief whip of the ruling party in the National Assembly. She was appointed deputy minister of home affairs in May 2002, and replaced Mangosuthu Buthelezi as minister of home affairs in 2004. That same year she jumped four places on the ANC's National to National list, from 24 to 20.

In 1993 Mapisa-Nqakula was elected to the position of secretary general within the ANCWL. She lost the position, but remained within the NEC of the Women's League at their 1997 conference, and was elected president of the League in 2003. In 2002 she was elected to the ANC NEC, and she now also serves on the NWC.

Her current mission is to redeem home affairs after the many 'lost years' under Buthelezi. Whether it is a 'mission impossible' or not, there are few commentators who are willing to say that she is meeting the challenge.

Housing: Lindiwe Sisulu

Lindiwe Sisulu attended high school in Swaziland. She returned to South Africa in the 1970s, and participated in student politics. She was arrested and detained in 1975, and left the country after her release. In the late 1970s she worked within MK and underwent military training, specializing in intelligence. In the 1980s she studied teaching in Swaziland, before furthering her studies as a historian in Swaziland and Britain. She worked throughout the 1980s variously as a teacher, lecturer and journalist.

On returning to South Africa in 1990, she re-entered formal alliance politics, working as a personal assistant to Jacob Zuma, then the head of ANC intelligence. During the transition years, she continued to work for ANC intelligence structures, as well as participating in the ANC's team at CODESA 1.

In 1994 Sisulu was elected to parliament, where she initially served as a backbencher. In 1995 she became the first chairperson of the intelligence committee. She left the post after the break-up of the GNU to take up an appointment as deputy minister of home affairs in Mandela's cabinet. She was retained in the post by Mbeki in 1999, but later appointed minister of intelligence after the death of Joe Nhlanhla in 2001. In 1997 Sisulu was elected to the ANC's NEC (58th), and was returned to the NEC at the 2002 Stellenbosch conference (13th). She currently serves on the ANC's NWC.

She is widely held to have performed dynamically in her current portfolio, with a valuable 'mapping exercise' of what is needed on the housing front and a change of approach underpinned by the concept of 'human settlement'.

Intelligence: Ronnie Kasrils

Ronnie Kasrils joined the ANC as a twenty-two-year-old in 1960. In 1961 he became a founding member of MK, and left the country the following year to undergo military training in the Soviet Union. For the next twenty-seven years, he served the ANC in exile across Africa and in the UK. In 1990 he returned to South Africa as part of Operation Vula. Kasrils has served on the ANC's NEC since 1987, and the SACP's central committee since 1986.

In 1994 he was appointed deputy minister of defence in Mandela's cabinet, an important post, given the preoccupation with the transformation of state and liberation security apparatus at the time. In 1999 Mbeki appointed Kasrils to the post of minister of water and forestry affairs. In 2004 Kasrils returned to security issues, when he was appointed minister of intelligence – a post that has proved to be even more controversial than expected, with the ongoing power struggle with the head of the National Intelligence Agency (NIA), Billy Masetla. Kasrils finally sacked Masetla in 2005.

Justice and constitutional development: Brigitte Mabandla

Brigitte Mabandla left South Africa for exile following the Soweto uprising. She gained her LLB at the University of Zambia in 1979, before embarking on an academic career lecturing law in Botswana for five years. In 1986 she was appointed legal advisor to the ANC's legal and constitutional affairs department in Lusaka. During this time she served on the Skweyiya Commission, tasked with investigating human rights abuses in ANC camps.

After returning to South Africa in 1990, Mabandla was appointed to the ANC's constitutional committee and negotiating team, a position she held until 1994. During this time she co-founded with Dullah Omar the Centre for Law at the University of the Western Cape, overseeing and coordinating research relating to the rights of women and children.

In 1997 Mabandla was elected to the ANC's NEC (34th), and she was returned to the NEC in 2002 (27th). She currently serves on the ANC's NWC.

In 1994 she was elected to parliament, and in 1995 she was appointed to Mandela's cabinet as deputy minister of arts, culture, science and technology, replacing Winnie Mandela, a position she held until 2003, when she replaced Sankie Mthembi-Mahanyele as minister of housing. In 2004, Mbeki appointed her minister of justice.

Despite her NGO background, Mabandla's appointment did not inspire much enthusiasm with the human rights community, who regard her as generally too weak to stand up to her more conservative and pragmatic colleagues in cabinet, especially in the security portfolios. Suffering from a variety of ailments that force her to delegate responsibilities, she has been repeatedly overshadowed by the more robust approach of her deputy minister, Johnny de Lange, with whom relations gradually soured as the public furore surrounding the package of judicial reform laws grew in late 2005 and early 2006.

Labour: Membathisi Mdladlana

Membathisi Mdladlana entered into organized politics through his primary profession of schoolteacher. In the early 1980s he was appointed as the Western Cape representative to the National Education Crisis Committee, an affiliate of the UDF, in his capacity as a school principal. In 1985 he became chairperson of the South African Democratic Teachers' Union (SADTU), a position he held until 1990, when he was elected national president of the organization. With the unbanning of the ANC, he retained his position as headmaster of Andile Primary School in Cape Town, while organizing branch structures for the ANC in the Western Cape.

In 1994 he was elected to parliament as a backbencher for the ANC, where he served as a member of the education and home affairs committees. In 1995 he was appointed as a whip within the ANC caucus. In July 1998 he was appointed to Mandela's cabinet to replace outgoing minister of labour, Tito Mboweni. Mbeki retained the minister in 1999, and reappointed him in 2004. In 2002 he was elected to the ANC's NEC (38th) for the first time. His rising profile within the ANC is reflected in his climb up the electoral lists:

in 1999 he was elected from 36th position on the list, and he moved up to 19th position in 2004.

Minerals and energy affairs: Buyelwa Patience Sonjica

Buyelwa Sonjica became politically active through the Black Consciousness movement in 1976. She qualified as a teacher the following year, and began work in the field. She was active within the UDF after its establishment in 1983, and joined the South African Democratic Teachers' Union.

After the unbanning of the ANC in 1990, she became active in the Eastern Cape structures of the ANC and ANCWL. She was elected to the regional executive committee for both organizations in 1992, and served on the working committee for the region as well. She does not serve on any ANC or ANCWL committees at a national level.

In 1994 Sonjica was elected to parliament for the ANC, and served as a whip for the party. In 1999 she was appointed chairperson of the water and forestry portfolio committee, a position she held until 2003, when she was appointed deputy minister of arts and culture. In 2004 Mbeki appointed her minister of water affairs and forestry. Sonjica was appointed as minister of minerals and energy in May 2006, swapping portfolios with Lindiwe Hendricks, who took over water affairs.

Provincial and local government: Sydney Mufamadi

At forty-five, Sydney Mufamadi remains one of the youngest senior members of the ANC and cabinet. He entered politics while still in high school in the Venda homeland. After school he moved to Johannesburg, and initially worked as a teacher before joining the General and Allied Workers' Union. He was elected general secretary in 1982, at the age of twenty-three. After the formation of the UDF the following year, he was appointed publicity secretary for the organization in the Transvaal. In 1985, in his capacity as a trade unionist, he helped to organize COSATU, and was elected assistant general at their inaugural rally in 1985.

After the unbanning of the ANC and SACP in 1990, he entered formal party structures, and was named as one of the SACP's twenty-two-person interim leadership group. Mufamadi participated in the CODESA negotiations as an ANC representative, and later in the transitional executive council.

Mufamadi continues to serve as a central committee member of the SACP. He was elected to the ANC's NEC in 1994 (6th place), and returned in 1997 (11th) and 2002 (7th). He currently serves on the ANC's NWC. He climbed the ANC's electoral list from 20th in 1999 to 11th in 2004.

Mufamadi holds an MSc from the University of London, and is currently studying towards a PhD in political economy.

In 1994 Mandela appointed him to the senior cabinet position of minister of safety and security – the youngest member of the first cabinet at thirty-five years of age. In 1999, President Mbeki deployed him to the provincial and local government portfolio, a challenging tenure in which he oversaw the transformation of local government during the demarcation process and the local government elections in 2000. Mbeki has cited local and provincial government as a key site of delivery and development and retained Mufamadi in this position after the 2004 elections.

Public enterprises: Alec Erwin

The former Federation of South African Trade Unions (FOSATU) and COSATU organizer and SACP member continues to change his ideological spots and increase his profile and popularity. Alec Erwin studied and lectured economics at the University of Natal in the 1970s, while working for NGOs associated with the trade union movement. In 1979 he was elected general secretary of FOSATU, and in 1983 education secretary of the same organization. After the formation of COSATU, he was appointed education secretary of the new union. From 1988 to 1993, he served the National Union of Mineworkers as national education officer. After the unbanning of the ANC in 1990, he became a senior member of the party in Natal. Having ideologically aligned himself with the anti-SACP 'workerist' traditions of the union movement, Erwin joined the SACP after 1990, and was elected to the central committee of the party.

He was elected to the ANC's NEC in 1994 at No. 45 on the list, and has returned in 25th place in 1997 and 20th place in 2002. Erwin did not stand for re-election to the SACP central committee in 2002, a position he was unlikely to keep ('Mbekites' Essop Pahad and Jeff Radebe lost their seats, and Fraser-Moleketi declined to stand). Erwin served as deputy minister of finance from 1994 to 1996, and succeeded Trevor Manuel as minister of trade and industry in 1996.

Erwin's reputation has soared abroad for his negotiating skills in international forums (notably the WTO). Some pundits have speculated that he may leave cabinet for a post with an international body. But Erwin was reappointed to the cabinet as minister of public enterprises, where his negotiating skills and relationships with the unions will be hard-pressed in implementing the government's plans to privatize government assets and parastatals, and in driving a more comprehensive industrial policy.

Public service and administration: Geraldine Fraser-Moleketi

Geraldine Fraser-Moleketi cut her teeth in the Unity Movement politics of the Western Cape as a student in the late 1970s. She left South Africa for exile in Zimbabwe in 1980 to join the ANC. She was elected deputy chairperson of the SACP in 1988, and retained the position and membership of the central committee until 2002, when the rank and file dropped her in a move widely interpreted as a protest to her pro-business government policies.

Fraser-Moleketi returned to South Africa in 1990, and worked full time for the SACP and ANC until her election to parliament in 1994. She was elected to the ANC's NEC in 1997 in 17th place, and again in 2002, in 14th position. Her rising profile in the ANC is reflected in her positions on the ANC list: 61st in 1994, 6th in 1999 and 9th in 2004.

She served as an MP in parliament, chairing the subcommittee on rules in the National Assembly from 1994 to 1995. In 1995 she was appointed deputy minister of welfare and population development in Mandela's cabinet, before being appointed minister of the same portfolio following the break-up of the GNU. In 1999 she was appointed minister of public service and administration by President Mbeki, and was retained in 2004.

Public works: Thoko Didiza

A veritable rising star within the ANC government, Thoko Didiza became active in youth, civics, women's and church networks in the 1980s, and was appointed the Young Women's Christian Association (YWCA) deputy secretary general in 1993.

It is worth noting that Didiza was never formally aligned with either the ANCYL or the ANCWL, and has forged a name for herself through the main body of the organization. She only entered formal tripartite alliance politics in 1994, and was appointed deputy minister of agriculture and land affairs in Mandela's cabinet (1994–99) at the age of twenty-eight. She was elected in last (60th) place to the ANC's NEC at the 1997 Mafikeng conference, and was elected to the NWC thereafter. Mbeki appointed her as minister of agriculture and land affairs in 1999. In 2002 she was elected in 4th place to the NEC.

Her rise within the ANC is illustrated by her climb up the party's election list. In 1999 she was elected to parliament from No. 32 on the National to National list. She was elected in 6th place in 2004.

Didiza, who has a firm understanding of the challenges facing agriculture and land affairs, was recently appointed to head public works following the death of Stella Sigcau. Didiza's experience and ability to navigate complex challenges, as shown in her tenure in agriculture and land affairs, could boost public works, which is supposed to serve as a strong push towards the realization of accelerated shared economic growth policy (ASGISA).

Safety and security: Charles Nqakula

Charles Nqakula entered politics as a journalist in the Eastern Cape. He was banned while working for the *Daily Dispatch*, and later exiled to the 'homeland' of the Ciskei (he was not allowed to enter the RSA). In 1983 the UDF appointed him as publicity secretary, but after an arrest in the same year, he left the Ciskei for exile outside South Africa's borders. After joining MK, he underwent military training in the USSR.

In 1988 Nqakula was smuggled back into South Africa as an Operation Vula operative. He remained underground until the unbanning of political organizations in 1991. In 1991 he was elected deputy general secretary of the SACP, and became general secretary of the party after the assassination of Chris Hani in 1992. He was re-elected general secretary in 1995, and in 1998 was elected national chairperson of the SACP. In 1994 he was elected to the NEC of the ANC (34th), and was re-elected in 1997 (32nd) and 2002 (11th).

He served within the SACP head office until 1999, when he was deployed to parliament, where he acted as parliamentary counsellor to Thabo Mbeki. He was appointed the deputy minister of home affairs in 2001, and as minister of safety and security after the death of Steve Tshwete in May 2002. His rising profile within the formal structures of the ANC is evident in his positions on the electoral list: 28th in 1999 and 14th in 2004.

Science and technology: Mosibudi Mangena

An interesting and inspired – as well as surprise – appointment to the cabinet in 2004, Mosibudi Mangena entered the Black Consciousness movement in the 1970s through the student association SASO. He remained in student politics until his exile in Botswana, where he became affiliated to the Black Consciousness Movement of Azania (BCMA). He was elected chairperson of the central committee of the BCMA, a position he held until 1994, when he was elected president of AZAPO.

AZAPO chose not to stand in the 1994 elections, and Mangena was only elected to parliament in 1999. In 2001, Thabo Mbeki appointed him deputy minister of education, where he was popular within the department for his hard work and dedication. Mbeki rewarded him in 2004 with a ministerial position in the science and technology ministry.

Social development: Zola Skweyiya

A veteran of both the ANC and the cabinet, Zola Skweyiya joined the ANC at the age of fourteen in 1956. He studied at Fort Hare, but did not complete his degree. He left the country for exile, where he joined MK and underwent military training. He obtained a law degree in East Germany in 1978. Skweyiya rose to a senior level within the exile structures, establishing the ANC offices in Dar es Salaam and serving the organization as their representative at the OAU from 1982 to 1985. He was recalled to Lusaka in 1985 to set up and oversee the legal and constitutional department.

Skweyiya returned to South Africa in 1990, and served the ANC in numerous capacities in the transition years, including membership of the ANC's negotiating commission.

In 1994 Skweyiya was elected to parliament, and was appointed minister of public service and administration in Mandela's cabinet. In 1999 Mbeki appointed him to the portfolio of social development (previously welfare and population development). He was retained in the position in 2004.

Skweyiya is a member of the ANC's NEC (24th in 1994, 24th in 1997, and 9th in 2002) and NWC.

Sport and recreation: Makhenkesi Stofile

Makhenkesi Stofile trained in theology at the University of Fort Hare, after which he entered the Presbyterian Church as a minister in 1975. In the

1980s, Stofile studied in Germany and the USA. In 1983 he was elected regional secretary of the UDF in the Eastern Cape, and remained active in UDF politics until the unbanning of the ANC in 1990. In 1990 he was elected regional chairperson of the ANC in the Eastern Cape, and served in the ANC's interim leadership structures during the transition.

Stofile was elected onto the ANC's NEC in 1991, and up to 1996 served the organization at national head office as the ANC's treasurer general. Since 1996, he has not sat on the NEC. In 1994 Stofile was elected to the National Assembly, and was appointed chief whip of the ruling party, a position he held until 1996, when he was deployed to the Eastern Cape as premier of the province. His one and a half terms were not particularly productive, and the national government had to step in on numerous occasions to run the affairs of the province. During this time, the ANC in the Eastern Cape became increasingly fractured due to infighting and power struggles.

In 2004 Mbeki appointed Stofile to the ministry of sport and recreation – something that suits his background and personal passion: he was actively engaged in sport (specifically rugby) as a coach and administrator throughout the 1970s, 1980s and early 1990s.

Minister in the office of the president: Essop Pahad

Essop Pahad entered politics through the Transvaal Indian Youth Congress in the late 1950s, where he sat on the executive committee as secretary. During this time he joined the ANC and, after its banning, the organization's underground. While at Wits University he became active in student politics, which led to his arrest and a banning order. In 1964 he left the country for exile.

In exile Pahad linked up with the ANC and SACP, undergoing military training in Angola and furthering his studies in Moscow. He later also attended the University of Sussex, obtaining an MA and PhD, where he formed a close relationship with Thabo Mbeki. Pahad served on the ANC's political and military council in London, before returning to South Africa in 1990.

Pahad has served on the ANC's NEC and the SACP's central committee. In 1994 he was elected to the NEC in 54th position, 45th in 1997, and 28th in 2002. In 2002 he did not gain re-election to the SACP's central committee.

In 1994 Pahad was elected to parliament, and served as the parliamentary counsellor to Deputy President Thabo Mbeki until 1996, when he was appointed deputy minister in the office of the deputy president. In 1999 he was appointed minister in the office of the president, and he was reappointed in 2004.

Trade and industry: Mandisi Mpahlwa

Mandisi Mpahlwa qualified as an electrician in the early 1980s. He worked in the Transkei for the Umtata municipality thereafter, but left to go into exile in 1985.

His spells in exile and within the ANC after returning to South Africa seem relatively unremarkable. He was retained as a volunteer throughout this period, and continued to work for his family's business in Umtata until his election to parliament in 1994. In 1995 and 1996 he studied economics through the University of London. In 1997 he was appointed chairperson of the portfolio committee on finance, a position he held until the end of the first parliament.

In 1999 he was appointed deputy minister of finance, where he earned a fine reputation for detail and policy implementation. There are very high hopes for Mpahlwa; in 2004 he replaced Alec Erwin as the minister for trade and industry – a hard act to follow – in a department with considerable domestic and international challenges.

Transport: Jeff Radebe

Jeff Radebe qualified as a lawyer at the University of Zululand, and completed his articles in 1976. In the same year he joined the ANC after the student uprisings in Soweto, and left South Africa for exile the following year, where he underwent military training.

He was infiltrated back into the country to establish underground structures for the ANC and SACP, but was arrested and sentenced to six years on Robben Island in 1986. On the island he was active in the ANC's political department, heading the committee by the time of the release of political prisoners in 1990.

During the transition he served as deputy chairman, and later chairman, of the ANC's Southern Natal structures. In 1991 he was appointed secretary of the SACP. Radebe has served on both the NEC of the ANC and the central committee of the SACP. He was elected to the NEC in 16th position in 1994, 14th in 1997, and 19th in 2002. He currently serves on the NWC of the ANC. In 2002 he was not re-elected to the SACP central committee after his relationship with the SACP soured with his implementation of centre-right policies in ministerial appointments.

In 1994 Radebe was elected to parliament and appointed minister of public works in the first cabinet. In 1999 he was appointed minister of public enterprise by Thabo Mbeki. After Dullah Omar fell ill, Radebe acted as transport minister from 2000, and Mbeki appointed him to this position in 2004.

Water affairs and forestry: Lindiwe Benedicta Hendricks

A qualified lawyer, Lindiwe Hendricks served as a member of parliament from 1994 to 1999. She was also a member of the justice and constitutional development committee. She served as deputy minister of trade and industry from 1999 to 2005, after which she was appointed minister of minerals and energy.

Hendricks was appointed to minerals and energy after a cabinet reshuffle that followed the dismissal of Jacob Zuma as deputy president. After Mlambo-Ngcuka was appointed deputy president following the sacking of Zuma, the minerals and energy ministry was left vacant, and Hendricks stepped in. Hendricks served minerals and energy for barely more than six months. In mid-2006, she was appointed as minister of water affairs and forestry, a clean portfolio swap with Buyelwa Sonjica. The transition from trade and industry to minerals and energy and to water affairs and forestry should not be a difficult one for Hendricks, who served different portfolios at ANC branch level.

Sources: These pen portraits are drawn from a number of sources, including:
- www.info.gov.za
- www.sahistory.org.za
- www.gcis.gov.za
- www.mg.co.za
- www.iol.co.za

Appendix B

The Constitutional Court

Chief Justice Pius Nkonzo Langa

Pius Langa was born in the Eastern Transvaal on 25 March 1939. He matriculated in 1960 through private study and obtained a Bachelor of Law degree (B Iuris) in 1973, and a Bachelor of Law degree (LLB) in 1976 through the University of South Africa.

He was admitted as an advocate of the Supreme Court of South Africa in Natal in June 1977. He practised at the Durban bar and attained the rank of senior counsel in January 1994.

Justice Langa was appointed as justice of the Constitutional Court of South Africa in October 1994, became deputy president of that court with effect from August 1997, and was appointed deputy chief justice of South Africa with effect from November 2001.

At the bar, his work involved both civil and criminal matters, with a predominance of political trials. He appeared in most of the more significant political trials, mainly in the former Natal, the Eastern Cape and Cape Town. His practice reflected the struggle against the apartheid dispensation, and his clientele thus included the underprivileged, various civic bodies, trade unions, and people charged under the security legislation and with activities designed to hasten the end of the apartheid system and to bring about a democratic South Africa.

As an advocate, Justice Langa was a member of the Democratic Lawyers' Association (DLA), and served on its executive. In 1987, he served on the steering committee which preceded the formation of the National Association of Democratic Lawyers (NADEL); he became a founder-member of NADEL and served as its president from 1988 until his resignation in 1994, when he was appointed as a justice of the Constitutional Court.

Justice Langa has served on the boards and as a trustee of various law-related institutions, such as the Community Legal Services Unit (CLSU), Centre for Development Studies (CDS), Centre for Applied Legal Studies (CALS), Legal Resources Trust (LRT) and the Centre for Socio-Legal Studies

(University of Natal). He was centrally involved in the founding of the South African Legal Defence Fund (SALDEF). He served as commissioner on the Human Rights Commission (later to be known as the Human Rights Committee) for several years, and attended, participated in and organized conferences, workshops and seminars on human rights issues, in South Africa and in a number of countries abroad.

He has served in the structures of the UDF, was involved in the work of CODESA and of its successor, the Multi-Party Negotiations Forum. He was also a member of the constitutional committee of the ANC and was in the advisor group during the Groote Schuur and Pretoria 'talks about talks'. He was appointed as a member of the police board to assist with the transformation of the police services in terms of the national peace accord. He also chaired the technical committee to review and rationalize health legislation, served as a member of the commission of inquiry into unrest in prisons, and was a member of the commission of inquiry into the so-called 'Meiring report'.

Justice Tholakele Hope Madala

Tholakele Madala was born on 13 July 1937 at Kokstad. In 1956 he matriculated at St John's College in Umtata. He taught at the Lovedale Institution at Alice, in the Eastern Cape, and in Swaziland before taking up law in 1972 at the University of Natal (Pietermaritzburg). He was also instrumental in the establishment of the first legal aid clinic on the Pietermaritzburg campus, to assist the indigent and underprivileged. He lectured at the University of Transkei, initially full time, but later on a part-time basis. He practised as an attorney and was admitted as an advocate in 1982, handling numerous human rights cases. He established, together with other lawyers interested in the protection of the rights of the underprivileged, the Umtata Law Clinic, under the auspices of the then Umtata and Districts Lawyers Association. As an attorney, he became chairman of the Transkei Attorneys Association.

Judge Madala was a founder-member and director of Prisoners' Welfare Programmes (PRIWELPRO), an association established in 1985 to provide legal, financial and educational assistance to political detainees, prisoners, ex-prisoners and their families. From 1987 to 1990 he was vice-chairman of the Society of Advocates of Transkei. Between 1991 and 1993 he was chairman of the Society of Advocates of Transkei, and represented the society on the General Council of the Bar of South Africa.

He took silk in 1993 and was elevated to the bench in 1994, becoming the first black judge in the Eastern Cape and the fourth black judge to be so appointed in South Africa. In October 1994 he was appointed to the Constitutional Court of South Africa.

Justice Yvonne Mokgoro

Born on 19 October 1950 in Galeshewe Township near Kimberley, Yvonne Mokgoro matriculated at the local St Boniface High School in 1970. She obtained the B Iuris degree at the University of the North West in 1982, an LLB degree two years later, and completed her LLM in 1987. She also attended the University of Pennsylvania in the USA. She started her work experience as a nursing assistant and later worked as a salesperson, before her appointment as a clerk in the department of justice of the erstwhile Bophuthatswana. After completion of her LLB degree she was appointed maintenance officer and public prosecutor in the then Mmabatho Magistrate's Court. In 1984, Judge Mokgoro was appointed lecturer in the Department of Jurisprudence, University of the North West, where she rose through the ranks to associate professor. From 1992 to 1993 she served as associate professor at the University of the Western Cape, from where she moved to the Centre for Constitutional Analysis at the Human Sciences Research Council, serving as specialist researcher (human rights). Throughout her legal career, she has written extensively, presented papers to, and participated in, a myriad of national and international conferences in South Africa and abroad, mainly in socio-logical jurisprudence, and particularly on human rights and customary law, focusing on the impact of law on society generally, and on women and children specifically. She has served extensively as a resource person in this regard for non-governmental and community-based organizations and initiatives.

Deputy Chief Justice Dikgang Moseneke

Dikgang Moseneke was born in 1947 in Pretoria, where he completed primary and secondary schooling. At the age of fifteen, while in Standard 8, he was arrested, detained and convicted for participating in political activity opposed to the apartheid regime. Moseneke was sentenced to ten years' imprisonment, all of which he served on Robben Island.

While on Robben Island, Moseneke matriculated and thereafter obtained a BA degree (in English and Political Science) and a B Iuris degree. Subsequently, he completed his LLB degree. All three degrees were conferred by the University of South Africa. His professional career started in 1976 as an attorney's clerk. In 1978 Moseneke was admitted and practised as an attorney.

In 1983 he was called to the bar, where he practised as an advocate at the Johannesburg and Pretoria bars. Ten years later, in 1993, he was elevated to the status of senior counsel (SC).

In 1993, Moseneke served (together with, *inter alia*, CJ Chaskalson and JP Ngoepe) on the technical committee that drafted the 1993 Interim Constitution for a democratic South Africa. In 1994 Moseneke was appointed deputy chairman of the Independent Electoral Commission, which conducted the first democratic elections in South Africa. In September 1994, Moseneke was appointed to the Supreme Court [TPD] as an acting judge.

From 1995 to 2001, Moseneke left the bar to pursue a full-time corporate career in the following capacities (he has since resigned all these corporate positions):

- Chairman of Telkom South Africa Ltd (Since October 1994)
- Chairman of African Merchant Bank
- Chairman of Metropolitan Life Ltd
- Chairman of African Bank Investments Ltd
- Chief executive of New Africa Investments Ltd
- Director of New Africa Publications (Pty) Ltd
- Director of Phaphama Holdings (Pty) Ltd
- Director of Urban Brew (Pty) Ltd
- Chairman of Alisa Car Rental (Pty) Ltd (Hertz)
- Director of Life Officers' Association.

Before his appointment to the Constitutional Court, Moseneke was a judge of the High Court in Pretoria. He is a founder member of the Black Lawyers Association (BLA) and of NADEL. From 1986 Moseneke was appointed visiting law professor at Columbia Law School, University of Columbia, New York.

Justice Bess Nkabinde (born Motsatsi)

Bess Nkabinde was born in Silwerkrans (North West Province) in 1959. She is married and has four children. She matriculated at Mariasdal High School (Tweespruit, OFS) in 1979. She obtained a BProc degree at the University of Zululand in 1983, and an LLB from the University of the North West in 1986. She also attended Damelin College, where she was awarded a diploma in industrial relations with distinction. Her professional career began in 1984, when she worked as a state law advisor, doing legislative drafting in Bophuthatswana. She did this until 1988, when she was admitted as an advocate. In 1989 she did her pupillage at the Johannesburg bar. From 1990 until 1999 she practised as an advocate at the North West bar. Her practice was in civil, commercial and matrimonial, as well as criminal, matters. In 1993 she attended a judicial training programme in Canada, and from 1994 to 1995 she was involved in investigating and leading evidence in the commission of inquiry into the mutiny of warders at Mogwase Prison. Between February and October 1999, she served as acting judge of the High Court of the Bophuthatswana provincial division. In November of the same year, she became judge of this court. In 2000 she served one term as acting judge of the Labour Court in Johannesburg, and then another term in the same position in 2003. In that year, she was appointed to serve on the special tribunal on civil matters likely to emanate from investigations by the special investigative units (established in terms of Act No. 74 of 1996). From October 2004 to May 2005, she once again served as acting judge of the Labour Appeal Court, and from June to November 2005, she was acting judge of the Supreme Court of Appeal.

Justice Sandile Ngcobo

Sandile Ngcobo began his legal education at the University of Zululand in 1972. He studied there until 1975, when he obtained his BProc degree with distinction in constitutional law, mercantile law and accounting. Ngcobo spent the period from July 1976 until July 1977 in detention. From 1983 until 1985 he studied at the University of Natal and was awarded his LLB degree, after which he participated in an orientation course on the United States' legal system at the Georgetown Law Center in Washington, DC. Ngcobo spent the next year studying for his LLM at Harvard Law School, concentrating on constitutional law, labour law, international legal process and international human rights.

He was admitted as an attorney in 1981, and worked as a law clerk to the late The Hon A Leon Higginbotham Jr, former chief judge of the Third Circuit Federal Court of Appeals, USA, from 1986 to 1987. In 1988 he was admitted as an advocate. In 1994 Ngcobo took up the post of part-time lecturer on constitutional litigation at the University of Natal, Durban. He was retained as one of the counsel to advise the ministerial legal task team that drafted the Labour Relations Act in 1995. He served as the acting High Court judge of the Cape of Good Hope provincial division and was appointed judge of the High Court of the Cape of Good Hope provincial division on 1 September 1996. He also served as judge on the amnesty committee of the Truth and Reconciliation Commission. Ngcobo was appointed chairperson of the Rules Board for Courts of Law in October 1998, as an honorary Professor of Law at the University of Cape Town, in February 1999, and as acting judge president of the Labour Court and Labour Appeal Court with effect from February 1999.

Justice Kate O'Regan

Born in Liverpool, England, on 17 September 1957, Kate O'Regan grew up in Cape Town, where she matriculated from Springfield Convent in 1974. She obtained her LLB degree *cum laude* from the University of Cape Town in 1980, and an LLM degree with first-class honours from the University of Sydney in 1981.

From 1982 to 1985 she worked for a firm of attorneys in Johannesburg specializing in labour law and land rights. During this time she was an executive member of the Industrial Aid Society, an advice officer for the unemployed, as well as a roster lawyer for Actstop and the Black Sash.

Thereafter she spent three years at the London School of Economics obtaining a PhD. Her research was on interdicts restraining strike actions. In mid-1988, Judge O'Regan joined the labour unit at UCT as a senior researcher. In 1990 she was appointed a senior lecturer in the law faculty at UCT, where she taught civil procedure, evidence and labour law, and introduced a course on 'Women in the legal system'. In 1992 she was promoted to associate professor. During her years at UCT she was a founder member of both the Institute of Development Law and the Law, Race and Gender Research Project. In 1992 she also became a trustee of the Legal Resources Centre.

Justice O'Regan has written articles for a wide range of academic journals and newspapers on matters relating to labour law, land and housing, race and gender equality, and constitutional law.

Justice Albie (Albert Louis) Sachs

Albie Sachs was born in Johannesburg on 30 January 1935, matriculated at the South African College School (SACS) in Cape Town in 1950, and attended the University of Cape Town, where he obtained the degrees BA and LLB. He started his practice as an advocate at the Cape Town bar in 1957 and worked mainly in the civil rights sphere until he was himself twice detained without trial by the security police.

In 1966 he went into exile in England, where he completed a PhD at the University of Sussex (1971) and taught in the Law Faculty of the University of Southampton (1970–1977). He was the first Nuffield Fellow of Socio-Legal Studies at Bedford College, London, and Wolfson College, Cambridge. In 1977 he took up a position as professor of law at the Eduardo Mondlane University in Maputo, Mozambique. From 1983 onwards he served as director of research in the ministry of justice. After nearly being killed by a car bomb in 1988, he returned to England. The next year he worked as professor at the Law School and in the Department of International Affairs at Columbia University in New York.

Later that year, Judge Sachs became the founding director of the South Africa Constitution Studies Centre, based at the Institute of Commonwealth Studies at the University of London. In 1992 the centre moved to the University of the Western Cape, where he was made professor extraordinary. He was also appointed honorary professor in the Law Faculty at the University of Cape Town. He took an active part in the negotiations for a new constitution as a member of the constitutional committee of the ANC and of the national executive of that organization.

Author of many books on human rights, he has been awarded honorary doctorates of law by the Universities of Southampton, York (Toronto), Antwerp and the William Mitchell College of Law.

For a number of years he has been a member of the UNESCO International Bioethics Committee, and helped to draft the international declaration on the human genome. He has written extensively on culture, gender rights and the environment. His book, *The Jail Diary of Albie Sachs*, was dramatized for the Royal Shakespeare Company and broadcast by the BBC.

Another autobiographical book, *The Soft Vengeance of a Freedom Fighter*, which deals with his recovery from a car bomb attack and his eventual appointment to the Constitutional Court, is presently being dramatized for film.

Justice Thembile Skweyiya

Thembile Skweyiya was born in Worcester in the Western Cape. He is married to Sayo Nomakhosi Skweyiya, and they have four children. Skweyiya attended primary school in Cape Town, where his parents settled. In 1959 he matriculated at the Healdtown Institution in the Eastern Cape. He was awarded a Bachelor of Social Science degree by the University of Natal in 1963 and an LLB by the same university in 1967. From 1968 to 1970, Skweyiya served his articles of clerkship in an attorney's office. In 1970 he was admitted as an advocate of the Supreme Court of South Africa, and became a member of the Society of Advocates in Natal.

From 1971 to 1996 he practised as an advocate in Durban. His practice dealt almost exclusively in commercial and civil matters. From about the end of 1979, however, Skweyiya's work became more varied and he began handling cases not only in Durban, but in all Supreme Court divisions in southern Africa.

From about 1981, the bulk of his work involved human rights and civil liberties cases. However, from the time Skweyiya took silk in 1989, the focus of his practice shifted back to commercial and civil work.

Skweyiya has held many positions in community organizations, as well as in the world of business, for example:

- As the chairperson of Worldwide African Investment holding (Pty) Ltd, KFM Radio (Pty) Ltd and Zenex Oil Ltd.
- As the deputy chairperson of Fortune Beverages Ltd and the SA Tourism Board.
- As the director and vice chairperson of Fasic Investment Ltd.
- As a director of Fedics Group Ltd, Lion Match (Pty) Ltd, Gold Circle Racing and Gaming, the Premier Group Ltd, Southern Bank of Africa Ltd.
- As a member of the regional advisory board of Nedcor Bank KwaZulu-Natal.

Justice Johann van der Westhuizen

Johann van der Westhuizen was born in Windhoek, in Namibia. He went to school there and in Pretoria, where he now lives. He received a BA Law *cum laude* from the University of Pretoria in 1973; an LLB *cum laude* from the University of Pretoria in 1975; and an LLD from the same university in 1980. He received the Grotius medal – awarded by the Pretoria bar council to the University of Pretoria's best final-year law student – in 1975.

Van der Westhuizen was admitted as an advocate in 1976. He was the professor (from 1980 to 1998) and head (from 1980 to 1994) of the Department of Legal History, Comparative Law and Legal Philosophy in the University of Pretoria's Faculty of Law. He was the founding director of the university's Centre for Human Rights from 1986 to 1998, and joined the Transvaal provincial division of the High Court of South Africa in 1999. He was an associate member of the Pretoria bar (1989 to 1998), and a member of the national council and board of trustees of Lawyers for Human Rights (1990 to 2001). He joined the Constitutional Court on 1 February 2004. He was intimately involved in the drafting of South Africa's final Constitution in 1995 and 1996: he was a member of the Independent Panel of Recognized Constitutional Experts, which advised the Constitutional Assembly, and was part of the technical refinement team, responsible for the final drafting and editing process.

He convened task groups at the multiparty negotiating process in 1993, resulting in the adoption of the Interim Constitution, and the Transitional Executive Council in 1994, and coordinated the equality legislation project of the ministry of justice and the South African Human Rights Commission in 1998.

Van der Westhuizen was involved in human rights litigation and argued numerous appeals against the censorship of socially and politically significant films such as *Roots*, *Cry Freedom* and *A Dry White Season*. He also acted as a consultant and in-house advocate for the Legal Resources Centre and Lawyers for Human Rights in Pretoria.

Justice Zakeria Mohammed Yacoob

Born on 3 March 1948, Zakeria Mohammed Yacoob became blind at the age of sixteen months as a result of meningitis. He attended the Arthur Blaxall School for the Blind, Durban, during the period 1956 to 1966, after which he studied for a BA degree at University College, Durban (now the University of Durban-Westville) from 1967 to 1969, majoring in English and Private Law. He completed a Bachelor of Law degree at the University of Durban-Westville in 1972. He was admitted as advocate by the Natal provincial division of the Supreme Court, as it was then known, on 12 March 1973.

Justice Yacoob represented victims of attempted unfair evictions or people who were required to pay unfair tariffs and charges, and represented a group of persons who became known as the 'Durban Six' in negotiations with the British government when they occupied the offices of the British Consulate in Durban during September–October 1984 in protest against apartheid and unjust laws in an effort to persuade the British government to help. He also represented their case before the Secretary-General and representatives of certain member countries of the United Nations in New York, and was part of a team that defended officials and members of the UDF and its affiliates on charges of treason and certain statutory offences during the period 1985 until 1988 in a trial that became known as the Delmas Treason Trial.

He also represented the accused in the political trial that became known as the Vula Trial, which involved high-ranking members of the ANC during the period 1990 to 1991, while sustaining a significant and diverse commercial and general legal practice.

Justice Yacoob was a member of the executive of the Natal Indian Congress from 1981 to 1991. In that capacity he both helped to organize and participated in protest action; helped to write, produce and distribute pamphlets, brochures and other publicity material; and helped to plan, organize, participated in and addressed numerous mass meetings aimed at supporting the struggle against apartheid.

He served as a member of the Society of Advocates of Natal for several years and took silk in May 1991. He was appointed a judge of the Constitutional Court on 1 February 1998. He is married with two children, and has lived in Durban virtually all his life.

Sources: These pen portraits are drawn from various sources, including:
- www.info.gov.za
- www.sahistory.org.za
- www.gcis.gov.za
- www.constitutionalcourt.org.za

Notes

Except where specifically referenced, quotations derive from interviews conducted by the author for the research purposes of this book. Biographical and related material has in some cases been taken directly from government, media and other websites but may not have been explicitly referenced.

Introduction

1 CODESA: Convention for a Democratic South Africa.

2 'Resolution on Social Transformation', www.anc.org.za/ancdocs/history/conf/conference52/resolutions

3 See Steven Lukes's classic work, *Power: A Radical View* (London: Macmillan, 1974). It describes different prisms for understanding power. The one-dimensional view of power involves a 'focus on *behaviour* in the making of *decisions* on *issues* over which there is an observable *conflict* of (subjective) *interests*, seen as express policy preferences ...'

4 Nelson Polsby, *Community power and political theory* (New Haven and London: Yale University Press, 1963), pp. 3–4.

5 'To the extent that a person or group – consciously or unconsciously – creates or reinforces barriers to the public airing of policy conflicts, that person or group has power' – a negative articulation of power (and, therefore, to Lukes, a 'two-dimensional' view). See Peter Bachrach and Morton Baratz, *Power and poverty. Theory and practice* (New York: Oxford University Press, 1962), p. 8. Similarly, the American public intellectual C Wright Mills 'arrived at a position which held that power as the capacity to make and to carry out decisions even if others resist, functions as an independent social variable'.

6 This is Lukes's preferred three-dimensional view of power, which 'involves a *thoroughgoing critique* of the *behavioural focus* of the first two views as too individualistic and allows for consideration of the many ways in which *potential issues* are kept out of politics, whether through the operation of social forces and institutional practices or through individuals' decisions'. Lukes, *ibid.*, p. 24.

7 Bernard Loomer, 'Two Conceptions of Power', *Criterion*, 15:1 (1976), pp. 12–29. On uses of the concept in organizing, see Harry C Boyte, *CommonWealth: A Return to Citizen Politics* (New York: Free Press, 1989).

8 Harry C Boyte, 'A Different Kind of Politics: John Dewey and the Meaning of Citizenship in the 21st Century', *A PEGS Journal: The Good Society*, 2004 (originally, 2002 Dewey lecture, University of Michigan).

Chapter 1

1 I have some experience of this; I have made one attempt before, with others, as co-editor (with Sean Jacobs) of *Thabo Mbeki's World: The Politics and Ideology of the South African President* (Scottsville: University of Natal Press, 2002).

2 P Bond, *Elite Transition: From Apartheid to Neo-Liberalism in South Africa* (London: Pluto Press, 2002).

3 William Mervin Gumede, *Thabo Mbeki and the Battle for the Soul of the ANC* (Cape Town: Zebra Press, 2005).

4 Statement made by Dr Zola Skweyiya, minister for public service and administration, before the Presidential Review Commission, 7 November 1997: http://www.polity.org.za/html/govdocs/reports/presreview/chap2.html

5 Para 7.2.1.4. http://www.polity.org.za/html/govdocs/reports/presreview/chap7.html

6 http://www.suntimes.co.za/2000/05/14/insight/in12.htm

7 The Constitutional Court decision is regarded as a *locus classicus* – that is to say, setting a major precedent on how government must act within the law – and is now always cited by litigants challenging the lawfulness of government decisions, notwithstanding that on the facts of the SARFU case itself, the court said there was 'no basis for finding that the president had abdicated his responsibility' when confirming the appointment of the commission of inquiry into rugby. President of Republic of South Africa and Others v South African Rugby Football Union and Others 1999 (2) SA 14 (CC).

8 The other two members of the task force were Advocate Vincent Balaka SC, a practising member of the Johannesburg bar, and Advocate Empie van Schoor, a public servant who now holds a senior position in the department of public service and administration (DPSA). As members of the task force dropped off for various reasons, Van Schoor ended up holding the fort and worked day and night alongside the parliamentary ad hoc committee as it completed its

diligent work on the bill in late 1999 and early 2000.

9 The Open Democracy Campaign Group comprised: COSATU, Idasa, the Black Sash, the Legal Resources Centre, the Human Rights Committee, the South African Catholic Bishops Conference, the South African Council of Churches (SACC), the Environmental Monitoring Group, the Freedom of Expression Institute and the Human Rights Commission. I led Idasa's representation on this consortium.

10 http://www.10years.gov.za/review/documents.htm

11 *Bua Komanisi*, special edition, Vol. 5, Issue 1, May 2006, p. 30.

Chapter 2

1 I have chosen these years for a purpose: 1994 is the Government of National Unity (GNU) cabinet; 1996 is the post-GNU cabinet; 1999 marks Thabo Mbeki's first cabinet; 2003 includes two NNP deputy ministers who joined after the collapse of the DP–NNP alliance; 2004 is Mbeki's second cabinet.

2 Section 91(1) of the Constitution.

3 Section 91(2), *ibid.*

4 Section 92(2), *ibid.*

Chapter 3

1 Lekota is not unusual in having a moniker that has stuck. The 'Terror' refers not, as many apartheid securocrats assumed, and were encouraged to think, to his warrior qualities as a leading activist in the UDF, but his pugnacity on the soccer field.

2 This table is replicated from Vino Naidoo's chapter in the 2004/05 HSRC *State of the Nation Yearbook*, edited by J Daniel, R Southall and J Lutchman (Pretoria: HSRC Press, 2005), p. 115, which in turn was an adaptation from F Cloete, 'Summary and conclusions:

Towards a strategic framework for public sector transformation', in F Cloete and J Mokgoro (eds.), *Policies for public service transformation* (Cape Town: Juta, 1995).

3   *Ibid.*, p. 118.

4   http://www.polity.org.za/html/ govdocs/policy/sms-aug00.html

5   *Presidential Review Commission Report*, Chapter 2, p. 1, 1998: http://www.polity. org.za/html/govdocs/reports/ presreview/chap2.html

Chapter 4

1   At the end of a lenghty debate on 17 September 1998 and towards the end of a long and increasingly tetchy parliamentary session, De Lange found himself sufficiently riled by the snide asides of a National Party MP, Manie Schoeman, to approach him as the debate ended and trade blows with him. National Assembly Speaker, Frene Ginwala, had left the chamber and was in the lift up to her office when the contretemps commenced, but arrived in time to catch the end of it on her TV screen. Ginwala, often compared to a strict headmistress by the more boyish members of the ANC caucus, commanded both De Lange and Schoeman to be outside her office the following Monday. Ironically, Schoeman crossed the floor to the ANC in 1999.

2   Opening speech of Nelson Mandela at the ANC's 45th national conference in December 1994, cited at www.anc.org. za/ancdocs/pubs/umrabulo/articles/ cadrepolicy.html

3   C Murray and L Nijzink, *Building Representative Democracy: South Africa's legislatures and the Constitution* (Cape Town, EU Parliamentary Support Programme, 2002), p. 60.

4   *Ibid.*, p. 60.

5   *Op cit.*, p. 66.

6   *Op cit.*, p. 66.

7   See http://www.pmg.org.za/docs/2002/ appendices/020820finalreport.htm

8   De Lange was appointed deputy minister of justice in 2004. His protégé and close colleague, Fatima Chohan, succeeded him as chairperson of the justice committee and has since sustained the energy and volume of work of her predecessor.

9   The FA folded into the DA.

10 Sheila Camerer of the NP and later DA; Chairperson: Johnny de Lange, ANC; Luwellyn Landers, ANC; Bernard Molewa, ANC; Jacobus van der Merwe, IFP. In addition to these five, Fatima Chohan has served nine years on the committee.

11 S Jacobs, G Power, R Calland, *Real Politics: The Wicked Issues* (Cape Town: Idasa/British Council, 2001), p. 58.

12 '"Storm in Sari" blew hot and cold over her appointment', *Sunday Independent*, 9 May 2004, p. 4.

Chapter 5

1   Anthony Sampson, *Who Runs this Place? The Anatomy of Britain in the 21st Century* (London: John Murray, 2004), p. 9.

2   *ANC Today*, Vol. 2, No. 21, 24–30 May 2002.

3   Having first conceded that there is 'bullying of the left' [inside the ANC alliance], what Cronin actually then said was: 'Well, of course, we shouldn't be surprised. Let's step back. We're involved in a multi-class process. The SACP all the way back in 1928 made this strategic choice. The fact that it made it in 1928 doesn't mean that, because we've stuck to it for this long, it's right now, but we may have made it and stuck by it for good reasons. Part of what we said was that there would be considerable turbulence in the post-independence situation, that the unity of the whole national liberation movement would be difficult to build, because of sheer

oppression and persecution and so forth. Those would be the organizational challenges of the post-independence, post-democracy breakthrough period. The challenges would be much more to maintain the dialectic and to struggle for popular working-class dominance, over a complicated multi-class front, a front to which nonetheless we were committed, we said at the time, and that's what we're living through. So if there's marginalization, shouting down, suppression of views and perspectives, it might have to do with individuals who are nasty, with Stalinist tendencies. It might have to do with a lack of imagination or any number of factors. But finally for me, a class analysis is also an important tool for understanding what we're living through. I think [a] characteristic of a lot of left people, including comrades inside of the SACP and COSATU, is that there's the assumption that we're living through a kind of tragedy, the sort of Stalin era is a version of it; or what's happened in Africa with Zanu and so forth, is another.' For the transcript of the whole interview, see: http://www.comms.dcu.ie/sheehanh/za/cronin02.htm

4 From Cronin's first interview with Helen Sheehan in April 2001, at http://www.comms.dcu.ie/sheehanh/za/cronin-aah01.htm

5 http://www.anc.org.za/ancdocs/ngcouncils/2005/org_report.html

6 According to Motlanthe's 2005 NGC report, membership had dropped to 385 000 at the time of the 1997 Mafikeng conference, risen to 416 000 by the time of Stellenbosch in 2002, and settled down at 401 000 in February 2005.

7 http://www.anc.org.za/ancdocs/ngcouncils/2005/org_design.html

Chapter 6

1 F Tregenna, 'The Post-Apartheid Transition in South Africa: What role, outcomes and prospects for the working class?', paper presented at the 2nd International Conference on Marxism and the Challenges of the 21st Century, Havana, Cuba, May 2004.

2 *Accelerating Transformation: COSATU's engagement with policy and legislative processes during South Africa's First Term Democratic Governance*, collective work of COSATU's parliamentary office, with contributions from Neil Coleman, Oupa Bodibe, Fiona Tregenna and Kenneth Creamer. All of the submissions are available at www.cosatu.org.za

3 'So many questions', *Sunday Times*, 19 March 2006, p. 21.

4 Tregenna, *ibid.*, p. 11.

5 See McKinley's paper summarizing his position on the alliance at http://www.dsp.org.au/links/back/issue16/McKinley.html

6 Tregenna, *ibid.*, p. 3.

7 http://www.nytimes.com/2004/06/27/magazine/27LULA.html

8 Tregenna, *ibid.*, p. 7.

9 'Neo-liberalism, reformism, populism and ultra-leftism', paper presented by Jeremy Cronin, SACP deputy general secretary, to the monthly SACP Gauteng Province Political Education School, 28 August 2005. The paper begins with a similarly clear exposition of 'neo-liberalism', describing how contemporary obsession with the free market has warped traditional models of liberalism, which contained progressive elements, including the emphasis on individual human rights.

10 COSATU paper for COSATU/ANC Bilateral 9/10 February 2002: http://www.cosatu.org.za/docs/2005/declarations.pdf

11 COSATU paper, 2002, *ibid.*, footnote 1, p. 2.

12 COSATU central committee statement, August 2005.

Chapter 7

1 'The Third Cabinet: Implications and Practice' in *ePoliticsSA*, edition 4, 2004, Political Information Monitoring Services (PIMS), Idasa: www.idasa.org.za

Chapter 8

1 A piece in the *Sunday Times* of 25 July 2004, 'Echoing their master's voice', began as follows: 'Fear and loathing stalk the SABC newsroom as a new breed of ANC acolyte rewrites the news to fit the government agenda, writes Chris Barron. To say the SABC is not a happy place is putting it mildly. Fear and discontent stalk the newsroom at Auckland Park as former ANC political commissar Snuki Zikalala forces his underlings to toe the government line.'
2 Names, portraits and biographical data of the SABC board members and the executive are available on http://www.sabc.co.za/portal/site/corporate/menuitem.2dd409d7e2136ee48891f2e75401aeb9/.]
3 Transcript, 'Advocacy and Lobbying Programme', No. 11, Democracy Radio, Idasa, 2001, quoted in S Jacobs, 'Public Sphere, Power and Democratic Politics: Media and Policy Debates in Post-Apartheid South Africa', doctoral thesis, University of London, 2004.
4 Jacobs, *ibid.*, 2004, p. 229.
5 Jacobs, *ibid.*, 2004, p. 235.

Chapter 9

1 'Don't turn the Bench into a political bull's eye, says Court', *Sunday Times*, 13 June 1999.
2 'Blacks' Genes are corrupt – white "racist" judge sparks anger', *City Press*, 13 February 2005.
3 JP Hlophe, 'Report on racism in the Cape Provincial Division', p. 32.

4 Information received from the Registrar's Office, Cape Provincial Division, 5 April 2006.
5 See 'Racial tension rocks Joburg Bar' by Mpumelelo Mkhabela, *City Press*, 26 June 2005, p. 6.
6 www.anc.org.za/ancdocs/pr/2005
7 www.da.org.za: The DA's judicial review: threats to judicial independence in South Africa.
8 Survey, 30 April 2004, General Council of the Bar, cited in *ePoliticsSA*, 'Debating the Transformation of the Bar – Rhetoric and Substance', edition 3, 2005, www.idasa.org.za
9 *ePoliticsSA*, 'Debating the Transformation of the Bar – Rhetoric and Substance', edition 3, 2005, www.idasa.org.za, *ibid.*, p. 3.
10 JAG Griffith, *The Politics of the Judiciary*, third edition (London: Fontana, 1985), p. 194.
11 Griffith, *ibid.*, p. 15.
12 Pharmaceutical Manufacturers Association of South Africa and Another: In re Ex parte President of the Republic of South Africa and Others 2000 (2) SA 674 (CC).
13 The President of the Republic of South Africa and Another v Modderklip Boerdery (Pty) Ltd CCT 20/04 and Modderfontein Squatters, Greater Benoni Municipality and Modderklip Boerdery (Pty) Ltd v The President of South Africa; President of the RSA and Others v Modderklip Boerdery (Pty) Ltd 2004 (6) SA 40 (SCA).
14 Section 178 of the final Constitution establishes the Judicial Services Commission and sets out its mandate as well as the structure of its composition.
15 www.constitutionalcourt.org.za/site/transcript
16 www.constitutionalcourtorg.za/site/judges/transcript/albertlouissachs.html

17 President of the Republic of South Africa and Others v South African Rugby Football Union and Others 1999 (2) SA 14 (CC).

18 Max du Plessis, 'Between Apology and Utopia – the Constitutional Court and Public Opinion', *South African Journal of Human Rights*, No. 18, 2002, p. 2.

19 United Democratic Movement v President of the Republic of South Africa and Others CCT23/02. Reported at 2003 (1) SA 495 (CC) [the 'floor-crossing case'].

20 www.idasa.org.za/epoliticssa 2005

21 Section 46 (1) (d) of the final Constitution.

22 Soobramoney v Minister of Health, KwaZulu-Natal 1998 (1) SA 765 (CC).

23 Alfred Cockrell, 'Rainbow Jurisprudence', *SAJHR*, No. 12, 2002. Reviewed in an equally thought-provoking and useful article by Iain Currie, 'Judicious Avoidance', *SAJHR*, No. 15, p. 138.

24 Minister of Health and Others v Treatment Action Campaign and others. CCT9/02. Reported as 2002 (5) SA 721 (CC) [the 'TAC case']. The main hearing date was 2 May 2002, with judgment delivered on 5 July 2002. The floor-crossing hearing was on 6 August 2002, with judgment delivered on 4 October 2002.

25 Judgment in the floor-crossing case, *ibid.*, pp. 27 and 28, paragraphs 48, 49 and 50. As a postscript to the judgment, during the floor-crossing window in September 2003, just six months before the 2004 general elections, ten of the UDM's fourteen National Assembly members of parliament crossed the floor, nine of them to the ANC. Undoubtedly, the UDM was struggling politically, but the idea that there had been a shift in public opinion sufficient to legitimize such a decimation of the party's representation in parliament was completely undermined by the result that the UDM duly obtained in April 2004, when it won

two-thirds of the percentage share of the vote it had won in 1999 and returned nine MPs to the National Assembly.

26 Government of the Republic of South Africa and Others v Grootboom and Others CCT11/00 2001(1) SA 46.

27 Sandra Liebenberg, 'South Africa's evolving jurisprudence on socio-economic rights: An effective tool in challenging poverty?', *Law Democracy and Development*, No. 6, 2002.

28 Theunis Roux, 'Legitimating Trans-formation: Political Resource Allocation in the South African Constitutional Court', 9 June 2004, p. 5: www.law.wits.ac.za/cals/it/pdf/norway_paper.pdf.

29 Siri Gloppen, *Social Rights Litigation as Transformation: South African perspectives, in Democratising Development: The Politics of Socio-economic Rights in South Africa* (Leiden: Marthinus Nijhoff Publishers, 2005), p. 167.

30 Saras Jagwanth and Christina Murray, 'Ten Years of Transformation: How has Gender Equality in South Africa Fared?' *Canadian Journal of Women and the Law*, 14.2, 2002, p. 255.

31 Jagwanth and Murray, *ibid.*, p. 282.

32 'Moseneke is the perfect candidate to transform our justice system', *Sunday Times*, 17 November 2002.

33 Review by David Penna of H Klug's 'Constituting Democracy: Law, Globalism and South Africa's Political Reconstruction', *Cambridge Studies in Law and Society* (New York and Cambridge: Cambridge University Press, 2000), at www.h-net.org/reviews/

34 This table is an adaptation of a similar table prepared by the *South African Journal on Human Rights*, which every year in its final volume of the year contains a valuable set of notes and comments, as well as statistics, on the Constitutional Court for the previous year. The 2005 review of the 2004 year,

in *SAJHR*, No. 21, 2005, summarizes the law relating to the tenure of the Constitutional Court: In terms of Section 4 of the Judges' Remuneration and Conditions of Employment Act 47 of 2001, Constitutional Court judges' terms have been extended to fifteen years in situations where their twelve-year term has expired or they have reached the age of seventy before they have completed fifteen years of active service as a judge, provided that they do not reach the age of seventy-five before this point.

35 In Bhe and Others v Magistrate, Khayelitsha and Others CCT 49/03; Shibi v Sithole and Others CCT 69/03; South African Human Rights Commission and Another v President of the Republic of South Africa and Another CCT 50/03, Ngcobo J dissents from the majority view that it is inappropriate to develop the indigenous rule of male primogeniture. In advocating for the development and strengthening of indigenous law separately from that of the common law, Ngobo J locates the origin of the rules of indigenous law within traditional society, at the heart of which, he submits, is the family unit. Ngobo J describes the family unit as being an integral part of traditional society, and defends the rules of primogeniture by defining the duties of the successor, which include providing guidance to minors, overseeing the well-being of the family, and generally ensuring certainty (paragraphs 80 to 81).

36 Griffiths, *ibid.*, p. 234.

Chapter 10

1 Samantha Fleming, Collette Herzenberg and Cherrel Africa, 'Civil Society, Public Participation and Bridging the Inequality Gap in South Africa', Idasa study for the Centre for Civil Society,

University of Natal, 2003. www.vkzam. ac.za/ccs/default.asp?3,28

2 Idasa study, *ibid.*, p. 27.

3 M Swilling and B Russel, 'The size and scope of the non-profit sector in South Africa', Graduate School of Public and Development Management at the University of the Witwatersrand, Johannesburg, 2001.

4 South Africa Summary Country Report: Open Society Institute Justice Initiative 2004 Monitoring Study at http://www.opendemocracy. org.za/documents/SA2004OSJIMoni- toringStudySummaryRTKday.doc

5 See Michael Sachs, '"We don't want the fucking vote". Social movements and demagogues in South Africa's young democracy', *South African Labour Bulletin*, Vol. 27, No. 6, December 2003, p. 23.

6 Ebrahim Fakir, 'Institutional Restruc- turing, State-Civil Society Relationships and Social Movements', *Development Update*, 2004.

7 Interview with Trevor Ngwane, *New Left Review* No. 22, July–August 2003.

8 Fakir, *ibid.*, p. 33.

9 Steven Friedman, 'Getting better than world class – the challenge of governing post-apartheid South Africa', *Social Research, an International Quarterly of the Social Sciences, South Africa – the second decade*, Vol. 72, Fall 2005, pp. 773 to 775.

10 Sandra Liebenberg, 'South Africa's evolving jurisprudence on socio- economic rights: An effective tool in challenging poverty?', *Law Democracy and Development*, No. 6, 2002.

Conclusion

1 'Alas poor Brett, no one ever knew him', *Mail & Guardian*, 31 October 2005.

2 'Roger Kebble's Vow', *Mail & Guardian* online, 4 October 2005: http://www. mg.co.za/articleP..aspx?articleid=

252756&area=/breaking_news/
breaking_news__national/

3   According to the SA Embassy website
in Mali, 'The Timbuktu Manuscripts
Project was officially launched by
President Mbeki and President
Amadou Toumani Toure of Mali as
Africa's very first New Partnership
for Africa's Development cultural
project on Africa Day, 25 May 2003.
The preservation of the Timbuktu
Manuscripts is a Presidential Project
co-ordinated by The Presidency and
the Department of Arts and Culture
through the National Archives.
President Mbeki first noted the
existence of these manuscripts, which
are believed to be more than 800 years
old, during a visit to the Institut Des
Hautes et de la Recherche Islamique
(IHERI-AB) as part of his State visit to
Mali in 2001. He subsequently undertook
that South Africa would assist with the
preservation of the Manuscripts through
exchange training and infrastructure-
development programmes.' According to
the government website, the National
Archives of South Africa will lead the
programme to build the infrastructure
and develop skills in conservation
and preservation management for the
staff at IHERI-AB. A trust fund for
the preservation of the manuscripts
was launched on 29 May 2003. See:
http://www.saembassy.org/
Art%20and%20Culture.htm

4   http://www.armsdeal-vpo.co.za/
articles06/fat_land.html

5   *Mail & Guardian* online, *ibid.*

6   *Bua Komanisi*, Vol. 5, No. 1, May 2006,
special edition.

7   The imported menswear retailer, much
loved by certain members of the
'stratum of emerging black capitalists',
as described by *Bua Komanisi*.

8   http://en.wikipedia.org/wiki/Comprador

9   According to newspaper reports, a
discussion document was tabled at
the NEC by the organization's deputy
secretary general, Sankie Mthembi-
Mahanyele, which, among other things,
explores the possibility of a policy to
limit ANC members' business interests
and BEE holdings: 'ANC turns on
Fat Cat Comrades', *Sunday Times*,
6 August 2006. This was quickly
followed by Thabo Mbeki's watershed
speech on ethical values at the Annual
Nelson Mandela lecture: see http://
www.dfa.gov.za/docs/speeches/2006/
mbeko729.htm

10   See W Robinson, 'Social Theory and
Globalization: The Rise of a Trans-
national State', *Theory and Society*,
Vol. 30, No. 2, 2001.

11   Between January 1986 and December
1988, Judge Braam Lategan heard 65
criminal cases in the Cape Provincial
Division of the Supreme Court. In
those 65 cases, he sentenced 29 people
to death, the highest number of any
judge serving during that time. He
was responsible for 24.27 per cent of
death penalties imposed, despite
hearing only 8.09 per cent of cases. He
also had the second highest personal
percentage of death sentences imposed
at 48.33 per cent of all his cases,
resulting in the accused sentenced to
death. In addition, he imposed 10 of
the 18 discretionary death sentences
during the two-year period. C Murray,
J Sloth-Nielsen, C Tredoux, 'The Death
Penalty in the Cape Provincial Division'
in *South African Human Rights Journal*,
1989, pp. 154–182.

12   N Alexander, *An Ordinary Country:
Issues in the Transition from Apartheid to
Democracy in South Africa* (Scottsville:
University of Natal Press, 2002), p. 64.

Index

Freedom Front Plus 102, 217, 281
Freedom Park Trust 98
FRELIMO 149
Friedman, Steven 201, 223
Frye, Isobel 1, 3–5, 7
Furlan, Luiz 144

Gauntlett, Jeremy 206
'Gautrain' project 156
GEAR 4, 57, 128, 140, 144–6, 150, 152–3, 286
Geffen, Nathan 201
Gender Commission 12, 125
General and Allied Workers' Union 292
George, Mluleki 200, 284
Gerwel, Jakes 22, 26–8, 36, 257–8
Gibson, Douglas 167
Gilbertson, Brian 269
Gilder, Barry 39, 70
Ginwala, Frene 90, 105, 111, 122
Gloppen, Siri 234
Godsell, Bobby 269
Goldberg, Prof. Denis 65
Golding, Marcell 99
Goldstone, Justice Richard 229, 235, 240
Goniwe, Mbulelo 110
Gordhan, Pravin 9, 80–81, 89, 92, 93, 95, 98, 159
Govender, Pregs 97, 118
Government Communication and Information Service (GCIS) 37, 49, 50, 189, 198
Government of National Unity 23, 101, 184, 282, 286, 288, 289, 294
GQ 55, 188, 189
Graham, Paul 236
Green, Pippa 188, 197
Greenberg, Stan 174–5
Greyling, Lance 176, 177

Griffith, John 211–12, 214, 242
Grootboom case 215, 233–4
'groupthink' 25, 169
Growth, Employment and Redistribution *see* GEAR
Guardian 163
Gumbi, Mojanku 8, 19, 27, 28–9, 30–31, 32, 33, 41, 61, 235, 239–40, 271
Gumede, William 18, 145
Gwagwa, Thembeka 142
Gwala, Xolani 199

Habib, Adam 174, 201
Haffajee, Ferial 188, 194, 195, 196, 197
handlangers 18–19, 63, 177, 181–2
Hanekom, Derek 51
Hangana, Elizabeth 101
Hani, Chris 153, 295
Hani, Limpho 98
Harding, Avril 167, 177
Hardwick, Stephen 90, 110
Harmony Gold 99
Hartley, Wyndham 196
Harvard University 58
Haysom, Fink 22, 27, 30
Hazell, Anthony 168
Heard, Tony 19, 38, 189, 190, 191
Heath, Justice Willem 105
Hefer, Justice Joos 216
Hefer Commission 216, 258
Hendricks, Prof. Denver 72
Hendricks, Lindiwe 217, 292, 299
Herald 203
Hersh, Seymour 262
Heywood, Mark 202
Higginbotham, Hon A Leon, Jr 306
Higher Education Bill 47
Hindle, Duncan 72
Hirsch, Alan 28, 37, 197

HIV/AIDS 4, 13, 17, 41, 75, 97, 117, 157, 160, 161, 189–91, 223, 230, 250–52, 259, 288
Hlophe, Justice John 205–7, 210, 236, 268
Hobbes, Thomas 244
Hofmeyr, Willie 34, 110
Hogan, Barbara 10, 59, 107–8, 114
Holomisa, Bantu 101, 108, 175, 228
Holomisa, Patekile 114
homelands 272
Hoosein, Haniff 176
Hopkins, Harry 19
Hosken Consolidated Investments 99
House of Lords (UK) 212
Howard, Randall 139, 142
Howie, Justice Craig Telfer 217
Human Rights Commission 12, 13, 22, 125, 273, 302
Human Sciences Research Council (HSRC) 194, 201, 266
Hutton, Will 58

ICFTU 137
Idasa 29, 31, 119, 130, 150, 164, 167, 170, 177, 184, 188, 194, 200, 201, 203, 228, 236, 241, 244, 245, 246, 252–7, 267
IFP 32, 70, 71, 102, 106, 107, 108, 167, 173, 178–82, 183, 184, 227, 258, 283, 285
Ilizwi 203
Imvume 12
Independent Democrats (ID) 167, 169–70, 175–8, 183, 184, 198, 227, 266
Independent Electoral Commission (IEC) 31, 68, 239, 265–8, 304